PENGUIN CLASSICS

THE CIVILIZATION OF THE
RENAISSANCE IN ITALY

JACOB BURCKHARDT was born in Basel in 1818. He intended to join the Church and studied theology before losing his faith. Between 1839 and 1842 he studied at the University of Berlin, devoting himself to history, and attended seminars given by Leopold von Ranke, the most famous living historian of the time. Burckhardt took his doctorate in 1843 and lectured at the University of Basel. In 1853 he published *The Age of Constantine the Great*, which was followed two years later by a historical guide to the art treasures of Italy, *The Cicerone*. These two books won Burckhardt a chair, and in 1855 he became Professor of Architecture and History at the Zurich Polytechnic. While there he wrote *The Civilization of the Renaissance in Italy*. Returning to Basel in 1858, he remained there for the rest of his life, lecturing at the university; in his own words, he 'lived exclusively for [his] work as a teacher'. He published little, apart from *The Architecture of the Renaissance in Italy* (1867). After his death in 1897 his remaining works, mainly lecture notes, were published. *Rubens*, *Essays on the History of Art in Italy* and *Cultural History of Greece* appeared in 1898, followed by the *Reflections on World History* (1905) and the *Historical Fragments* (1929).

PETER BURKE is Reader in Cultural History, University of Cambridge, Fellow of Emmanuel College, Cambridge, and author of *The Italian Renaissance*, *Popular Culture in Early Modern Europe* and *History and Social Theory*.

From 1980 until his death in 1992, Peter Murray was Emeritus Professor of the History of Art at the University of London. He taught at the Courtauld Institute from 1949 to 1967 and served there as the first Witt Librarian, until he succeeded Sir Nikolaus Pevsner in the chair of Art History at Birkbeck College. He was President of the Society of Architectural Historians of Great Britain and Chairman of the Society of Renaissance Studies. He published an annotated edition of Burckhardt's *Architecture of the Italian Renaissance* in 1985 (Penguin 1987) and his own books include *The Architecture of the Italian Renaissance* (third edition, 1986) and *Renaissance Architecture*, as well as *The Penguin*

Dictionary of Art and Artists with his wife Linda (the sixth edition of which was published in 1989), with whom he also wrote *The Art of the Renaissance*, first published in 1963.

JACOB BURCKHARDT

THE
CIVILIZATION
OF THE
RENAISSANCE
IN ITALY

Translated by S. G. C. Middlemore
With a new Introduction by Peter Burke
and Notes by Peter Murray

PENGUIN BOOKS

PENGUIN BOOKS

Published by the Penguin Group
Penguin Books Ltd, 27 Wrights Lane, London W8 5TZ, England
Penguin Putnam Inc., 375 Hudson Street, New York, New York 10014, USA
Penguin Books Australia Ltd, Ringwood, Victoria, Australia
Penguin Books Canada Ltd, 10 Alcorn Avenue, Toronto, Ontario, Canada M4V 3B2
Penguin Books (NZ) Ltd, 182–190 Wairau Road, Auckland 10, New Zealand

Penguin Books Ltd, Registered Offices: Harmondsworth, Middlesex, England

This edition first published 1990
9 10

Printed in England by Clays Ltd, St Ives plc
Filmset in 10/12 pt Monophoto Bembo

CONTENTS

THE CIVILIZATION OF THE RENAISSANCE IN ITALY

PART I
The State as a Work of Art

PART II
The Development of the Individual

PART III
The Revival of Antiquity

98920

PART IV

The Discovery of the World and of Man

PART V

Society and Festivals

PART VI

Morality and Religion

Introduction

JACOB BURCKHARDT AND THE
ITALIAN RENAISSANCE

Jacob Burckhardt was not only one of the greatest historians of the nineteenth century; he remains one of the most accessible to modern readers. Born in 1818, the same year as Karl Marx, Burckhardt belonged to one of the best-known Basel families; monuments to seventeenth-century Burckhardts can still be seen in the cathedral there. Jacob Burckhardt senior was a clergyman of scholarly interests, who collected coins and medals and wrote on local history, and at the age of seventeen Jacob junior followed in his father's footsteps and carried out research on behalf of a German professor who was writing a book on the Swiss humanist Glareanus. Burckhardt was intended for the Church and studied theology, at his father's suggestion, before losing his faith and deciding to be a scholar. Between 1839 and 1842 he studied at the university of Berlin. He followed courses on ancient history, the history of architecture, and Arabic. He also attended the seminars of the most famous living historian of the time, Leopold von Ranke, and wrote a paper for him on an early medieval topic, the achievement of Charles Martell.

Burckhardt disliked Ranke as a person but admired him as a historian. He considered publishing the paper on Charles Martell and becoming a medievalist, but decided against both. His visits to Italy, from 1837 onwards, and his friendship with one of the younger professors, Franz Kugler, had fired him with enthusiasm for cultural history and for the classical and Renaissance world. He returned to Basel in 1843, took his doctorate, and began to lecture in the university on a wide range of topics, including the history of painting, the Middle Ages, the Counter-Reformation in Switzerland, and the Roman emperors. At first he combined his academic duties with the task of editing a conservative paper, the *Basler Zeitung*, for four or five hours a day.

However, he came to feel an increasing dislike for politics, and also for the 'degrading *métier* of journalist', and in 1846, when his friend Kugler asked for help in preparing a second edition of his successful *Handbook of Art History*, Burckhardt gave up the newspaper in order to spend more time on his research. The first-fruits of this research were a major book on *The Age of Constantine the Great*, published in 1853, when the author was 35, followed two years later by an extremely successful historical guide to the art treasures of Italy, *The Cicerone*.

These two books won Burckhardt a chair. He was called to the Zurich Polytechnic when it opened its doors in 1855, to be the professor of architecture and art history. He lectured on the Renaissance, and it was here that he wrote his most famous work, *The Civilization of the Renaissance in Italy*. However, he returned to Basel as soon as he could, in 1858, and remained there for the rest of his life. From this time onwards Burckhardt 'lived exclusively for his work as a teacher', as he put it himself, lecturing to a handful of students during the week and to the general public on Saturdays on history and art history, and refusing the flattering invitation to succeed Ranke in Berlin.

Burckhardt published little after 1860, apart from *The Architecture of the Renaissance in Italy* (1867), a relatively technical study presented more or less in note form (but attentive all the same to the social and political context of building). It was only after his death, in 1897, that his remaining studies, for the most part notes for his lectures, appeared in print. His *Rubens*, *Essays on the History of Art in Italy* and *Cultural History of Greece* all appeared in 1898, followed by *Reflections on World History* (1905) and *Judgements on History and Historians* (1929).

The young Burckhardt was ardent, sentimental and artistic. He wore his hair long, he played the piano and composed music, he sketched, he wrote poetry (and even published some, anonymously, in 1853). It is easy to understand what attracted him to Kugler, another unconventional academic who composed songs and wrote plays as well as studying art history. 'Giacomo Burcardo' (as he called himself when he was fifteen) seems to have identified with Italy even before he had seen it, and when he visited the country he found it a welcome escape from the Protestant piety of Basel, where art and its history were suspect to some people as 'worldly' pursuits. He had a circle of friends of both sexes to whom he wrote lively and sentimental letters, not infrequently signed 'Saltimbanck'.

It is at first sight a little difficult to reconcile this person, or persona, with that of the elderly Professor Burckhardt, a close-cropped, dignified and solitary bachelor of modest and conservative tastes, who lived in two rooms above a baker's shop in the old town. He withdrew from political and social life and concentrated on his teaching and on being what he called 'a good private individual'. However, he continued to play the piano and to indulge what he once called 'my passion for travel, my mania for natural scenery and my interest in art'.

Like a good old-fashioned Swiss republican, he disliked pomp and pretentiousness and expressed this dislike in his style of life. At least one foreign visitor failed to recognize the distinguished scholar he had come to see, only to be told, 'If you must speak to Jacob Burckhardt, you must make do with me.' The professor was, however, a familiar figure in the Basel of the 1880s and the early 1890s, walking to his lectures (as we see him in a famous photograph), with a large blue portfolio of illustrations under his arm. The reaction of Basel to Burckhardt's death suggests that he was loved as well as respected in his native city and was indeed something of a local institution, a position which he retains to this day. It was in Basel that two of Burckhardt's books, on Rubens and on the history of Italian art, were posthumously published, as well as a complete edition of his letters and a massive seven-volume intellectual biography, the life-work of a fellow-citizen, the cultural historian Werner Kaegi.

As a lecturer Burckhardt was incisive, ironic and caustic, as may well be imagined from an inspection of his *Reflections on World History* and *Historical Fragments*, in which one can almost hear him talking. He impressed even the 24-year-old Nietzsche, who wrote that listening to Burckhardt talk on 'Great Men in History' was the first time in his life that he had enjoyed a lecture. He used to memorize his lectures and deliver them without notes as if he were thinking aloud; but it is said that even his asides had been rehearsed. These asides (which have their equivalents in *The Renaissance in Italy*) include many disapproving references to the contemporary world. Burckhardt had a hearty dislike for the French Revolution, for the United States (which he never visited), for mass democracy, uniformity, industrialism, militarism, nationalism, the railways, and what he called 'the whole power and money racket' – developments which he saw to be both connected and inevitable. In the age of the unification of Germany and Italy he condemned the modern centralized state, 'worshipped as a god', as he put it, 'and ruling like a sultan'. He preferred to be a good citizen and a good European (fluent not only in German, Italian and the dialect of Basel, but in French and even English).

Burckhardt's conception of history was a very different one from that of many of his contemporaries. He rejected both the positivism and the Hegelianism which fascinated so many of his contemporaries all over Europe. As a student at the university of Berlin, he wrote regretfully that the philosophy of history was taught by followers of Hegel, 'whom I cannot understand'. As a professor at the university of Basel, he told his students that his lectures on the study of history would offer 'no philosophy of history'. According to Burckhardt, there was no such thing; the idea of the philosophy of history was a contradiction in terms, 'for history co-ordinates, and hence is unphilosophical, while philosophy subordinates, and hence is unhistorical'. In other words, history is unsystematic and systems are unhistorical.

This view is further from British historical empiricism than it may look. Unlike many practising historians, Burckhardt was not philosophically illiterate. Despite his claim to be unfit for speculation and abstract thought, he was well acquainted with the ideas of Hegel and Schopenhauer as well as with those of the young Nietzsche, with whom he used to go for walks discussing ideas. Although he was sceptical of the claims made for grand philosophical systems, his vision of the past was not completely free of philosophical presuppositions, as we shall see.

In any case, Burckhardt's position was as far from positivism as it was from Hegel. Where the positivists saw history as a science, and historians as collecting 'facts' from the documents and giving what they considered to be an 'objective' account of what had 'actually' happened, Burckhardt saw history as an art. He regarded history as a form of imaginative literature, akin to poetry. He wanted 'to write in a readable style', to appeal to 'thinking readers of all classes' rather than to his fellow-scholars, and to concentrate on what was interesting in the past rather than attempting to be exhaustive. He disliked heaping up what he called 'mere facts' or 'external facts': 'One really needs to use only such facts as are characteristic of an idea, or a clear sign of the time'. If Burckhardt has to be labelled, the adjectives 'sceptical', 'relativist' and, perhaps, 'intuitive' are probably less misleading than most.

In the preface to the first edition of his *Age of Constantine*, in 1852, the author declared that he was 'well aware that his treatment may be impugned as being subjective', but explained that 'In works of general history there is room for differences of opinion on fundamental premises and aims, so that the same fact may seem essential and important to one writer, for example, and to another mere rubbish utterly without interest'. What he offered was a personal interpretation, or better, 'view' or 'vision' (*Anschauung*); what he called a 'sketch of the whole' (*Gesamtschilderung*). The visual metaphors are revealing; there are many of them in the work of this connoisseur of painting, sculpture and architecture. What metaphors like 'outlines' (*Umrisse*) or 'image' (*Bild*) reveal is the distance between Burckhardt and the tradition of narrative history. Where others wanted to tell a story, Burckhardt's aim was to paint the portrait of an age.

The term 'sketch' was probably employed not only out of modesty but also to suggest the impossibility of reaching definitive conclusions about the past. In a similar way, in 1860, Burckhardt described his study of the Italian Renaissance as an 'essay' (*Versuch*) 'in the strictest sense of the word', explaining that 'To each eye . . . the outlines of a given civilization [*Kulturepoche*] present a different picture', and that 'the same studies which have served for this work might easily, in other hands, not only receive a wholly different treatment and application, but lead also to essentially different conclusions'.

In the preface to the second edition of *Constantine*, in 1880, Burckhardt felt the need to explain his approach in a little more detail, describing the book as 'not so much a complete historical account as an integrated description, from the viewpoint of cultural history'. As early as 1848 he had been planning a series of books on 'cultural history' (*Kulturgeschichte*).

Exactly what Burckhardt meant by 'cultural history' is not easy to explain, just as it is difficult to translate the German term *Kultur* into English. As an approximation we may say that he employed the term in two senses. He used it in a narrow sense to refer to the arts, and in a wide sense to describe his holistic view of what we call 'a culture'. The ambiguity is revealing. What it reveals is the centrality of the arts in Burckhardt's world-view, as in his life. After all, throughout his career he both taught and wrote art history, from his early contributions to Kinkel's handbook to the study of Rubens in his old age. One of his pupils, Heinrich Wölfflin, achieved fame as an art historian, and described his master as primarily a historian of art. *The Renaissance in Italy* was originally intended to include a discussion of the art of the period, and came to exclude art only because Burckhardt planned a separate volume on the subject.

Burckhardt's concern for cultural history became more exclusive with the passing of the years. His reaction to the Franco-Prussian war of 1870 was to regard 'all mere "events" in the past', such as battles, as without value and to declare that 'From now on in my lectures, I shall emphasize only cultural history.' His lectures on ancient Greece did in fact concentrate on the Greek view of life and mentality (*Denkweise*).

At this point the contrast between Burckhardt's kind of history and that of Leopold von Ranke is at its plainest. The younger man acknowledged a considerable intellectual debt to the teaching of his master, and he retained a lifelong admiration for Ranke's *History of the Popes* and for his account of Germany in the age of the Reformation. For his part Ranke praised Burckhardt's seminar papers and his *Age of Constantine* and recommended him for a chair at the university of Munich. However, the paths of these two great historians gradually diverged. Ranke's later works were more narrowly political than the earlier ones, while Burckhardt became increasingly preoccupied with cultural history.

This kind of history was already the central theme of the book Burckhardt published in 1860, at the age of forty-two, the book generally regarded as his masterpiece: *The Civilization* (or *Culture*) of *the Renaissance in Italy* (*Die Kultur der Renaissance in Italien*). He once wrote that a great historical subject 'must needs cohere sympathetically and mysteriously to the author's inmost being', and this was certainly true for him in this case. He was very much in sympathy with the period and its artistic achievements, and also with the region he had chosen, Italy.

Like other northerners, from Goethe to Ibsen, from Wagner to Warburg, Burckhardt found that his encounter with southern Europe, and with Italy in particular, was a major event in his life. This attraction was in part a kind of psychological compensation (the 21-year-old Burckhardt described Italy as 'a necessary supplement to my whole being and life'). Italy was for him the Other, attractively different from the Switzerland he left behind, with sun instead of rain, wine instead of beer, and an outward-going people instead of an inward-looking one. His sketchbooks give some idea of the fascination this country had for him. His letters, too, are full of vivid descriptions, verbal vignettes of Italy and the Italians. At the age of twenty-eight he was writing from Italy lamenting the necessity to leave and declaring that 'I now know that I shall never really be happy again away from Rome', its streets and gardens, a city where 'there is not the smallest trace of industry', while 'leisure has made politeness flourish like an art'.

Rome also appealed to Burckhardt's historical imagination. 'Part of the pleasure of Rome is that it keeps one perpetually guessing and arranging the ruins of the ages that lie so mysteriously, layer upon layer.' It was in Rome in 1847 that the idea of writing a book on the Renaissance in Italy first started to his mind (much as the idea of writing about the decline and fall of the Roman empire had started to the mind of Gibbon). It was in Rome in 1848, when revolutions were breaking out all over Europe, that Burckhardt decided that he would work on 'The Age of Raphael'.

The book that he dreamed of writing in 1847–8 was published in 1860. In some respects it is a companion-piece to the *Cicerone*, published five years earlier, for it assumes some knowledge of the art of the period, and concentrates on the culture which made the art possible. It was in the *Cicerone* that Burckhardt first stressed what he called the 'realism' or 'naturalism' of the Renaissance (in the work of Ghiberti and Donatello, for example), and also the new concern for individuality.

In other respects *The Renaissance in Italy* is a companion-piece to *Constantine the Great*. The earlier book had been concerned with the 'crisis' of classical culture, its 'senescence', in other words the transition from the classical to the medieval. The later book deals with the end of the Middle Ages and with the revival of antiquity. *Constantine* deals with the rise of other-worldliness in the fourth century, *The Renaissance* with the rise of worldliness in the fifteenth and sixteenth centuries. The aim of both books is not, like most nineteenth-century works of history, to tell a story, but to portray an age by cutting what the author elsewhere called 'cross-sections' (*Querdurchschnitte*) through the period and emphasizing 'the constant, the recurrent, and the typical' (*das sich Wiederholende, Konstante, Typische*). The book on Constantine was presented as a series of studies, omitting whatever 'could not be woven as a living element into the texture of the whole', for example 'property and wealth, industry and trade'. In a similar way the Renaissance book, with its subtitle 'an essay', virtually omitted economic life (from guild organization to commercial capitalism).

On what criteria did Burckhardt decide what to include? In order to understand his approach better, it may be useful to make yet a third juxtaposition, this time between the essay on the Renaissance and the lectures he gave a few years later, in 1868–9 and 1870–71, under the title 'Introduction to the Study of History'. These lectures are organized around the idea of three 'powers', the state, religion and culture, and their reciprocal interaction. 'Culture' is defined as the realm of the spontaneous, including 'social intercourse, technologies, arts, literatures and sciences'. According to Burckhardt, 'There are primarily political and primarily religious epochs, and finally epochs which seem to live for the great purposes of culture.' Ancient Egypt, Mexico and Peru are examples of 'culture determined by the state'. The world of Islam illustrates 'culture determined by religion', while the Greek *polis* reveals 'the state determined by culture'.

The Renaissance is clearly another example of an epoch which lives 'for the great purposes of culture', and Burckhardt devotes the four central chapters of his book to culture, framing them by an introduction on politics and a conclusion on religion. The first chapter illustrates the effect of culture on politics. It concentrates on the rise of a new, self-conscious conception of the state, which may be illustrated from the Florentine and Venetian concern with gathering what would later be called statistics. It is this new conception which Burckhardt calls 'the state as a work of art' (*Der Staat als Kunstwerk*). In a similar manner the last chapter concentrates on the effect of culture on religion, characterizing the religious attitudes of Renaissance Italians as both subjective and worldly.

Set in this frame come four chapters on the culture of the Renaissance. Of these, Chapter Three, 'The Revival of Antiquity', is the most conventional. Chapter Five, 'Society and Festivals', illustrates Burckhardt's relatively wide conception of culture as including not only the visual arts, literature and music, but also costume, language, etiquette, cleanliness, and festivals sacred and profane, from Corpus Christi to Carnival. The most famous chapters, however, are the remaining two, dealing with what Burckhardt called 'The Development of the Individual' and 'The Discovery of the World and of Man'.

Perhaps the most famous statement in this famous book is the following:

> In the Middle Ages . . . man was conscious of himself only as a member of a race, people, party, family, or corporation – only through some general category. In Italy this veil first melted into air; an *objective* treatment of the state and all the things of this world became possible. The *subjective* side at the same time asserted itself with corresponding emphasis; man became a spiritual *individual*, and recognized himself as such.

It is this insight – or theory – which determines the selection of the concrete examples not only for this chapter but for the whole book. Machiavelli's *Prince* stands for Renaissance objectivity and the idea of the state as a work of art, while autobiographies like those of Pius II and Benvenuto Cellini, and the poems of Petrarch, with their 'abundance of pictures of the inmost soul', illustrate the 'subjective side' of the period.

A major theme of *The Renaissance in Italy* is that 'it was not the revival of antiquity alone, but its union with the genius of the Italian people [*dem italienischen Volksgeist*], which achieved the conquest of the Western world'. The historic importance of Italy is that it was the place where the medieval 'veil' first 'melted into air'. The Italian was, as he put it, 'the first-born among the sons of modern Europe', just as Petrarch was 'one of the first truly modern men'. However, Burckhardt the historian, like Burckhardt the traveller, also found Italians fascinating for their own sake. The 'many-sided men' Leon Battista Alberti and Leonardo da Vinci are described as 'giants' who tower over their contemporaries: 'The colossal outlines of Leonardo's nature can never be more than dimly and distantly conceived.' The city-states of Renaissance Italy, like those of ancient Greece, exerted a strong attraction on a historian who came from a patrician family in a city which had continued to be ruled by its patricians until the 1830s. In this case one might talk of an elective affinity between Burckhardt and his subject. In his view, perhaps coloured by nostalgia for the world of his childhood, these city-states had enjoyed a harmonious mode of existence which the modern world had lost.

Yet the violent political history of Renaissance Italy also fascinated

Burckhardt: the civil war between two noble families of Perugia, for example, the Oddi and the Baglioni, or the 'insane thirst for blood' of Cesare Borgia, which leads the historian to speculate on what might have happened had Cesare not been seriously ill on the occasion of his father's death. 'What a conclave would that have been, in which, armed with all his weapons, he had extorted his election from a college whose numbers he had judiciously reduced by poison . . . In pursuing such a hypothesis the imagination loses itself in an abyss.'

It is with reference to comments like this that the intellectual historian Peter Gay, contrasting the 'sober moderation' of Burckhardt's own life with 'the extravagant violence on which he concentrates', diagnoses 'a secret infatuation with enormities'. I would rather speak of Burckhardt's ambivalence, and place more stress on the northerner's perception of the hot-blooded south as the Other, and also on the German cultural tradition of fascination with the demonic, a tradition which runs from Goethe through Wagner and Nietzsche to Thomas Mann.

What is the place of Burckhardt's essay in the history of historical writing? The idea of writing on cultural rather than political history was not a new one. Giorgio Vasari's *Lives of the Artists* (1550) is an early example of cultural history as well as one of Burckhardt's sources. Voltaire's *Essay on Manners* (1756) is closer to Burckhardt's combination of what we might call 'socio-cultural' history, since it deals with topics such as literature, learning, systems of values (such as chivalry) and even tablecloths and table manners from Charlemagne to the beginning of the seventeenth century. Closer still to *The Renaissance in Italy* is a relatively neglected work by an eighteenth-century Italian scholar, Saverio Bettinelli's *Revival of Italy* (1775), which deals with Italy's *risorgimento* in the fields of learning, art and social life after the year 1000 (the term *risorgimento* had not yet acquired its modern political meaning).

A central concept in Voltaire's *Essay on Manners* is that of the 'spirit' or 'genius' of an age, of a people, of laws, of chivalry, of Catholicism, of commerce and so on. Voltaire had no monopoly of the concept, which can be found in contemporary French writers, such as Montesquieu, and also in British ones, such as William Robertson and David Hume. In the late eighteenth century it attracted some German philosophers of history, notably Johann Gottfried Herder, who emphasized the distinctive character or spirit of each people, their *Volksgeist*, and

Georg Wilhelm Friedrich Hegel, who placed more stress on the 'spirit of the age' (*Zeitgeist*).

Despite Burckhardt's avowed rejection of the philosophers of history, his work shows clear traces of their ideas. The chapter on 'The State as a Work of Art', for example, parallels Hegel's discussion in his *Lectures on the Philosophy of History* of the political system of ancient Greece as 'the political work of art' (*Das politische Kunstwerk*), while the chapter 'The Development of the Individual' echoes Hegel's discussion of 'individuality', objectivity and subjectivity. Sir Ernst Gombrich goes as far as to say that Burckhardt's work was 'built on Hegelian foundations', pointing in particular to the idea of the *Zeitgeist*. Gombrich is surely right to suggest that the idea of the cultural unity of a period like the Renaissance is central to Burckhardt's thought. It underlies his attempt to see the age as a whole and also the organization of his essay. As we have just seen, however, this idea was not peculiar to Hegel, while Burckhardt rejected the distinctively Hegelian view of history as the long march of the 'world spirit'.

Again, it may not be fanciful to suggest that the concern with the polarities of objective and subjective in *The Renaissance in Italy* owes something, consciously or unconsciously, to the philosophy of Schopenhauer, 'our philosopher', as Burckhardt used to call him on his walks with Nietzsche. It was Schopenhauer's *World as Will and Idea* that Burckhardt was echoing when he contrasted the systematic character of science, which subordinates, with the unsystematic character of history, which co-ordinates.

Burckhardt also owed a good deal to earlier studies of the Italian Renaissance. The basic idea of a revival of classical antiquity was formulated during the period itself, from Petrarch to Vasari, who first used the abstract noun 'Renaissance' (*rinascità*). In the eighteenth and nineteenth centuries the idea was elaborated. Voltaire suggested that the Renaissance, 'the time of Italy's glory', was one of the only four periods in human history worthy of consideration by a thinking person, or a person of taste. The relationship between liberty and culture in the Italian city-states was underlined by Burckhardt's fellow-countryman Sismondi in his *History of the Italian Republics in the Middle Ages* (1807–18). In his *History of Painting in Italy* (1817) Stendhal revealed his fascination with individuals such as Cesare Borgia and Pope Julius II, suggesting that it was no accident that great painters appeared in 'this century of passions'.

Closest of all to Burckhardt in their approach were two scholars who published their studies in the 1850s, when he was already working on his book. Italian humanism was placed firmly on the historical map in *The Revival of Classical Antiquity* (1859) by Georg Voigt, who was appointed to the chair of history at Munich, for which Ranke had wanted to recommend Burckhardt. Voigt described the Middle Ages in terms of what he called 'the corporative tendency', and the Renaissance, from Petrarch onwards, in terms of 'individuality and its rights'. In his *Renaissance* (written in 1842 and published in 1855), a volume in his *History of France*, Jules Michelet characterized the period as one of 'the discovery of the world, the discovery of man'. Voigt's and Michelet's anticipations of Burckhardt's famous formulations suggest that *The Renaissance in Italy* was a true child of its time. It is Burckhardt, however, with whom posterity associates the definition of the Renaissance in terms of the development of the individual and the discovery of the world and of man, and this is a fair verdict in the sense that it was he who organized his whole essay around these ideas (together with that of 'modernity'), rather than around the more conventional concept of the revival of antiquity.

The Renaissance in Italy was not an instant success. The first 200 copies were in fact rather slow to sell, and it was nine years before a second edition was required. The book gradually grew in popularity, however, reaching its tenth German edition in 1908 and its fourteenth edition in 1925. The 421 illustrations chosen by Ludwig Goldscheider doubtless added to the work's popularity. It was translated into French in 1885, into Polish in 1905, into Italian in 1911. Burckhardt appeared in English translation relatively early, in 1878, just after the first three volumes of the massive *Renaissance in Italy* (1875–86) by his imitator John Addington Symonds. The new editions of 1890, 1898, 1929, 1937, 1944, 1950 and now 1989 (not counting reprints) suggest that it has acquired the status of a classic. So has the translation, by Samuel Middlemore, a journalist who later lectured at the Malvern School of Art.

Like other classics, *The Renaissance in Italy* has had many critics. After more than 120 years of increasingly specialized research, it is easy to point out exaggerations, rash generalizations and other weaknesses in this famous essay. It is doubtful, for example, whether any historian of the Italian Renaissance working today would be prepared to write, as Burckhardt did, that in this period 'women stood on a footing of perfect equality with men'; there is too much evidence to the contrary. Now that the history of science has become professionalized, with its own journals and research centres, Burckhardt's discussion of astrology, alchemy and so on has come to look rather amateurish. Some of his interpretations of Renaissance texts have been challenged, for example his reading of Petrarch's famous letter describing his ascent of Mont Ventoux in Provence. For Burckhardt, this letter is a literal description of an event in Petrarch's life and also an illustration of the awakening of the modern sense of natural beauty. More recent scholars, however, see the letter as an allegory, describing the ascent of the soul to God, and emphasize its quotations from the Bible and St Augustine.

There are also what might be called 'structural' weaknesses in the essay. Burckhardt himself, who confided the task of revising his book to someone else – to Bernhard Kugler (the son of his old teacher Franz) – wrote to him cheerfully admitting to its lack of concern with the economic foundations of cultural life. The criticism has been voiced many times since. It has also become commonplace to refer to the lack of concern with change shown by Burckhardt in a study concerned with some three hundred years of Italian history, from Dante to the Counter-Reformation. This impression of immobility is the result of Burckhardt's successful attempt to demonstrate the lateral connections between different domains of Renaissance life. This weakness, in other words, is no accident but the perhaps inevitable price of Burckhardt's achievement. A weakness it remains none the less.

Burckhardt has also been criticized for his lack of knowledge of and sympathy for the Middle Ages, in contrast to which he defines his Renaissance. Adjectives like 'childish' no longer seem appropriate when applied to this period (or indeed to any other). The suggestion that medieval men did not feel themselves to be individuals but were conscious of themselves 'only through some general category' does not easily square with the existence of twelfth-century autobiographies such as those of Abelard and Guibert of Nogent. Indeed, the concept of 'the development of the individual' is difficult to pin down. Is self-consciousness the criterion of individualism? Or is it the desire for glory, 'the modern sense of fame' as Burckhardt called it? Did medieval knights not seek fame through their achievements in battles and tournaments? In this case, as in that of the economic foundations of the Renaissance, the old Burckhardt came to agree with his later critics. 'As far as individualism is concerned', he once remarked, 'I don't believe in it any more'.

Another of Burckhardt's problematic central concepts is 'modernity'. To describe Renaissance Italians as the first modern men encourages us to see them in our own image and forget the many differences between us and them. Another problem with modernity is that it keeps changing. What looked modern in 1860 does not necessarily strike late twentieth-century eyes as modern at all. In any case, the sociological debate over 'modernization' has made us aware of the dangers of assuming that there is only one path to the future, that history is a one-way street. It is as misleading to describe the changes in European culture and society in the fifteenth and sixteenth centuries as 'Italianization' as it is to describe more recent changes as 'Americanization'. The appeal of Italy in one instance and the United States in the other needs to be explained, and account has to be taken of conscious or unconscious divergences from the model, its adaptation to local circumstances.

Burckhardt's view of the Renaissance may be easy to criticize, but it is also difficult to replace. Much the same goes for his vision of cultural history. To late twentieth-century eyes, Burckhardt's view of an epoch as a whole no longer seems completely convincing. He says too little, for example, about the cultural conflicts between the humanists and the scholastic philosophers of the Renaissance, or between one kind of humanist and another. He constructed his image of the Renaissance out of a relatively narrow range of literary texts. All the same, his work has been an inspiration to later cultural historians, despite their rejection of some of his conclusions. The great Dutch historian Johan Huizinga wrote his *Waning of the Middle Ages* (1919) as a kind of riposte to Burckhardt, emphasizing the theme of decay rather than rebirth and the culture of France and Flanders rather than that of Italy. At the same time, his book paints the portrait of an age in Burckhardtian style. It is a work of imagination, intuition, vision. Faithful to his principle that 'God is to be found in detail' (*Der Liebe Gott steckt im Detail*), the German scholar Aby Warburg produced short essays on Renaissance Italy, miniatures rather than a broad canvas. Yet he, like Huizinga, started from the place where Burckhardt had left off. So did Warburg's friend Ernst Cassirer, who criticized Burckhardt for omitting from his essay any serious consideration of the philosophy of the period, but adopted a Burckhardtian framework for his *The Individual and the Cosmos in Renaissance Philosophy* (1927). Georg Misch's monumental *History of Autobiography* (3 vols., 1907–62) discussed medieval examples which invalidate Burckhardt's view of Renaissance individualism, yet Misch spent his long career answering a question which Burckhardt had formulated.

Although he found celebrity an embarrassment, Burckhardt had (and continues to have) many claims to fame. His book on *The Age of Constantine the Great* is a remarkable essay on an age of cultural crisis and transition. His *Cicerone* first brought him to the notice of a wide public, and still gives him a place in the history of art history. His posthumously published cultural history of Greece is still considered important by classical scholars of the calibre of the late Arnaldo Momigliano, who stresses its novelty and its potential value for future research. The acute, pessimistic observations on the present and the future to be found in Burckhardt's letters and in his reflections on world history have attracted increasing attention in our own time. Like the Norman aristocrat Alexis de Tocqueville, this Basel patrician may be regarded as a 'prophet of a mass age'. His emphasis on the subjectivity of historical writing and on cultural relativism, heretical in his own day, is now widely shared. His concern with patterns of culture and with changing concepts of the person has appealed to social anthropologists (from Ruth Benedict to Clifford Geertz) as well as to socio-cultural historians. However, Burckhardt's name continues to be most closely associated with the period and the country which he made his own: with the Renaissance in Italy.

FURTHER READING

Baron, Hans, 'Burckhardt's *Civilization of the Renaissance* a Century after its Publication', *Renaissance News*, 1960, pp. 207–22.

Burckhardt and the Renaissance a Hundred Years After, Lawrence, Kan., University of Kansas Press, 1960.

Dru, Alexander, ed., *The Letters of Jacob Burckhardt*, London, Routledge & Kegan Paul, 1955.

Ferguson, Wallace K., *The Renaissance in Historical Thought: Five Centuries of Interpretation*, Cambridge, Mass., Houghton Mifflin, 1948.

Gay, Peter, 'Burckhardt: the Poet of Truth', in his *Style in History*, London, Jonathan Cape, 1975.

Gilbert, Felix, 'Burckhardt's Student Years', *Journal of the History of Ideas*, 47, 1986, pp. 249–74.

Gilbert, Felix, 'Ranke as the Teacher of Jacob Burckhardt', forthcoming.

Gilmore, Myron P., 'Burckhardt as a Social Historian', *Society and History in the Renaissance*, Washington, Folger, 1960, pp. 27–33.

Gombrich, Ernst H., *In Search of Cultural History*, Oxford, Oxford University Press, 1969.

Janssen, E. M., *Jacob Burckhardt und die Renaissance*, Assen, Netherlands, van Gorcum, 1970.

Kaegi, Werner, *Jacob Burckhardt: eine Biographie*, 7 vols., Basle, Schwabe, 1947–82.

Meinecke, Friedrich, 'Ranke und Burckhardt', 1948, English trans. in *German History*, ed. Hans Kohn, London, Routledge & Kegan Paul, 1954, pp. 142–56.

Momigliano, Arnaldo, 'Introduction to the *Griechische Kulturgeschichte* by Jacob Burckhardt', 1955, English trans. in his *Essays in Ancient and Modern Historiography*, Oxford, Blackwell, 1977, Ch. 17.

Nelson, Benjamin, and Trinkaus, Charles, Introduction to Burckhardt, *The Civilization of the Renaissance in Italy*, New York, Harper & Row, 1958.

Nelson, N., 'Individualism as a Criterion of the Renaissance', *Journal of English and Germanic Philology*, 32, 1933, pp. 316–34.

Rüsen, Jörn, 'Jacob Burckhardt: Political Standpoint and Historical Insight on the Border of Post-Modernism', *History and Theory*, 24, 1985.

Salin, Edgar, *Burckhardt und Nietzsche*, 1938, second edn, Heidelberg, Rowohlt, 1948.

Trevor-Roper, H. R., 'The Faustian Historian', in his *Historical Essays*, London, Macmillan, 1957, pp. 273–8.

Weintraub, Karl J., *Visions of Culture*, Chicago, University of Chicago Press, 1966, Ch. 3.

White, Hayden, 'Burckhardt: the Ironic Vision', in his *Metahistory*, Baltimore and London, Johns Hopkins University Press, 1973, pp. 230–64.

THE
CIVILIZATION
OF THE
RENAISSANCE
IN ITALY

PART I

The State as a Work of Art

INTRODUCTION

THIS WORK bears the title of an essay in the strictest sense of the word. No one is more conscious than the writer with what limited means and strength he has addressed himself to a task so arduous. And even if he could look with greater confidence upon his own researches, he would hardly thereby feel more assured of the approval of competent judges. To each eye, perhaps, the outlines of a given civilization present a different picture; and in treating of a civilization which is the mother of our own, and whose influence is still at work among us, it is unavoidable that individual judgement and feeling should tell every moment both on the writer and on the reader. In the wide ocean upon which we venture, the possible ways and directions are many; and the same studies which have served for this work might easily, in other hands, not only receive a wholly different treatment and application, but lead also to essentially different conclusions. Such indeed is the importance of the subject, that it still calls for fresh investigation, and may be studied with advantage from the most varied points of view. Meanwhile we are content if a patient hearing is granted us, and if this book be taken and judged as a whole. It is the most serious difficulty of the history of civilization that a great intellectual process must be broken up into single, and often into what seem arbitrary categories, in order to be in any way intelligible. It was formerly our intention to fill up the gaps in this book by a special work on the art of the Renaissance – an intention, however, which we have been able to fulfil only in part.[1] The struggle between the popes and the Hohenstaufen left Italy in a political condition which differed essentially from that of other countries of the West. While in France, Spain and England the feudal system was so organized that, at the close of its existence, it was naturally transformed into a unified monarchy, and while in Germany it helped to maintain, at least outwardly, the unity of the empire, Italy had shaken it off almost entirely. The emperors of the fourteenth century, even in the most favourable case, were no longer received and respected as feudal lords, but as possible leaders and supporters of powers already in existence; while the papacy, with its creatures and allies, was strong enough to hinder national unity in the future, not strong enough itself to bring about that unity. Between the two lay a multitude of political units – republics and despots – in part of long standing, in part of recent origin, whose existence was founded simply on their power to maintain it.[2] In them for the first time we detect the modern political spirit of Europe, surrendered freely to its own instincts, often displaying the worst features of an unbridled egotism, outraging every right, and killing every germ of a healthier culture. But, wherever this vicious tendency is overcome or in any way compensated, a new fact appears in history – the state as the outcome of reflection and calculation, the state as a work of art. This new life displays itself in a hundred forms, both in the republican and in the despotic states, and determines their inward constitution, no less than their foreign policy. We shall limit ourselves to the consideration of the completer and more clearly defined type, which is offered by the despotic states.

The internal condition of the despotically governed states had a memorable counterpart in the Norman empire of Lower Italy and Sicily, after its transformation by the emperor Frederick II. Bred amid treason and peril in the neighbourhood of the Saracens, Frederick, the first ruler of the modern type who sat upon a throne, had early accustomed himself to a thoroughly objective treatment of affairs. His acquaintance with the internal condition and administration of the Saracenic states was close and intimate; and the mortal struggle in which he was engaged with the papacy compelled him, no less than his adversaries, to bring into the field all the resources at his command. Frederick's measures (especially after the year 1231) are aimed at the complete destruction of the feudal state, at the transformation of the people into a multitude destitute of will and of the means of resistance, but profitable in the utmost degree to the exchequer. He centralized, in a manner hitherto unknown in the West, the whole judicial and political administration. No office was henceforth to be filled by popular election, under penalty of the devastation of the offending district and of the enslavement of its inhabitants. The taxes, based on a comprehensive assessment, and distributed in accordance with Muhammadan usages, were collected by those cruel and vexatious methods without which, it is true, it is impossible to obtain any money from

Orientals. Here, in short, we find, not a people, but simply a disciplined multitude of subjects, who were forbidden, for example, to marry out of the country without special permission, and under no circumstances were allowed to study abroad. The university of Naples was the first we know of to restrict the freedom of study, while the East, in these respects at all events, left its youth unfettered. It was after the example of Muhammadan rules that Frederick traded on his own account in all parts of the Mediterranean, reserving to himself the monopoly of many commodities, and restricting in various ways the commerce of his subjects. The Fatimite Caliphs, with all their esoteric unbelief, were, at least in their earlier history, tolerant of all the differences in the religious faith of their people; Frederick, on the other hand, crowned his system of government by a religious inquisition, which will seem the more reprehensible when we remember that in the persons of the heretics he was persecuting the representatives of a free municipal life. Lastly, the internal police, and the kernel of the army for foreign service, was composed of Saracens who had been brought over from Sicily to Nocera and Lucera – men who were deaf to the cry of misery and careless of the ban of the Church. At a later period the subjects, by whom the use of weapons had long been forgotten, were passive witnesses of the fall of Manfred and of the seizure of the government by Charles of Anjou; the latter continued to use the system which he found already at work.

At the side of the centralizing emperor appeared a usurper of the most peculiar kind: his vicar and son-in-law, Ezzelino da Romano. He stands as the representative of no system of government or administration, for all his activity was wasted in struggles for supremacy in the eastern part of Upper Italy; but as a political type he was a figure of no less importance for the future than his imperial protector Frederick. The conquests and usurpations which had hitherto taken place in the Middle Ages rested on real or pretended inheritance and other such claims, or else were effected against unbelievers and excommunicated persons. Here for the first time the attempt was openly made to found a throne by wholesale murder and endless barbarities, by the adoption, in short, of any means with a view to nothing but the end pursued. None of his successors, not even Cesare Borgia, rivalled the colossal guilt of Ezzelino; but the example once set was not forgotten, and his fall led to no return of justice among the nations, and served as no warning to future transgressors.

It was in vain at such a time that St Thomas Aquinas, a born subject of Frederick, set up the theory of a constitutional monarchy, in which the prince was to be supported by an upper house named by himself, and a representative body elected by the people. Such theories found no echo outside the lecture-room, and Frederick and Ezzelino were and remain for Italy the great political phenomena of the thirteenth century. Their personality, already half legendary, forms the most important subject of *The Hundred Old Tales*, whose original composition falls certainly within this century. In them Ezzelino is spoken of with the awe which all mighty impressions leave behind them. His person became the centre of a whole literature from the chronicle of eye-witnesses to the half-mystical tragedy of later poets.

DESPOTS OF THE FOURTEENTH CENTURY

The tyrannies, great and small, of the fourteenth century afford constant proof that examples such as these were not thrown away. Their misdeeds cried forth loudly and have been circumstantially told by historians. As states depending for existence on themselves alone, and scientifically organized with a view to this object, they present to us a higher interest than that of mere narrative.

The deliberate adaptation of means to ends, of which no prince out of Italy had at that time a conception, joined to almost absolute power within the limits of the state, produced among the despots both men and modes of life of a peculiar character. The chief secret of government in the hands of the prudent ruler lay in leaving the incidence of taxation so far as possible where he found it, or as he had first arranged it. The chief sources of income were: a land tax, based on a valuation; definite taxes on articles of consumption and duties on exported and imported goods; together with the private fortune of the ruling house. The only possible increase was derived from the growth of business and of general prosperity. Loans, such as we find in the free cities, were here unknown; a well-planned confiscation was held a preferable means of raising money, provided only that it left public credit unshaken – an end attained, for example, by the truly oriental practice of deposing and plundering the director of the finances.

Out of this income the expenses of the little court, of the bodyguard, of the mercenary troops, and of the public buildings were met, as well as of the buffoons and men of talent who belonged to the personal attendants of the prince. The illegitimacy of his rule isolated the tyrant and surrounded him with constant danger; the most honourable alliance which he could form was with intellectual merit, without regard to its origin. The liberality of the northern princes of the thirteenth century was confined to the knights, to the nobility which served and sang. It was otherwise with the Italian despot. With his thirst for fame and his passion for monumental works, it was talent, not birth, which he needed. In the company of the poet and the scholar he felt himself in a new position, almost, indeed in possession of a new legitimacy.

No prince was more famous in this respect than the ruler of Verona, Can Grande della Scala, who numbered among the illustrious exiles whom he entertained at his court representatives of the whole of Italy. The men of letters were not ungrateful. Petrarch, whose visits at the courts of such men have been so severely censured, sketched an ideal picture of a prince of the fourteenth century. He demands great things from his patron, the lord of Padua, but in a manner which shows that he holds him capable of them.

> Thou must not be the master but the father of thy subjects, and must love them as thy children; yea, as members of thy body. Weapons, guards and soldiers thou mayest employ against the enemy – with thy subjects goodwill is sufficient. By citizens, of course, I mean those who love the existing order; for those who daily desire change are rebels and traitors, and against such a stern justice may take its course.

Here follows, worked out in detail, the purely modern fiction of the omnipotence of the state. The prince is to take everything into his charge, to maintain and restore churches and public buildings, to keep up the municipal police,[3] to drain the marshes, to look after the supply of wine and corn; so to distribute the taxes that the people can recognize their necessity; he is to support the sick and the helpless, and to give his protection and society to distinguished scholars, on whom his fame in after ages will depend.

But whatever might be the brighter sides of the system, and the merits of individual rulers, yet the men of the fourteenth century were not without a more or less distinct consciousness of the brief and uncertain tenure of most of these despotisms. Inasmuch as political institutions like these are naturally secure in proportion to the size of the territory in which they exist, the larger principalities were constantly tempted to swallow up the smaller. Whole hecatombs of petty rulers were sacrificed at this time to the Visconti alone. As a result of this outward danger an inward ferment was in ceaseless activity; and the effect of the situation on the character of the ruler was generally of the most sinister kind. Absolute power, with its temptations to luxury and unbridled selfishness, and the perils to which he was exposed from enemies and conspirators, turned him almost inevitably into a tyrant in the worst sense of the word. Well for him if he could trust his nearest relations! But where all was illegitimate, there could be no regular law of inheritance, either with regard to the succession or to the division of the ruler's property; and consequently the heir, if incompetent or a minor, was liable in the interest of the family itself to be supplanted by an uncle or cousin of more resolute character. The acknowledgement or exclusion of the bastards was a fruitful source of contest; and most of these families in consequence were plagued with a crowd of discontented and vindictive kinsmen. This circumstance gave rise to continual outbreaks of treason and to frightful scenes of domestic bloodshed. Sometimes the pretenders lived abroad in exile, and like the Visconti, who practised the fisherman's craft on the Lake of Garda, viewed the situation with patient indifference. When asked by a messenger of his rival when and how he thought of returning to Milan, one gave the reply, 'By the same means as those by which I was expelled, but not till his crimes have outweighed my own.' Sometimes, too, the despot was sacrificed by his relations, with the view of saving the family, to the public conscience which he had too grossly outraged. In a few cases the government was in the hands of the whole family, or at least the ruler was bound to take their advice; and here, too, the distribution of property and influence often led to bitter disputes.

The whole of this system excited the deep and persistent hatred of the Florentine writers of that epoch. Even the pomp and display, with which the despot was perhaps less anxious to gratify his own vanity than to impress the popular imagination, awakened their keenest sarcasm. Woe to an adventurer if he fell into their hands, like the upstart Doge Agnello of Pisa (1364), who used to ride out with a golden sceptre, and show himself at the window of his house, 'as relics are shown', reclining on embroidered drapery and cushions, served like a pope or emperor, by kneeling attendants. More often, however, the old Florentines speak on this subject in a tone of lofty seriousness. Dante saw and characterized well the vulgarity and commonplace which marked the ambition of the new princes. 'What mean their trumpets and their bells, their horns and their flutes; but come, hangman – come, vultures?' The castle of the tyrant, as pictured by the popular mind, is a lofty and solitary building, full of dungeons and listening-tubes, the home of cruelty and misery.[4] Misfortune is foretold to all who enter the service of the despot, who even becomes at last himself an object of pity: he must needs be the enemy of all good and honest men; he can trust no one, and can read in the faces of his subjects the expectation of his fall. 'As despotisms rise, grow, and are consolidated, so grows in their midst the hidden element which must produce their dissolution and ruin.' But the deepest ground of dislike has not been stated; Florence was then the scene of the richest development of human individuality, while for the despots no other individuality could be suffered to live and thrive but their own and that of their nearest dependants. The control of the individual was rigorously carried out, even down to the establishment of a system of passports.[5]

The astrological superstitions and the religious unbelief of many of the tyrants gave, in the minds of their contemporaries, a peculiar colour to this awful and God-forsaken existence. When the last Carrara could no longer defend the walls and gates of the plague-stricken Padua, hemmed in on all sides by the Venetians (1405), the soldiers of the guard heard him cry to the devil 'to come and kill me'.

The most complete and instructive type of the tyranny of the fourteenth century is to be found unquestionably among the Visconti of Milan, from the death of the Archbishop Giovanni onwards (1354). The family likeness which shows itself between Bernabò and the worst of the Roman emperors is unmistakable; the most important public object was the prince's boar-hunting; whoever interfered with it was put to death with torture; the terrified people were forced to maintain 5,000 boar-hounds, with strict responsibility for their health and safety. The taxes were extorted by every conceivable sort of compulsion; seven daughters of the prince received a dowry of 100,000 gold florins apiece; and an enormous treasure was collected. On the death of his wife (1384) an order was issued 'to the subjects' to share his grief, as once they had shared his joy, and to wear mourning for a year. The coup de main (1385) by which his nephew Giangaleazzo got him into his power – one of those brilliant plots which make the heart of even late historians beat more quickly – was strikingly characteristic of the man.

In Giangaleazzo that passion for the colossal which was common to most of the despots shows itself on the largest scale. He undertook, at the cost of 300,000 golden florins, the construction of gigantic dykes, to divert in case of need the Mincio from Mantua and the Brenta from Padua, and thus to render these cities defenceless. It is not impossible, indeed, that he thought of draining away the lagoons of Venice. He founded that most wonderful of all convents, the Certosa of Pavia, and the cathedral of Milan, 'which exceeds in size and splendour all the churches of Christendom'. The Palace in Pavia, which his father Galeazzo began and which he himself finished, was probably by far the most magnificent of the princely dwellings of Europe. There he transferred his famous library, and the great collection of relics of the saints, in which he placed a peculiar faith. It would have been strange indeed if a prince of this character had not also cherished the highest ambitions in political matters. King Wenceslaus made him Duke (1395); he was hoping for nothing less than the kingdom of Italy or the imperial crown, when (1402) he fell ill and died. His whole territories are said to have paid him in a single year, besides the regular contribution of 1,200,000 gold florins, no less than 800,000 more in extraordinary subsidies. After his death the dominions which he had brought together by every sort of violence fell to pieces; and for a time even the original nucleus could with difficulty be maintained by his successors. What might have become of his sons Giovanni Maria (died 1412) and Filippo Maria (died 1417), had they lived in a different country and among other traditions, cannot be said. But, as heirs of their house, they inherited that monstrous capital of cruelty and cowardice which had been accumulated from generation to generation.

Giovanni Maria, too, is famed for his dogs, which were no longer, however, used for hunting but for tearing human bodies. Tradition has preserved their names, like those of the bears of the Emperor Valentinian I. In May 1409, when war was going on, and the starving populace cried to him in the streets, *Pace! Pace!*, he let loose his mercenaries upon them, and 200 lives were sacrificed; under penalty of the gallows it was forbidden to utter the words *pace* and *guerra*, and the priests were ordered, instead of *dona nobis pacem*, to say *tranquillitatem*. At last a band of conspirators took advantage of the moment when Facino Cane, the chief *condottiere* of the insane ruler, lay ill at Pavia, and cut down Giovanni Maria in the church of San Gottardo at Milan;

the dying Facino on the same day made his officers swear to stand by the heir Filippo Maria, whom he himself urged his wife to take for a second husband. His wife, Beatrice di Tenda, followed his advice. We shall have occasion to speak of Filippo Maria later on.

And in times like these Cola di Rienzi was dreaming of founding on the rickety enthusiasm of the corrupt population of Rome a new state which was to comprise all Italy. By the side of rulers such as those whom we have described, he seems no better than a poor deluded fool.

DESPOTS OF THE FIFTEENTH CENTURY

The despotisms of the fifteenth century show an altered character. Many of the less important tyrants, and some of the greater, like the Scala and the Carrara, had disappeared, while the more powerful ones, aggrandized by conquest, had given to their systems each its characteristic development. Naples, for example, received a fresh and stronger impulse from the new Aragonese dynasty. A striking feature of this epoch is the attempt of the *condottieri* to found independent dynasties of their own. Facts and the actual relations of things, apart from traditional estimates, are alone regarded; talent and audacity win the great prizes. The petty despots, to secure a trustworthy support, begin to enter the service of the larger states, and become themselves *condottieri*, receiving in return for their services money and impunity for their misdeeds, if not an increase of territory. All, whether small or great, must exert themselves more, must act with greater caution and calculation, and must learn to refrain from too wholesale barbarities; only so much wrong is permitted by public opinion as is necessary for the end in view, and this the impartial bystander certainly finds no fault with. No trace is here visible of that half-religious loyalty by which the legitimate princes of the West were supported; personal popularity is the nearest approach we can find to it. Talent and calculation are the only means of advancement. A character like that of Charles the Bold, which wore itself out in the passionate pursuit of impracticable ends, was a riddle to the Italians. 'The Swiss were only peasants, and if they were all killed, that would be no satisfaction for the Burgundian nobles who might fall in the war. If the duke got possession of all Switzerland without a struggle, his income would not be 5,000 ducats the greater.' The medieval features in the character of

Charles, his chivalrous aspirations and ideals, had long become unintelligible to the Italians. The diplomatists of the South, when they
saw him strike his officers and yet keep them in his service, when he
maltreated his troops to punish them for a defeat, and then threw the
blame on his counsellors in the presence of the same troops, gave him
up for lost. Louis XI, on the other hand, whose policy surpasses that of
the Italian princes in their own style, and who was an avowed admirer
of Francesco Sforza, must be placed in all that regards culture and
refinement far below these rulers.

Good and evil lie strangely mixed together in the Italian states of the
fifteenth century. The personality of the ruler is so highly developed,
often of such deep significance, and so characteristic of the conditions
and needs of the time, that to form an adequate moral judgement on it
is no easy task.[6]

The foundation of the system was and remained illegitimate, and
nothing could remove the curse which rested upon it. The imperial
approval or investiture made no change in the matter, since the people
attached little weight to the fact that the despot had bought a piece of
parchment somewhere in foreign countries, or from some stranger
passing through his territory. If the emperor had been good for
anything – so ran the logic of uncritical common sense – he would
never have let the tyrant rise at all. Since the Roman expedition of
Charles IV, the emperors had done nothing more in Italy than sanction
a tyranny which had arisen without their help; they could give it no
other practical authority than what might flow from an imperial
charter. The whole conduct of Charles in Italy was a scandalous
political comedy. Matteo Villani relates how the Visconti escorted
him round their territory, and at last out of it; how he went about like
a hawker selling his wares (privileges, etc.) for money; what a mean
appearance he made in Rome, and how at the end, without even
drawing the sword, he returned with replenished coffers across the
Alps. Sigismund came, on the first occasion at least (1414), with the
good intention of persuading John XXIII to take part in his council; it
was on that journey, when pope and emperor were gazing from the
lofty tower of Cremona on the panorama of Lombardy, that their
host, the tyrant Gabrino Fondolo, was seized with the desire to throw
them both over. On his second visit Sigismund came as a mere
adventurer; for more than half a year he remained shut up in Siena,
like a debtor in gaol, and only with difficulty, and at a later period,

succeeded in being crowned in Rome. And what can be thought of
Frederick III? His journeys to Italy have the air of holiday-trips or
pleasure-tours made at the expense of those who wanted him to confirm
their prerogatives, or whose vanity it flattered to entertain an emperor.
The latter was the case with Alfonso of Naples, who paid 150,000
florins for the honour of an imperial visit. At Ferrara, on his second
return from Rome (1469), Frederick spent a whole day without
leaving his chamber, distributing no less than eighty titles; he created
knights, counts, doctors, notaries – counts, indeed, of different degrees,
as, for instance, counts palatine, counts with the right to create doctors
up to the number of five, counts with the rights to legitimatize
bastards, to appoint notaries, and so forth. The chancellor, however,
expected in return for the patents in question a gratuity which was
thought excessive at Ferrara. The opinion of Borso, himself created
Duke of Modena and Reggio in return for an annual payment of
4,000 gold florins, when his imperial patron was distributing titles and
diplomas to all the little court, is not mentioned. The humanists, then
the chief spokesmen of the age, were divided in opinion according to
their personal interests, while the emperor was greeted by some of
them with the conventional acclamations of the poets of imperial
Rome. Poggio confessed that he no longer knew what the coronation
meant; in the old times only the victorious Imperator was crowned;
and then he was crowned with laurel.

With Maximilian I begins not only the general intervention of
foreign nations, but a new imperial policy with regard to Italy. The
first step – the investiture of Lodovico il Moro with the duchy of
Milan and the exclusion of his unhappy nephew – was not of a kind to
bear good fruits. According to the modern theory of intervention,
when two parties are tearing a country to pieces, a third may step in
and take its share, and on this principle the empire acted. But right and
justice were appealed to no longer. When Louis XII was expected in
Genoa (1502), and the imperial eagle was removed from the hall of the
ducal palace and replaced by painted lilies, the historian Senarega
asked what, after all, was the meaning of the eagle which so many
revolutions had spared, and what claims the empire had upon Genoa.
No one knew more about the matter than the old phrase that Genoa
was a *camera imperii*. In fact, nobody in Italy could give a clear answer
to any such questions. At length, when Charles V held Spain and the
empire together, he was able by means of Spanish forces to make good

imperial claims; but it is notorious that what he thereby gained turned to the profit, not of the empire, but of the Spanish monarchy.

Closely connected with the political illegitimacy of the dynasties of the fifteenth century was the public indifference to legitimate birth, which to foreigners – for example, to Comines – appeared so remarkable. The two things went naturally together. In northern countries, as in Burgundy, the illegitimate offspring were provided for by a distinct class of appanages, such as bishoprics and the like; in Portugal an illegitimate line maintained itself on the throne only by constant effort; in Italy, on the contrary, there no longer existed a princely house where, even in the direct line of descent, bastards were not patiently tolerated. The Aragonese monarchs of Naples belonged to the illegitimate line, Aragon itself falling to the lot of the brother of Alfonso I. The great Frederick of Urbino was, perhaps, no Montefeltro at all. When Pius II was on his way to the Congress of Mantua (1459), eight bastards of the house of Este rode to meet him at Ferrara, among them the reigning duke Borso himself and two illegitimate sons of his illegitimate brother and predecessor Lionello. The latter had also had a lawful wife, herself an illegitimate daughter of Alfonso I of Naples by an African woman. The bastards were often admitted to the succession where the lawful children were minors and the dangers of the situation were pressing; and a rule of seniority became recognized, which took no account of pure or impure birth. The fitness of the individual, his worth and capacity, were of more weight than all the laws and usages which prevailed elsewhere in the West. It was the age, indeed, in which the sons of the popes were founding dynasties. In the sixteenth century, through the influence of foreign ideas and of the Counter-Reformation which then began, the whole question was judged more strictly: Varchi discovers that the succession of the legitimate children 'is ordered by reason, and is the will of heaven from eternity'. Cardinal Ippolito de' Medici founded his claim to the lordship of Florence on the fact that he was perhaps the fruit of a lawful marriage, and at all events son of a gentlewoman, and not, like Duke Alessandro, of a servant girl. At this time began those morganatic marriages of affection which in the fifteenth century, on grounds either of policy or morality, would have had no meaning at all.

But the highest and the most admired form of illegitimacy in the fifteenth century was presented by the *condottiere*, who, whatever may have been his origin, raised himself to the position of an independent ruler. At bottom, the occupation of Lower Italy by the Normans in the eleventh century was of this character. Such attempts now began to keep the peninsula in a constant ferment.

It was possible for a *condottiere* to obtain the lordship of a district even without usurpation, in the case when his employer, through want of money or troops, provided for him in this way; under any circumstances the *condottiere*, even when he dismissed for the time the greater part of his forces, needed a safe place where he could establish his winter quarters, and lay up his stores and provisions. The first example of a captain thus portioned is John Hawkwood, who was invested by Gregory XI with the lordship of Bagnacavallo and Cotignola. When with Alberigo de Barbiano Italian armies and leaders appeared upon the scene, the chances of founding a principality, or of increasing one already acquired, became more frequent. The first great bacchanalian outbreak of military ambition took place in the duchy of Milan after the death of Giangaleazzo (1402). The policy of his two sons was chiefly aimed at the destruction of the new despotisms founded by the *condottieri*; and from the greatest of them, Facino Cane, the house of Visconti inherited, together with his widow, a long list of cities, and 400,000 golden florins, not to speak of the soldiers of her first husband whom Beatrice di Tenda brought with her. From henceforth that thoroughly immoral relation between the governments and their *condottieri*, which is characteristic of the fifteenth century, became more and more common. An old story – one of those which are true and not true, everywhere and nowhere – describes it as follows: The citizens of a certain town (Siena seems to be meant) had once an officer in their service who had freed them from foreign aggression; daily they took counsel how to recompense him, and concluded that no reward in their power was great enough, not even if they made him lord of the city. At last one of them rose and said, 'Let us kill him and then worship him as our patron saint.' And so they did, following the example set by the Roman senate with Romulus. In fact, the *condottieri* had reason to fear none so much as their employers; if they were successful, they became dangerous, and were put out of the way like Roberto Malatesta just after the victory he had won for Sixtus IV (1482); if they failed, the vengeance of the Venetians on Carmagnola showed to what risks they were exposed (1432).[7] It is characteristic of the moral aspect of the situation that the *condottieri* had often to give their wives and children as hostages, and notwithstanding this, neither felt nor inspired confidence. They must have been heroes of abnegation, natures like Belisarius himself, not to be cankered by hatred and bitterness; only the most perfect goodness could save them from the most monstrous iniquity. No wonder then if we find them full of contempt for all sacred things, cruel and treacherous to their fellows – men who cared nothing whether or no they died under the ban of the Church. At the same time, and through the force of the same conditions, the genius and capacity of many among them attained the highest conceivable development, and won for them the admiring devotion of their followers; their armies are the first in modern history in which the personal credit of the leader is the one moving power. A brilliant example is shown in the life of Francesco Sforza; no prejudice of birth could prevent him from winning and turning to account when he needed it a boundless devotion from each individual with whom he had to deal; it happened more than once that his enemies laid down their arms at the sight of him, greeting him reverently with uncovered heads, each honouring in him 'the common father of the men-at-arms'. The race of the Sforza has this special interest, that from the very beginning of its history we seem able to trace its endeavours after the crown. The foundation of its fortune lay in the remarkable fruitfulness of the family; Francesco's father, Jacopo, himself a cele-brated man, had twenty brothers and sisters, all brought up roughly at Cotignola, near Faenza, amid the perils of one of the endless Rom-agnole vendettas between their own house and that of the Pasolini. The family dwelling was a mere arsenal and fortress; the mother and daughters were as warlike as their kinsmen. In his thirteenth year Jacopo ran away and fled to Panicale to the papal *condottiere* Boldrino – the man who even in death continued to lead his troops, the word of order being given from the bannered tent in which the embalmed body lay, till at last a fit leader was found to succeed him. Jacopo, when he had at length made himself a name in the service of different *condottieri*, sent for his relations, and obtained through them the same advantages that a prince derives from a numerous dynasty. It was these relations who kept the army together when he lay a captive in the Castel dell'Uovo at Naples; his sister took the royal envoys prisoner with her own hands, and saved him by this reprisal from death. It was an indication of the breadth and the range of his plans that in monetary affairs Jacopo was thoroughly trustworthy; even in his defeats he consequently found credit with the bankers. He habitually protected the peasants against the licence of his troops, and reluctantly destroyed or injured a conquered city. He gave his well-known mistress, Lucia, the mother of Francesco, in marriage to another, in order to be free for a princely alliance. Even the marriages of his relations were arranged on a definite plan. He kept clear of the impious and profligate life of his contemporaries, and brought up his son Francesco to the three rules: 'Let other men's wives alone; strike none of your followers, or, if you do, send the injured man far away; don't ride a hard-mouthed horse, or one that drops his shoe.' But his chief source of influence lay in the qualities, if not of a great general, at least of a great soldier. His frame was powerful, and developed by every kind of exercise; his peasant's face and frank manners won general popularity; his memory was marvellous, and after the lapse of years could recall the names of his followers, the number of their horses, and the amount of their pay. His education was purely Italian: he devoted his leisure to the study of history, and had Greek and Latin authors translated for his use. Francesco, his still more famous son, set his mind from the first on founding a powerful state, and through brilliant generalship and a faithlessness which hesitated at nothing, got possession of the great city of Milan (1447–50).

His example was contagious. Aeneas Sylvius wrote about this time: 'In our change-loving Italy, where nothing stands firm, and where no ancient dynasty exists, a servant can easily become a king.' One man in particular, who styles himself 'the man of fortune', filled the imagination of the whole country: Giacomo Piccinino, the son of Niccolò. It was a burning question of the day if he, too, would succeed in founding a princely house. The greater states had an obvious interest in hindering it, and even Francesco Sforza thought it would be all the better if the list of self-made sovereigns were not enlarged. But the troops and captains sent against him, at the time, for instance, when he was aiming at the lordship of Siena, recognized their interest in supporting him: 'If it were all over with him, we should have to go back and plough our fields.' Even while besieging him at Orbetello, they supplied him with provisions; and he got out of his straits with honour. But at last fate overtook him. All Italy was betting on the result, when (1465), after a visit to Sforza at Milan, he went to King Ferrante at Naples. In spite of the pledges given, and of his high connections, he was murdered in the Castel Nuovo. Even the *condottieri,* who had obtained their dominions by inheritance, never felt themselves safe. When Roberto Malatesta and Frederick of Urbino died on the same day (1482), the one at Rome, the other at Bologna, it was found that each had recommended his state to the care of the other. Against a class of men who themselves stuck at nothing, everything was held to be permissible. Francesco Sforza, when quite young, had married a rich Calabrian heiress, Polissena Russa, Countess of Montalto, who bore him a daughter; an aunt poisoned both mother and child, and seized the inheritance.

From the death of Piccinino onwards, the foundations of new states by the *condottieri* became a scandal not to be tolerated. The four great powers, Naples, Milan, the papacy and Venice, formed among themselves a political equilibrium which refused to allow of any disturbance. In the States of the Church, which swarmed with petty tyrants, who in part were, or had been, *condottieri*, the nephews of the popes, since the time of Sixtus IV, monopolized the right to all such undertakings. But at the first sign of a political crisis, the soldiers of fortune appeared again upon the scene. Under the wretched administration of Innocent VIII it was near happening that a certain Boccalino, who had formerly served in the Burgundian army, gave himself and the town of Osimo, of which he was master, up to the Turkish forces; fortunately, through the intervention of Lorenzo the Magnificent, he proved willing to be paid off, and took himself away. In the year 1495, when the wars of Charles VIII had turned Italy upside down, the *condottiere* Vidovero, of Brescia, made trial of his strength: he had already seized the town of Cesena and murdered many of the nobles and the burghers; but the citadel held out, and he was forced to withdraw. He then, at the head of a band lent him by another scoundrel, Pandolfo Malatesta of Rimini, son of the Roberto already spoken of, and Venetian *condottiere*, wrested the town of Castelnuovo from the Archbishop of Ravenna. The Venetians, fearing that worse would follow, and urged also by the pope, ordered Pandolfo, 'with the kindest intentions', to take an opportunity of arresting his good friend: the arrest was made, though 'with great regret', whereupon the order came to bring the prisoner to the gallows. Pandolfo was considerate enough to strangle him in prison, and then show his corpse to the people. The last notable example of such usurpers is the famous castellan of Musso, who, during the confusion in the Milanese territory which followed the battle of Pavia (1525), improvised a sovereignty on the Lake of Como.

THE SMALLER DESPOTISMS

It may be said in general of the despotisms of the fifteenth century that the greatest crimes are most frequent in the smallest states. In these, where the family was numerous and all the members wished to live in a manner befitting their rank, disputes respecting the inheritance were unavoidable. Bernardo Varano of Camerino put two of his brothers to death (1434), wishing to divide their property among his sons. Where the ruler of a single town was distinguished by a wise, moderate and humane government, and by zeal for intellectual culture, he was generally a member of some great family, or politically dependent on it. This was the case, for example, with Alessandro Sforza, Prince of Pesaro (d. 1473), brother of the great Francesco, and step-father of Frederick of Urbino. Prudent in administration, just and affable in his rule, he enjoyed, after years of warfare, a tranquil reign, collected a noble library, and passed his leisure in learned or religious conversation. A man of the same class was Giovanni II Bentivoglio of Bologna (1462–1506), whose policy was determined by that of the Este and the Sforza. What ferocity and bloodthirstiness is found, on the other hand, among the Varani of Camerino, the Malatesta of Rimini, the Manfreddi of Faenza, and above all among the Baglioni of Perugia. We find a striking picture of the events in the last-named family, towards the close of the fifteenth century, in the admirable historical narratives of Graziani and Matarazzo.

The Baglioni were one of those families whose rule never took the shape of an avowed despotism. It was rather a leadership exercised by means of their vast wealth and of their practical influence in the choice of public officers. Within the family one man was recognized as head; but deep and secret jealousy prevailed among the members of the different branches. Opposed to the Baglioni stood another aristocratic party, led by the family of the Oddi. In 1487 the city was turned into a camp, and the houses of the leading citizens swarmed with bravos; scenes of violence were of daily occurrence. At the burial of a German student, who had been assassinated, two colleges took arms against one another; sometimes the bravos of the different houses even joined battle in the public square. The complaints of the merchants and artisans were vain; the papal governors and *nipoti* held their tongues, or took themselves off on the first opportunity. At last the Oddi were forced to abandon Perugia, and the city became a beleaguered fortress under the absolute despotism of the Baglioni, who used even the cathedral as barracks. Plots and surprises were met with cruel vengeance; in the year 1491, after 130 conspirators who had forced their way into the city were killed and hung up at the Palazzo Comunale, thirty-five altars were erected in the square, and for three days mass was performed and processions held, to take away the curse which rested on the spot. A nephew of Innocent VIII was in open day run through in the street. A nephew of Alexander VI, who was sent to smooth matters over, was dismissed with public contempt. All the while the two leaders of the ruling house, Guido and Ridolfo, were holding frequent interviews with Suor Colomba of Rieti, a Dominican nun of saintly reputation and miraculous powers, who under penalty of some great disaster ordered them to make peace – naturally in vain. Nevertheless the chronicle takes the opportunity to point out the devotion and piety of the better men in Perugia during this reign of terror. When in 1494 Charles VIII approached, the Baglioni from Perugia and the exiles encamped in and near Assisi conducted the war with such ferocity that every house in the valley was levelled to the ground. The fields lay untilled, the peasants were turned into plundering and murdering savages, the fresh-grown bushes were filled with stags and wolves, and the beasts grew fat on the bodies of the slain, on so-called 'Christian flesh'. When Alexander VI withdrew (1495) into Umbria before Charles VIII, then returning from Naples, it occurred to him, when at Perugia, that he might now rid himself of the Baglioni once for all; he proposed to Guido a festival or tournament, or something else of the same kind, which would bring the whole family together. Guido, however, was of the opinion 'that the most impressive spectacle of all would be to see the whole military force of Perugia collected in a body', whereupon the pope abandoned his project. Soon after, the exiles made another attack in which nothing but the personal heroism of the Baglioni won them the victory. It was then that Simonetto Baglione, a lad of scarcely eighteen, fought in the square with a handful of followers against hundreds of the enemy: he fell at last with more than twenty wounds, but recovered himself when Astorre Baglione came to his help, and mounting on horseback in gilded armour with a falcon on his helmet, 'like Mars in bearing and in deeds, plunged into the struggle'.

At that time Raphael, a boy of twelve years of age, was at school under Pietro Perugino. The impressions of these days are perhaps immortalized in the small, early pictures of St Michael and St George: something of them, it may be, lives eternally in the great painting of St Michael: and if Astorre Baglione has anywhere found his apotheosis, it is in the figure of the heavenly horseman in the Heliodorus.[8]

The opponents of the Baglioni were partly destroyed, partly scattered in terror, and were henceforth incapable of another enterprise of the kind. After a time a partial reconciliation took place, and some of the exiles were allowed to return. But Perugia became none the safer or more tranquil: the inward discord of the ruling family broke out in frightful excesses. An opposition was formed against Guido and Ridolfo and their sons Gianpaolo, Simonetto, Astorre, Gismondo, Gentile, Marcantinio and others, by two great-nephews, Grifone and Carlo Barciglia; the latter of the two was also nephew of Varano, Prince of Camerino, and brother-in-law of one of the former exiles, Ieronimo della Penna. In vain did Simonetto, warned by sinister presentiment, entreat his uncle on his knees to allow him to put Penna to death: Guido refused. The plot ripened suddenly on the occasion of the marriage of Astorre with Lavinia Colonna, at midsummer 1500. The festival began and lasted several days amid gloomy forebodings, whose deepening effect is admirably described by Matarazzo. Varano fed and encouraged them with devilish ingenuity: he worked upon Grifone by the prospect of undivided authority, and by stories of an imaginary intrigue of his wife Zenobia with Gianpaolo. Finally each conspirator was provided with a victim. (The Baglioni lived all of them in separate houses, mostly on the site of the present castle.) Each received fifteen of the bravos at hand; the remainder were set on the watch. In the night of 15 July the doors were forced, and Guido, Astorre, Simonetto and Gismondo were murdered; the others succeeded in escaping.

As the corpse of Astorre lay by that of Simonetto in the street, the spectators, 'and especially the foreign students', compared him to an ancient Roman, so great and imposing did he seem. In the features of Simonetto could still be traced the audacity and defiance which death itself had not tamed. The victors went round among the friends of the family, and did their best to recommend themselves; they found all in tears and preparing to leave for the country. Meantime the escaped Baglioni collected forces without the city, and on the following day forced their way in, Gianpaolo at their head, and speedily found adherents among others whom Barciglia had been threatening with death. When Grifone fell into their hands near Sant' Ercolano, Gianpaolo handed him over for execution to his followers. Barciglia and Penna fled to Varano, the chief author of the tragedy, at Camerino; and in a moment, almost without loss, Gianpaolo became master of the city.

Atalanta, the still young and beautiful mother of Grifone, who the day before had withdrawn to a country house with the latter's wife Zenobia and two children of Gianpaolo, and more than once had repulsed her son with a mother's curse, now returned with her daughter-in-law in search of the dying man. All stood aside as the two women approached, each man shrinking from being recognized as the slayer of Grifone, and dreading the malediction of the mother. But they were deceived: she herself besought her son to pardon him who had dealt the fatal blow, and he died with her blessing. The eyes of the crowd followed the two women reverently as they crossed the square with blood-stained garments. It was Atalanta for whom Raphael afterwards painted the world-famed *Deposition*, with which she laid her own maternal sorrows at the feet of a yet higher and holier suffering.[9]

The cathedral, in the immediate neighbourhood of which the greater part of this tragedy had been enacted, was washed with wine and consecrated afresh. The triumphal arch, erected for the wedding, still remained standing, painted with the deeds of Astorre and with the laudatory verses of the narrator of these events, the worthy Matarazzo.

A legendary history, which is simply the reflection of these atrocities, arose out of the early days of the Baglioni. All the members of this family from the beginning were reported to have died an evil death – twenty-seven on one occasion together; their houses were said to have been once before levelled to the ground, and the streets of Perugia paved with the bricks – and more of the same kind. Under Paul III the destruction of their palaces really took place.

For a time they seemed to have formed good resolutions, to have brought their own party into order, and to have protected the public officials against the arbitrary acts of the nobility. But the old curse broke out again like a smouldering fire. In 1520 Gianpaolo was enticed to Rome under Leo X, and there beheaded; one of his sons, Orazio, who ruled in Perugia for a short time only, and by the most violent means, as the partisan of the Duke of Urbino (himself threatened by the pope), once more repeated in his own family the horrors of the past. His uncle and three cousins were murdered, whereupon the duke sent him word that enough had been done. His brother, Malatesta Baglione, the Florentine general, has made himself immortal by the treason of 1530; and Malatesta's son Ridolfo, the last of the house, attained, by the murder of the legate and the public officers in the year 1534, a brief but sanguinary authority.

Here and there we meet with the names of the rulers of Rimini. Unscrupulousness, impiety, military skill and high culture have been seldom combined in one individual as in Sigismondo Malatesta (d. 1467). But the accumulated crimes of such a family must at last outweigh all talent, however great, and drag the tyrant into the abyss. Pandolfo, Sigismondo's nephew, who has been mentioned already, succeeded in holding his ground, for the sole reason that the Venetians refused to abandon their *condottiere*, whatever guilt he might be chargeable with; when his subjects, after ample provocation, bombarded him in his castle at Rimini (1497), and afterwards allowed him to escape, a Venetian commissioner brought him back, stained as he was with fratricide and every other abomination. Thirty years later the Malatesta were penniless exiles. In the year 1527, as in the time of Cesare Borgia, a sort of epidemic fell on the petty tyrants; few of them outlived this date, and none to their own good. At Mirandola, which was governed by insignificant princes of the house of Pico, lived in the year 1533 a poor scholar, Lilio Gregorio Giraldi, who had fled from the sack of Rome to the hospitable hearth of the aged Giovanni Francesco Pico, nephew of the famous Giovanni; the discussions as to the sepulchral monument which the prince was constructing for himself gave rise to a treatise, the dedication of which bears the date of April in this year. The postscript is a sad one – 'In October of the same year the unhappy prince was attacked in the night and robbed of life and throne by his brother's son; and I myself escaped narrowly, and am now in the deepest misery.'

A pseudo-despotism without characteristic features, such as Pandolfo Petrucci exercised from the year 1490 in Siena, then torn by faction, is hardly worth a closer consideration. Insignificant and malicious, he governed with the help of a professor of jurisprudence and of an astrologer, and frightened his people by an occasional murder. His pastime in the summer months was to roll blocks of stone from the top of Monte Amiata, without caring what or whom they hit. After succeeding, where the most prudent failed, in escaping from the devices of Cesare Borgia, he died at last forsaken and despised. His sons maintained a qualified supremacy for many years afterwards.

THE GREATER DYNASTIES

In treating of the chief dynasties of Italy, it is convenient to discuss the Aragonese, on account of its special character, apart from the rest. The feudal system, which from the days of the Normans had survived in the form of a territorial supremacy of the barons, gave a distinctive colour to the political constitution of Naples; while elsewhere in Italy, excepting only in the southern part of the ecclesiastical dominion, and in a few other districts, a direct tenure of land prevailed, and no hereditary powers were permitted by the law. The great Alfonso, who reigned in Naples from 1435 onwards (d. 1458), was a man of another kind than his real or alleged descendants. Brilliant in his whole existence, fearless in mixing with his people, dignified and affable in intercourse, admired rather than blamed even for his old man's passion for Lucrezia d'Alagnam, he had the one bad quality of extravagance, from which, however, the natural consequence followed. Unscrupulous financiers were long omnipotent at court, till the bankrupt king robbed them of their spoils; a crusade was preached as a pretext for taxing the clergy; when a great earthquake happened in the Abruzzi, the survivors were compelled to make good the contributions of the dead. By such means Alfonso was able to entertain distinguished guests with unrivalled splendour; he found pleasure in ceaseless expense, even for the benefit of his enemies, and in rewarding literary work knew absolutely no measure. Poggio received 500 pieces of gold for translating Xenophon's *Cyropaedeia*.

Ferrante, who succeeded him, passed as his illegitimate son by a Spanish lady, but was not improbably the son of a half-caste Moor of Valencia. Whether it was his blood or the plots formed against his life by the barons which embittered and darkened his nature, it is certain that he was equalled in ferocity by none among the princes of his time. Restlessly active, recognized as one of the most powerful political minds of the day, and free from the vices of the profligate, he concentrated all his powers, among which must be reckoned profound dissimulation and an irreconcilable spirit of vengeance, on the destruction of his opponents. He had been wounded in every point in which a ruler is open to offence; for the leaders of the barons, though related to him by marriage, were yet the allies of his foreign enemies. Extreme measures became part of his daily policy. The means for this struggle with his barons, and for his external wars, were exacted in the same Muhammadan fashion which Frederick II had introduced: the government alone dealt in oil and corn; the whole commerce of the country was put by Ferrante into the hands of a wealthy merchant, Francesco Coppola, who had entire control of the anchorage on the coast, and shared the profits with the king. Deficits were made up by forced loans, by executions and confiscations, by open simony, and by contributions levied on the ecclesiastical corporations. Besides hunting, which he practised regardless of all rights of property, his pleasures were of two kinds: he liked to have his opponents near him, either alive in well-guarded prisons, or dead and embalmed, dressed in the costume which they wore in their lifetime. He would chuckle in talking of the captives with his friends, and made no secret whatever of the museum of mummies. His victims were mostly men whom he had got into his power by treachery; some were even seized while guests at the royal table. His conduct to his first minister, Antolello Petrucci, who had grown sick and grey in his service, and from whose increasing fear of death he extorted 'present after present', was literally devilish. At length the suspicion of complicity with the last conspiracy of the barons gave the pretext for his arrest and execution. With him died Coppola. The way in which all this is narrated in Caracciolo and Porzio makes one's hair stand on end.

The elder of the king's sons, Alfonso, Duke of Calabria, enjoyed in later years a kind of co-regency with his father. He was a savage, brutal profligate, who in point of frankness alone had the advantage of Ferrante, and who openly avowed his contempt for religion and its usages. The better and nobler features of the Italian despotisms are not to be found among the princes of this line; all that they possessed of the art and culture of their time served the purposes of luxury or display. Even the genuine Spaniards seem to have almost always degenerated in Italy; but the end of this cross-bred house (1494 and 1503) gives clear proof of a want of blood. Ferrante died of mental care and trouble; Alfonso accused his brother Federigo, the only honest member of the family, of treason, and insulted him in the vilest manner. At length, though he had hitherto passed for one of the ablest generals in Italy, he lost his head and fled to Sicily, leaving his son, the younger Ferrante, a prey to the French and to domestic treason. A dynasty which had ruled as this had done must at least have sold its life dear, if its children were ever to hope for a restoration. But, as Comines one-sidedly and yet on the whole rightly observes on this occasion, '*Jamais homme cruel ne fut plus hardi*': there was never a more cruel man.

The despotism of the dukes of Milan, whose government from the time of Giangaleazzo onwards was an absolute monarchy of the most thoroughgoing sort, shows the genuine Italian character of the fifteenth century. The last of the Visconti, Filippo Maria (1412–47), is a character of peculiar interest, and of which fortunately an admirable description has been left us. What a man of uncommon gifts and high position can be made by the passion of fear is here shown with what may be called a mathematical completeness. All the resources of the state were devoted to the one end of securing his personal safety, though happily his cruel egotism did not degenerate into a purposeless thirst for blood. He lived in the Citadel of Milan, surrounded by magnificent gardens, arbours and lawns. For years he never set foot in the city, making his excursions only in the country, where lay several of his splendid castles; the flotilla which, drawn by the swiftest horses, conducted him to them along canals constructed for the purpose, was so arranged as to allow of the application of the most rigorous etiquette. Whoever entered the Citadel was watched by a hundred eyes; it was forbidden even to stand at the window, lest signs should be given to those without. All who were admitted among the personal followers of the prince were subjected to a series of the strictest examinations; then, once accepted, were charged with the highest diplomatic commissions, as well as with the humblest personal services – both in this court being alike honourable. And this was the man who conducted long and difficult wars, who dealt habitually with political affairs of the first importance, and every day sent his plenipotentiaries to all parts of Italy. His safety lay in the fact that none of his servants trusted the others, that his *condottieri* were watched and misled by spies, and that the ambassadors and higher officials were baffled and kept apart by artificially nourished jealousies, and in particular by the device of coupling an honest man with a knave. His inward faith, too, rested upon opposed and contradictory systems; he believed in blind necessity, and in the influence of the stars, and offering prayers at one and the same time to helpers of every sort; he was a student of the ancient authors, as well as of French tales of chivalry. And yet the same man, who would never suffer death to be mentioned in his presence, and caused his dying favourites to be removed from the castle, that no shadow might fall on the abode of happiness, deliberately hastened his own death by closing up a wound, and, refusing to be bled, died at last with dignity and grace.

His son-in-law and successor, the fortunate *condottiere* Francesco Sforza (1450–66), was perhaps of all the Italians of the fifteenth century the man most after the heart of his age. Never was the triumph of genius and individual power more brilliantly displayed than in him; and those who would not recognize his merit were at least forced to wonder at him as the spoilt child of fortune. The Milanese claimed it openly as an honour to be governed by so distinguished a master; when he entered the city the thronging populace bore him on horseback into the cathedral, without giving him the chance to dismount. Let us listen to the balance-sheet of his life, in the estimate of Pope Pius II, a judge in such matters:

> In the year 1459, when the duke came to the congress at Mantua, he was sixty (really fifty-eight) years old; on horseback he looked like a young man; of a lofty and imposing figure, with serious features, calm and affable in conversation, princely in his whole bearing, with a combination of bodily and intellectual gifts unrivalled in our time, unconquered on the field of battle – such was the man who raised himself from a humble position to the control of an empire. His wife was beautiful and virtuous, his children were like the angels of heaven; he was seldom ill, and all his chief wishes were fulfilled. And yet he was not without misfortune. His wife, out of jealousy, killed his mistress; his old comrades and friends, Troilo and Brunoro, abandoned him and went over to King Alfonso; another, Ciarpollone, he was forced to hang for treason; he had to suffer it that his brother Alessandro set the French upon him; one of his sons formed intrigues against him, and was imprisoned; the March of Ancona, which he had won in war, he lost again the same way. No man enjoys so unclouded a fortune, that he has not somewhere to struggle with adversity. He is happy who has but few troubles.

With this negative definition of happiness the learned pope dismisses the reader. Had he been able to see into the future, or been willing to stop and discuss the consequences of an uncontrolled despotism, one pervading fact would not have escaped his notice – the absence of all guarantee for the future. Those children, beautiful as angels, carefully and thoroughly educated as they were, fell victims, when they grew up, to the corruption of a measureless egotism. Galeazzo Maria (1466–76), solicitous only of outward effect, took pride in the beauty of his hands, in the high salaries he paid, in the financial credit he enjoyed, in his treasure of two million pieces of gold, in the distinguished people who surrounded him, and in the army and birds of chase which he maintained. He was fond of the sound of his own voice, and spoke well, most fluently, perhaps, when he had the chance of insulting a Venetian ambassador. He was subject to caprices, such as having a room painted with figures in a single night; and, what was worse, to fits of senseless debauchery and of revolting cruelty to his nearest friends. To a handful of enthusiasts, he seemed a tyrant too bad to live; they murdered him, and thereby delivered the state into the power of his brothers, one of whom, Lodovico il Moro, threw his nephew into prison, and took the government into his own hands. From this usurpation followed the French intervention, and the disasters which befell the whole of Italy.

Lodovico Sforza, called 'il Moro', the Moor, is the most perfect type of the despot of that age, and, as a kind of natural product, almost disarms our moral judgement. Notwithstanding the profound immorality of the means he employed, he used them with perfect ingeniousness; no one would probably have been more astonished than himself to learn that for the choice of means as well as of ends a human being is morally responsible; he would rather have reckoned it as a singular virtue that, so far as possible, he had abstained from too free a use of the punishment of death. He accepted as no more than his due the almost fabulous respect of the Italians for his political genius. In 1496 he boasted that the Pope Alexander was his chaplain, the Emperor Maximilian his *condottiere*, Venice his chamberlain, and the King of France his courier, who must come and go at his bidding. With marvellous presence of mind he weighed, even in his last extremity (1499), all possible means of escape, and at length decided, to his honour, to trust to the goodness of human nature; he rejected the proposal of his brother, the Cardinal Ascanio, who wished to remain in the Citadel of Milan, on the ground of a former quarrel: 'Monsignore, take it not ill, but I trust you not, brother though you be'; and appointed to the command of the castle, 'that pledge of his return', a man to whom he had always done good, but who nevertheless betrayed him. At home the Moor was a good and useful ruler, and to the last he reckoned on his popularity both in Milan and in Como. In later years (after 1496) he had overstrained the resources of his state, and at Cremona had ordered, out of pure expediency, a respectable citizen, who had spoken against the new taxes, to be quietly strangled. Since that time, in holding audiences, he kept his visitors away from his person by means of a bar, so that in conversing with him they were compelled to speak at the top of their voices. At his court, the most brilliant in Europe, since that of Burgundy had ceased to exist, immorality of the worst kind was prevalent; the daughter was sold by the father, the wife by the husband, the sister by the brother. The prince himself was incessantly active, and, as son of his own deeds, claimed relationship with all who, like himself, stood on their personal merits — with scholars, poets, artists and musicians. The academy which he founded served rather for his own purposes than for the instruction of scholars; nor was it the fame of the distinguished men who surrounded him which he heeded, so much as their society and their services. It is certain that Bramante was scantily paid at first; Leonardo, on the other hand, was up to 1496 suitably remunerated — and besides, what kept him at the court, if not his own free will? The world lay open to him, as perhaps to no other mortal man of that day; and if proof were wanting of the loftier element in the nature of Lodovico il Moro, it is found in the long stay of the enigmatic master at his court. That afterwards Leonardo entered the service of Cesare Borgia and Francis I was probably due to the interest he felt in the unusual and striking character of the two men.

After the fall of the Moor, his sons were badly brought up among strangers. The elder, Massimiliano, had no resemblance to him; the younger, Francesco, was at all events not without spirit. Milan, which in those years changed its rulers so often, and suffered so unspeakably in the change, endeavoured to secure itself against a reaction. In the year 1512 the French, retreating before the arms of Maximilian and the Spaniards, were induced to make a declaration that the Milanese had taken no part in their expulsion, and, without being guilty of rebellion, might yield themselves to a new conqueror. It is a fact of some political importance that in such moments of transition the unhappy city, like Naples at the flight of the Aragonese, was apt to fall a prey to gangs of (often highly aristocratic) scoundrels.

The house of Gonzaga at Mantua and that of Montefeltro of

Urbino were among the best ordered and richest in men of ability during the second half of the fifteenth century. The Gonzaga were a tolerably harmonious family; for a long period no murder had been known among them, and their dead could be shown to the world without fear. The Marquis Francesco Gonzaga[10] and his wife, Isabella of Este, in spite of some few irregularities, were a united and respectable couple, and brought up their sons to be successful and remarkable men at a time when their small but most important state was exposed to incessant danger. That Francesco, either as statesman or as soldier, should adopt a policy of exceptional honesty, was what neither the emperor, nor Venice, nor the King of France could have expected or desired; but certainly since the battle of the Taro (1495), so far as military honour was concerned, he felt and acted as an Italian patriot, and imparted the same spirit to his wife. Every deed of loyalty and heroism, such as the defence of Faenza against Cesare Borgia, she felt as a vindication of the honour of Italy. Our judgement of her does not need to rest on the praises of the artists and writers who made the fair princess a rich return for her patronage; her own letters show her to us as a woman of unshaken firmness, full of kindliness and humorous observation. Bembo, Bandello, Ariosto and Bernardo Tasso sent their works to this court, small and powerless as it was, and empty as they found its treasury. A more polished and charming circle was not to be seen in Italy, since the dissolution (1508) of the old court of Urbino; and in one respect, in freedom of movement, the society of Ferrara was inferior to that of Mantua. In artistic matters Isabella had an accurate knowledge, and the catalogue of her small but choice collection can be read by no lover of art without emotion.

In the great Federigo (1444–82), whether he were a genuine Montefeltro or not, Urbino possessed a brilliant representative of the princely order. As a *condottiere* he shared the political morality of soldiers of fortune, a morality of which the fault does not rest with them alone; as ruler of his little territory he adopted the plan of spending at home the money he had earned abroad, and taxing his people as lightly as possible. Of him and his two successors, Guidobaldo and Francesco Maria, we read: 'They erected buildings, furthered the cultivation of the land, lived at home, and gave employment to a large number of people: their subjects loved them.' But not only the state, but the court too, was a work of art and organization, and this in every sense of the word. Federigo had 500 persons in his service; the arrangements of the court were as complete as in the capitals of the greatest monarchs, but nothing was wasted; all had its object, and all was carefully watched and controlled. The court was no scene of vice and dissipation: it served as a school of military education for the sons of other great houses, the thoroughness of whose culture and instruction was made a point of honour by the duke. The palace which he built, if not one of the most splendid, was classical in the perfection of its plan; there was placed the greatest of his treasures, the celebrated library. Feeling secure in a land where all gained profit or employment from his rule, and where none were beggars, he habitually went about unarmed and almost unaccompanied; alone among the princes of his time he ventured to walk in an open park, and to take his frugal meals in an open chamber, while Livy, or in time of fasting some devotional work, was read to him. In the course of the same afternoon he would listen to a lecture on some classical subject, and thence would go to the monastery of the Clarisses and talk of sacred things through the grating with the abbess. In the evening he would overlook the martial exercises of the young people of his court on the meadow of San Francesco, known for its magnificent view, and saw to it well that all the feats were done in the most perfect manner. He strove always to be affable and accessible to the utmost degree, visiting the artisans who worked for him in their shops, holding frequent audiences, and, if possible, attending to the requests of each individual on the same day that they were presented. No wonder that the people, as he walked along the street, knelt down and cried: 'Dio ti mantenga, signore!' He was called by thinking people 'the light of Italy'. His gifted son Guidobaldo, visited by sickness and misfortune of every kind, was able at the last (1508) to give his state into the safe hands of his nephew Francesco Maria (nephew also of Pope Julius II), who at least succeeded in preserving the territory from any permanent foreign occupation. It is remarkable with what confidence Guidobaldo yielded and fled before Cesare Borgia and Francesco before the troops of Leo X; each knew that his restoration would be all the easier and the more popular the less the country suffered through a fruitless defence. When Lodovico made the same calculation at Milan, he forgot the many grounds of hatred which existed against him. The court of Guidobaldo has been made immortal as the high school of polished manners by Baldassare Castiglione, who represented his eclogue 'Thyrsis' before, and in honour of, that society (1506), and who afterwards (1518) laid the scene of the dialogue of his *Cortigiano* in the circle of the accomplished Duchess Elisabetta Gonzaga.

The government of the family of Este at Ferrara, Modena and Reggio displays curious contrasts of violence and popularity. Within the palace frightful deeds were perpetrated; a princess was beheaded (1425) for alleged adultery with a step-son; legitimate and illegitimate children fled from the court, and even abroad their lives were threatened by assassins sent in pursuit of them (1471). Plots from without were incessant; the bastard of a bastard tried to wrest the crown from the lawful heir, Ercole I; this latter is said afterwards (1493) to have poisoned his wife on discovering that she, at the instigation of her brother Ferrante of Naples, was going to poison him. This list of tragedies is closed by the plot of two bastards against their brothers, the ruling Duke Alfonso I and Cardinal Ippolito (1506), which was discovered in time, and punished with imprisonment for life. The financial system in this state was of the most perfect kind, and necessarily so, since none of the large or second-rate powers of Italy were exposed to such danger and stood in such constant need of armaments and fortifications. It was the hope of the rulers that the increasing prosperity of the people would keep pace with the increasing weight of taxation, and the Marquis Niccolò (d. 1441) used to express the wish that his subjects might be richer than the people of other countries. If the rapid increase of the population be a measure of prosperity actually attained, it is certainly a fact of importance that in the year 1497, notwithstanding the wonderful extension of the capital, no houses were to be let. Ferrara is the first really modern city in Europe; large and well-built quarters sprang up at the bidding of the ruler: here, by the concentration of the official classes and the active promotion of trade, was formed for the first time a true capital; wealthy fugitives from all parts of Italy, Florentines especially, settled and built their palaces at Ferrara. But the indirect taxation, at all events, must have reached a point at which it could only just be borne. The government, it is true, took measures of alleviation which were also adopted by other Italian despots, such as Galeazzo Maria Sforza: in time of famine corn was brought from a distance and seems to have been distributed gratuitously; but in ordinary times it compensated itself by the monopoly, if not of corn, of many other of the necessaries of life – fish, salt, meat, fruit and vegetables, which last were carefully planted on and near the walls of the city. The most considerable source of income, however, was the annual sale of public offices, a usage which was common throughout Italy, and about the working of which at Ferrara we have more precise information. We read, for example, that at the new year 1502 the majority of the officials bought their places at '*prezzi salati*'; public servants of the most various kinds, custom-house officers, bailiffs (*massari*), notaries, '*podestà*', judges and even captains, i.e. lieutenant-governors of provincial towns, are quoted by name. As one of the 'devourers of the people' who paid dearly for their places, and who were 'hated worse than the devil', Tito Strozza – let us hope not the famous Latin poet – is mentioned. About the same time every year the dukes were accustomed to make a round of visits in Ferrara, the so-called '*andar per ventura*', in which they took presents from, at any rate, the more wealthy citizens. The gifts, however, did not consist of money, but of natural products.

It was the pride of the duke for all Italy to know that at Ferrara the soldiers received their pay and the professors at the university their salary not a day later than it was due; that the soldiers never dared lay arbitrary hands on a citizen or peasant; that the town was impregnable to assault; and that vast sums of coined money were stored up in the citadel. To keep two sets of accounts seemed unnecessary: the Minister of Finance was at the same time manager of the ducal household. The buildings erected by Borso (1430–71), by Ercole I (till 1505), and by Alfonso I (till 1534), were very numerous, but of small size; they are characteristic of a princely house which, with all its love of splendour – Borso never appeared but in embroidery and jewels – indulged in no ill-considered expense. Alfonso may perhaps have foreseen the fate which was in store for his charming little villas, the Belvedere with its shady gardens, and Montana with its fountains and beautiful frescoes.

It is undeniable that the dangers to which these princes were constantly exposed developed in them capacities of a remarkable kind. In so artificial a world only a man of consummate address could hope to succeed; each candidate for distinction was forced to make good his claims by personal merit and show himself worthy of the crown he sought. Their characters are not without dark sides; but in all of them lives something of those qualities which Italy then pursued as its ideal. What European monarch of the time laboured for his own culture as, for instance, Alfonso I? His travels in France, England and the Netherlands were undertaken for the purpose of study: by means of them he gained an accurate knowledge of the industry and commerce of these countries.[11] It is ridiculous to reproach him with the turner's work which he practised in his leisure hours, connected as it was with his skill in the casting of cannon, and with the unprejudiced freedom with which he surrounded himself by masters of every art. The Italian princes were not, like their contemporaries in the North, dependent on the society of an aristocracy which held itself to be the only class worth consideration, and which infected the monarch with the same conceit. In Italy the prince was permitted and compelled to know and to use men of every grade in society; and the nobility, though by birth a caste, were forced in social intercourse to stand upon their personal qualifications alone. But this is a point which we shall discuss more fully in the sequel.

The feeling of the Ferrarese towards the ruling house was a strange compound of silent dread, of the truly Italian sense of well-calculated interest, and of the loyalty of the modern subject: personal admiration was transferred into a new sentiment of duty. The city of Ferrara raised in 1451 a bronze equestrian statue to their Prince Niccolò, who had died ten years earlier; Borso (1454) did not scruple to place his own statue, also of bronze, but in a sitting posture, hard by in the market; in addition to which the city, at the beginning of his reign, decreed to him a 'marble triumphal pillar'. A citizen who, when abroad in Venice, had spoken ill of Borso in public was informed against on his return home, and condemned to banishment and the confiscation of his goods; a loyal subject was with difficulty restrained from cutting him down before the tribunal itself, and with a rope round his neck the offender went to the duke and begged for a full pardon. The government was well provided with spies, and the duke inspected personally the daily list of travellers which the inn-keepers were strictly ordered to present. Under Borso, who was anxious to leave no distinguished stranger unhonoured, this regulation served a hospitable purpose; Ercole I used it simply as a measure of precaution. In Bologna, too, it was then the rule, under Giovanni II Bentivoglio, that every passing traveller who entered at one gate must obtain a ticket in order to go out at another. An unfailing means of popularity was the sudden dismissal of oppressive officials. When Borso arrested in person his chief and confidential counsellors, when Ercole I removed and disgraced a tax-gatherer who for years had been sucking the blood of the people, bonfires were lighted and the bells were pealed in their honour. With one of his servants, however, Ercole let things go too far. The director of the police, or by whatever name we should choose to call him (*capitano di giustizia*), was Gregorio Zampante of Lucca – a native being unsuited for an office of this kind. Even the sons and brothers of the duke trembled before this man; the fines he inflicted amounted to hundreds and thousands of ducats, and torture was applied even before the hearing of a case: bribes were accepted from wealthy criminals, and their pardon obtained from the duke by false representations. Gladly would the people have paid any sum to this ruler for sending away the 'enemy of God and man'. But Ercole had knighted him and made him godfather to his children; and year by year Zampante laid by 2,000 ducats. He dared only eat pigeons bred in his own house, and could not cross the street without a band of archers and bravos. It was time to get rid of him; in 1496 two students and a converted Jew whom he had mortally offended killed him in his house while he was taking his siesta, and then rode through the town on horses held in waiting, raising the cry, 'Come out! Come out! We have slain Zampante!' The pursuers came too late, and found them already safe across the frontier. Of course it now rained satires – some of them in the form of sonnets, others of odes.

It was wholly in the spirit of this system that the sovereign imposed his own respect for useful servants on the court and on the people. When in 1469 Borso's privy councillor Lodovico Casella died, no court of law or place of business in the city, and no lecture-room at the university, was allowed to be open: all had to follow the body to San Domenico, since the duke intended to be present. And, in fact, 'the first of the house of Este who attended the corpse of a subject' walked, clad in black, after the coffin, weeping, while behind him came the relatives of Casella, each conducted by one of the gentlemen of the court: the body of the plain citizen was carried by nobles from the church into the cloister, where it was buried. Indeed this official sympathy with princely emotion first came up in the Italian states. At the root of the practice may be a beautiful, humane sentiment; the utterance of it, especially in the poets, is, as a rule, of equivocal sincerity. One of the youthful poems of Ariosto, on the death of Leonora of Aragon, wife of Ercole I, contains besides the inevitable graveyard flowers, which are scattered in the elegies of all ages, some thoroughly modern features:

This death had given Ferrara a blow which it would not get over for years: its benefactress was now its advocate in heaven, since earth was not worthy of her; truly the angel of Death did not come to her, as to us common mortals, with blood-stained scythe, but fair to behold [*onesta*] and with so kind a face that every fear was allayed.

But we meet, also, with a sympathy of a different kind. Novelists, depending wholly on the favour of their patrons, tell us the love-stories of the prince, even before his death, in a way which, to later times, would seem the height of indiscretion, but which then passed simply as an innocent compliment. Lyrical poets even went so far as to sing the illicit flames of their lawfully married lords, e.g. Angelo Poliziano, those of Lorenzo the Magnificent, and Gioviano Pontano, with a singular gusto, those of Alfonso of Calabria. The poem in question betrays unconsciously the odious disposition of the Aragonese ruler; in these things too, he must needs be the most fortunate, else woe be to those who are more successful! That the greatest artists, for example Leonardo, should paint the mistresses of their patrons was no more than a matter of course.

But the house of Este was not satisfied with the praises of others; it undertook to celebrate them itself. In the Palazzo Schifanoia Borso caused himself to be painted in a series of historical representations, and Ercole (from 1472 on) kept the anniversary of his accession to the throne by a procession which was compared to the feast of Corpus Christi; shops were closed as on Sunday; in the centre of the line walked all the members of the princely house (bastards included) clad in embroidered robes. That the crown was the fountain of honour and authority, that all personal distinction flowed from it alone, had been long expressed at this court by the Order of the Golden Spur – an order which had nothing in common with medieval chivalry. Ercole I added to the spur a sword, a gold-laced mantle and a grant of money, in return for which there is no doubt that regular service was required.

The patronage of art and letters for which this court has obtained a world-wide reputation was exercised through the university, which was one of the most perfect in Italy, and by the gift of places in the personal or official service of the prince; it involved consequently no additional expense. Boiardo, as a wealthy country gentleman and high official, belonged to this class. At the time when Ariosto began to distinguish himself, there existed no court, in the true sense of the word, either at Milan or Florence, and soon there was none either at

Urbino or at Naples. He had to content himself with a place among the musicians and jugglers of Cardinal Ippolito till Alfonso took him into his service. It was otherwise at a later time with Torquato Tasso, whose presence at court was jealously sought after.

THE OPPONENTS OF THE DESPOTS

In face of this centralized authority, all legal opposition within the borders of the state was futile. The elements needed for the restoration of a republic had been for ever destroyed, and the field prepared for violence and despotism. The nobles, destitute of political rights, even where they held feudal possessions, might call themselves Guelphs or Ghibellines at will, might dress up their bravos in padded hose and feathered caps or how else they pleased; thoughtful men like Machiavelli knew well enough that Milan and Naples were too 'corrupt' for a republic. Strange judgements fall on these two so-called parties, which now served only to give an official sanction to personal and family disputes. An Italian prince, whom Agrippa of Nettesheim advised to put them down, replied that their quarrels brought him more than 12,000 ducats a year in fines. And when in the year 1500, during the brief return of Lodovico il Moro to his states, the Guelphs of Tortona summoned a part of the neighbouring French army into the city, in order to make an end once for all of their opponents, the French certainly began by plundering and ruining the Ghibellines, but finished by doing the same to the Guelphs, till Tortona was utterly laid waste. In Romagna, the hotbed of every ferocious passion, these two names had long lost all political meaning. It was a sign of the political delusion of the people that they not seldom believed the Guelphs to be the natural allies of the French and the Ghibellines of the Spaniards. It is hard to see that those who tried to profit by this error got much by doing so. France, after all her interventions, had to abandon the peninsula at last, and what became of Spain, after she had destroyed Italy, is known to every reader.

But to return to the despots of the Renaissance. A pure and simple mind, we might think, would perhaps have argued that, since all power is derived from God, these princes, if they were loyally and honestly supported by all their subjects, must in time themselves improve and lose all traces of their violent origin. But from characters and imaginations inflamed by passion and ambition, reasoning of this kind could not be expected. Like bad physicians, they thought to cure the disease by removing the symptoms, and fancied that if the tyrant were put to death, freedom would follow of itself. Or else, without reflecting even to this extent, they sought only to give a vent to the universal hatred, or to take vengeance for some family misfortune or personal affront. Since the governments were absolute, and free from all legal restraints, the opposition chose its weapons with equal freedom. Boccaccio declares openly:

> Shall I call the tyrant king or prince, and obey him loyally as my lord? No, for he is the enemy of the commonwealth. Against him I may use arms, conspiracies, spies, ambushes and fraud; to do so is a sacred and necessary work. There is no more acceptable sacrifice than the blood of a tyrant.

We need not occupy ourselves with individual cases; Machiavelli, in a famous chapter of his *Discorsi*, treats of the conspiracies of ancient and modern times from the days of the Greek tyrants downwards, and classifies them with cold-blooded indifference according to their various plans and results. We need make but two observations, first on the murders committed in church, and next on the influence of classical antiquity. So well was the tyrant guarded that it was almost impossible to lay hands upon him elsewhere than at solemn religious services; and on no other occasion was the whole family to be found assembled together. It was thus that the Fabrianese murdered the members of their ruling house, the Chiavelli, during high mass (1435), the signal being given by the words of the Creed, '*Et incarnatus est.*' At Milan the Duke Giovan Maria Visconti (1412) was assassinated at the entrance of the church of San Gottardo, Galeazzo Maria Sforza (1476) in the church of Santo Stefano, and Lodovico il Moro only escaped (1484) the daggers of the adherents of the widowed Duchess Bona through entering the church of Sant' Ambrogio by another door than that by which he was expected. There was no intentional impiety in the act; the assassins of Galeazzo did not fail to pray before the murder to the patron saint of the church, and to listen devoutly to the first mass. It was, however, one cause of the partial failure of the conspiracy of the Pazzi against Lorenzo and Giuliano Medici (1478), that the brigand Montesecco, who had bargained to commit the murder at a banquet, declined to undertake it in the cathedral of Florence. Certain of the clergy 'who were familiar with the sacred place, and consequently had no fear' were induced to act in his stead.

As to the imitation of antiquity, the influence of which on moral and more especially on political questions we shall often refer to, the example was set by the rulers themselves, who, both in their conception of the state and in their personal conduct, took the old Roman empire avowedly as their model. In like manner their opponents, when they set to work with a deliberate theory, took pattern by the ancient tyrannicides. It may be hard to prove that in the main point – in forming the resolve itself – they consciously followed a classical example; but the appeal to antiquity was no mere phrase. The most striking disclosures have been left us with respect to the murderers of Galeazzo Sforza – Lampugnani, Olgiati and Visconti. Though all three had personal ends to serve, yet their enterprise may be partly ascribed to a more general reason. About this time Cola de' Montani, a humanist and professor of eloquence, had awakened among many of the young Milanese nobility a vague passion for glory and patriotic achievements, and had mentioned to Lampugnani and Olgiati his hope of delivering Milan. Suspicion was soon aroused against him: he was banished from the city, and his pupils were abandoned to the fanaticism he had excited. Some ten days before the deed they met together and took a solemn oath in the monastery of Sant' Ambrogio. 'Then,' says Olgiati, 'in a remote corner I raised my eyes before the picture of the patron saint, and implored his help for ourselves and for all *his* people.' The heavenly protector of the city was called on to bless the undertaking, as was afterwards St Stephen, in whose church it was fulfilled. Many of their comrades were now informed of the plot, nightly meetings were held in the house of Lampugnani, and the conspirators practised for the murder with the sheaths of their daggers. The attempt was successful, but Lampugnani was killed on the spot by the attendants of the duke; the others were captured. Visconti was penitent, but Olgiati through all his tortures maintained that the deed was an acceptable offering to God, and exclaimed while the executioner was breaking his ribs, 'Courage, Girolamo! Thou wilt long be remembered; death is bitter, but glory is eternal.'

But however idealistic the object and purpose of such conspiracies may appear, the manner in which they were conducted betrays the influence of that worst of all conspirators, Catiline – a man in whose thoughts freedom had no place whatever. The annals of Siena tell us expressly that the conspirators were students of Sallust, and the fact is indirectly confirmed by the confession of Olgiati. Elsewhere, too, we meet with the name of Catiline, and a more attractive pattern of the conspirator, apart from the end he followed, could hardly be discovered.

Among the Florentines, whenever they got rid of, or tried to get rid of, the Medici, tyrannicide was a practice universally accepted and approved. After the flight of the Medici in 1494, the bronze group of Donatello – Judith with the dead Holofernes – was taken from their collection, and placed before the Palazzo della Signoria, on the spot where the *David* of Michelangelo now stands, with the inscription, '*Exemplum salutis publicae cives posuere* 1495'.[12] No example was more popular than that of the younger Brutus, who, in Dante, lies with Cassius and Judas Iscariot in the lowest pit of hell, because of his treason to the empire. Pietro Paolo Boscoli, whose plot against Giuliano, Giovanni and Giulio Medici failed (1513), was an enthusiastic admirer of Brutus, and in order to follow his steps, only waited to find a Cassius. Such a partner he met with in Agostino Capponi. His last utterances in prison – a striking evidence of the religious feeling of the time – show with what an effort he rid his mind of these classical imaginations, in order to die like a Christian. A friend and the confessor both had to assure him that St Thomas Aquinas condemned conspirators absolutely; but the confessor afterwards admitted to the same friend that St Thomas drew a distinction and permitted conspiracies against a tyrant who had forced himself on a people against their will.

After Lorenzino Medici had murdered the Duke Alessandro (1537), and then escaped, an apology for the deed appeared, which is probably his own work, and certainly composed in his interest, in which he praises tyrannicide as an act of the highest merit; on the supposition that Alessandro was a legitimate Medici, and, therefore, related to him, if only distantly, he boldly compares himself with Timoleon, who slew his brother for his country's sake. Others, on the same occasion, made use of the comparison with Brutus, and that Michelangelo himself, even late in life, was not unfriendly to ideas of this kind, may be inferred from his bust of Brutus in the Bargello. He left it unfinished, like nearly all his works, but certainly not because the murder of Cesare was repugnant to his feeling, as the couplet beneath declares.

A popular radicalism in the form in which it is opposed to the monarchies of later times is not to be found in the despotic states of the Renaissance. Each individual protested inwardly against despotism but was rather disposed to make tolerable or profitable terms with it, than to combine with others for its destruction. Things must have been as bad as at Camerino, Fabriano or Rimini before the citizens united to destroy or expel the ruling house. They knew in most cases only too well that this would but mean a change of masters. The star of the republics was certainly on the decline.

THE REPUBLICS: VENICE AND FLORENCE

The Italian municipalities had, in earlier days, given signal proof of that force which transforms the city into the state. It remained only that these cities should combine in a great confederation; and this idea was constantly recurring to Italian statesmen, whatever differences of form it might from time to time display. In fact, during the struggles of the twelfth and thirteenth centuries, great and formidable leagues actually were formed by the cities; and Sismondi[13] is of the opinion that the time of the final armaments of the Lombard confederation against Barbarossa (from 1168 on) was the moment when a universal Italian league was possible. But the more powerful states had already developed characteristic features which made any such scheme impracticable. In their commercial dealings they shrank from no measures, however extreme, which might damage their competitors; they held their weaker neighbours in a condition of helpless dependence – in short, they each fancied they could get on by themselves without the assistance of the rest, and thus paved the way for future usurpation. The usurper was forthcoming when long conflicts between the nobility and the people, and between the different factions of the nobility, had awakened the desire for a strong government, and when bands of mercenaries ready and willing to sell their aid to the highest bidder had superseded the general levy of the citizens, which party leaders now found unsuited to their purposes. The tyrants destroyed the freedom of most of the cities; here and there they were expelled, but not thoroughly, or only for a short time; and they were always restored, since the inward conditions were favourable to them, and the opposing forces were exhausted.

Among the cities which maintained their independence are two of deep significance for the history of the human race: Florence, the city of incessant movement, which has left us a record of the thoughts and aspirations of each and all who, for three centuries, took part in this movement, and Venice, the city of apparent stagnation and of political secrecy. No contrast can be imagined stronger than that which is offered us by these two, and neither can be compared to anything else which the world had hitherto produced.

Venice recognized itself from the first as a strange and mysterious creation – the fruits of a higher power than human ingenuity. The solemn foundation of the city was the subject of a legend. On 25 March 413, at midday, the emigrants from Padua laid the first stone at the Rialto, that they might have a sacred, inviolable asylum amid the devastations of the barbarians. Later writers attributed to the founders the presentiment of the future greatness of the city; M. Antonio Sabellico, who has celebrated the event in the dignified flow of his hexameters, makes the priest who completes the act of consecration cry to heaven, 'When we hereafter attempt great things, grant us prosperity! Now we kneel before a poor altar; but if our vows are not made in vain, a hundred temples, O God, of gold and marble shall arise to Thee.' The island city at the end of the fifteenth century was the jewel-casket of the world. It is so described by the same Sabellico, with its ancient cupolas, its leaning towers, its inlaid marble façades, its compressed splendour, when the richest decoration did not hinder the practical employment of every corner of space. He takes us to the crowded piazza before San Giacometto at the Rialto, where the business of the world is transacted, not amid shouting and confusion, but with the subdued hum of many voices; where in the porticoes round the square and in those of the adjoining streets sit hundreds of money-changers and goldsmiths, with endless rows of shops and warehouses above their heads. He describes the great Fondaco of the Germans beyond the bridge, where their goods and their dwellings lay, and before which their ships are drawn up side by side in the canal; higher up is a whole fleet laden with wine and oil, and parallel with it, on the shore swarming with porters, are the vaults of the merchants; then from the Rialto to the square of St Mark come the inns and the perfumers' cabinets. So he conducts the reader from one quarter of the city to another till he comes at last to the two hospitals which were among those institutions of public utility nowhere so numerous as at Venice. Care for the people, in peace as well as in war, was characteristic of this government, and its attention to the wounded, even to those of the enemy, excited the admiration of other states.

Public institutions of every kind found in Venice their pattern; the pensioning of retired servants was carried out systematically, and included a provision for widows and orphans. Wealth, political security and acquaintance with other countries had matured the understanding of such questions. These slender fair-haired men with quiet cautious steps and deliberate speech differed but slightly in costume and bearing from one another; ornaments, especially pearls, were reserved for the women and girls. At that time the general prosperity, notwithstanding the losses sustained from the Turks, was still dazzling; the stores of energy which the city possessed and the prejudice in its favour diffused throughout Europe enabled it at a much later time to survive the heavy blows which were inflicted by the discovery of the sea route to the Indies, by the fall of the Mamelukes in Egypt, and by the war of the League of Cambrai.

Sabellico, born in the neighbourhood of Tivoli, and accustomed to the frank loquacity of the scholars of his day, remarks elsewhere with some astonishment that the young nobles who came of a morning to hear his lectures could not be prevailed on to enter into political discussions. 'When I ask them what people think, say and expect about this or that movement in Italy, they all answer with one voice that they know nothing about the matter.' Still, in spite of the strict imposition of the state, much was to be learned from the more corrupt members of the aristocracy by those who were willing to pay enough for it. In the last quarter of the fifteenth century there were traitors among the highest officials; the popes, the Italian princes, and even second-rate *condottieri* in the service of the government had informers in their pay, sometimes with regular salaries; things went so far that the Council of Ten found it prudent to conceal important political news from the Council of the Pregadi, and it was even supposed that Lodovico il Moro had control of a definite number of votes among the latter. Whether the hanging of single offenders and the high rewards – such as a life-pension of sixty ducats paid to those who informed against them – were of much avail, it is hard to decide; one of the chief causes of this evil, the poverty of many of the nobility, could not be removed in a day. In the year 1492 a proposal was urged by two of that order, that the state should spend 70,000 ducats for the relief of those poorer nobles who held no public office; the matter was near coming before the Great Council, in which it might have had a majority, when the Council of Ten interfered in time and banished the two proposers for life to Nicosia in Cyprus. About this time a Soranzo was hanged, though not in Venice itself, for sacrilege, and a Contarini put in chains for burglary; another of the same family came in 1499 before the Signoria, and complained that for many years he had been without an office, that he had only sixteen ducats a year and nine children, that his debts amounted to sixty ducats, that he knew no trade and had lately been turned on to the streets. We can understand why some of the wealthier nobles built houses, sometimes whole rows of them, to provide free lodging for their needy comrades. Such works figure in wills among deeds of charity.

But if the enemies of Venice ever founded serious hopes upon abuses of this kind, they were greatly in error. It might be thought that the commercial activity of the city, which put within reach of the humblest a rich reward for their labour, and the colonies on the eastern shores of the Mediterranean would have diverted from political affairs the dangerous elements of society. But had not the political history of Genoa, notwithstanding similar advantages, been of the stormiest? The cause of the stability of Venice lies rather in a combination of circumstances which were found in union nowhere else. Unassailable from its position, it had been able from the beginning to treat of foreign affairs with the fullest and calmest reflection and ignore nearly altogether the parties which divided the rest of Italy, to escape the entanglement of permanent alliances, and to set the highest price on those which it thought fit to make. The keynote of the Venetian character was, consequently, a spirit of proud and contemptuous isolation, which, joined to the hatred felt for the city by the other states of Italy, gave rise to a strong sense of solidarity within. The inhabitants meanwhile were united by the most powerful ties of interest in dealing both with the colonies and with the possessions on the mainland, forcing the population of the latter, that is, of all the towns up to Bergamo, to buy and sell in Venice alone. A power which rested on means so artificial could only be maintained by internal harmony and unity; and this conviction was so widely diffused among the citizens that the conspirator found few elements to work upon. And the discontented, if there were such, were held so far apart by the division between the noble and the burgher that a mutual understanding was not easy. On the other hand, within the ranks of the nobility itself, travel, commercial enterprise and the incessant wars with the Turks saved the wealthy and dangerous from that fruitful source of conspiracies – idleness. In these wars they were spared, often to a criminal extent, by the general in command, and the fall of the city was predicted by a Venetian Cato, if this fear of the nobles 'to give one another pain' should continue at the expense of justice. Nevertheless this free movement in the open air gave the Venetian aristocracy, as a whole, a healthy bias.

And when envy and ambition called for satisfaction an official victim was forthcoming, and legal means and authorities were ready. The moral torture, which for years the Doge Francesco Foscari (d. 1457) suffered before the eyes of all Venice, is a frightful example of a vengeance possible only in an aristocracy.[14] The Council of Ten, which had a hand in everything, which disposed without appeal of life and death, of financial affairs and military appointments, which included the Inquisitors among its number, and which overthrew Foscari, as it had overthrown so many powerful men before – this council was yearly chosen afresh from the whole governing body, the Gran Consiglio, and was consequently the most direct expression of its will. It is not probable that serious intrigues occurred at these elections, as the short duration of the office and the accountability which followed rendered it an object of no great desire. But violent and mysterious as the proceedings of this and other authorities might be, the genuine Venetian courted rather than fled their sentence, not only because the republic had long arms, and if it could not catch him might punish his family, but because in most cases it acted from rational motives and not from a thirst for blood. No state, indeed, has ever exercised a greater moral influence over its subjects, whether abroad or at home. If traitors were to be found among the Pregadi, there was ample compensation for this in the fact that every Venetian away from home was a born spy for his government. It was a matter of course that the Venetian cardinals at Rome sent home news of the transactions of the secret papal consistories. The Cardinal Domenico Grimani had the dispatches intercepted in the neighbourhood of Rome (1500) which Ascanio Sforza was sending to his brother Lodovico il Moro, and forwarded them to Venice; his father, then exposed to a serious accusation, claimed public credit for this service of his son before the Gran Consiglio; in other words, before all the world.

The conduct of the Venetian government to the *condottieri* in its pay has been spoken of already. The only further guarantee of their fidelity which could be obtained lay in their great number, by which treachery

was made as difficult as its discovery was easy. In looking at the
Venetian army list, one is only surprised that among forces of such
miscellaneous composition any common action was possible. In the
catalogue for the campaign of 1495 we find 15,526 horsemen, broken
up into a number of small divisions. Gonzaga of Mantua alone had as
many as 1,200, and Gioffredo Borgia 740; then follow six officers with
a contingent of 600 to 700, ten with 400, twelve with 400 to 200,
fourteen or thereabouts with 200 to 100, nine with 80, six with 50 to
60, and so forth. These forces were partly composed of old Venetian
troops, partly of veterans led by Venetian city or country nobles; the
majority of the leaders were, however, princes and rulers of cities or
their relatives. To these forces must be added 24,000 infantry – we are
not told how they were raised or commanded – with 3,300 additional
troops, who probably belonged to the special services. In time of peace
the cities of the mainland were wholly unprotected or occupied by
insignificant garrisons. Venice relied, if not exactly on the loyalty, at
least on the good sense of its subjects; in the war of the League of
Cambrai (1509) it absolved them, as is well known, from their oath of
allegiance, and let them compare the amenities of a foreign occupation
with the mild government to which they had been accustomed. As
there had been no treason in their desertion of St Mark, and consequently no punishment was to be feared, they returned to their old
masters with the utmost eagerness. This war, we may remark parenthetically, was the result of a century's outcry against the Venetian
desire for aggrandizement. The Venetians, in fact, were not free from
the mistake of those over-clever people who will credit their opponents
with no irrational and inconsiderate conduct. Misled by this optimism,
which is, perhaps, a peculiar weakness of aristocracies, they had utterly
ignored not only the preparations of Muhammad II for the capture of
Constantinople, but even the armaments of Charles VIII, till the
unexpected blow fell at last. The League of Cambrai was an event of
the same character, in so far as it was clearly opposed to the interests of
the two chief members, Louis XII and Julius II. The hatred of all Italy
against the victorious city seemed to be concentrated in the mind of
the pope, and to have blinded him to the evils of foreign intervention;
and as to the policy of Cardinal d'Amboise and his king, Venice ought
long before to have recognized it as a piece of malicious imbecility,
and to have been thoroughly on its guard. The other members of the
League took part in it from that envy which may be a salutary

corrective to great wealth and power, but which in itself is a beggarly sentiment. Venice came out of the conflict with honour, but not without lasting damage.

A power, whose foundations were so complicated, whose activity and interests filled so wide a stage, cannot be imagined without a systematic oversight of the whole, without a regular estimate of means and burdens, of profits and losses. Venice can fairly make good its claim to be the birthplace of statistical science, together, perhaps, with Florence, and followed by the more enlightened despotisms. The feudal state of the Middle Ages knew of nothing more than catalogues of signorial rights and possessions (urbaria); it looked on production as a fixed quantity, which it approximately is, so long as we have to do with landed property only. The towns, on the other hand, throughout the West must from very early times have treated production, which with them depended on industry and commerce, as exceedingly variable; but, even in the most flourishing times of the Hanseatic League, they never got beyond a simple commercial balance-sheet. Fleets, armies, political power and influence fall under the debit and credit of a trader's ledger. In the Italian states a clear political consciousness, the pattern of Muhammadan administration, and the long and active exercise of trade and commerce combined to produce for the first time a true science of statistics.[15] The absolute monarchy of Frederick II in Lower Italy was organized with the sole object of securing a concentrated power for the death-struggle in which he was engaged. In Venice, on the contrary, the supreme objects were the enjoyment of life and power, the increase of inherited advantages, the creation of the most lucrative forms of industry, and the opening of new channels for commerce.

The writers of the time speak of these things with the greatest freedom. We learn that the population of the city amounted in the year 1422 to 190,000 souls; the Italians were, perhaps, the first to reckon, not according to hearths, or men able to bear arms, or people able to walk, and so forth, but according to animae, and thus to get the most neutral basis for further calculation. About this time, when the Florentines wished to form an alliance with Venice against Filippo Maria Visconti, they were for the moment refused, in the belief, resting on accurate commercial returns, that a war between Venice and Milan, that is, between seller and buyer, was foolish. Even if the duke simply increased his army, the Milanese, through the heavier taxation they must pay, would become worse customers. 'Better let the Florentines be defeated, and then, used as they are to the life of a free city, they will settle with us and bring their silk and woollen industry with them, as the Lucchese did in their distress.' The speech of the dying Doge Mocenigo (1423) to a few of the senators whom he had sent for to his bedside is still more remarkable. It contains the chief elements of a statistical account of the whole resources of Venice. I cannot say whether or where a thorough elucidation of this perplexing document exists; by way of illustration, the following facts may be quoted. After repaying a war-loan of four million ducats, the public debt (il monte) still amounted to six million ducats; the current trade (so it seems) ten million, which yielded, the text informs us, a profit of four million. The 3,000 navigli, the 300 navi, and the 45 galleys were manned respectively by 17,000, 8,000 and 11,000 seamen (more than 200 for each galley). To these must be added 16,000 shipwrights. The houses in Venice were valued at seven million, and brought in a rent of half a million.[16] There were 1,000 nobles whose income ranged from 70 to 4,000 ducats. In another passage the ordinary income of the state in that same year is put at 1,100,000 ducats; through the disturbance of trade caused by the wars it sank about the middle of the century to 800,000 ducats.

If Venice, by this spirit of calculation, and by the practical turn which she gave it, was the first fully to represent one important side of modern political life, in that culture, on the other hand, which Italy then prized most highly she did not stand in the front rank. The literary impulse, in general, was here wanting, and especially that enthusiasm for classical antiquity which prevailed elsewhere.[17] The aptitude of the Venetians, says Sabellico, for philosophy and eloquence was in itself not less remarkable than for commerce and politics. George of Trebizond, who, in 1459, laid the Latin translation of Plato's Laws at the feet of the doge, was appointed professor of philology with a yearly salary of 150 ducats, and finally dedicated his Rhetoric to the Signoria. If, however, we look through the history of Venetian literature which Francesco Sansovino has appended to his well-known book, we shall find in the fourteenth century almost nothing but history, and special works on theology, jurisprudence and medicine; and in the fifteenth century, till we come to Ermolao Barbaro and Aldo Manucci, humanistic culture is, for a city of such importance, most scantily represented. The library which Cardinal Bessarion bequeathed to the state (1468) narrowly escaped dispersion and destruction. Learning was certainly cultivated at the university of Padua, where, however, the physicians and the jurists – the latter as the authors of legal opinions – received by far the highest pay. The share of Venice in the poetical creations of the country was long insignificant, till, at the beginning of the sixteenth century, her deficiencies were made good. Even the art of the Renaissance was imported into the city from without, and it was not before the end of the fifteenth century that she learned to move in this field with independent freedom and strength. But we find more striking instances still of intellectual backwardness. This government, which had the clergy so thoroughly in its control, which reserved to itself the appointment to all important ecclesiastical offices, and which, one time after another, dared to defy the court of Rome, displayed an official piety of a most singular kind. The bodies of saints and other relics imported from Greece after the Turkish conquest were bought at the greatest sacrifices and received by the doge in solemn procession. For the coat without a seam it was decided (1455) to offer 10,000 ducats, but it was not to be had. These measures were not the fruit of any popular excitement, but of the tranquil resolutions of the heads of the government, and might have been omitted without attracting any comment, and at Florence, under similar circumstances, would certainly have been omitted. We shall say nothing of the piety of the masses, and of their firm belief in the indulgences of an Alexander VI. But the state itself, after absorbing the Church to a degree unknown elsewhere, had in truth a certain ecclesiastical element in its composition, and the doge, the symbol of the state, appeared in twelve great processions (*andate*) in a half-clerical character. They were almost all festivals in memory of political events, and competed in splendour with the great feasts of the Church; the most brilliant of all, the famous marriage with the sea, fell on Ascension Day.

The most elevated political thought and the most varied forms of human development are found united in the history of Florence, which in this sense deserves the name of the most modern state in the world. Here the whole people are busied with what in the despotic cities is the affair of a single family. That wondrous Florentine spirit, at once keenly critical and artistically creative, was incessantly transforming the social and political condition of the state, and as incessantly describing and judging the change. Florence thus became the home of political doctrines and theories, of experiments and sudden changes, but also, like Venice, the home of statistical science, and alone and above all other states in the world, the home of historical representation in the modern sense of the phrase. The spectacle of ancient Rome and a familiarity with its leading writers were not without influence; Giovanni Villani confesses that he received the first impulse to his great work at the jubilee of the year 1300, and began it immediately on his return home. Yet how many among the 200,000 pilgrims of that year may have been like him in gifts and tendencies and still did not write the history of their native cities! For not all of them could encourage themselves with the thought, 'Rome is sinking; my native city is rising, and ready to achieve great things, and therefore I wish to relate its past history, and hope to continue the story to the present time, and as long as my life shall last.' And besides the witness to its past, Florence obtained through its historians something further – a greater fame than fell to the lot of any other city of Italy.

Our present task is not to write the history of this remarkable state, but merely to give a few indications of the intellectual freedom and independence for which the Florentines were indebted to this history.

In no other city of Italy were the struggles of political parties so bitter, of such early origin, and so permanent. The descriptions of them, which belong, it is true, to a somewhat later period, give clear evidence of the superiority of Florentine criticism.

And what a politician is the great victim of these crises, Dante Alighieri, matured alike by home and by exile! He uttered his scorn of the incessant changes and experiments in the constitution of his native city in verses of adamant, which will remain proverbial so long as political events of the same kind recur; he addressed his home in words of defiance and yearning which must have stirred the hearts of his countrymen. But his thoughts ranged over Italy and the whole world; and if his passion for the Empire, as he conceived it, was no more than an illusion, it must yet be admitted that the youthful dreams of a new-born political speculation are in his case not without a poetical grandeur. He is proud to be the first who trod this path, certainly in the footsteps of Aristotle, but in his own way independently. His ideal emperor is a just and humane judge, dependent on God only, the heir of the universal sway of Rome to which belonged the sanction of nature, of right and of the will of God. The conquest of the world was, according to this view, rightful, resting on a divine judgement between Rome and the other nations of the earth, and God gave his approval to this Empire, since under it he became Man, submitting at his birth to the census of the Emperor Augustus, and at his death to the judgement of Pontius Pilate. We may find it hard to appreciate these and other arguments of the same kind, but Dante's passion never fails to carry us with him. In his letters he appears as one of the earliest publicists, and is perhaps the first layman to publish political tracts in this form. He began early. Soon after the death of Beatrice he addressed a pamphlet on the state of Florence 'to the Great ones of the Earth', and the public utterances of his later years, dating from the time of his banishment, are all directed to emperors, princes and cardinals. In these letters and in his book *De Vulgari Eloquio* the feeling, bought with such bitter pains, is constantly recurring that the exile may find elsewhere than in his native place an intellectual home in language and culture, which cannot be taken from him. On this point we shall have more to say in the sequel.

To the two Villani, Giovanni as well as Matteo, we owe not so much deep political reflection as fresh and practical observations, together with the elements of Florentine statistics and important notices of other states. Here too trade and commerce had given the impulse to economical as well as political science. Nowhere else in the world was such accurate information to be had on financial affairs. The wealth of the papal court at Avignon, which at the death of John XXII amounted to 25 million gold florins, would be incredible on any less trustworthy authority. Here only, at Florence, do we meet with colossal loans like that which the King of England contracted from the Florentine houses of Bardi and Peruzzi, who lost to His Majesty the sum of 1,365,000 gold florins (1338) – their own money and that of their partners – and nevertheless recovered from the shock.[18] Most important facts are here recorded as to the condition of Florence at this time:[19] the public income (over 300,000 gold florins) and expenditure; the population of the city, here only roughly estimated, according to the consumption of bread, in *bocche*, i.e. mouths, put at 90,000, and the population of the whole territory; the excess of 300 to 500 male children among the 5,800 to 6,000 annually baptized; the schoolchildren, of whom 8,000 to 10,000 learned reading, 1,000 to 1,200 in six schools arithmetic; and besides these, 600 scholars who were taught Latin grammar and logic in four schools. Then follow the statistics of the churches and monasteries; of the hospitals, which held more than a thousand beds; of the wool-trade, with its most valuable details; of the mint, the provisioning of the city, the public officials, and so on. Incidentally we learn many curious facts; how, for instance, when the public funds (*monte*) were first established, in the year 1353, the Franciscans spoke from the pulpit in favour of the measure, the Dominicans and Augustinians against it. The economical results of the black death were and could be observed and described nowhere else in all Europe as in this city. Only a Florentine could have left it on record how it was expected that the scanty population would have made everything cheap, and how instead of that labour and commodities doubled in price; how the common people at first would do no work at all, but simply gave themselves up to enjoyment; how in the city itself servants and maids were not to be had except at extravagant wages; how the peasants would only till the best lands, and left the rest uncultivated; and how the enormous legacies bequeathed to the poor at the time of the plague seemed afterwards useless, since the poor had either died or had ceased to be poor. Lastly, on the occasion of a great bequest, by which a childless philanthropist left six *danari* to every beggar in the city, the attempt is made to give a comprehensive statistical account of Florentine mendicancy.

This statistical view of things was at a later time still more highly cultivated at Florence. The noteworthy point about it is that, as a rule, we can perceive its connection with the higher aspects of history, with art, and with culture in general. An inventory of the year 1422 mentions, within the compass of the same document, the seventy-two exchange offices which surrounded the Mercato Nuovo; the amount of coined money in circulation (2 million golden florins); the then new industry of gold spinning; the silk wares; Filippo Brunellesco, then busy in digging classical architecture from its grave; and Leonardo Aretino, secretary of the republic, at work at the revival of ancient literature and eloquence; lastly, it speaks of the general prosperity of the city, then free from political conflicts, and of the good fortune of Italy, which had rid itself of foreign mercenaries. The Venetian statistics quoted above, which date from about the same year, certainly give evidence of larger property and profits and of a more extensive scene of action; Venice had long been mistress of the seas before Florence sent out its first galleys (1422) to Alexandria. But no reader can fail to recognize the higher spirit of the Florentine documents. These and similar lists recur at intervals of ten years, systematically arranged and tabulated, while elsewhere we find at best occasional notices. We can form an approximate estimate of the property and the business of the first Medici; they paid for charities, public buildings and taxes from 1434 to 1471 no less than 663,755 gold florins, of which more than 400,000 fell on Cosimo alone, and Lorenzo il Magnifico was delighted that the money had been so well spent.[20] In 1478 we have again a most important and in its way complete view of the commerce and trades of this city, some of which may be wholly or partly reckoned among the fine arts – such as those which had to do with damasks and gold or silver embroidery, with woodcarving and intarsia, with the sculpture of arabesques in marble and sandstone, with portraits in wax, and with jewellery and work in gold. The inborn talent of the Florentines for the systematization of outward life is shown by their books on agriculture, business and domestic economy, which are markedly superior to those of other European people in the fifteenth century. It has been rightly decided to publish selections of these works, although no little study will be needed to extract clear and definite results from them. At all events, we have no difficulty in recognizing the city, where dying parents begged the government in their wills to fine their sons 1,000 florins if they declined to practise a regular profession.

For the first half of the sixteenth century probably no state in the world possesses a document like the magnificent description of Florence by Varchi. In descriptive statistics, as in so many things besides, yet another model is left to us, before the freedom and greatness of the city sank into the grave.[21]

This statistical estimate of outward life is, however, uniformly accompanied by the narrative of political events to which we have already referred.

Florence not only existed under political forms more varied than those of the free states of Italy and of Europe generally, but it reflected upon them far more deeply. It is a faithful mirror of the relations of individuals and classes to a variable whole. The pictures of the great civic democracies in France and in Flanders, as they are delineated in Froissart, and the narratives of the German chroniclers of the fourteenth century, are in truth of high importance; but in comprehensiveness of thought and in the rational development of the story none will bear comparison with the Florentines. The rule of the nobility, the tyrannies, the struggles of the middle class with the proletariat, limited and unlimited democracy, pseudo-democracy, the primacy of a single house, the theocracy of Savonarola, and the mixed forms of government which prepared the way for the Medicean despotism – all are so described that the inmost motives of the actors are laid bare to the light. At length Machiavelli in his Florentine history (down to 1492) represents his native city as a living organism and its development as a natural and individual process; he is the first of the moderns who has risen to such a conception. It lies without our province to determine whether and in what points Machiavelli may have done violence to history, as is notoriously the case in his life of Castruccio Castracani – a fancy picture of the typical despot. We might find something to say against every line of the *Storie Fiorentine*, and yet the great and unique value of the whole would remain unaffected. And his contemporaries and successors, Jacopo Pitti, Guicciardini, Segni, Varchi, Vettori, what a circle of illustrious names! And what a story it is which these masters tell us! The great and memorable drama of the last decades of the Florentine republic is here unfolded. The voluminous record of the collapse of the highest and most original life which the world could then show may appear to one but as a collection of curiosities, may awaken in another a devilish delight at the shipwreck of so much nobility and grandeur, to a third may seem like a great historical assize; for all it will be an object of thought and study to the end of time. The evil, which was for ever troubling the peace of the city, was its rule over once powerful and now conquered rivals like Pisa – a rule of which the necessary consequence was a chronic state of violence. The only remedy, certainly an extreme one and which none but Savonarola could have persuaded Florence to accept, and that only with the help of favourable chances, would have been the well-timed dissolution of Tuscany into a federal union of free cities. At a later period this scheme, then no more than the dream of a past age, brought (1548) a patriotic citizen of Lucca to the scaffold. From this evil and from the ill-starred Guelph sympathies of Florence for a foreign prince, which familiarized it with foreign intervention, came all the disasters which followed. But who does not admire the people, which was wrought up by its venerated preacher to a mood of such sustained loftiness, that for the first time in Italy it set the example of sparing a conquered foe, while the whole history of its past taught nothing but vengeance and extermination? The glow which melted patriotism into one with moral regeneration may seem, when looked at from a distance, to have soon passed away; but its best results shine forth again in the memorable siege of 1529–30. They were 'fools', as Guicciardini then wrote, who drew down this storm upon Florence, but he confesses himself that they achieved things which seemed incredible; and when he declares that sensible people would have got out of the way of the danger, he means no more than that Florence ought to have yielded itself silently and ingloriously into the hands of its enemies. It would no doubt have preserved its splendid suburbs and gardens, and the lives and prosperity of countless citizens; but it would have been the poorer by one of its greatest and most ennobling memories.

In many of their chief merits the Florentines are the pattern and the earliest type of Italians and modern Europeans generally; they are so also in many of their defects. When Dante compares the city which was always mending its constitution with the sick man who is continually changing his posture to escape from pain, he touches with the comparison a permanent feature of the political life of Florence. The great modern fallacy that a constitution can be made, can be manufactured by a combination of existing forces and tendencies,[22] was constantly cropping up in stormy times; even Machiavelli is not wholly free from it. Constitutional artists were never wanting who by an ingenious distribution and division of political power, by indirect elections of the most complicated kind, by the establishment of nominal offices, sought to found a lasting order of things, and to satisfy or to deceive the rich and the poor alike. They naïvely fetch their examples from classical antiquity, and borrow the party names *ottimati*, *aristocrazia*, as a matter of course. The world since then has become used to these expressions and given them a conventional European sense, whereas all former party names were purely national, and either characterized the cause at issue or sprang from the caprice of accident. But how a name colours or discolours a political cause!

But of all who thought it possible to construct a state, the greatest beyond all comparison was Machiavelli. He treats existing forces as living and active, takes a large and an accurate view of alternative possibilities, and seeks to mislead neither himself nor others. No man could be freer from vanity or ostentation; indeed, he does not write for the public, but either for princes and administrators or for personal friends. The danger for him does not lie in an affectation of genius or in a false order of ideas, but rather in a powerful imagination which he evidently controls with difficulty. The objectivity of his political judgement is sometimes appalling in its sincerity; but it is the sign of a time of no ordinary need and peril, when it was a hard matter to believe in right, or to credit others with just dealing. Virtuous indignation at his expense is thrown away upon us who have seen in what sense political morality is understood by the statesmen of our own century. Machiavelli was at all events able to forget himself in his cause. In truth, although his writings, with the exception of very few words, are altogether destitute of enthusiasm, and although the Florentines themselves treated him at last as a criminal, he was a patriot in the fullest meaning of the word. But free as he was, like most of his contemporaries, in speech and morals, the welfare of the state was yet his first and last thought.

His most complete programme for the construction of a new political system at Florence is set forth in the memorial to Leo X, composed after the death of the younger Lorenzo Medici, Duke of Urbino (d. 1519), to whom he had dedicated his *Prince*. The state was by that time in extremities and utterly corrupt, and the remedies proposed are not always morally justifiable; but it is most interesting to see how he hopes to set up the republic in the form of a moderate democracy, as heiress to the Medici. A more ingenious scheme of concessions to the pope, to the pope's various adherents, and to the different Florentine interests cannot be imagined; we might fancy ourselves looking into the works of a clock. Principles, observations, comparisons, political forecasts and the like are to be found in numbers in the *Discorsi*, among them flashes of wonderful insight. He recognizes, for example, the law of a continuous though not uniform development in republican institutions, and requires the constitution to be flexible and capable of change, as the only means of dispensing with bloodshed and banishments. For a like reason, in order to guard against private violence and foreign interference – 'the death of all freedom' – he wishes to see introduced a judicial procedure (*accusa*) against hated citizens, in place of which Florence had hitherto had nothing but the court of scandal. With a masterly hand the tardy and involuntary decisions are characterized, which at critical moments play so important a part in republican states. Once, it is true, he is misled by his imagination and the pressure of events into unqualified praise of the people, which chooses its officers, he says, better than any prince, and which can be cured of its errors by 'good advice'. With regard to the government of Tuscany, he has no doubt that it belongs to his native city, and maintains, in a special *Discorso*, that the reconquest of Pisa is a question of life or death; he deplores that Arezzo, after the rebellion of 1502, was not razed to the ground; he admits in general that Italian republics must be allowed to expand freely and add to their territory in order to enjoy peace at home, and not to be themselves attacked by others, but declares that Florence had always begun at the wrong end, and from the first made deadly enemies of Pisa, Lucca and Siena, while Pistoia, 'treated like a brother', had voluntarily submitted to her.

It would be unreasonable to draw a parallel between the few other republics which still existed in the fifteenth century and this unique city – the most important workshop of the Italian, and indeed of the modern European spirit. Siena suffered from the gravest organic maladies, and its relative prosperity in art and industry must not mislead us on this point. Aeneas Sylvius looks with longing from his native town over to the 'merry' German imperial cities, where life is embittered by no confiscations of land and goods, by no arbitrary officials, and by no political factions.[23] Genoa scarcely comes within range of our task, as before the time of Andrea Doria it took almost no part in the Renaissance. Indeed, the inhabitant of the Riviera was proverbial among Italians for his contempt of all higher culture. Party conflicts here assumed so fierce a character, and disturbed so violently the whole course of life, that we can hardly understand how, after so many revolutions and invasions, the Genoese ever contrived to return to an endurable condition. Perhaps it was owing to the fact that nearly all who took part in public affairs were at the same time almost without exception active men of business. The example of Genoa shows in a striking manner with what insecurity wealth and vast commerce, and with what internal disorder the possession of distant colonies, are compatible.

Lucca is of small significance in the fifteenth century.

FOREIGN POLICY

As the majority of the Italian states were in their internal constitution works of art, that is, the fruit of reflection and careful adaptation, so was their relation to one another and to foreign countries also a work of art.

That nearly all of them were the result of recent usurpations was a fact which exercised as fatal an influence in their foreign as in their internal policy. Not one of them recognized another without reserve; the same play of chance which had helped to found and consolidate one dynasty might upset another. Nor was it always a matter of choice with the despot whether to keep quiet or not. The necessity of movement and aggrandizement is common to all illegitimate powers. Thus Italy became the scene of a 'foreign policy' which gradually, as in other countries also, acquired the position of a recognized system of public law. The purely objective treatment of international affairs, as free from prejudice as from moral scruples, attained a perfection which sometimes is not without a certain beauty and grandeur of its own. But as a whole it gives us the impression of a bottomless abyss.

Intrigues, armaments, leagues, corruption and treason make up the outward history of Italy at this period. Venice in particular was long accused on all hands of seeking to conquer the whole peninsula, or gradually so to reduce its strength that one state after another must fall into her hands. But on a closer view it is evident that this complaint did not come from the people, but rather from the courts and official classes, which were commonly abhorred by their subjects, while the mild government of Venice had secured for it general confidence.[24] Even Florence, with its restive subject cities, found itself in a false position with regard to Venice, apart from all commercial jealousy and from the progress of Venice in Romagna. At last the League of Cambrai actually did strike a serious blow at the state which all Italy ought to have supported with united strength.

The other states, also, were animated by feelings no less unfriendly, and were at all times ready to use against one another any weapon which their evil conscience might suggest. Lodovico il Moro, the Aragonese kings of Naples and Sixtus IV – to say nothing of the smaller powers – kept Italy in a constant perilous agitation. It would have been well if the atrocious game had been confined to Italy; but it lay in the nature of the case that intervention and help should at last be sought from abroad – in particular from the French and the Turks.

The sympathies of the people at large were throughout on the side of France. Florence had never ceased to confess with shocking *naïveté* its old Guelph preference for the French. And when Charles VIII actually appeared on the south of the Alps, all Italy accepted him with an enthusiasm which to himself and his followers seemed unaccountable. In the imagination of the Italians, to take Savonarola for an example, the ideal picture of a wise, just and powerful saviour and ruler was still living, with the difference that he was no longer the emperor invoked by Dante, but the Capetian King of France. With his departure the illusion was broken; but it was long before all understood how completely Charles VIII, Louis XII and Francis I had mistaken their true relation to Italy, and by what inferior motives they were led. The princes, for their part, tried to make use of France in a wholly different way. When the Franco-English wars came to an end, when Louis XI began to cast about his diplomatic nets on all sides, and Charles of Burgundy to embark on his foolish adventures, the Italian Cabinets came to meet them at every point. It became clear that the intervention of France was only a question of time, even though the claims on Naples and Milan had never existed, and that the old interference with Genoa and Piedmont was only a type of what was to follow. The Venetians, in fact, expected it as early as 1462. The mortal terror of the Duke Galeazzo Maria of Milan during the Burgundian war, in which he was apparently the ally of Charles as well as of Louis, and consequently had reason to dread an attack from both, is strikingly shown in his correspondence. The plan of an equilibrium of the four chief Italian powers, as understood by Lorenzo the Magnificent, was but the assumption of a cheerful optimistic spirit, which had outgrown both the recklessness of an experimental policy and the superstitions of Florentine Guelphism, and persisted in hoping for the best. When Louis XI offered him aid in the war against Ferrante of Naples and Sixtus IV, he replied, 'I cannot set my own advantage above the safety of all Italy; would to God it never came into the mind of the French kings to try their strength in this country! Should they ever do so, Italy is lost.' For the other princes, the King of France was alternately a bugbear to themselves and to their enemies, and they threatened to call him in whenever they saw no more convenient way out of their difficulties. The popes, in their turn, fancied that they could make use of France without any danger to themselves, and even Innocent VIII imagined that he could withdraw to sulk in the North, and return as a conqueror to Italy at the head of a French army.

Thoughtful men, indeed, foresaw the foreign conquest long before the expedition of Charles VIII. And when Charles was back again on the other side of the Alps, it was plain to every eye that an era of intervention had begun. Misfortune now followed on misfortune; it was understood too late that France and Spain, the two chief invaders, had become great European powers, that they would be no longer satisfied with verbal homage, but would fight to the death for influence and territory in Italy. They had begun to resemble the centralized Italian states, and indeed to copy them, only on a gigantic scale. Schemes of annexation or exchange of territory were for a time indefinitely multiplied. The end, as is well known, was the complete victory of Spain, which, as sword and shield of the Counter-Reformation, long held the papacy among its other subjects. The melancholy reflections of the philosophers could only show them how those who had called in the barbarians all came to a bad end.

Alliances were at the same time formed with the Turks too, with as little scruple or disguise; they were reckoned no worse than any other political expedients. The belief in the unity of Western Christendom had at various times in the course of the Crusades been seriously shaken, and Frederick II had probably outgrown it. But the fresh advance of the oriental nations, the need and the ruin of the Greek empire, had revived the old feeling, though not in its former strength, throughout Western Europe. Italy, however, was a striking exception to this rule. Great as was the terror felt for the Turks, and the actual danger from them, there was yet scarcely a government of any consequence which did not conspire against other Italian states with Muhammad II and his successors. And when they did not do so, they still had the credit of it; nor was it worse than the sending of emissaries to poison the cisterns of Venice, which was the charge brought against the heirs of Alfonso, King of Naples. From a scoundrel like Sigismondo Malatesta nothing better could be expected than that he should call the Turks into Italy. But the Aragonese monarchs of Naples, from whom Muhammad – at the instigation, we read, of other Italian governments, especially of Venice – had once wrested Otranto (1480), afterwards hounded on the Sultan Bajazet II against the Venetians. The same charge was brought against Lodovico il Moro. 'The blood of the slain, and the misery of the prisoners in the hands of the Turks, cry to God for vengeance against him,' says the state historian. In Venice, where the government was informed of everything, it was known that Giovanni Sforza, ruler of Pesaro, the cousin of the Moor, had entertained the Turkish ambassadors on their way to Milan. The two most respectable among the popes of the fifteenth century, Nicholas V and Pius II, died in the deepest grief at the progress of the Turks, the latter indeed amid the preparations for a crusade which he was hoping to lead in person; their successors embezzled the contributions sent for this purpose from all parts of Christendom, and degraded the indulgences granted in return for them into a private commercial speculation. Innocent VIII consented to be gaoler to the fugitive Prince Djem, for a salary paid by the prisoner's brother Bajazet II, and Alexander VI supported the steps taken by Lodovico il Moro in Constantinople to further a Turkish assault upon Venice (1498), whereupon the latter threatened him with a Council. It is clear the notorious alliance between Francis I and Soliman II was nothing new or unheard of.

Indeed, we find instances of whole populations to whom it seemed no particular crime to go over bodily to the Turks. Even if it were only held out as a threat to oppressive governments, this is at least a proof that the idea had become familiar. As early as 1480 Battista Mantovano gives us clearly to understand that most of the inhabitants of the Adriatic coast foresaw something of this kind, and that Ancona in particular desired it. When Romagna was suffering from the oppressive government of Leo X, a deputy from Ravenna said openly to the legate, Cardinal Giulio Medici: 'Monsignore, the honourable Republic of Venice will not have us, for fear of a dispute with the Holy See; but if the Turk comes to Ragusa we will put ourselves into his hands.'

It was a poor but not wholly groundless consolation for the enslavement of Italy then begun by the Spaniards that the country was at least secured from the relapse into barbarism which would have awaited it under the Turkish rule. By itself, divided as it was, it could hardly have escaped this fate.

If, with all these drawbacks, the Italian statesmanship of this period deserves our praise, it is only on the ground of its practical and unprejudiced treatment of those questions which were not affected by fear, passion or malice. Here was no feudal system after the northern fashion, with its artificial scheme of rights; but the power which each possessed he held in practice as in theory. Here was no attendant nobility to foster in the mind of the prince the medieval sense of honour, with all its strange consequences; but princes and counsellors were agreed in acting according to the exigencies of the particular case and to the end they had in view. Towards the men whose services were used and towards allies, come from what quarter they might, no pride of caste was felt which could possibly estrange a supporter; and the class of the *condottieri*, in which birth was a matter of indifference, shows clearly enough in what sort of hands the real power lay; and lastly, the government, in the hands of an enlightened despot, had an incomparably more accurate acquaintance with its own country and that of its neighbours than was possessed by northern contemporaries, and estimated the economical and moral capacities of friend and foe down to the smallest particular. The rulers were, notwithstanding grave errors, born masters of statistical science. With such men negotiation was possible; it might be presumed that they would be convinced and their opinion modified when practical reasons were laid before them. When the great Alfonso of Naples was (1434) a prisoner of Filippo Maria Visconti, he was able to satisfy his gaoler that the rule of the House of Anjou instead of his own at Naples would make the French masters of Italy; Filippo Maria set him free without ransom and made an alliance with him. A northern prince would scarcely have acted in the same way, certainly not one whose morality in other respects was like that of Visconti. What confidence was felt in the power of self-interest is shown by the celebrated visit which Lorenzo the Magnificent, to the universal astonishment of the Florentines, paid the faithless Ferrante at Naples – a man who would be certainly tempted to keep him a prisoner, and was by no means too scrupulous to do so. For to arrest a powerful monarch, and then to let him go alive, after extorting his signature and otherwise insulting him, as Charles the Bold did to Louis XI at Peronne (1468), seemed madness to the Italians; so that Lorenzo was expected to come back covered with glory, or else not to come back at all. The art of political persuasion was at this time raised to a point – especially by the Venetian ambassadors – of which northern nations first obtained a conception from the Italians, and of which the official addresses give a most imperfect idea. These are mere pieces of humanistic rhetoric. Nor, in spite of an otherwise ceremonious etiquette, was there in case of need any lack of rough and frank speaking in diplomatic intercourse. A man like Machiavelli appears in his *Legazioni* in an almost pathetic light. Furnished with scanty instructions, shabbily equipped, and treated as an agent of inferior rank, he never loses his gift of free and wide observation or his pleasure in picturesque description.

A special division of this work will treat of the study of man individually and nationally, which among the Italians went hand in hand with the study of the outward conditions of human life.

WAR AS A WORK OF ART

It must here be briefly indicated by what steps the art of war assumed the character of a product of reflection. Throughout the countries of the West the education of the individual soldier in the Middle Ages was perfect within the limits of the then prevalent system of defence and attack: nor was there any want of ingenious inventors in the arts of besieging and of fortification. But the development both of strategy and of tactics was hindered by the character and duration of military service, and by the ambition of the nobles, who disputed questions of precedence in the face of the enemy, and through simple want of discipline caused the loss of great battles like Crécy and Maupertuis. Italy, on the contrary, was the first country to adopt the system of mercenary troops, which demanded a wholly different organization; and the early introduction of firearms did its part in making war a democratic pursuit, not only because the strongest castles were unable to withstand a bombardment, but because the skill of the engineer, of the gun-founder and of the artillerist – men belonging to another class than the nobility – was now of the first importance in a campaign. It was felt, with regret, that the value of the individual, which had been the soul of the small and admirably organized bands of mercenaries, would suffer from these novel means of destruction, which did their work at a distance; and there were *condottieri* who opposed to the utmost the introduction at least of the musket, which had been lately invented in Germany. We read that Paolo Vitelli, while recognizing and himself adopting the cannon, put out the eyes and cut off the hands of the captured *schioppettieri* of the enemy, because he held it unworthy that a gallant, and it might be noble, knight should be wounded and laid low by a common, despised foot soldier. On the whole, however, the new discoveries were accepted and turned to useful account, till the Italians became the teachers of all Europe, both in the building of fortifications and in the means of attacking them. Princes like Federigo of Urbino and Alfonso of Ferrara acquired a mastery of the subject compared to which the knowledge even of Maximilian I appears superficial. In Italy, earlier than elsewhere, there existed a comprehensive science and art of military affairs; here, for the first time, that impartial delight is taken in able generalship for its own sake which might, indeed, be expected from the frequent change of party and from the wholly unsentimental mode of action of the *condottieri.* During the Milano-Venetian war of 1451 and 1452, between Francesco Sforza and Jacopo Piccinino, the headquarters of the latter were attended by the scholar Gian Antonio Porcello dei Pandoni, commissioned by Alfonso of Naples to write a report of the campaign. It is written, not in the purest, but in a fluent Latin, a little too much in the style of the humanistic bombast of the day, is modelled on Caesar's *Commentaries*, and interspersed with speeches, prodigies and the like. Since for the past hundred years it had been seriously disputed whether Scipio Africanus or Hannibal was the greater, Piccinino through the whole book must needs be called Scipio and Sforza Hannibal. But something positive had to be reported, too, respecting the Milanese army; the sophist presented himself to Sforza, was led along the ranks, praised highly all that he saw, and promised to hand it down to posterity. Apart from him the Italian literature of the day is rich in descriptions of wars and strategic devices, written for the use of educated men in general as well as of specialists, while the con-temporary narratives of northerns, such as the *Burgundian War* by Diebold Schilling, still retain the shapelessness and matter-of-fact dry-ness of a mere chronicle. The greatest dilettante who has ever treated in that character of military affairs, Machiavelli, was then busy writing his *Arte della Guerra*. But the development of the individual soldier found its most complete expression in those public and solemn conflicts between one or more pairs of combatants which were practised long before the famous 'Challenge of Barletta' (1503). The victor was assured of the praises of poets and scholars, which were denied to the northern warrior. The result of these combats was no longer regarded as a divine judgement, but as a triumph of personal merit, and to the minds of the spectators seemed to be both the decision of an exciting competition and a satisfaction for the honour of the army or the nation.

It is obvious that this purely rational treatment of warlike affairs allowed, under certain circumstances, of the worst atrocities, even in the absence of a strong political hatred, as, for instance, when the plunder of a city had been promised to the troops. After the forty days' devastation of Piacenza, which Sforza was compelled to permit to his soldiers (1447), the town long stood empty, and at last had to be peopled by force. Yet outrages like these were nothing compared with the misery which was afterwards brought upon Italy by foreign troops, and most of all by the Spaniards, in whom perhaps a touch of oriental blood, perhaps familiarity with the spectacles of the Inquisition, had unloosed the devilish element of human nature. After seeing them at work at Prato, Rome and elsewhere, it is not easy to take any interest of the higher sort in Ferdinand the Catholic and Charles V, who knew what these hordes were, and yet unchained them. The mass of documents which are gradually brought to light from the Cabinets of these rulers will always remain an important source of historical information; but from such men no fruitful political conception can be looked for.

THE PAPACY

The papacy and the dominions of the Church are creations of so peculiar a kind that we have hitherto, in determining the general characteristics of Italian states, referred to them only occasionally. The deliberate choice and adaptation of political expedients, which gives so great an interest to the other states, is what we find least of all at Rome, since here the spiritual power could constantly conceal or supply the defects of the temporal. And what fiery trials did this state undergo in the fourteenth and the beginning of the fifteenth century, when the papacy was led captive to Avignon! All, at first, was thrown into confusion; but the pope had money, troops and a great statesman and general, the Spaniard Albornoz, who again brought the ecclesiastical state into complete subjection. The danger of a final dissolution was still greater at the time of the schism, when neither the Roman nor the French pope was rich enough to reconquer the newly lost state; but this was done under Martin V, after the unity of the Church was restored, and done again under Eugenius IV, when the same danger was renewed. But the ecclesiastical state was and remained a thorough anomaly among the powers of Italy; in and near Rome itself, the papacy was defied by the great families of the Colonna, Orsini, Savelli and Anguilara; in Umbria, in the Marches and in Romagna, those civic republics had almost ceased to exist, for whose devotion the papacy had showed so little gratitude; their place had been taken by a crowd of princely dynasties, great or small, whose loyalty and obedience signified little. As self-dependent powers, standing on their own merits, they have an interest of their own; and from this point of view the most important of them have already been discussed.

Nevertheless, a few general remarks on the papacy can hardly be dispensed with. New and strange perils and trials came upon it in the course of the fifteenth century, as the political spirit of the nation began to lay hold upon it on various sides, and to draw it within the sphere of its action. The least of these dangers came from the populace or from abroad; the most serious had their ground in the characters of the popes themselves.

Let us, for this moment, leave out of consideration the countries beyond the Alps. At the time when the papacy was exposed to mortal danger in Italy, it neither received nor could receive the slightest assistance either from France, then under Louis XI, or from England, distracted by the Wars of the Roses, or from the then disorganized Spanish monarchy, or from Germany, but lately betrayed at the Council of Basel. In Italy itself there was a certain number of instructed and even uninstructed people whose national vanity was flattered by the Italian character of the papacy; the personal interests of very many depended on its having and retaining this character; and vast masses of the people still believed in the virtue of the papal blessing and consecration;[25] among them notorious transgressors like Vitelozzo Vitelli, who still prayed to be absolved by Alexander VI, when the pope's son had him strangled. But all these grounds of sympathy put together would not have sufficed to save the papacy from its enemies, had the latter been really in earnest, and had they known how to take advantage of the envy and hatred with which the institution was regarded.

And at the very time when the prospect of help from without was so small, the most dangerous symptoms appeared within the papacy itself. Living, as it now did, and acting in the spirit of the secular Italian principalities, it was compelled to go through the same dark experiences as they; but its own exceptional nature gave a peculiar colour to the shadows.

As far as the city of Rome itself is concerned, small account was taken of its internal agitations, so many were the popes who had returned after being expelled by popular tumult, and so greatly did the presence of the Curia minister to the interests of the Roman people. But Rome not only displayed at times a specific anti-papal radicalism, but in the most serious plots which were then contrived, gave proof of the working of unseen hands from without. It was so in the case of the conspiracy of Stefano Porcari against Nicholas V (1453), the very pope who had done most for the prosperity of the city. Porcari aimed at the complete overthrow of the papal authority, and had distinguished accomplices, who, though their names are not handed down to us, are certainly to be looked for among the Italian governments of the time. Under the pontificate of the same man, Lorenzo Valla concluded his famous declamation against the gift of Constantine with the wish for the speedy secularization of the states of the Church.[26]

The Catilinarian gang, with which Pius II had to contend (1460), avowed with equal frankness their resolution to overthrow the government of the priests, and its leader, Tiburzio, threw the blame on the soothsayers, who had fixed the accomplishment of his wishes for this very year. Several of the chief men of Rome, the Prince of Taranto and the *condottiere* Jacopo Piccinino were accomplices and supporters of Tiburzio. Indeed, when we think of the booty which was accumulated in the palaces of wealthy prelates – the conspirators had the Cardinal of Aquileia especially in view – we are surprised that, in an almost unguarded city, such attempts were not more frequent and more successful. It was not without reason that Pius II preferred to reside anywhere rather than in Rome, and even Paul II was exposed to no small anxiety through a plot formed by some discharged abbreviators, who, under the command of Platina, besieged the Vatican for twenty days. The papacy must sooner or later have fallen a victim to such enterprises, if it had not stamped out the aristocratic factions under whose protection these bands of robbers grew to a head.

This task was undertaken by the terrible Sixtus IV. He was the first pope who had Rome and the neighbourhood thoroughly under his control, especially after his successful attack on the House of Colonna, and consequently, both in his Italian policy and in the internal affairs of the Church, he could venture to act with a defiant audacity, and to set at nought the complaints and threats to summon a Council which arose from all parts of Europe. He supplied himself with the necessary funds by simony, which suddenly grew to unheard-of proportions, and which extended from the appointment of cardinals down to the granting of the smallest favours. Sixtus himself had not obtained the papal dignity without recourse to the same means.

A corruption so universal might sooner or later bring disastrous consequences on the Holy See, but they lay in the uncertain future. It was otherwise with nepotism, which threatened at one time to destroy the papacy altogether. Of all the *nipoti*, Cardinal Pietro Riario enjoyed at first the chief and almost exclusive favour of Sixtus. He soon drew upon him the eyes of all Italy, partly by the fabulous luxury of his life, partly through the reports which were current of his irreligion and his political plans. He bargained with Duke Galeazzo Maria of Milan (1473) that the latter should become King of Lombardy, and then aid him with money and troops to return to Rome and ascend the papal throne; Sixtus, it appears, would have voluntarily yielded to him. This plan, which, by making the papacy hereditary, would have ended in the secularization of the papal state, failed through the sudden death of Pietro. The second *nipote*, Girolamo Riario, remained a layman, and did not seek the pontificate. From this time the *nipoti*, by their endeavours to found principalities for themselves, became a new source of confusion to Italy. It had already happened that the popes tried to make good their feudal claims on Naples in favour of their relatives! But since the failure of Calixtus III, such a scheme was no longer practicable, and Girolamo Riario, after the attempt to conquer Florence (and who knows how many other places) had failed, was forced to content himself with founding a state within the limits of the papal dominions themselves. This was justifiable in so far as Romagna, with its princes and civic despots, threatened to shake off the papal supremacy altogether, and ran the risk of shortly falling a prey to Sforza or the Venetians, when Rome interfered to prevent it. But who, at times and in circumstances like these, could guarantee the continued obedience of *nipoti* and their descendants, now turned into sovereign rulers, to popes with whom they had no further concern? Even in his lifetime the pope was not always sure of his own son or nephew, and the temptation was strong to expel the *nipote* of a precedessor and replace him with one of his own. The reaction of the whole system on the papacy itself was of the most serious character; all means of compulsion, whether temporal or spiritual, were used without scruple for the most questionable ends, and to these all the other objects of the Apostolic See were made subordinate. And when they were attained, at whatever cost of revolutions and proscriptions, a dynasty was founded which had no stronger interest than the destruction of the papacy.

At the death of Sixtus, Girolamo was only able to maintain himself in his usurped principality of Forlì and Imola by the utmost exertions of his own, and by the aid of the House of Sforza, to which his wife belonged. In the conclave (1484) which followed the death of Sixtus –

that in which Innocent VIII was elected – an incident occurred which seemed to furnish the papacy with a new external guarantee. Two cardinals, who, at the same time, were princes of ruling houses, Giovanni d'Aragona, son of King Ferrante, and Ascanio Sforza, brother of the Moor, sold their votes with the most shameless effrontery; so that, at any rate, the ruling houses of Naples and Milan became interested, by their participation in the booty, in the continuance of the papal system. Once again, in the following conclave, when all the cardinals but five sold themselves, Ascanio received enormous sums in bribes, but without cherishing the hope that at the next election he would himself be the favoured candidate.

Lorenzo the Magnificent, for his part, was anxious that the House of Medici should not be sent away with empty hands. He married his daughter Maddalena to the son of the new pope – the first who publicly acknowledged his children – Franceschetto Cibò, and expected not only favours of all kinds for his own son, Cardinal Giovanni, afterwards Leo X, but also the rapid promotion of his son-in-law. But with respect to the latter, he demanded impossibilities. Under Innocent VIII there was no opportunity for the audacious nepotism by which states had been founded, since Franceschetto himself was a poor creature who, like his father the pope, sought power only for the lowest purpose of all – the acquisition and accumulation of money. The manner, however, in which father and son practised this occupation must have led sooner or later to a final catastrophe – the dissolution of the state. If Sixtus had filled his treasury by the sale of spiritual dignities and favours, Innocent and his son, for their part, established an office for the sale of secular favours, in which pardons for murder and manslaughter were sold for large sums of money. Out of every fine 150 ducats were paid into the papal exchequer, and what was over to Franceschetto. Rome, during the latter part of this pontificate, swarmed with licensed and unlicensed assassins; the factions, which Sixtus had begun to put down, were again as active as ever; the pope, well guarded in the Vatican, was satisfied with now and then laying a trap, in which a wealthy misdoer was occasionally caught. For Franceschetto the chief point was to know by what means, when the pope died, he could escape with well-filled coffers. He betrayed himself at last, on the occasion of a false report (1490) of his father's death; he endeavoured to carry off all the money in the papal treasury, and when this proved impossible, insisted that, at all events, the Turkish prince, Djem, should go with him, and serve as a living capital, to be advantageously disposed of, perhaps to Ferrante of Naples. It is hard to estimate the political possibilities of remote periods, but we cannot help asking ourselves the question, if Rome could have survived two or three pontificates of this kind. Even with reference to the believing countries of Europe, it was imprudent to let matters go so far that not only travellers and pilgrims, but a whole embassy of Maximilian, King of the Romans, were stripped to their shirts in the neighbourhood of Rome, and that envoys had constantly to turn back without setting foot within the city.

Such a condition of things was incompatible with the conception of power and its pleasures which inspired the gifted Alexander VI (1492–1503), and the first event that happened was the restoration, at least provisionally, of public order, and the punctual payment of every salary.

Strictly speaking, as we are now discussing phases of Italian civilization, this pontificate might be passed over, since the Borgias are no more Italian than the House of Naples. Alexander spoke Spanish in public with Cesare; Lucrezia, at her entrance to Ferrara, where she wore a Spanish costume, was sung to by Spanish buffoons; their confidential servants consisted of Spaniards, as did also the most ill-famed company of the troops of Cesare in the war of 1500; and even his hangman, Don Micheletto, and his poisoner, Sebastian Pinzon Cremonese, seem to have been of the same nation. Among his other achievements, Cesare, in true Spanish fashion, killed, according to the rules of the craft, six wild bulls in an enclosed court. But the Roman corruption, which seemed to culminate in this family, was already far advanced when they came to the city.

What they were and what they did has been often and fully described. Their immediate purpose, which, in fact, they attained, was the complete subjugation of the pontifical state. All the petty despots, who were mostly more or less refractory vassals of the Church, were expelled or destroyed; and in Rome itself the two great factions were annihilated, the so-called Guelph Orsini as well as the so-called Ghibelline Colonna. But the means employed were of so frightful a character that they must certainly have ended in the ruin of the papacy, had not the contemporaneous death of both father and son by poison suddenly intervened to alter the whole aspect of the situation. The moral indignation of Christendom was certainly no great source of danger to

Alexander; at home he was strong enough to extort terror and obedience; foreign rulers were won over to his side, and Louis XII even aided him to the utmost of his power. The mass of the people throughout Europe had hardly a conception of what was passing in Central Italy. The only moment which was really fraught with danger – when Charles VIII was in Italy – went by with unexpected fortune, and even then it was not the papacy as such that was in peril, but Alexander, who risked being supplanted by a more respectable pope.[27] The great, permanent and increasing danger for the papacy lay in Alexander himself, and, above all, in his son Cesare Borgia.

In the nature of the father, ambition, avarice and sensuality were combined with strong and brilliant qualities. All the pleasures of power and luxury he granted himself from the first day of his pontificate in the fullest measure. In the choice of means to this end he was wholly without scruple; it was known at once that he would more than compensate himself for the sacrifices which his election had involved,[28] and that the simony of the seller would far exceed the simony of the buyer. It must be remembered that the vice-chancellorship and other offices which Alexander had formerly held had taught him to know better and turn to more practical account the various sources of revenue than any other member of the Curia. As early as 1494, a Carmelite, Adam of Genoa, who had preached at Rome against simony, was found murdered in his bed with twenty wounds. Hardly a single cardinal was appointed without the payment of enormous sums of money.

But when the pope in course of time fell under the influence of his son Cesare Borgia, his violent measures assumed that character of devilish wickedness which necessarily reacts upon the ends pursued. What was done in the struggle with the Roman nobles and with the tyrants of Romagna exceeded in faithlessness and barbarity even that measure to which the Aragonese rulers of Naples had already accustomed the world; and the genius for deception was also greater. The manner in which Cesare isolated his father, murdering brother, brother-in-law and other relations or courtiers, whenever their favour with the pope or their position in any other respect became inconvenient to him, is literally appalling. Alexander was forced to acquiesce in the murder of his best-loved son, the Duke of Gandia, since he himself lived in hourly dread of Cesare.

What were the final aims of the latter? Even in the last months of his tyranny, when he had murdered the *condottieri* at Sinigaglia, and was to all intents and purposes master of the ecclesiastical state (1503), those who stood near him gave the modest reply that the duke merely wished to put down the factions and the despots, and all for the good of the Church only; that for himself he desired nothing more than the lordship of the Romagna, and that he had earned the gratitude of all the following popes by riding them of the Orsini and Colonna. But no one will accept this as his ultimate design. The Pope Alexander himself, in his discussions with the Venetian ambassador, went further than this, when committing his son to the protection of Venice: 'I will see to it,' he said, 'that one day the papacy shall belong either to him or to you.' Cesare certainly added that no one could become pope without the consent of Venice, and for this end the Venetian cardinals had only to keep well together. Whether he referred to himself or not we are unable to say; at all events, the declaration of his father is sufficient to prove his designs on the pontifical throne. We further obtain from Lucrezia Borgia a certain amount of indirect evidence, in so far as certain passages in the poems of Ercole Strozza may be the echo of expressions which she as Duchess of Ferrara may easily have permitted herself to use. Here, too, Cesare's hopes of the papacy are chiefly spoken of; but now and then a supremacy over all Italy is hinted at, and finally we are given to understand that as temporal ruler Cesare's projects were of the greatest, and that for their sake he had formerly surrendered his cardinalate. In fact, there can be no doubt whatever that Cesare, whether chosen pope or not after the death of Alexander, meant to keep possession of the pontifical state at any cost, and that this, after all the enormities he had committed, he could not as pope have succeeded in doing permanently. He, if anybody, could have secularized the States of the Church, and he would have been forced to do so in order to keep them. Unless we are much deceived, this is the real reason of the secret sympathy with which Machiavelli treats the great criminal; from Cesare, or from nobody, could it be hoped that he 'would draw the steel from the wound', in other words, annihilate the papacy – the source of all foreign intervention and of all the divisions of Italy. The intriguers who thought to divine Cesare's aims, when holding out to him hopes of the kingdom of Tuscany, seem to have been dismissed with contempt.

But all logical conclusions from his premises are idle, not because of the unaccountable genius which in fact characterized him as little as it did Wallenstein,[29] but because the means which he employed were not compatible with any large and consistent course of action. Perhaps, indeed, in the very excess of his wickedness some prospect of salvation for the papacy may have existed even without the accident which put an end to his rule.

Even if we assume that the destruction of the petty despots in the pontifical state had gained for him nothing but sympathy, even if we take as proof of his great projects the army, composed of the best soldiers and officers in Italy, with Leonardo da Vinci as chief engineer, which followed his fortunes in 1502, other facts nevertheless wear such a character of unreason that our judgement, like that of contemporary observers, is wholly at a loss to explain them. One fact of this kind is the devastation and maltreatment of the newly won state, which Cesare still intended to keep and to rule over. Another is the condition of Rome and of the Curia in the last decades of the pontificate. Whether it were that father and son had drawn up a formal list of proscribed persons, or that the murders were resolved upon one by one, in either case the Borgias were bent on the secret destruction of all who stood in their way or whose inheritance they coveted. Of this money and movable goods formed the smallest part; it was a much greater source of profit for the pope that the incomes of the clerical dignitaries in question were suspended by their death, and that he received the revenues of their offices while vacant, and the price of these offices when they were filled by the successors of the murdered men. The Venetian ambassador Paolo Capello announces in the year 1500: 'Every night four or five murdered men are discovered – bishops, prelates and others – so that all Rome is trembling for fear of being destroyed by the duke [Cesare].' He himself used to wander about Rome in the night-time with his guards, and there is every reason to believe that he did so not only because, like Tiberius, he shrank from showing his now repulsive features by daylight, but also to gratify his insane thirst for blood, perhaps even on the persons of those unknown to him.

As early as the year 1499 the despair was so great and so general that many of the papal guards were waylaid and put to death. But those whom the Borgias could not assail with open violence fell victims to their poison. For the cases in which a certain amount of discretion seemed requisite, a white powder of an agreeable taste was made use of, which did not work on the spot, but slowly and gradually, and which could be mixed without notice in any dish or goblet. Prince Djem had taken some of it in a sweet draught, before Alexander surrendered him to Charles VIII (1495), and at the end of their career father and son poisoned themselves with the same powder by accidentally tasting a sweetmeat intended for a wealthy cardinal. The official epitomizer of the history of the popes, Onofrio Panvinio, mentions three cardinals, Orsini, Ferrerio and Michiel, whom Alexander caused to be poisoned, and hints at a fourth, Giovanni Borgia, whom Cesare took into his own charge – though probably wealthy prelates seldom died in Rome at that time without giving rise to suspicions of this sort. Even tranquil scholars who had withdrawn to some provincial town were not out of reach of the merciless poison. A secret horror seemed to hang about the pope; storms and thunderbolts, crushing in walls and chambers, had in earlier times often visited and alarmed him; in the year 1500, when these phenomena were repeated, they were held to be *cosa diabolica*. The report of these events seems at last, through the well-attended jubilee of 1500, to have been carried far and wide throughout the countries of Europe, and the infamous traffic in indulgences did what else was needed to draw all eyes upon Rome. Besides the returning pilgrims, strange white-robed penitents came from Italy to the North, among them disguised fugitives from the papal state, who are not likely to have been silent. Yet none can calculate how far the scandal and indignation of Christendom might have gone before they became a source of pressing danger to Alexander. 'He would,' says Panvinio elsewhere, 'have put all the other rich cardinals and prelates out of the way, to get their property, had he not, in the midst of his great plans for his son, been struck down by death.' And what might not Cesare have achieved if, at the moment when his father died, he had not himself been laid upon a sickbed! What a conclave would that have been, in which, armed with all his weapons, he had extorted his election from a college whose numbers he had judiciously reduced by poison – and this at a time when there was no French army at hand! In pursuing such a hypothesis the imagination loses itself in an abyss.

Instead of this followed the conclave in which Pius III was elected, and, after his speedy death, that which chose Julius II – both elections the fruits of a general reaction.

Whatever may have been the private morals of Julius II, in all essential respects he was the saviour of the papacy. His familiarity with the course of events since the pontificate of his uncle Sixtus had given him a profound insight into the grounds and conditions of the papal authority. On these he founded his own policy, and devoted to it the whole force and passion of his unshaken soul. He ascended the steps of St Peter's chair without simony and amid general applause, and with him ceased, at all events, the undisguised traffic in the highest offices of the Church. Julius had favourites, and among them were some the reverse of worthy, but a special fortune put him above the temptation to nepotism. His brother, Giovanni della Rovere, was the husband of the heiress of Urbino, sister of the last Montefeltro Guidobaldo, and from this marriage was born, in 1491, a son, Francesco Maria della Rovere, who was at the same time papal *nipote* and lawful heir to the duchy of Urbino. What Julius elsewhere acquired, either on the field of battle or by diplomatic means, he proudly bestowed on the Church, not on his family; the ecclesiastical territory, which he found in a state of dissolution, he bequeathed to his successor completely subdued, and increased by Parma and Piacenza. It was not his fault that Ferrara too was not added to the dominions of the Church. The 700,000 ducats which were stored up in the Castel Sant' Angelo were to be delivered by the governor to none but the future pope. He made himself heir of the cardinals, and, indeed, of all the clergy who died in Rome, and this by the most despotic means; but he murdered or poisoned none of them.[30] That he should himself lead his forces to battle was for him an unavoidable necessity, and certainly did him nothing but good at a time when a man in Italy was forced to be either hammer or anvil, and when personality was a greater power than the most indisputable right. If, despite all his high-sounding 'Away with the barbarians!' he nevertheless contributed more than any man to the firm settlement of the Spaniards in Italy, he may have thought it a matter of indifference to the papacy, or even, as things stood, a relative advantage. And to whom, sooner than to Spain, could the Church look for a sincere and lasting respect, in an age when the princes of Italy cherished none but the sacrilegious projects against her? Be this as it may, the powerful, original nature, which could swallow no anger and conceal no genuine good-will, made on the whole the impression most desirable in his situation – that of the *pontefice terribile*.[31] He could even, with a comparatively clear conscience, venture to summon a Council to Rome, and so bid defiance to that outcry for a Council which was raised by the opposition all over Europe. A ruler of this stamp needed some great outward symbol of his conceptions; Julius found it in the reconstruction of St Peter's. The plan of it, as Bramante wished to have it, is perhaps the grandest expression of power in unity which can be imagined. In other arts besides architecture the face and the memory of the pope live on in their most ideal form, and it is not without significance that even the Latin poetry of those days gives proof of a wholly different enthusiasm for Julius than that shown for his pre-decessors. The entry into Bologna, at the end of the *Iter Julii Secundi*, by the Cardinal Adriano da Corneto, has a splendour of its own, and Giovan Antonio Flaminio, in one of the finest elegies, appealed to the patriot in the pope to grant his protection to Italy.

In a constitution of his Lateran Council, Julius had solemnly de-nounced the simony of the papal elections. After his death in 1513, the money-loving cardinals tried to evade the prohibition by proposing that the endowments and offices hitherto held by the chosen candi-date should be equally divided among themselves, in which case they would have elected the best-endowed cardinal, the incompetent Raphael Riario. But a reaction, chiefly arising from the younger members of the Sacred College, who, above all things, desired a liberal pope, rendered the miserable combination futile; Giovanni Medici was elected – the famous Leo X.

We shall often meet with him in treating of the noonday of the Renaissance; here we wish only to point out that under him the papacy was again exposed to great inward and outward dangers. Among these we do not reckon the conspiracy of the Cardinals Petrucci, De Saulis, Riario and Corneto (1517), which at most could have occasioned a change of persons, and to which Leo found the true antidote in the unheard-of creation of thirty-one new cardinals, a measure which had the additional advantage of rewarding, in some cases at least, real merit.

But some of the paths which Leo allowed himself to tread during the first two years of his office were perilous to the last degree. He seriously endeavoured to secure, by negotiation, the kingdom of Naples for his brother Giuliano, and for his nephew Lorenzo a powerful North Italian state, to comprise Milan, Tuscany, Urbino and Ferrara. It is clear that the pontifical state, thus hemmed in on all sides, would have become a mere Medicean appanage, and that, in fact, there would have been no further need to secularize it.

The plan found an insuperable obstacle in the political conditions of the time. Giuliano died early. To provide for Lorenzo, Leo undertook to expel the Duke Francesco Maria della Rovere from Urbino, but reaped from the war nothing but hatred and poverty, and was forced, when in 1519 Lorenzo followed his uncle to the grave, to hand over the hard-won conquests to the Church. He did on compulsion and without credit what, if it had been done voluntarily, would have been to his lasting honour. What he attempted against Alfonso of Ferrara, and actually achieved against a few petty despots and *condottieri*, was assuredly not of a kind to raise his reputation. And this was at a time when the monarchs of the West were yearly growing more and more accustomed to political gambling on a colossal scale, of which the stakes were this or that province of Italy. Who could guarantee that, since the last decades had seen so great an increase of their power at home, their ambition would stop short of the States of the Church? Leo himself witnessed the prelude of what was fulfilled in the year 1527; a few bands of Spanish infantry appeared — of their own accord, it seems — at the end of 1520, on the borders of the pontifical territory, with a view of laying the pope under contribution, but were driven back by the papal forces. The public feeling, too, against the corruptions of the hierarchy had of late years been drawing rapidly to a head, and men with an eye for the future, like the younger Pico della Mirandola, called urgently for reform. Meantime Luther had already appeared upon the scene.

Under Adrian VI (1522–3), the few and timid improvements, carried out in the face of the great German Reformation, came too late. He could do little more than proclaim his horror of the course which things had taken hitherto, of simony, nepotism, prodigality, brigandage and profligacy. The danger from the side of the Lutherans was by no means the greatest; an acute observer from Venice, Girolamo Negro, uttered his fears that a speedy and terrible disaster would befall the city of Rome itself.

Under Clement VII the whole horizon of Rome was filled with vapours, like that leaden veil which the scirocco drew over the Campagna, and which made the last months of summer so deadly. The pope was no less detested at home than abroad. Thoughtful people were filled with anxiety, hermits appeared upon the streets and squares of Rome, foretelling the fate of Italy and of the world, and calling the pope by the name of Antichrist; the faction of the Colonna raised its head defiantly; the indomitable Cardinal Pompeo Colonna, whose mere existence was a permanent menace to the papacy, ventured to surprise the city in 1526, hoping, with the help of Charles V, to become pope then and there, as soon as Clement was killed or captured. It was no piece of good fortune for Rome that the latter was able to escape to the Castel Sant' Angelo, and the fate for which he himself was reserved may well be called worse than death.

By a series of those falsehoods, which only the powerful can venture on, but which bring ruin upon the weak, Clement brought about the advance of the Germano-Spanish army under Bourbon and Frundsberg (1527). It is certain that the Cabinet of Charles V intended to inflict on him a severe castigation, and that it could not calculate beforehand how far the zeal of its unpaid hordes would carry them. It would have been vain to attempt to enlist men in Germany without paying any bounty, if it had not been well known that Rome was the object of the expedition. It may be that the written orders to Bourbon will be found some day or other, and it is not improbable that they will prove to be worded mildly. But historical criticism will not allow itself to be led astray. The Catholic king and emperor owed it to his luck and nothing else that pope and cardinals were not murdered by his troops. Had this happened, no sophistry in the world could clear him of his share in the guilt. The massacre of countless people of less consequence, the plunder of the rest, and all the horrors of torture and traffic in human life show clearly enough what was possible in the *Sacco di Roma*.

Charles seems to have wished to bring the pope, who had fled a second time to the Castel Sant' Angelo, to Naples, after extorting from him vast sums of money, and Clement's flight to Orvieto must have happened without any connivance on the part of Spain. Whether the emperor ever thought seriously of the secularization of the States of the Church, for which everybody was quite prepared, and whether he was really dissuaded from it by the representations of Henry VIII of England, will probably never be made clear.

But if such projects really existed, they cannot have lasted long: from the devastated city arose a new spirit of reform both in Church and state. It made itself felt in a moment. Cardinal Sadoleto, one witness of many, thus writes:

> If through our suffering a satisfaction is made to the wrath and justice of
> God, if these fearful punishments again open the way to better laws and

morals, then is our misfortune perhaps not of the greatest ... What
belongs to God He will take care of; before us lies a life of reformation,
which no violence can take from us. Let us so rule our deeds and
thoughts as to seek in God only the true glory of the priesthood and our
own true greatness and power.

In point of fact, this critical year, 1527, so far bore fruit that the
voices of serious men could again make themselves heard. Rome
had suffered too much to return, even under a Paul III, to the gay
corruption of Leo X.

The papacy, too, when its sufferings became so great, began to
excite a sympathy half religious and half political. The kings could not
tolerate that one of their number should arrogate to himself the rights
of papal gaoler, and concluded (18 August 1527) the Treaty of Amiens,
one of the objects of which was the deliverance of Clement. They
thus, at all events, turned to their own account the unpopularity which
the deeds of the imperial troops had excited. At the same time the
emperor became seriously embarrassed, even in Spain, where the
prelates and grandees never saw him without making the most urgent
remonstrances. When a general deputation of the clergy and laity, all
clothed in mourning, was projected, Charles, fearing that troubles
might arise out of it, like those of the insurrection quelled a few years
before, forbade the scheme. Not only did he not dare to prolong the
maltreatment of the pope, but he was absolutely compelled, even
apart from all considerations of foreign politics, to be reconciled with
the papacy which he had so grievously wounded. For the temper of
the German people, which certainly pointed to a different course,
seemed to him, like German affairs generally, to afford no foundation
for a policy. It is possible, too, as a Venetian maintains, that the
memory of the sack of Rome lay heavy on his conscience, and tended
to hasten that expiation which was sealed by the permanent subjection
of the Florentines to the Medicean family of which the pope was a
member. The *nipote* and new duke, Alessandro Medici, was married to
the natural daughter of the emperor.

In the following years the plan of a Council enabled Charles to keep
the papacy in all essential points under his control, and at one and the
same time to protect and to oppress it. The greatest danger of all –
secularization – the danger which came from within, from the popes
themselves and their *nipoti*, was adjourned for centuries by the German

Reformation. Just as this alone had made the expedition against Rome (1527) possible and successful, so did it compel the papacy to become once more the expression of a world-wide spiritual power, to raise itself from the soulless debasement in which it lay, and to place itself at the head of all the enemies of this Reformation. The institution thus developed during the latter years of Clement VII, and under Paul III, Paul IV, and their successors, in the face of the defection of half Europe, was a new, regenerated hierarchy, which avoided all the great and dangerous scandals of former times, particularly nepotism, with its attempts at territorial aggrandizement, and which, in alliance with the Catholic princes, and impelled by a new-born spiritual force, found its chief work in the recovery of what had been lost. It only existed and is only intelligible in opposition to the seceders. In this sense it can be said with perfect truth that the moral salvation of the papacy is due to its mortal enemies. And now its political position, too, though certainly under the permanent tutelage of Spain, became impregnable; almost without effort it inherited, on the extinction of its vassals, the legitimate line of Este and the house of della Rovere, the duchies of Ferrara and Urbino. But without the Reformation – if, indeed, it is possible to think it away – the whole ecclesiastical state would long ago have passed into secular hands.

PATRIOTISM

In conclusion, let us briefly consider the effect of these political circumstances on the spirit of the nation at large.

It is evident that the general political uncertainty in Italy during the fourteenth and fifteenth centuries was of a kind to excite in the better spirits of the time a patriotic disgust and opposition. Dante and Petrarch, in their day, proclaimed loudly a common Italy, the object of the highest efforts of all her children. It may be objected that this was only the enthusiasm of a few highly instructed men, in which the mass of the people had no share; but it can hardly have been otherwise even in Germany, although in name at least that country was united, and recognized in the emperor one supreme head. The first patriotic utterances of German literature, if we except some verses of the *Minnesänger*, belong to the humanists of the time of Maximilian I and after, and read like an echo of Italian declamations. And yet, as a matter of fact, Germany had been long a nation in a truer sense than

Italy ever was since the Roman days. France owes the consciousness of its national unity mainly to its conflicts with the English, and Spain has never permanently succeeded in absorbing Portugal, closely related as the two countries are. For Italy, the existence of the ecclesiastical state, and the conditions under which alone it could continue, were a permanent obstacle to national unity, an obstacle whose removal seemed hopeless. When, therefore, in the political intercourse of the fifteenth century, the common fatherland is sometimes emphatically named, it is done in most cases to annoy some other Italian state. But those deeply serious and sorrowful appeals to national sentiment were not heard again till later, when the time for unity had gone by, when the country was inundated with Frenchmen and Spaniards. The sense of local patriotism may be said in some measure to have taken the place of this feeling, though it was but a poor equivalent for it.

PART II

The Development of the Individual

PERSONALITY

IN THE character of these states, whether republics or despotisms, lies not the only but the chief reason for the early development of the Italian. To this it is due that he was the first-born among the sons of modern Europe.

In the Middle Ages both sides of human consciousness – that which was turned within as that which was turned without – lay dreaming or half awake beneath a common veil. The veil was woven of faith, illusion and childish prepossession, through which the world and history were seen clad in strange hues. Man was conscious of himself only as a member of a race, people, party, family or corporation – only through some general category. In Italy this veil first melted into air; an *objective* treatment and consideration of the state and of all the things of this world became possible. The *subjective* side at the same time asserted itself with corresponding emphasis; man became a spiritual *individual*,[32] and recognized himself as such. In the same way the Greek had once distinguished himself from the barbarian, and the Arab had felt himself an individual at a time when other Asiatics knew themselves only as members of a race. It will not be difficult to show that this result was due above all to the political circumstances of Italy.

In far earlier times we can here and there detect a development of free personality which in northern Europe either did not occur at all, or could not display itself in the same manner. The band of audacious wrongdoers in the tenth century described to us by Liudprand, some of the contemporaries of Gregory VII (for example, Benzo of Alba) and a few of the opponents of the first Hohenstaufen show us characters of this kind. But at the close of the thirteenth century Italy began to swarm with individuality; the ban laid upon human personality was dissolved; and a thousand figures meet us each in its own special shape and dress. Dante's great poem would have been impossible in any other country of Europe, if only for the reason that they all still lay under the spell of race. For Italy the august poet, through the wealth of individuality which he set forth, was the most national herald of his time. But this unfolding of the treasures of human nature in literature and art – this many-sided representation and criticism – will be discussed in separate chapters; here we have to deal only with the psychological fact itself. This fact appears in the most decisive and unmistakable form. The Italians of the fourteenth century knew little of false modesty or of hypocrisy in any shape; not one of them was afraid of singularity, of being and seeming unlike his neighbours.

Despotism, as we have already seen, fostered in the highest degree the individuality not only of the tyrant or *condottiere* himself,[33] but also of the men whom he protected or used as his tools – the secretary, minister, poet and companion. These people were forced to know all the inward resources of their own nature, passing or permanent; and their enjoyment of life was enhanced and concentrated by the desire to obtain the greatest satisfaction from a possibly very brief period of power and influence.

But even the subjects whom they ruled over were not free from the same impulse. Leaving out of account those who wasted their lives in secret opposition and conspiracies, we speak of the majority who were content with a strictly private station, like most of the urban population of the Byzantine empire and the Muhammadan states. No doubt it was often hard for the subjects of a Visconti to maintain the dignity of their persons and families, and multitudes must have lost in moral character through the servitude they lived under. But this was not the case with regard to individuality; for political impotence does not hinder the different tendencies and manifestations of private life from thriving in the fullest vigour and variety. Wealth and culture, so far as display and rivalry were not forbidden to them, a municipal freedom which did not cease to be considerable, and a Church which, unlike that of the Byzantine or of the Muhammadan world, was not identical with the state – all these conditions undoubtedly favoured the growth of individual thought, for which the necessary leisure was furnished by the cessation of party conflicts. The private man, indifferent to politics, and busied partly with serious pursuits, partly with the interests of a dilettante, seems to have been first fully formed in these despotisms of the fourteenth century. Documentary evidence cannot, of course, be required on such a point. The novelists, from whom we might expect information, describe to us oddities in plenty, but only from one point of view and in so far as the needs of the story demand. Their scene, too, lies chiefly in the republican cities.

In the latter, circumstances were also, but in another way, favourable to the growth of individual character. The more frequently the governing party was changed, the more the individual was led to make the utmost of the exercise and enjoyment of power. The statesmen and popular leaders, especially in Florentine history, acquired so marked a personal character that we can scarcely find, even exceptionally, a parallel to them in contemporary history, hardly even in Jacob von Artevelde.

The members of the defeated parties, on the other hand, often came into a position like that of the subjects of the despotic states, with the difference that the freedom or power already enjoyed, and in some cases the hope of recovering them, gave a higher energy to their individuality. Among these men of involuntary leisure we find, for instance, an Agnolo Pandolfini (d. 1446), whose work on domestic economy[34] is the first complete programme of a developed private life. His estimate of the duties of the individual as against the dangers and thanklessness of public life is in its way a true monument of the age.

Banishment, too, has this effect above all, that it either wears the exile out or develops whatever is greatest in him. 'In all our more populous cities,' says Gioviano Pontano, 'we see a crowd of people who have left their homes of their own free will; but a man takes his virtues with him wherever he goes.' And, in fact, they were by no means only men who had been actually exiled, but thousands left their native place voluntarily, because they found its political or economical condition intolerable. The Florentine emigrants at Ferrara and the Lucchese in Venice formed whole colonies by themselves.

The cosmopolitanism which grew up in the most gifted circles is in itself a high stage of individualism. Dante, as we have already said, finds a new home in the language and culture of Italy, but goes beyond even this in the words, 'My country is the whole world.' And when his recall to Florence was offered him on unworthy conditions, he wrote back: 'Can I not everywhere behold the light of the sun and the stars; everywhere meditate on the noblest truths, without appearing ingloriously and shamefully before the city and the people? Even my bread will not fail me.' The artists exult no less defiantly in their freedom from the constraints of fixed residence. 'Only he who has learned everything,' says Ghiberti,[35] 'is nowhere a stranger; robbed of his fortune and without friends, he is yet the citizen of every country, and can fearlessly despise the changes of fortune.' In the same strain an exiled humanist writes: 'Wherever a learned man fixes his seat, there is home.'[36]

An acute and practised eye might be able to trace, step by step, the increase in the number of complete men during the fifteenth century. Whether they had before them as a conscious object the harmonious development of their spiritual and material existence is hard to say; but several of them attained it, so far as is consistent with the imperfection of all that is earthly. It may be better to renounce the attempt at an estimate of the share which fortune, character and talent had in the life of Lorenzo il Magnifico. But look at a personality like that of Ariosto, especially as shown in his satires. In what harmony are there expressed the pride of the man and the poet, the irony with which he treats his own enjoyment, the most delicate satire, and the deepest goodwill!

When this impulse to the highest individual development was combined with a powerful and varied nature, which had mastered all the elements of the culture of the age, then arose the 'all-sided man' – *l'uomo universale* – who belonged to Italy alone. Men there were of encyclopedic knowledge in many countries during the Middle Ages, for this knowledge was confined within narrow limits; and even in the twelfth century there were universal artists, but the problems of architecture were comparatively simple and uniform, and in sculpture and painting the matter was of more importance than the form. But in Italy at the time of the Renaissance we find artists who in every branch created new and perfect works, and who also made the greatest impression as men. Others, outside the arts they practised, were masters of a vast circle of spiritual interests.

Dante, who, even in his lifetime, was called by some a poet, by others a philosopher, by others a theologian, pours forth in all his writings a stream of personal force by which the reader, apart from the interest of the subject, feels himself carried away. What power of will must the steady, unbroken elaboration of the *Divine Comedy* have required! And if we look at the matter of the poem, we find that in the whole spiritual or physical world there is hardly an important subject which the poet has not fathomed, and on which his utterances – often only a few words – are not the most weighty of his time. For the plastic arts he is of the first importance, and this for better reasons than the few references to contemporary artists – he soon became himself the source of inspiration.

The fifteenth century is, above all, that of the many-sided men. There is no biography which does not, besides the chief work of its hero, speak of other pursuits all passing beyond the limits of dilettantism. The Florentine merchant and statesman was often learned in both the classical languages; the most famous humanists read the *Ethics* and *Politics* of Aristotle to him and his sons; even the daughters of the house were highly educated. It is in these circles that private education was first treated seriously. The humanist, on his side, was compelled to the most varied attainments, since his philological learning was not limited, as it is now, to the theoretical knowledge of classical antiquity, but had to serve the practical needs of daily life. While studying Pliny, he made collections of natural history; the geography of the ancients was his guide in treating of modern geography; their history was his pattern in writing contemporary chronicles, even when composed in Italian; he not only translated the comedies of Plautus, but acted as manager when they were put on the stage; every effective form of ancient literature down to the dialogues of Lucian he did his best to imitate; and besides all this, he acted as magistrate, secretary and diplomatist – not always to his own advantage.

But among these many-sided men, some who may truly be called all-sided tower above the rest. Before analysing the general phases of life and culture of this period, we may here, on the threshold of the fifteenth century, consider for a moment the figure of one of these giants – Leon Battista Alberti (b. 1404?, d. 1472). His biography,[37] which is only a fragment, speaks of him but little as an artist, and makes no mention at all of his great significance in the history of architecture. We shall now see what he was, apart from these special claims to distinction.

In all by which praise is won, Leon Battista was from his childhood the first. Of his various gymnastic feats and exercises we read with astonishment how, with his feet together, he could spring over a man's head; how, in the cathedral, he threw a coin in the air till it was heard to ring against the distant roof; how the wildest horses trembled under him. In three things he desired to appear faultless to others, in walking, in riding, and in speaking. He learned music without a master, and yet his compositions were admired by professional judges. Under the pressure of poverty, he studied both civil and canonical law for many years, till exhaustion brought on a severe illness. In his twenty-fourth year, finding his memory for words weakened, but his sense of facts unimpaired, he set to work at physics and mathematics. And all the while he acquired every sort of accomplishment and dexterity, cross-examining artists, scholars and artisans of all descriptions, down to the cobblers, about the secrets and peculiarities of their craft. Painting and modelling he practised by the way, and especially excelled in admirable likenesses from memory. Great admiration was excited by his mysterious camera obscura, in which he showed at one time the stars and the moon rising over rocky hills, at another wide landscapes with mountains and gulfs receding into dim perspective, and with fleets advancing on the waters in shade or sunshine. And that which others created he welcomed joyfully, and held every human achievement which followed the laws of beauty for something almost divine. To all this must be added his literary works, first of all those on art, which are landmarks and authorities of the first order for the Renaissance of form, especially in architecture; then his Latin prose writings – novels and other works – of which some have been taken for productions of antiquity; his elegies, eclogues and humorous dinner-speeches. He also wrote an Italian treatise on domestic life[38] in four books; and even a funeral oration on his dog. His serious and witty sayings were thought worth collecting, and specimens of them, many columns long, are quoted in his biography. And all that he had and knew he imparted, as rich natures always do, without the least reserve, giving away his chief discoveries for nothing. But the deepest spring of his nature has yet to be spoken of – the sympathetic intensity with which he entered into the whole life around him. At the sight of noble trees and waving cornfields he shed tears; handsome and dignified old men he honoured as 'a delight of nature', and could never look at them enough. Perfectly formed animals won his goodwill as being specially favoured by nature; and more than once, when he was ill, the sight of a beautiful landscape cured him. No wonder that those who saw him in this close and mysterious communion with the world ascribed to him the gift of prophecy. He was said to have foretold a bloody catastrophe in the family of Este, the fate of Florence, and the death of the popes years before they happened, and to be able to read into the countenances and the hearts of men. It need not be added that an iron will pervaded and sustained his whole personality; like all the great men of the Renaissance, he said, 'Men can do all things if they will.'

And Leonardo da Vinci was to Alberti as the finisher to the beginner, as the master to the dilettante. Would only that Vasari's work were here supplemented by a description like that of Alberti! The colossal outlines of Leonardo's nature can never be more than dimly and distantly conceived.

GLORY

To this inward development of the individual corresponds a new sort of outward distinction – the modern form of glory.[39]

In the other countries of Europe the different classes of society lived apart, each with its own medieval caste sense of honour. The poetical fame of the troubadours and Minnesingers was peculiar to the knightly order. But in Italy social equality had appeared before the time of the tyrannies or the democracies. We there find early traces of a general society, having, as will be shown more fully later on, a common ground in Latin and Italian literature; and such a ground was needed for this new element in life to grow in. To this must be added that the Roman authors, who were now zealously studied, are filled and saturated with the conception of fame, and that their subject itself – the universal empire of Rome – stood as a permanent ideal before the minds of Italians. From henceforth all the aspirations and achievements of the people were governed by a moral postulate, which was still unknown elsewhere in Europe.

Here, again, as in all essential points, the first witness to be called is Dante. He strove for the poet's garland with all the power of his soul. As publicist and man of letters, he laid stress on the fact that what he did was new, and that he wished not only to be, but to be esteemed, the first in his own walks. But even in his prose writings he touches on the inconveniences of fame; he knows how often personal acquaintance with famous men is disappointing, and explains how this is due partly to the childish fancy of men, partly to envy, and partly to the imperfections of the hero himself. And in his great poem he firmly maintains the emptiness of fame, although in a manner which betrays that his heart was not set free from the longing for it. In paradise the sphere of Mercury is the seat of such blessed ones as on earth strove after glory and thereby dimmed 'the beams of true love'. It is characteristic that the lost souls in hell beg of Dante to keep alive for them their memory and fame on earth, while those in purgatory only entreat his prayers and those of others for their deliverance. And in a famous passage, the passion for fame – '*lo gran disio dell'eccellenza*' – is reproved for the reason that intellectual glory is not absolute, but relative to the times, and may be surpassed and eclipsed by greater successors.

The new race of poet-scholars which arose soon after Dante quickly made themselves masters of this fresh tendency. They did so in a double sense, being themselves the most acknowledged celebrities of Italy, and at the same time, as poets and historians, consciously disposing of the reputation of others. An outward symbol of this sort of fame was the coronation of the poets, of which we shall speak later on.

A contemporary of Dante, Albertinus Musattus or Mussatus, crowned poet at Padua by the bishop and rector, enjoyed a fame which fell little short of deification. Every Christmas Day the doctors and students of both colleges at the university came in solemn procession before his house with trumpets and, as it seems, with burning tapers, to salute him and bring him presents. His reputation lasted till, in 1318, he fell into disgrace with the ruling tyrant of the House of Carrara.

This new incense, which once was offered only to saints and heroes, was given in clouds to Petrarch, who persuaded himself in his later years that it was but a foolish and troublesome thing. His letter 'To Posterity' is the confession of an old and famous man, who is forced to gratify the public curiosity. He admits that he wishes for fame in the times to come, but would rather be without it in his own day. In his dialogue on fortune and misfortune, the interlocutor, who maintains the futility of glory, has the best of the contest. But, at the same time, Petrarch is pleased that the autocrat of Byzantium knows him as well by his writings as Charles IV knows him. And in fact, even in his lifetime, his fame extended far beyond Italy. And the emotion which he felt was natural when his friends, on the occasion of a visit to his native Arezzo (1350), took him to the house where he was born, and told him how the city had provided that no change should be made in it. In former times the dwellings of certain great saints were preserved and revered in this way, like the cell of St Thomas Aquinas in the Dominican convent at Naples, and the Portiuncula of St Francis near Assisi; and one or two great jurists also enjoyed the half-mythical reputation which led to this honour. Towards the close of the fourteenth century the people at Bagnolo, near Florence, called an old building the 'Studio' of Accursius (b. *c.* 1150), but, nevertheless, suffered it to be destroyed. It is probable that the great incomes and the political influence which some jurists obtained as consulting lawyers made a lasting impression on the popular imagination.

To the cultus of the birthplaces of famous men must be added that of their graves, and, in the case of Petrarch, of the spot where he died. In memory of him Arquà became a favourite resort of the Paduans, and was dotted with graceful little villas. At this time there were no 'classic spots' in northern Europe, and pilgrimages were only made to pictures and relics. It was a point of honour for the different cities to possess the bones of their own and foreign celebrities; and it is most remarkable how seriously the Florentines, even in the fourteenth century – long before the building of Santa Croce – laboured to make their cathedral a pantheon. Accorso, Dante, Petrarch, Boccaccio and the jurist Zanobi della Strada were to have had magnificent tombs there erected to them. Late in the fifteenth century, Lorenzo il Magnifico applied in person to the Spoletans, asking them to give up the corpse of the painter Fra Filippo Lippi for the cathedral, and received the answer that they had none too many ornaments to the city, especially in the shape of distinguished people, for which reason they begged him to spare them; and, in fact, he had to be contented with erecting a cenotaph. And even Dante, in spite of all the applications to which Boccaccio urged the Florentines with bitter emphasis, remained sleeping tranquilly by the side of San Francesco at Ravenna, 'among ancient tombs of emperors and vaults of saints, in more honourable company than thou, O Home, couldst offer him'. It even happened that a man once took away unpunished the lights from the altar on which the crucifix stood, and set them by the grave, with the words, 'Take them; thou art more worthy of them than He, the Crucified One!'

And now the Italian cities began again to remember their ancient citizens and inhabitants. Naples, perhaps, had never forgotten its tomb of Virgil, since a kind of mythical halo had become attached to the name.

The Paduans, even in the sixteenth century, firmly believed that they possessed not only the genuine bones of their founder, Antenor, but also those of the historian Livy.[40] 'Sulmona,' says Boccaccio, 'bewails that Ovid lies buried far away in exile; and Parma rejoices that Cassius sleeps within its walls.' The Mantuans coined a medal in 1257 with the bust of Virgil, and raised a statue to represent him. In a fit of aristocratic insolence, the guardian of the young Gonzaga, Carlo Malatesta, caused it to be pulled down in 1392, and was afterwards forced, when he found the fame of the old poet too strong for him, to set it up again. Even then, perhaps, the grotto, a couple of miles from the town, where Virgil was said to have meditated, was shown to strangers, like the 'Scuola di Virgilio' at Naples. Como claimed both the Plinys for its own, and at the end of the fifteenth century erected statues in their honour, sitting under graceful baldachins on the façade of the cathedral.

History and the new topography were now careful to leave no local celebrity unnoticed. At the same period the northern chronicles only here and there, among the list of popes, emperors, earthquakes and comets, put in the remark that at such a time this or that famous man 'flourished'. We shall elsewhere have to show how, mainly under the influence of this idea of fame, an admirable biographical literature was developed. We must here limit ourselves to the local patriotism of the topographers who recorded the claims of their native cities to distinction.

In the Middle Ages, the cities were proud of their saints and of the bones and relics in their churches. With these the panegyrist of Padua in 1450, Michele Savonarola, begins his list; from them he passes to 'the famous men who were no saints, but who, by their great intellect and force [virtus] deserve to be added [adnecti] to the saints' – just as in classical antiquity the distinguished man came close upon the hero. The further enumeration is most characteristic of the time. First comes Antenor, the brother of Priam, who founded Padua with a band of Trojan fugitives; King Dardanus, who defeated Attila in the Euganean hills, followed him in pursuit and struck him dead at Rimini with a chess-board; the Emperor Henry IV, who built the cathedral; a King Marcus, whose head was preserved in Monselice; then a couple of cardinals and prelates as founders of colleges, churches and so forth; the famous Augustinian theologian, Fra Alberto; a string of philosophers beginning with Paolo Veneto and the celebrated Pietro of Albano; the jurist Paolo Padovano; then Livy and the poets Petrarch, Mussato, Lovato. If there is any want of military celebrities in the list, the poet consoles himself for it by the abundance of learned men whom he has to show, and by the more durable character of intellectual glory, while the fame of the soldier is buried with his body, or, if it lasts, owes its permanence only to the scholar. It is nevertheless honourable to the city that foreign warriors lie buried here by their own wish, like Pietro de' Rossi of Parma, Filippo Arcelli of Piacenza, and especially Gattamelata of Narni (d. 1443), whose brazen equestrian statue, 'like a Caesar in triumph', already stood by the church of the Santo. The author then names a crowd of jurists and physicians, nobles 'who had not only, like so many others, received, but deserved, the honour of knighthood'. Then follows a list of famous mechanicians, painters and musicians, which is closed by the name of a fencing-master Michele Rosso, who, as the most distinguished man in his profession, was to be seen painted in many places.

By the side of these local temples of fame, which myth, legend, popular admiration and literary tradition combined to create, the poet-scholars built up a great pantheon of world-wide celebrity. They made collections of famous men and famous women, often in direct imitation of Cornelius Nepos, the pseudo-Suetonius, Valerius Maximus, Plutarch (*Mulierum virtutes*), Hieronymus (*De viris illustribus*) and others; or they wrote of imaginary triumphal processions and Olympian assemblies, as was done by Petrarch in his *Trionfo della fama*, and Boccaccio in the *Amorosa visione*, with hundreds of names, of which three-fourths at least belong to antiquity and the rest to the Middle Ages.[41] By and by this new and comparatively modern element was treated with greater emphasis; the historians began to insert descriptions of character, and collections arose of the biographies of distinguished contemporaries, like those of Filippo Villani, Vespasiano Fiorentino, Bartolommeo Facio and lastly of Paolo Giovio.

The north of Europe, until Italian influence began to tell upon its writers – for instance, on Trithemius, the first German who wrote the lives of famous men – possessed only either legends of the saints, or descriptions of princes and churchmen partaking largely of the character of legends and showing no traces of the idea of fame, that is, of distinction won by a man's personal efforts. Poetical glory was still confined to certain classes of society, and the names of northern artists are only known to us at this period in so far as they were members of certain guilds or corporations.

The poet-scholar in Italy had, as we have already said, the fullest consciousness that he was the giver of fame and immortality, or, if he chose, of oblivion. Boccaccio complains of a fair one to whom he had done homage, and who remained hard-hearted in order that he might go on praising her and making her famous, and he gives her a hint that he will try the effect of a little blame. Sannazaro, in two magnificent sonnets, threatens Alfonso of Naples with eternal obscurity on account of his cowardly flight before Charles VIII. Angelo Poliziano seriously exhorts (1491) King John of Portugal to think betimes of his immortality in reference to the new discoveries in Africa, and to send him materials to Florence, there to be put into shape (*operosius excolenda*), otherwise it would befall him as it had befallen all the others whose deeds, unsupported by the help of the learned, 'lie hidden in the vast heap of human frailty'. The king, or his humanistic chancellor, agreed to this, and promised that at least the Portuguese chronicles of African affairs should be translated into Italian and sent to Florence to be done into Latin. Whether the promise was kept is not known. These pretensions are by no means so groundless as they may appear at first sight; for the form in which events, even the greatest, are told to the living and to posterity is anything but a matter of indifference. The Italian humanists, with their mode of exposition and their Latin style, had long the complete control of the reading world of Europe, and till last century the Italian poets were more widely known and studied than those of any other nation. The baptismal name of the Florentine Amerigo Vespucci was given, on account of his book of travels, to a new quarter of the globe, and if Paolo Giovio, with all his superficiality and graceful caprice, promised himself immortality, his expectation has not altogether been disappointed.

Amid all these preparations outwardly to win and secure fame, the curtain is now and then drawn aside, and we see with frightful evidence a boundless ambition and thirst after greatness, independent of all means and consequences. Thus, in the Preface to Machiavelli's Florentine history, in which he blames his predecessors Leonardo, Aretino and Poggio for their too considerate reticence with regard to the political parties in the city: 'They erred greatly and showed that they understood little the ambition of men and the desire to perpetuate a name. How many who could distinguish themselves by nothing praiseworthy strove to do so by infamous deeds! Those writers did not consider that actions which are great in themselves, as is the case with the actions of rulers and of states, always seem to bring more glory than blame, of whatever kind they are and whatever the result of them may be.' In more than one remarkable and dreadful undertaking the motive assigned by serious writers is the burning desire to achieve something great and memorable. This motive is not a mere extreme case of ordinary vanity, but something demonic, involving a surrender of the will, the use of any means, however atrocious, and even an indifference to success itself. In this sense, for example, Machiavelli conceives the character of Stefano Porcari; of the murderers of Galeazzo Maria Sforza (p. 54), the documents tell us about the same; and the assassination of Duke Alessandro of Florence (1537) is ascribed by Varchi himself to the thirst for fame which tormented the murderer Lorenzino Medici. Still more stress is laid on this motive by Paolo Giovio. Lorenzino, according to him, pilloried by a pamphlet of Molza, broods over a deed whose novelty shall make his disgrace forgotten, and ends by murdering his kinsmen and prince. These are characteristic features of this age of overstrained and despairing passions and forces, and reminds us of the burning of the temple of Diana at Ephesus in the time of Philip of Macedon.

RIDICULE AND WIT

The corrective, not only of this modern desire for fame, but of all highly developed individuality, is found in ridicule, especially when expressed in the victorious form of wit. We read in the Middle Ages how hostile armies, princes and nobles provoked one another with symbolical insult, and how the defeated party was loaded with symbolical outrage. Here and there, too, under the influence of classical literature, wit began to be used as a weapon in theological disputes, and the poetry of Provence produced a whole class of satirical compositions. Even the Minnesingers, as their political poems show, could adopt this tone when necessary. But wit could not be an independent element in life till its appropriate victim, the developed individual with personal pretensions, had appeared. Its weapons were then by no means limited to the tongue and the pen, but included tricks and practical jokes – the so-called *burle* and *beffe* – which form a chief subject of many collections of novels.

The Hundred Old Tales, which must have been composed about the end of the thirteenth century, have as yet neither wit, the fruit of contrast, nor the *burla*, for their subject; their aim is merely to give simple and elegant expression to wise sayings and pretty stories or fables. But if anything proves the great antiquity of the collection, it is precisely this absence of satire. For with the fourteenth century comes Dante, who, in the utterance of scorn, leaves all other poets in the world far behind, and who, if only on account of his great picture of the deceivers, must be called the chief master of colossal comedy. With Petrarch begin the collections of witty sayings after the pattern of Plutarch (Apophthegmata, etc.).

What stores of wit were concentrated in Florence during this century is most characteristically shown in the novels of Franco Sacchetti. These are, for the most part, not stories but answers, given under certain circumstances – shocking pieces of *naïveté*, with which silly folks, court jesters, rogues and profligate women make their retort. The comedy of the tale lies in the startling contrast of this real or assumed *naïveté* with conventional morality and the ordinary relations of the world – things are made to stand on their heads. All means of picturesque representation are made use of, including the introduction of certain North Italian dialects. Often the place of wit is taken by mere insolence, clumsy trickery, blasphemy and obscenity; one or two jokes told of *condottieri* are among the most brutal and malicious which are recorded. Many of the *burle* are thoroughly comic, but many are only real or supposed evidence of personal superiority, of triumph over another. How much people were willing to put up with, how often the victim was satisfied with getting the laugh on his side by a retaliatory trick, cannot be said; there was much heartless and pointless malice mixed up with it all, and life in Florence was no doubt often made unpleasant enough from this cause.[42] The inventors and retailers of jokes soon became inevitable figures, and among them there must have been some who were classical – far superior to all the mere court-jesters, to whom competition, a changing public and the quick apprehension of the audience, all advantages of life in Florence, were wanting. Some Florentine wits went starring among the despotic courts of Lombardy and Romagna, and found themselves much better rewarded than at home, where their talent was cheap and plentiful. The better type of these people is the amusing man (*l'uomo piacevole*), the worse is the buffoon and the vulgar parasite who presents himself at weddings and banquets with the argument, 'If I am not invited, the fault is not mine.' Now and then the latter combine to pluck a young spendthrift, but in general they are treated and despised as parasites, while wits of higher position bear themselves like princes, and consider their talent as something sovereign. Dolcibene, whom Charles IV had pronounced to be the 'king of Italian jesters', said to him at Ferrara: 'You will conquer the world, since you are my friend and the pope's; you fight with the sword, the pope with his bulls, and I with my tongue.' This is no mere jest, but the foreshadowing of Pietro Aretino.

The two most famous jesters about the middle of the fifteenth century were a priest near Florence, Arlotto (1483), for more refined wit (*facezie*), and the court-fool of Ferrara, Gonnella, for buffoonery. We can hardly compare their stories with those of the Parson of Kalenberg and Till Eulenspiegel, since the latter arose in a different and half-mythical manner, as fruits of the imagination of a whole people, and touch rather on what is general and intelligible to all, while Arlotto and Gonnella were historical beings, coloured and shaped by local influences. But if the comparison be allowed, and extended to the jests of the non-Italian nations, we shall find in general that the joke in the French *fabliaux*, as among the Germans, is chiefly directed to the attainment of some advantage or enjoyment, while the wit of Arlotto and the practical jokes of Gonnella are an end in themselves, and exist simply for the sake of the triumph of production. (Till Eulenspiegel again forms a class by himself, as the personified quiz, mostly pointless enough, of particular classes and professions.) The court-fool of the Este saved himself more than once by his keen satire and refined modes of vengeance.

The type of the *uomo piacevole* and the *buffone* long survived the freedom of Florence. Under Duke Cosimo flourished Barlacchia, and at the beginning of the seventeenth century Francesco Ruspoli and Curzio Marignolli. In Pope Leo X the genuine Florentine love of jesters showed itself strikingly. This prince, whose taste for the most refined intellectual pleasures was insatiable, endured and desired at his table a number of witty buffoons and jack-puddings, among them two monks and a cripple; at public feasts he treated them with deliberate scorn as parasites, setting before them monkeys and crows in the place of savoury meats. Leo, indeed, showed a peculiar fondness for the *burla*; it belonged to his nature sometimes to treat his own favourite pursuits – music and poetry – ironically, parodying them with his factotum, Cardinal Bibbiena. Neither of them found it beneath him to fool an honest old secretary till he thought himself a master of the art of music. The *improvvisatore*, Baraballo of Gaeta, was brought so far by Leo's flattery that he applied in all seriousness for the poet's coronation on the Capitol. On the anniversary of St Cosmas and St Damian, the patrons of the House of Medici, he was first compelled, adorned with laurel and purple, to amuse the papal guests with his recitations, and at last, when all were ready to split with laughter, to mount a gold-harnessed elephant in the court of the Vatican, sent as a present to Rome by Emmanuel the Great of Portugal, while the pope looked down from above through his eyeglass. The brute, however, was so terrified by the noise of the trumpets and kettledrums, and the cheers of the crowd, that there was no getting him over the bridge of Sant' Angelo.

The parody of what is solemn or sublime, which here meets us in the case of a procession, had already taken an important place in poetry.[43] It was naturally compelled to choose victims of another kind than those of Aristophanes, who introduced the great tragedians into his plays. But the same maturity of culture which at a certain period produced parody among the Greeks did the same in Italy. By the close of the fourteenth century the love-lorn wailings of Petrarch's sonnets and others of the same kind were taken off by caricaturists; and the solemn air of this form of verse was parodied in lines of mystic twaddle. A constant invitation to parody was offered by the *Divine Comedy*, and Lorenzo il Magnifico wrote the most admirable travesty in the style of the *Inferno* (*Simposio* or *I Beoni*). Luigi Pulci obviously imitates the *improvvisatori* in his *Morgante*, and both his poetry and Boiardo's are in part, at least, a half-conscious parody of the chivalrous poetry of the Middle Ages. Such a caricature was deliberately undertaken by the great parodist Teofilo Folengo (about 1520). Under the name of Limerno Pitocco, he composed the *Orlandino*, in which chivalry appears only as a ludicrous setting for a crowd of modern figures and ideas. Under the name of Merlinus Coccaius he described the journeys and exploits of his fantastic vagabonds (also in the same spirit of parody) in half-Latin hexameters, with all the affected pomp of the learned Epos of the day (*opus macaronicorum*). Since then caricature has been constantly, and often brilliantly, represented on the Italian Parnassus.

About the middle period of the Renaissance a theoretical analysis of wit was undertaken, and its practical application in good society was regulated more precisely. The theorist was Gioviano Pontano. In his work on speaking, especially in the third and fourth books, he tries by means of the comparison of numerous jokes, or *facetiae*, to arrive at a general principle. How wit should be used among people of position is taught by Baldassare Castiglione in his *Cortigiano*.[44] Its chief function is naturally to enliven those present by the repetition of comic or graceful stories and sayings; personal jokes, on the contrary, are discouraged on the ground that they wound unhappy people, show too much honour to wrong-doers, and make enemies of the powerful and the spoiled children of fortune; and even in repetition, a wide reserve in the use of dramatic gestures is recommended to the gentleman. Then follows, not only for purposes of quotation, but as patterns for future jesters, a large collection of puns and witty sayings, methodically arranged according to their species, among them some that are admirable. The doctrine of Giovanni della Casa, some twenty years later, in his guide to good manners,[45] is much stricter and more cautious; with a view to the consequences, he wishes to see the desire of triumph banished altogether from jokes and *burle*. He is the herald of a reaction, which was certain sooner or later to appear.

Italy had, in fact, become a school for scandal, the like of which the world cannot show, not even in France at the time of Voltaire. In him and his comrades there was assuredly no lack of the spirit of negation; but where, in the eighteenth century, was to be found the crowd of suitable victims, that countless assembly of highly and characteristically developed human beings, celebrities of every kind, statesmen, churchmen, inventors and discoverers, men of letters, poets and artists, all of whom then gave the fullest and freest play to their individuality? This host existed in the fifteenth and sixteenth centuries, and by its side the general culture of the time had educated a poisonous brood of impotent wits, of born critics and railers, whose envy called for hecatombs of victims; and to all this was added the envy of the famous men among themselves. In this the philologists notoriously led the way – Filelfo, Poggio, Lorenzo Valla and others – while the artists of the fifteenth century lived in peaceful and friendly competition with one another. The history of art may take note of the fact.

Florence, the great market of fame, was in this point, as we have said, in advance of other cities. 'Sharp eyes and bad tongues' is the description given of the inhabitants. An easygoing contempt of everything and everybody was probably the prevailing tone of society. Machiavelli, in the remarkable Prologue to his *Mandragola*, refers rightly or wrongly the visible decline of moral force to the general habit of evil-speaking, and threatens his detractors with the news that he can say sharp things as well as they. Next to Florence comes the papal court, which had long been a rendezvous of the bitterest and wittiest tongues. Poggio's *Facetiae* are dated from the Chamber of Lies (*bugiale*) of the apostolic notaries; and when we remember the number of disappointed place-hunters, of hopeless competitors and enemies of the favourites, of idle, profligate prelates there assembled, it is intelligible how Rome became the home of the savage pasquinade as well as of more philosophical satire. If we add to this the widespread hatred borne to the priests, and the well-known instinct of the mob to lay any horror to the charge of the great, there results an untold mass of infamy. Those who were able protected themselves best by contempt both of the false and true accusations, and by brilliant and joyous display. More sensitive natures sank into utter despair when they found themselves deeply involved in guilt, and still more deeply in slander. In course of time calumny became universal, and the strictest virtue was most certain of all to challenge the attacks of malice. Of the great pulpit orator, Fra Egidio of Viterbo, whom Leo made a cardinal on account of his merits, and who showed himself a man of the people and a brave monk in the calamity of 1527, Giovio gives us to understand that he preserved his ascetic pallor by the smoke of wet straw and other means of the same kind. Giovio is a genuine Curial in these matters. He generally begins by telling his story, then adds that he does not believe it, and then hints at the end that perhaps after all there may be something in it. But the true scapegoat of Roman scorn was the pious and moral Adrian VI. A general agreement seemed to be made to take him only on the comic side. He fell out from the first with the formidable Francesco Berni, threatening to have thrown into the Tiber not, as people said, the statue of Pasquino, but the writers of the satires themselves. The vengeance for this was the famous *Capitolo* against Pope Adriano, inspired not exactly by hatred, but by contempt for the comical Dutch barbarian; the more savage menaces were reserved for the cardinals who had elected him. The plague, which then was prevalent in Rome, was ascribed to him; Berni and others sketch the environment of the pope with the same sparkling untruthfulness with which the modern *feuilletoniste* turns black into white, and everything into anything. The biography which Paolo Giovio was commissioned to write by the Cardinal of Tortosa, and which was to have been a eulogy, is for anyone who can read between the lines an unexampled piece of satire. It sounds ridiculous – at least for the Italians of that time – to hear how Adrian applied to the Chapter of Saragossa for the jaw-bone of St Lambert; how the devout Spaniards

decked him out till he looked 'like a right well-dressed pope'; how he
came in a confused and tasteless procession from Ostia to Rome, took
counsel about burning or drowning Pasquino, would suddenly break
off the most important business when dinner was announced; and
lastly, at the end of an unhappy reign, how he died of drinking too
much beer – whereupon the house of his physician was hung with
garlands by midnight revellers, and adorned with the inscription,
'*Liberatori Patriae S.P.Q.R.*' It is true that Giovio had lost his money
in the general confiscation of public funds, and had only received a
benefice by way of compensation because he was 'no poet', that is to
say, no pagan. But it was decreed that Adrian should be the last great
victim. After the disaster which befell Rome in 1527, slander visibly
declined along with the unrestrained wickedness of private life.

But while it was still flourishing was developed, chiefly in Rome, the
greatest railer of modern times, Pietro Aretino. A glance at his life and
character will save us the trouble of noticing many less distinguished
members of his class.

We know him chiefly in the last thirty years of his life (1527–56),
which he passed in Venice, the only asylum possible for him. From
hence he kept all that was famous in Italy in a kind of state of siege,
and here were delivered the presents of the foreign princes who
needed or dreaded his pen. Charles V and Francis I both pensioned
him at the same time, each hoping that Aretino would do some
mischief to the other. Aretino flattered both, but naturally attached
himself more closely to Charles, because he remained master in Italy.
After the emperor's victory at Tunis in 1535, this tone of adulation
passed into the most ludicrous worship, in observing which it must
not be forgotten that Aretino constantly cherished the hope that
Charles would help him to a cardinal's hat. It is probable that he
enjoyed special protection as Spanish agent, as his speech or silence
could have no small effect on the smaller Italian courts and on public
opinion in Italy. He affected utterly to despise the papal court because
he knew it so well; the true reason was that Rome neither could nor
would pay him any longer. Venice, which sheltered him, he was wise
enough to leave unassailed. The rest of his relations with the great is
mere beggary and vulgar extortion.

Aretino affords the first great instance of the abuse of publicity to
such ends. The polemical writings which a hundred years earlier

Poggio and his opponents interchanged are just as infamous in their tone and purpose, but they were not composed for the press, but for a sort of private circulation. Aretino made all his profit out of a complete publicity, and in a certain sense may be considered the father of modern journalism. His letters and miscellaneous articles were printed periodically, after they had already been circulated among a tolerably extensive public.

Compared with the sharp pens of the eighteenth century, Aretino had the advantage that he was not burdened with principles, neither with liberalism nor philanthropy nor any other virtue, nor even with science; his whole baggage consisted of the well-known motto, '*Veritas odium parit*'. He never, consequently, found himself in the false position of Voltaire, who was forced to disown his *Pucelle* and conceal all his life the authorship of other works. Aretino put his name to all he wrote, and openly gloried in his notorious *Ragionamenti*. His literary talent, his clear and sparkling style, his varied observation of men and things, would have made him a considerable writer under any circumstances, destitute as he was of the power of conceiving a genuine work of art, such as a true dramatic comedy; and to the coarsest as well as the most refined malice he added a grotesque wit so brilliant that in some cases it does not fall short of that of Rabelais.

In such circumstances, and with such objects and means, he set to work to attack or circumvent his prey. The tone in which he appealed to Clement VII not to complain or to think of vengeance, but to forgive, at the moment when the wailings of the devastated city were ascending to the Castel Sant' Angelo, where the pope himself was a prisoner, is the mockery of a devil or a monkey. Sometimes, when he is forced to give up all hope of presents, his fury breaks out into a savage howl, as in the *Capitolo* to the Prince of Salerno, who after paying him for some time refused to do so any longer. On the other hand, it seems that the terrible Pierluigi Farnese, Duke of Parma, never took any notice of him at all. As this gentleman had probably renounced altogether the pleasures of a good reputation, it was not easy to cause him any annoyance; Aretino tried to do so by comparing his personal appearance to that of a constable, a miller and a baker. Aretino is most comical of all in the expression of whining mendicancy, as in the *Capitolo* to Francis I; but the letters and poems made up of menaces and flattery cannot, notwithstanding all that is ludicrous in them, be read without the deepest disgust. A letter like that one of his written to Michelangelo[46] in November 1545 is alone of its kind; along with all the admiration he expresses for the *Last Judgement* he charges him with irreligion, indecency and theft from the heirs of Julius II, and adds in a conciliating postscript, 'I only want to show you that if you are *divino*, I am not *d'acqua*.' Aretino laid great stress upon it – whether from the insanity of conceit or by way of caricaturing famous men – that he himself should be called divine, as one of his flatterers had already begun to do; and he certainly attained so much personal celebrity that his house at Arezzo passed for one of the sights of the place. There were indeed whole months during which he never ventured to cross his threshold at Venice, lest he should fall in with some incensed Florentine like the younger Strozzi. Nor did he escape the cudgels and the daggers of his enemies, although they failed to have the effect which Berni prophesied him in a famous sonnet. Aretino died in his house, of apoplexy.

The differences he made in his modes of flattery are remarkable: in dealing with non-Italians he was grossly fulsome; people like Duke Cosimo of Florence he treated very differently. He praised the beauty of the then youthful prince, who in fact did share this quality with Augustus in no ordinary degree; he praised his moral conduct, with an oblique reference to the financial pursuits of Cosimo's mother Maria Salviati, and concluded with a mendicant whine about the bad times and so forth. When Cosimo pensioned him, which he did liberally, considering his habitual parsimony – to the extent, at last, of 160 ducats a year – he had doubtless an eye to Aretino's dangerous character as Spanish agent. Aretino could ridicule and revile Cosimo, and in the same breath threaten the Florentine agent that he would obtain from the duke his immediate recall; and if the Medicean prince felt himself at last to be seen through by Charles V he would not care for Aretino's jokes and rhymes against him to circulate at the imperial court. A curiously qualified piece of flattery was that addressed to the notorious Marquis of Marignano, who as castellan of Musso had attempted to found an independent state. Thanking him for the gift of a hundred crowns, Aretino writes: 'All the qualities which a prince should have are present in you, and all men would think so, were it not that the acts of violence inevitable at the beginning of all undertakings cause you to appear a trifle rough [*aspro*].'

It has often been noticed as something singular that Aretino only reviled the world, and not God also. The religious belief of a man who lived as he did is a matter of perfect indifference, as are also the edifying writings which he composed for reasons of his own.[47] It is in fact hard to say why he should have been a blasphemer. He was no professor, or theoretical thinker or writer; and he could extort no money from God by threats or flattery, and was consequently never goaded into blasphemy by a refusal. A man like him does not take trouble for nothing.

It is a good sign of the present spirit of Italy that such a character and such a career have become a thousand times impossible. But historical criticism will always find in Aretino an important study.

PART III

The Revival of Antiquity

NOW THAT this point in our historical view of Italian civilization has been reached, it is time to speak of the influence of antiquity, the 'new birth' of which has been one-sidedly chosen as the name to sum up the whole period. The conditions which have been hitherto described would have sufficed, apart from antiquity, to upturn and to mature the national mind; and most of the intellectual tendencies which yet remain to be noticed would be conceivable without it. But both what has gone before and what we have still to discuss are coloured in a thousand ways by the influence of the ancient world; and though the essence of the phenomena might still have been the same without the classical revival, it is only with and through this revival that they are actually manifested to us. The Renaissance would not have been the process of world-wide significance which it is, if its elements could be so easily separated from one another. We must insist upon it, as one of the chief propositions of this book, that it was not the revival of antiquity alone, but its union with the genius of the Italian people, which achieved the conquest of the Western world. The amount of independence which the national spirit maintained in this union varied according to circumstances. In the modern Latin literature of the period, it is very small, while in plastic art, as well as in other spheres, it is remarkably great; and hence the alliance between two distant epochs in the civilization of the same people, because concluded on equal terms, proved justifiable and fruitful. The rest of Europe was free either to repel or else partly or wholly to accept the mighty impulse which came forth from Italy. Where the latter was the case we may as well be spared the complaints over the early decay of medieval faith and civilization. Had these been strong enough to hold their ground, they would be alive to this day. If those elegiac natures which long to see them return could pass but one hour in the midst of them, they would gasp to be back in modern air. That in a great historical process of this kind flowers of exquisite beauty may perish without being made immortal in poetry or tradition is undoubtedly true; nevertheless, we cannot wish the process undone. The general result of it consists in this – that by the side of the Church which had hitherto held the countries of the West together (though it was unable to do so much longer) there arose a new spiritual influence which, spreading itself abroad from Italy, became the breath of life for all the more instructed minds in Europe. The worst that can be said of the movement is that it was anti-popular, that through it Europe became for the first time sharply divided into the cultivated and uncultivated classes. The reproach will appear groundless when we reflect that even now the fact, though clearly recognized, cannot be altered. The separation, too, is by no means so cruel and absolute in Italy as elsewhere. The most artistic of her poets, Tasso, is in the hands of even the poorest.

The civilization of Greece and Rome, which, ever since the four-teenth century, obtained so powerful a hold on Italian life, as the source and basis of culture, as the object and ideal of existence, partly also as an avowed reaction against preceding tendencies – this civilization had long been exerting a partial influence on medieval Europe, even beyond the boundaries of Italy. The culture of which Charlemagne was a representative was, in face of the barbarism of the seventh and eighth centuries, essentially a Renaissance, and could appear under no other form. Just as in the Romanesque architecture of the North, beside the general outlines inherited from antiquity, remarkable direct imitations of the antique also occur, so too monastic scholarship had not only gradually absorbed an immense mass of materials from Roman writers, but the style of it, from the days of Einhard onwards, shows traces of conscious imitations.

But the resuscitation of antiquity took a different form in Italy from that which it assumed in the North. The wave of barbarism had scarcely gone by before the people, in whom the former life was but half effaced, showed a consciousness of its past and a wish to reproduce it. Elsewhere in Europe men deliberately and with reflection borrowed this or the other element of classical civilization; in Italy the sympathies both of the learned and of the people were naturally engaged on the side of antiquity as a whole, which stood to them as a symbol of past greatness. The Latin language, too, was easy to an Italian, and the numerous monuments and documents in which the country abounded facilitated a return to the past. With this tendency other elements – the popular character which time had now greatly modified, the political institutions imported by the Lombards from Germany, chivalry and other northern forms of civilization, and the influence of religion and the Church – combined to produce the modern Italian spirit, which was destined to serve as the model and ideal for the whole Western world.

How antiquity began to work in plastic art, as soon as the flood of barbarism had subsided, is clearly shown in the Tuscan buildings of the twelfth and in the sculptures of the thirteenth centuries. In poetry, too, there will appear no want of similar analogies to those who hold that the greatest Latin poet of the twelfth century, the writer who struck the keynote of a whole class of Latin poems, was an Italian. We mean the author of the best pieces in the so-called *Carmina Burana*.[48] A frank enjoyment of life and its pleasures, as whose patrons the gods of heathendom are invoked, while Catos and Scipios hold the place of the saints and heroes of Christianity, flows in full current through the rhymed verses. Reading them through at a stretch, we can scarcely help coming to the conclusion that an Italian, probably a Lombard, is speaking; in fact, there are positive grounds for thinking so. To a certain degree these Latin poems of the *clerici vagantes* of the twelfth century, with all their remarkable frivolity, are, doubtless, a product in which the whole of Europe had a share; but the writer of the song 'De Phyllide et Flora' and the 'Aestuans Interius' can have been a northerner as little as the polished Epicurean observer to whom we owe 'Dum Dianae vitrea sero lampas oritur'. Here, in truth, is a reproduction of the whole ancient view of life, which is all the more striking from the medieval form of the verse in which it is set forth. There are many works of this and the following centuries, in which a careful imitation of the antique appears both in the hexameter and pentameter of the metre and in the classical, often mythological, character of the subject, and which yet have not anything like the same spirit of antiquity about them. In the hexameter chronicles and other works of Guglielmus Appulus and his successors (from about 1100), we find frequent traces of a diligent study of Virgil, Ovid, Lucan, Statius and Claudian; but this classical form is, after all, a mere matter of archaeology, as is the classical subject in collectors like Vincent of Beauvais, or in the mythological and allegorical writer, Alanus ab Insulis. The Renaissance is not a mere fragmentary imitation or compilation, but a new birth; and the signs of this are visible in the poems of the unknown *clericus* of the twelfth century.

But the great and general enthusiasm of the Italians for classical antiquity did not display itself before the fourteenth century. For this a development of civic life was required, which took place only in Italy, and there not till then. It was needful that noble and burgher should first learn to dwell together on equal terms, and that a social world should arise which felt the want of culture, and had the leisure and the means to obtain it. But culture, as soon as it freed itself from the fantastic bonds of the Middle Ages, could not at once and without help find its way to the understanding of the physical and intellectual world. It needed a guide, and found one in the ancient civilization, with its wealth of truth and knowledge in every spiritual interest. Both the form and the substance of this civilization were adopted with admiring gratitude; it became the chief part of the culture of the age. The general condition of the country was favourable to this transformation. The medieval empire, since the fall of the Hohenstaufen, had either renounced, or was unable to make good, its claims on Italy. The popes had migrated to Avignon. Most of the political powers actually in existence owed their origin to violent and illegitimate means. The spirit of the people, now awakened to self-consciousness, sought for some new and stable ideal on which to rest. And thus the vision of the world-wide empire of Italy and Rome so possessed the popular mind that Cola di Rienzi could actually attempt to put it in practice. The conception he formed of his task, particularly when tribune for the first time, could only end in some extravagant comedy; nevertheless, the memory of ancient Rome was no slight support to the national sentiment. Armed afresh with its culture, the Italian soon felt himself in truth citizen of the most advanced nation in the world.

It is now our task to sketch this spiritual movement, not indeed in all its fullness, but in its most salient features, and especially in its first beginnings.[49]

THE RUINS OF ROME

Rome itself, the city of ruins, now became the object of a wholly different sort of piety from that of the time when the *Mirabilia Romae* and the collection of William of Malmesbury were composed. The imaginations of the devout pilgrim, or of the seeker after marvels and treasures, are supplanted in contemporary records by the interests of the patriot and the historian. In this sense we must understand Dante's words, that the stones of the walls of Rome deserve reverence, and that the ground on which the city is built is more worthy than men say. The jubilees, incessant as they were, have scarcely left a single devout record in literature properly so called. The best thing that Giovanni Villani brought back from the jubilee of the year 1300 was the resolution to write his history which had been awakened in him by the sight of the ruins of Rome. Petrarch gives evidence of a taste divided between classical and Christian antiquity. He tells us how often with Giovanni Colonna he ascended the mighty vaults of the Baths of Diocletian, and there in the transparent air, amid the wide silence, with the broad panorama stretching far around them, they spoke, not of business or political affairs, but of the history which the ruins beneath their feet suggested, Petrarch appearing in their dialogues as the partisan of classical, Giovanni of Christian antiquity; then they would discourse of philosophy and of the inventors of the arts. How often since that time, down to the days of Gibbon and Niebuhr, have the same ruins stirred men's minds to the same reflections!

This double current of feeling is also recognizable in the *Dittamondo* of Fazio degli Uberti, composed about the year 1360 — a description of visionary travels, in which the author is accompanied by the old geographer Solinus, as Dante was by Virgil. They visit Bari in memory of St Nicholas, and Monte Gargano of the archangel Michael, and in Rome the legends of Aracoeli and of Santa Maria in Trastevere are mentioned. Still, the pagan splendour of ancient Rome unmistakably exercises a greater charm upon them. A venerable matron in torn garments — Rome herself is meant — tells them of the glorious past, and gives them a minute description of the old triumphs; she then leads the strangers through the city and points out to them the seven hills and many of the chief ruins — '*che comprender potrai, quanto fui bella*'.

Unfortunately this Rome of the schismatic and Avignonese popes was no longer, in respect of classical remains, what it had been some generations earlier. The destruction of 140 fortified houses of the Roman nobles by the senator Brancaleone in 1257 must have wholly altered the character of the most important buildings then standing: for the nobles had no doubt ensconced themselves in the loftiest and best-preserved of the ruins.[50] Nevertheless, far more was left than we now find, and probably many of the remains had still their marble incrustation, their pillared entrances and their other ornaments, where we now see nothing but the skeleton of brickwork. In this state of things, the first beginnings of a topographical study of the old city were made.

In Poggio's walks through Rome[51] the study of the remains themselves is for the first time more intimately combined with that of the ancient authors and inscriptions – the latter he sought out from among all the vegetation in which they were embedded – the writer's imagination is severely restrained, and the memories of Christian Rome carefully excluded. The only pity is that Poggio's work was not fuller and was not illustrated with sketches. Far more was left in his time than was found by Raphael eighty years later. He saw the tomb of Caecilia Metella and the columns in front of one of the temples on the slope of the Capitol, first in full preservation, and then afterwards half destroyed, owing to that unfortunate quality which marble possesses of being easily burnt into lime. A vast colonnade near the Minerva fell piecemeal a victim to the same fate. A witness in the year 1443 tells us that this manufacture of lime still went on, 'which is a shame, for the new buildings are pitiful, and the beauty of Rome is in its ruins'. The inhabitants of that day, in their peasant's cloaks and boots, looked to foreigners like cowherds; and in fact the cattle were pastured in the city up to the Banchi. The only opportunities for social gatherings were the services at church, on which occasion it was possible to get a sight of the beautiful women.

In the last years of Eugenius IV (d. 1447) Blondus of Forlì[52] wrote his *Roma Instaurata*, making use of Frontinus and of the old *Libri Regionali*, as well as, it seems, of Anastasius. His object is not only the description of what existed, but still more the recovery of what was lost. In accordance with the dedication to the pope, he consoles himself for the general ruin by the thought of the precious relics of the saints in which Rome was so rich.

With Nicholas V (1447–55) that new monumental spirit which was distinctive of the age of the Renaissance appeared on the papal throne. The new passion for embellishing the city brought with it on the one hand a fresh danger for the ruins, on the other a respect for them, as forming one of Rome's claims to distinction. Pius II was wholly possessed by antiquarian enthusiasm, and if he speaks little of the antiquities of Rome, he closely studied those of all other parts of Italy, and was the first to know and describe accurately the remains which abounded in the districts for miles around the capital. It is true that, both as priest and cosmographer, he was interested alike in classical and Christian monuments and in the marvels of nature. Or was he doing violence to himself when he wrote that Nola was more highly honoured by the memory of St Paulinus than by all its classical reminiscences and by the heroic struggle of Marcellus? Not, indeed, that his faith in relics was assumed; but his mind was evidently rather disposed to an inquiring interest in nature and antiquity, to a zeal for monumental works, to a keen and delicate observation of human life. In the last years of his papacy, afflicted with the gout and yet in the most cheerful mood, he was borne in his litter over hill and dale to Tusculum, Alba, Tibur, Ostia, Falerii and Otriculum, and whatever he saw he noted down. He followed the line of the Roman roads and aqueducts, and tried to fix the boundaries of the old tribes who dwelt round the city. On an excursion to Tivoli with the great Federigo of Urbino the time was happily spent in talk on the military system of the ancients, and particularly on the Trojan war. Even on his journey to the Congress of Mantua (1459) he searched, though unsuccessfully, for the labyrinth of Clusium mentioned by Pliny, and visited the so-called villa of Virgil on the Mincio. That such a pope should demand a classical Latin style from his abbreviators, is no more than might be expected. It was he who, in the war with Naples, granted an amnesty to the men of Arpinum, as countrymen of Cicero and Marius, after whom many of them were named. It was to him alone, as both judge and patron, that Blondus could dedicate his *Roma Triumphans*, the first great attempt at a complete exposition of Roman antiquity.

Nor was the enthusiasm for the classical past of Italy confined at this period to the capital. Boccaccio had already called the vast ruins of Baiae 'old walls, yet new for modern spirits'; and since this time they were held to be the most interesting sight near Naples. Collections of antiquities of all sorts now became common. Ciriaco of Ancona (d. 1457) travelled, not only through Italy, but through other countries of the old world, and brought back with him countless inscriptions and sketches. When asked why he took all this trouble, he replied, 'To wake the dead.' The histories of the various cities of Italy had from the earliest times laid claim to some true or imagined connection with Rome, had alleged some settlement or colonization which started from the capital; and the obliging manufacturers of pedigrees seem constantly to have derived various families from the oldest and most famous blood of Rome. So highly was the distinction valued that men clung to it even in the light of the dawning criticism of the fifteenth century. When Pius II was at Viterbo he said frankly to the Roman deputies who begged him to return, 'Rome is as much my home as Siena, for my House, the Piccolomini, came in early times from the capital to Siena, as is proved by the constant use of the names Aeneas and Sylvius in my family.' He would probably have had no objection to be held a descendant of the Julii. Paul II, a Barbo of Venice, found his vanity flattered by deducing his House, notwithstanding an adverse pedigree, according to which it came from Germany, from the Roman Ahenobarbus, who led a colony to Parma, and whose successors were driven by party conflicts to migrate to Venice. That the Massimi claimed descent from Q. Fabius Maximus, and the Cornaro from the Cornelii, cannot surprise us. On the other hand, it is a strikingly exceptional fact for the sixteenth century that the novelist Bandello tried to connect his blood with a noble family of Ostrogoths (i. nov. 23).

To return to Rome. The inhabitants, 'who then called themselves Romans', accepted greedily the homage which was offered them by the rest of Italy. Under Paul II, Sixtus IV and Alexander VI magnificent processions formed part of the carnival, representing the scene most attractive to the imagination of the time – the triumph of the Roman Imperator. The sentiment of the people expressed itself naturally in this shape and others like it. In this mood of public feeling, a report arose that on 18 April 1485 the corpse of a young Roman lady of the classical period – wonderfully beautiful and in perfect preservation – had been discovered.[53] Some Lombard masons digging out an ancient tomb on an estate of the convent of Santa Maria Nuova, on the Appian Way, beyond the tomb of Caecilia Metella, were said to have found a marble sarcophagus with the inscription, 'Julia, daughter of Claudius'. On this basis the following story was built. The Lombards disappeared with the jewels and treasure which were found with the corpse in the sarcophagus. The body had been coated with an antiseptic essence, and was as fresh and flexible as that of a girl of fifteen the hour after death. It was said that she still kept the colours of life, with eyes and mouth half open. She was taken to the palace of the *conservatori* on the Capitol; and then a pilgrimage to see her began. Among the crowd were many who came to paint her; 'for she was more beautiful than can be said or written, and, were it said or written, it would not be believed by those who had not seen her'. By the order of Innocent

VIII she was secretly buried one night outside the Pincian Gate; the empty sarcophagus remained in the court of the *conservatori*. Probably a coloured mask of wax or some other material was modelled in the classical style on the face of the corpse, with which the gilded hair of which we read would harmonize admirably. The touching point in the story is not the fact itself, but the firm belief that an ancient body, which was now thought to be at last really before men's eyes, must of necessity be far more beautiful than anything of modern date.

Meanwhile the material knowledge of old Rome was increased by excavations. Under Alexander VI the so-called 'grotesques', that is, the mural decorations of the ancients, were discovered, and the Apollo of the Belvedere was found at Porto d'Anzio. Under Julius II followed the memorable discoveries of the Laocoön, of the Venus of the Vatican, of the Torso of the Cleopatra. The palaces of the nobles and the cardinals began to be filled with ancient statues and fragments. Raphael undertook for Leo X that ideal restoration of the whole ancient city which his (or Castiglione's) celebrated letter (1518 or 1519) speaks of.[54] After a bitter complaint over the devastations which had not even then ceased, and which had been particularly frequent under Julius II, he beseeches the pope to protect the few relics which were left, to testify to the power and greatness of that divine soul of antiquity whose memory was inspiration to all who were capable of higher things. He then goes on with penetrating judgement to lay the foundations of a comparative history of art, and concludes by giving the definition of an architectural survey which has been accepted since his time; he requires the ground plan, section and elevation separately of every building that remained. How archeology devoted itself after his day to the study of the venerated city and grew into a special science, and how the Vitruvian Academy at all events proposed to itself great aims, cannot here be related. Let us rather pause at the days of Leo X, under whom the enjoyment of antiquity combined with all other pleasures to give to Roman life a unique stamp and consecration. The Vatican resounded with song and music, and their echoes were heard through the city as a call to joy and gladness, though Leo did not succeed thereby in banishing care and pain from his own life, and his deliberate calculation to prolong his days by cheerfulness was frustrated by an early death. The Rome of Leo, as described by Paolo Giovio, forms a picture too splendid to turn away from, unmistakable as are also its darker aspects – the slavery of those who were struggling to rise; the secret misery of the prelates, who, notwithstanding heavy debts, were forced to live in a style befitting their rank; the system of literary patronage, which drove men to be parasites or adventurers; and, lastly, the scandalous maladministration of the finances of the state. Yet the same Ariosto who knew and ridiculed all this so well gives in the sixth satire a longing picture of his expected intercourse with the accomplished poets who would conduct him through the city of ruins, of the learned counsel which he would there find for his own literary efforts, and of the treasures of the Vatican library. These, he says, and not the long-abandoned hope of Medicean protection, were the real baits which attracted him, when he was asked to go as Ferrarese ambassador to Rome.

But the ruins within and outside Rome awakened not only archeological zeal and patriotic enthusiasm, but an elegiac or sentimental melancholy. In Petrarch and Boccaccio we find touches of this feeling. Poggio Bracciolini often visited the temple of Venus at Rome, in the belief that it was that of Castor and Pollux, where the senate used so often to meet, and would lose himself in memories of the great orators Crassus, Hortensius, Cicero. The language of Pius II, especially in describing Tivoli, has a thoroughly sentimental ring, and soon afterwards (1467) appeared the first pictures of ruins, with a commentary by Polifilo.[55] Ruins of mighty arches and colonnades, half hid in plane-trees, laurels, cypresses and brushwood, figure in his pages. In the sacred legends it became the custom, we can hardly say how, to lay the scene of the birth of Christ in the ruins of a magnificent palace.[56] That artificial ruins became afterwards a necessity of landscape gardening is only a practical consequence of this feeling.

THE CLASSICS

But the literary bequests of antiquity, Greek as well as Latin, were of far more importance than the architectural, and indeed than all the artistic remains which it had left. They were held in the most absolute sense to be the springs of all knowledge. The literary conditions of that age of great discoveries have been often set forth; no more can be here attempted than to point out a few less-known features of the picture.

Great as was the influence of the old writers on the Italian mind in the fourteenth century and before, yet that influence was due rather to the wide diffusion of what had long been known than to the discovery of much that was new. The most popular Latin poets, historians, orators and letter-writers, together with a number of Latin translations of single works of Aristotle, Plutarch and a few other Greek authors, constituted the treasure from which a few favoured individuals in the time of Petrarch and Boccaccio drew their inspiration. The former, as is well known, owned and kept with religious care a Greek Homer, which he was unable to read. A complete Latin translation of the *Iliad* and *Odyssey*, though a very bad one, was made at Petrarch's suggestion, and with Boccaccio's help, by a Calabrian Greek, Leonzio Pilato. But with the fifteenth century began the long list of new discoveries, the systematic creation of libraries by means of copies, and the rapid multiplication of translations from the Greek.

Had it not been for the enthusiasm of a few collectors of that age, who shrank from no effort or privation in their researches, we should certainly possess only a small part of the literature, especially that of the Greeks, which is now in our hands. Pope Nicholas V, when only a simple monk, ran deeply into debt through buying manuscripts or having them copied. Even then he made no secret of his passion for the two great interests of the Renaissance, books and buildings. As pope he kept his word. Copyists wrote and spies searched for him through half the world. Perotto received 500 ducats for the Latin translation of Polybius; Guarino, 1,000 gold florins for that of Strabo, and he would have been paid 500 more but for the death of the pope. Filelfo was to have received 10,000 gold florins for a metrical translation of Homer, and was only prevented by the pope's death from coming from Milan to Rome. Nicholas left a collection of 5,000 or, according to another way of calculating, 9,000 volumes, for the use of the members of the Curia, which became the foundation of the library of the Vatican. It was to be preserved in the palace itself, as its noblest ornament, like the library of Ptolemy Philadelphus at Alexandria. When the plague (1450) drove him and his court to Fabriano, whence then, as now, the best paper was procured, he took his translators and compilers with him, that he might run no risk of losing them.

The Florentine Niccolò Niccoli, a member of that accomplished circle of friends which surrounded the elder Cosimo de' Medici, spent his whole fortune in buying books. At last, when his money was all gone, the Medici put their purse at his disposal for any sum which his purpose might require. We owe to him the completion of Ammianus Marcellinus, of the *De Oratore* of Cicero, and other works; he persuaded Cosimo to buy the best manuscript of Pliny from a monastery at Lubeck. With noble confidence he lent his books to those who asked for them, allowed all comers to study them in his own house, and was ready to converse with the students on what they had read. His collection of 800 volumes, valued at 6,000 gold florins, passed after his death, through Cosimo's intervention, to the monastery of San Marco, on the condition that it should be accessible to the public.

Of the two great book-finders, Guarino and Poggio, the latter, on the occasion of the Council of Constance and acting partly as the agent of Niccoli, searched industriously among the abbeys of South Germany. He there discovered six orations of Cicero, and the first complete Quintilian, that of St Gall, now at Zurich; in thirty-two days he is said to have copied the whole of it in a beautiful handwriting. He was able to make important additions to Silius Italicus, Manilius, Lucretius, Valerius Flaccus, Asconius Pedianus, Columella, Celsus, Aulus Gellius, Statius and others; and with the help of Leonardo Aretino he unearthed the last twelve comedies of Plautus, as well as the Verrine orations.

The famous Greek, Cardinal Bessarion, in whom patriotism was mingled with a zeal for letters, collected, at a great sacrifice, 600 manuscripts of pagan and Christian authors. He then looked round for some receptacle where they could safely lie until his unhappy country, if she ever regained her freedom, could reclaim her lost literature. The Venetian government declared itself ready to erect a suitable building, and to this day the Biblioteca Marciana retains a part of these treasures.[57]

The formation of the celebrated Medicean library has a history of its own, into which we cannot here enter. The chief collector for Lorenzo il Magnifico was Johannes Lascaris. It is well known that the collection, after the plundering in the year 1494, had to be recovered piecemeal by the Cardinal Giovanni Medici, afterwards Leo X.

The library of Urbino, now in the Vatican, was wholly the work of the great Federigo of Montefeltro (p. 46ff). As a boy he had begun to collect; in after years he kept thirty or forty scrittori employed in various places, and spent in the course of time no less than 30,000 ducats on the collection. It was systematically extended and completed, chiefly by the help of Vespasiano, and his account of it forms an ideal picture of a library of the Renaissance. At Urbino there were catalogues of the libraries of the Vatican, of St Mark at Florence, of the

Visconti at Pavia, and even of the library at Oxford. It was noted with pride that in richness and completeness none could rival Urbino. Theology and the Middle Ages were perhaps most fully represented. There was a complete Thomas Aquinas, a complete Albertus Magnus, a complete Bonaventura. The collection, however, was a many-sided one, and included every work on medicine which was then to be had. Among the 'moderns' the great writers of the fourteenth century – Dante and Boccaccio, with their complete works – occupied the first place. Then followed twenty-five select humanists, invariably with both their Latin and Italian writings and with all their translations. Among the Greek manuscripts the fathers of the Church far outnumbered the rest; yet in the list of the classics we find all the works of Sophocles, all of Pindar, and all of Menander. The last must have quickly disappeared from Urbino, else the philologists would have soon edited it.

We have, further, a good deal of information as to the way in which manuscripts and libraries were multiplied. The purchase of an ancient manuscript, which contained a rare, or the only complete, or the only existing text of an old writer, was naturally a lucky accident of which we need take no further account. Among the professional copyists those who understood Greek took the highest place, and it was they especially who bore the honourable name of *scrittori*. Their number was always limited, and the pay they received very large. The rest, simply called *copisti*, were partly mere clerks who made their living by such work, partly schoolmasters and needy men of learning who desired an addition to their income. The copyists at Rome in the time of Nicholas V were mostly Germans or Frenchmen – 'barbarians' as the Italian humanists called them, probably men who were in search of favours at the papal court, and who kept themselves alive meanwhile by this means. When Cosimo de' Medici was in a hurry to form a library for his favourite foundation, the Badia below Fiesole, he sent for Vespasiano, and received from him the advice to give up all thoughts of purchasing books, since those which were worth getting could not be had easily, but rather to make use of the copyists; whereupon Cosimo bargained to pay him so much a day, and Vespasiano, with forty-five writers under him, delivered 200 volumes in twenty-two months. The catalogue of the works to be copied was sent to Cosimo by Nicholas V, who wrote it with his own hand. Ecclesiastical literature and the books needed for the choral services naturally held the chief place in the list.

The handwriting was that beautiful modern Italian which was already in use in the preceding century, and which makes the sight of one of the books of that time a pleasure. Pope Nicholas V, Poggio, Giannozzo Manetti, Niccolò Niccoli and other distinguished scholars themselves wrote a beautiful hand, and desired and tolerated none other. The decorative adjuncts, even when miniatures formed no part of them, were full of taste, as may be seen especially in the Laurentian manuscripts, with the light and graceful scrolls which begin and end the lines. The material used to write on, when the work was ordered by great or wealthy people, was always parchment; the binding, both in the Vatican and at Urbino, was a uniform crimson velvet with silver clasps. Where there was so much care to show honour to the contents of a book by the beauty of its outward form, it is intelligible that the sudden appearance of printed books was greeted at first with anything but favour. Federigo of Urbino 'would have been ashamed to own a printed book'.

But the weary copyists – not those who lived by the trade, but the many who were forced to copy a book in order to have it – rejoiced at the German invention. It was soon applied in Italy to the multiplication first of the Latin and then of the Greek authors, and for a long period nowhere but in Italy, yet it spread with by no means the rapidity which might have been expected from the general enthusiasm for these works. After a while the modern relation between author and publisher began to develop itself, and under Alexander VI, when it was no longer easy to destroy a book, as Cosimo could make Filelfo promise to do, the prohibitive censorship made its appearance.

The growth of textual criticism which accompanied the advancing study of languages and antiquity belongs as little to the subject of this book as the history of scholarship in general. We are here occupied, not with the learning of the Italians in itself, but with the reproduction of antiquity in literature and life. One word more on the studies themselves may still be permissible.

Greek scholarship was chiefly confined to Florence and to the fifteenth and the beginning of the sixteenth centuries.

The impulse which proceeded from Petrarch and Boccaccio, superficial as was their own acquaintance with Greek, was powerful, but did not tell immediately on their contemporaries; on the other hand, the study of Greek literature died out about the year 1520 with the last of the colony of learned Greek exiles, and it was a singular piece of fortune that northerners like Erasmus, the Stephani and Budaeus had meanwhile made themselves masters of the language. That colony had begun with Manuel Chrysoloras and his relation John, and with George of Trebizond. Then followed, about and after the time of the conquest of Constantinople, John Argyropulos, Theodore Gaza, Demetrios Chalcondylas, who brought up his sons Theophilos and Basilios to be excellent Hellenists, Andronikos Kallistos, Marcos Musuros and the family of the Lascaris, not to mention others. But after the subjection of Greece by the Turks was completed, the succession of scholars was maintained only by the sons of the fugitives and perhaps here and there by some Candian or Cypriot refugee. That the decay of Hellenistic studies began about the time of the death of Leo X was due partly to a general change of intellectual attitude, and to a certain satiety of classical influences which now made itself felt; but its coincidence with the death of the Greek fugitives was not wholly a matter of accident. The study of Greek among the Italians appears, if we take the year 1500 as our standard, to have been pursued with extraordinary zeal. The youths of that day learned to speak the language, and half a century later, like the Popes Paul III and Paul IV, they could still do so in their old age. But this sort of mastery of the study presupposes intercourse with native Greeks.

Besides Florence, Rome and Padua nearly always maintained paid teachers of Greek, and Verona, Ferrara, Venice, Perugia, Pavia and other cities occasional teachers. Hellenistic studies owed a priceless debt to the press of Aldo Manuzio at Venice, where the most important and voluminous writers were for the first time printed in the original. Aldo ventured his all in the enterprise; he was an editor and publisher whose like the world has rarely seen.

Along with this classical revival, oriental studies now assumed considerable proportions. The controversial writings of the great Florentine statesman and scholar, Giannozzo Manetti (d. 1459), against the Jews afford an early instance of a complete mastery of their language and science. His son Agnolo was from his childhood instructed in Latin, Greek and Hebrew. The father, at the bidding of Nicholas V, translated the whole Bible, as learned opinion of the time insisted on giving up the *Vulgata*.

Many other humanists devoted themselves before Reuchlin to the study of Hebrew, among them Pico della Mirandola, who was not satisfied with a knowledge of the Hebrew grammar and Scriptures, but penetrated into the Jewish Cabbalah and even made himself as familiar with the literature of the Talmud as any rabbi.

Among the oriental languages, Arabic was studied as well as Hebrew. The science of medicine, no longer satisfied with the older Latin translations of the great Arab physicians, had constant recourse to the originals, to which an easy access was offered by the Venetian consulates in the East, where Italian doctors were regularly kept. Hieronimo Ramusio, a Venetian physician, translated a great part of Avicenna from the Arabic and died at Damascus in 1486. Andrea Mongaio of Belluno, a disciple of the same Avicenna, lived long at Damascus, learnt Arabic, and improved on his master. The Venetian government afterwards appointed him professor of this subject at Padua.

We must here linger for a moment over Pico della Mirandola before passing on to the general effects of humanism. He was the only man who loudly and vigorously defended the truth and science of all ages against the one-sided worship of classical antiquity. He knew how to value not only Averroës and the Jewish investigators, but also the scholastic writers of the Middle Ages, according to the matter of their writings. He seems to hear them say,

> We shall live for ever, not in the schools of word-catchers, but in the circle of the wise, where they talk not of the mother of Andromache or of the sons of Niobe, but of the deeper causes of things human and divine; he who looks closely will see that even the barbarians had intelligence [mercurium], not on the tongue but in the breast.

Himself writing a vigorous and not inelegant Latin, and a master of clear exposition, he despised the purism of pedants and the current over-estimate of borrowed forms, especially when joined, as they often are, with one-sidedness, and involving indifference to the wider truth of the things themselves. Looking at Pico, we can guess at the lofty flight which Italian philosophy would have taken had not the Counter-Reformation annihilated the higher spiritual life of the people.

THE HUMANISTS

Who now were those who acted as mediators between their own age and a venerated antiquity, and made the latter a chief element in the culture of the former?

They were a crowd of the most miscellaneous sort, wearing one face today and another tomorrow; but they clearly felt themselves, and it was fully recognized by their time, that they formed a wholly new element in society. The *clerici vagantes* of the twelfth century may perhaps be taken as their forerunners – the same unstable existence, the same free and more than free views of life, and the germs at all events of the same pagan tendencies in their poetry. But now, as competitor with the whole culture of the Middle Ages, which was essentially clerical and was fostered by the Church, there appeared a new civilization, founding itself on that which lay on the other side of the Middle Ages. Its active representatives became influential because they knew what the ancients knew, because they tried to write as the ancients wrote, because they began to think, and soon to feel, as the ancients thought and felt. The tradition to which they devoted themselves passed at a thousand points into genuine reproduction.

Some modern writers deplore the fact that the germs of a far more independent and essentially national culture, such as appeared in Florence about the year 1300, were afterwards so completely swamped by the humanists. There was then, we are told, nobody in Florence who could not read; even the donkey-men sang the verses of Dante; the best Italian manuscripts which we possess belonged originally to Florentine artisans; the publication of a popular encyclopedia, like the *Tesoro* of Brunetto Latini, was then possible; and all this was founded on a strength and soundness of character due to the universal participation in public affairs, to commerce and travel, and to the systematic reprobation of idleness. The Florentines, it is urged, were at that time respected and influential throughout the whole world, and were called in that year, not without reason, by Pope Boniface VIII, 'the fifth element'. The rapid progress of humanism after the year 1400 paralysed native impulses. Henceforth men looked only to antiquity for the solution of every problem, and consequently allowed literature to sink into mere quotation. Nay, the very fall of civil freedom is partly to be ascribed to all this, since the new learning rested on obedience to authority, sacrificed municipal rights to Roman law, and thereby both sought and found the favour of the despots.

These charges will occupy us now and then at a later stage of our inquiry, when we shall attempt to reduce them to their true value, and to weigh the losses against the gains of this movement. For the present we must confine ourselves to showing how the civilization even of the vigorous fourteenth century necessarily prepared the way for the complete victory of humanism, and how precisely the greatest representatives of the national Italian spirit were themselves the men who opened wide the gate for the measureless devotion to antiquity in the fifteenth century.

To begin with Dante. If a succession of men of equal genius had presided over Italian culture, whatever elements their natures might have absorbed from the antique, they still could not fail to retain a characteristic and strongly marked national stamp. But neither Italy nor Western Europe produced another Dante, and he was and remained the man who first thrust antiquity into the foreground of national culture. In the *Divine Comedy* he treats the ancient and the Christian worlds, not indeed as of equal authority, but as parallel to one another. Just as at an earlier period of the Middle Ages types and antitypes were sought in the history of the Old and New Testaments, so does Dante constantly bring together a Christian and a pagan illustration of the same fact. It must be remembered that the Christian cycle of history and legend was familiar, while the ancient was relatively unknown, was full of promise and of interest, and must necessarily have gained the upper hand in the competition for public sympathy when there was no longer a Dante to hold the balance between the two.

Petrarch, who lives in the memory of most people nowadays chiefly as a great Italian poet, owed his fame among his contemporaries far rather to the fact that he was a kind of living representative of antiquity, that he imitated all styles of Latin poetry, endeavoured by his voluminous historical and philosophical writings not to supplant but to make known the works of the ancients, and wrote letters that, as treatises on matters of antiquarian interest, obtained a reputation which to us is unintelligible, but which was natural enough in an age without handbooks.

It was the same with Boccaccio. For two centuries, when but little was known of the *Decameron* north of the Alps, he was famous all over Europe simply on account of his Latin compilations on mythology, geography and biography. One of these, *De genealogia deorum*, contains in the fourteenth and fifteenth books a remarkable appendix, in which he discusses the position of the then youthful humanism with regard to the age. We must not be misled by his exclusive references to *poesia*, as closer observation shows that he means thereby the whole mental activity of the poet-scholars. This it is whose enemies he so vigorously combats – the frivolous ignoramuses who have no soul for anything but debauchery; the sophistical theologian, to whom Helicon, the Castalian fountain and the grove of Apollo where foolishness; the greedy lawyers, to whom poetry was a superfluity, since no money was to be made by it; finally the mendicant friars, described periphrastically, but clearly enough, who made free with their charges of paganism and immorality. Then follows the defence of poetry, the praise of it, and especially of the deeper and allegorical meanings which we must always attribute to it, and of that calculated obscurity which is intended to repel the dull minds of the ignorant.

And finally, with a clear reference to his own scholarly work, the writer justifies the new relation in which his age stood to paganism. The case was wholly different, he pleads, when the early Church had to fights its way among the heathen. Now – praised be Jesus Christ! – true religion was strengthened, paganism destroyed, and the victorious Church in possession of the hostile camp. It was now possible to touch and study paganism almost (*fere*) without danger. This is the argument invariably used in later times to defend the Renaissance.

There was thus a new cause in the world and a new class of men to maintain it. It is idle to ask if this cause ought not to have stopped short in its career of victory, to have restrained itself deliberately, and conceded the first place to purely national elements of culture. No conviction was more firmly rooted in the popular mind than that antiquity was the highest title to glory which Italy possessed.

There was a symbolical ceremony familiar to this generation of poet-scholars which lasted on into the fifteenth and sixteenth centuries, though losing the higher sentiment which inspired it – the coronation of the poets with the laurel wreath. The origin of this custom in the Middle Ages is obscure, and the ritual of the ceremony never became fixed. It was a public demonstration, an outward and visible expression of literary enthusiasm, and naturally its form was variable. Dante, for instance, seems to have understood it in the sense of a half-religious consecration; he desired to assume the wreath in the baptistery of San Giovanni, where, like thousands of other Florentine children, he had received baptism. He could, says his biographer, have anywhere received the crown in virtue of his fame, but desired it nowhere but in his native city, and therefore died uncrowned. From the same source we learn that the usage was till then uncommon, and was held to be inherited by the ancient Romans from the Greeks. The most recent source to which the practices could be referred is to be found in the Capitoline contests of musicians, poets and other artists, founded by Domitian in imitation of the Greeks and celebrated every five years, which may possibly have survived for a time the fall of the Roman empire; but as few other men would venture to crown themselves, as Dante desired to do, the question arises, to whom did this office belong? Albertino Mussato was crowned at Padua in 1310 by the bishop and the rector of the university. The university of Paris, the rector of which was then a Florentine (1341), and the municipal authorities of Rome, competed for the honour of crowning Petrarch. His self-elected examiner, King Robert of Anjou, would gladly have performed the ceremony at Naples, but Petrarch preferred to be crowned on the Capitol by the senator of Rome. This honour was long the highest object of ambition, and so it seemed to Jacobus Pizinga, an illustrious Sicilian magistrate. Then came the Italian journey of Charles IV, whom it amused to flatter the vanity of ambitious men and impress the ignorant multitude by means of gorgeous ceremonies. Starting from the fiction that the coronation of poets was a prerogative of the old Roman emperors, and consequently was no less his own, he crowned (15 May 1355) the Florentine scholar Zanobi della Strada at Pisa, to the great disgust of Boccaccio, who declined to recognize this 'laurea Pisana' as legitimate. Indeed, it might be fairly asked with what right this stranger, half Slavonic by birth, came to sit in judgement on the merits of Italian poets. But from henceforth the emperors crowned poets wherever they went on their travels; and in the fifteenth century the popes and other princes assumed the same right, till at last no regard whatever was paid to place or circumstances. In Rome, under Sixtus IV, the academy of Pomponius Laetus gave the wreath on its own authority. The Florentines had the good taste not to crown their famous humanists till after death. Carlo Aretino and Leonardo Aretino were thus crowned; the eulogy of the first was pronounced by Matteo Palmieri, of the latter by Giannozzo Manetti, before the members of the council and the whole people, the orator standing at the head of the bier, on which the corpse lay clad in a silken robe. Carlo Aretino was further honoured by a tomb in Santa Croce, which is among the most beautiful in the whole course of the Renaissance.[58]

UNIVERSITIES AND SCHOOLS

The influence of antiquity on culture, of which we have now to speak, presupposes that the new learning had gained possession of the universities. This was so, but by no means to the extent and with the results which might have been expected.

Few of the Italian universities show themselves in their full vigour till the thirteenth and fourteenth centuries, when the increase of wealth rendered a more systematic care for education possible. At first there were generally three sorts of professorships – one for civil law, another for canonical law, the third for medicine; in course of time professorships of rhetoric, of philosophy and of astronomy were added, the last commonly, though not always, identical with astrology. The salaries varied greatly in different cases. Sometimes a capital sum was paid down. With the spread of culture competition became so active that the different universities tried to entice away distinguished teachers from one another, under which circumstances Bologna is said to have sometimes devoted the half of its public income (20,000 ducats) to the university. The appointments were as a rule made only for a certain time, sometimes for only half a year, so that the teachers were forced to lead a wandering life, like actors. Appointments for life were, however, not unknown. Sometimes the promise was exacted not to teach elsewhere what had already been taught at one place. There were also voluntary, unpaid professors.

Of the chairs which have been mentioned, that of rhetoric was especially sought by the humanist; yet it depended only on his familiarity with the matter of ancient learning whether or no he could aspire to those of law, medicine, philosophy or astronomy. The inward conditions of the science of the day were as variable as the outward conditions of the teacher. Certain jurists and physicians received by far the largest salaries of all, the former chiefly as consulting lawyers for the suits and claims of the state which employed them. In Padua a lawyer of the fifteenth century received a salary of 1,000 ducats, and it was proposed to appoint a celebrated physician with a yearly payment of 2,000 ducats, and the right of private practice, the same man having previously received 700 gold florins at Pisa. When the jurist Bartolommeo Socini, professor at Pisa, accepted a Venetian appointment at Padua, and was on the point of starting on his journey, he was arrested by the Florentine government and only released on payment of bail to the amount of 18,000 gold florins. The high estimation in which these branches of science were held makes it intelligible why distinguished philologists turned their attention to law and medicine, while on the other hand specialists were more and more compelled to acquire something of a wide literary culture. We shall presently have occasion to speak of the work of the humanists in other departments of practical life.

Nevertheless, the position of the philologists, as such, even where the salary was large and did not exclude other sources of income, was on the whole uncertain and temporary, so that one and the same teacher could be connected with a great variety of institutions. It is evident that change was desired for its own sake, and something fresh expected from each newcomer, as was natural at a time when science was in the making, and consequently depended to no small degree on the personal influence of the teacher. Nor was it always the case that a lecturer on classical authors really belonged to the university of the town where he taught. Communication was so easy, and the supply of suitable accommodation, in monasteries and elsewhere, was so abundant, that a private undertaking was often practicable. In the first decades of the fifteenth century, when the university of Florence was at its greatest brilliance, when the courtiers of Eugenius IV and perhaps even of Martin V thronged the lecture-room, when Carlo Aretino and Filelfo were competing for the largest audience, there existed, not only an almost complete university among the Augustinians of Santo Spirito, not only an association of scholars among the Camaldolesi of the Angeli, but individuals of mark, either singly or in common, arranged to provide philosophical and philological teaching for themselves and others. Linguistic and antiquarian studies in Rome had next to no connection with the university (Sapienza), and depended almost exclusively either on the favour of individual popes and prelates, or on the appointments made in the papal chancery. It was not till Leo X (1513) that the great reorganization of the Sapienza took place, with its eighty-eight lecturers, among whom there were able men, though none of the first rank, at the head of the archeological department. But this new brilliancy was of short duration. We have already spoken briefly of the Greek professorships in Italy.

To form an accurate picture of the method of scientific instruction then pursued, we must turn away our eyes as far as possible from our present academic system. Personal intercourse between the teachers and the taught, public disputations, the constant use of Latin and often of Greek, the frequent changes of lecturers and the scarcity of books, gave the studies of that time a colour which we cannot represent to ourselves without effort.

There were Latin schools in every town of the least importance, not by any means merely as preparatory to higher education, but because, next to reading, writing and arithmetic, the knowledge of Latin was a necessity; and after Latin came logic. It is to be noted particularly that these schools did not depend on the Church, but on the municipality; some of them, too, were merely private enterprises.

This school system, directed by a few distinguished humanists, not only attained a remarkable perfection of organization, but became an instrument of higher education in the modern sense of the phrase. With the education of the children of two princely houses in North Italy institutions were connected which may be called unique of their kind.

At the court of Giovan Francesco Gonzaga at Mantua (reg. 1407–44) appeared the illustrious Vittorino da Feltre, one of those men who devote their whole life to an object for which their natural gifts constitute a special vocation.

He directed the education of the sons and daughters of the princely house, and one of the latter became under his care a woman of learning. When his reputation extended far and wide over Italy, and members of great and wealthy families came from long distances, even from Germany, in search of his instructions, Gonzaga was not only willing that they should be received, but seems to have held it an honour for Mantua to be the chosen school of the aristocratic world. Here for the first time gymnastics and all noble bodily exercises were treated along with scientific instruction as indispensable to a liberal education. Besides these pupils came others, whose instruction Vittorino probably held to be his highest earthly aim, the gifted poor, whom he supported in his house and educated, *per l'amore di Dio*, along with the high-born youths who here learned to live under the same roof with untitled genius. Gonzaga paid him a yearly salary of 300 gold florins, and contributed to the expenses caused by the poorer pupils. He knew that Vittorino never saved a penny for himself, and doubtless realized that the education of the poor was the unexpressed condition of his presence. The establishment was conducted on strictly religious lines, stricter indeed than many monasteries.

More stress was laid on pure scholarship by Guarino of Verona (1370–1460), who in the year 1429 was called to Ferrara by Niccolò d'Este to educate his son Lionello, and who, when his pupil was nearly grown up in 1436, began to teach at the university of eloquence and of the ancient languages. While still acting as tutor to Lionello, he had many other pupils from various parts of the country, and in his own house a select class of poor scholars, whom he partly or wholly supported. His evening hours till far into the night were devoted to hearing lessons or to instructive conversation. His house, too, was the home of a strict religion and morality. It signified little to him or to Vittorino that most of the humanists of their day deserved small praise in the matter of morals or religion. It is inconceivable how Guarino, with all the daily work which fell upon him, still found time to write translations from the Greek and voluminous original works.

Not only in these two courts, but generally throughout Italy, the education of the princely families was in part and for certain years in the hands of the humanists, who thereby mounted a step higher in the aristocratic world. The writing of treatises on the education of princes, formerly the business of theologians, fell now within their province.

From the time of Pier Paolo Vergerio the Italian princes were well taken care of in this respect, and the custom was transplanted into Germany by Aeneas Sylvius, who addressed detailed exhortations to two young German princes of the House of Habsburg on the subject of their further education, in which they are both urged, as might be expected, to cultivate and nurture humanism. Perhaps Aeneas was aware that in addressing these youths he was talking in the air, and therefore took measures to put his treatise into public circulation. But the relations of the humanists to the rulers will be discussed separately.

PROPAGATORS OF ANTIQUITY

We have here first to speak of those citizens, mostly Florentines, who made antiquarian interests one of the chief objects of their lives, and who were themselves either distinguished scholars or else distinguished dilettanti who maintained the scholars. They were of peculiar significance during the period of transition at the beginning of the fifteenth century, since it was in them that humanism first showed itself practically as an indispensable element in daily life. It was not till after this time that the popes and princes began seriously to occupy themselves with it.

Niccolò Niccoli and Giannozzo Manetti have been already spoken of more than once. Niccoli is described to us by Vespasiano as a man who would tolerate nothing around him out of harmony with his own classical spirit. His handsome long-robed figure, his kindly speech, his house adorned with the noblest remains of antiquity, made a singular impression. He was scrupulously cleanly in everything, most of all at table, where ancient vases and crystal goblets stood before him on the whitest linen.[59] The way in which he won over a pleasure-loving young Florentine to intellectual interests is too charming not to be here described. Piero de' Pazzi, son of a distinguished merchant, and himself destined to the same calling, fair to behold, and much given to the pleasures of the world, thought about anything rather than literature. One day, as he was passing the Palazzo del Podestà, Niccolò called the young man to him, and although they had never before exchanged a word, the youth obeyed the call of one so respected. Niccolò asked him who his father was. He answered, 'Messer Andrea de' Pazzi.' When he was further asked what his pursuit was, Piero replied, as young people are wont to do, 'I enjoy myself [*attendo a darmi buon tempo*].' Niccolò said to him, 'As son of such a father, and so fair to look upon, it is a shame that thou knowest nothing of the Latin language, which would be so great an ornament to thee. If thou learnest it not, thou wilt be good for nothing, and as soon as the flower of youth is over, wilt be a man of no consequence [*virtù*].' When Piero heard this, he straightway perceived that it was true, and said that he would gladly take pains to learn, if only he had a teacher. Whereupon Niccolò answered that he would see to that. And he found him a learned man for Latin and Greek, named Pontano, whom Piero treated as one of his own house, and to whom he paid 100 gold florins a year. Quitting all the pleasures in which he had hitherto lived, he studied day and night, and became a friend of all learned men and a noble-minded statesman. He learned by heart the whole *Aeneid* and many speeches of Livy, chiefly on the way between Florence and his country house at Trebbio. Antiquity was represented in another and higher sense by Giannozzo Manetti (1393–1459). Precocious from his first years, he was hardly more than a child when he had finished his apprenticeship in commerce, and became book-keeper in a bank. But soon the life he led seemed to him empty and perishable, and he began to yearn after science, through which alone man can secure im- mortality. He then busied himself with books as few laymen had done before him, and became, as has been said, one of the most profound scholars of his time. When appointed by the government as its representative magistrate and tax-collector at Pescia and Pistoia, he fulfilled his duties in accordance with the lofty ideal with which his religious feeling and humanistic studies combined to inspire him. He succeeded in collecting the most unpopular taxes which the Florentine state imposed, and declined payment for his services. As provincial governor he refused all presents, abhorred all bribes, checked gambling, kept the country well supplied with corn, was indefatigable in settling lawsuits amicably, and did wonders in calming inflamed passions by his goodness. The Pistoiese were never able to discover to which of the two political parties he leaned. As if to symbolize the common rights and interests of all, he spent his leisure hours in writing the history of the city, which was preserved, bound in a purple cover, as a sacred relic in the town hall. When he took his leave the city presented him with a banner bearing the municipal arms and a splendid silver helmet.

For further information as to the learned citizens of Florence at this period the reader must all the more be referred to Vespasiano,[60] who knew them all personally, because the tone and atmosphere in which he writes, and the terms and conditions on which he mixed in their society, are of even more importance than the facts which he records. Even in a translation, and still more in the brief indications to which we are here compelled to limit ourselves, this chief merit of his book is lost. Without being a great writer, he was thoroughly familiar with the subject he wrote on, and had a deep sense of its intellectual significance.

If we seek to analyse the charm which the Medici of the fifteenth century, especially Cosimo the Elder (d. 1464) and Lorenzo the Magnificent (d. 1492) exercised over Florence and over all their contemporaries, we shall find that it lay less in their political capacity than in their leadership in the culture of the age. A man in Cosimo's position – a great merchant and party leader, who also had on his side all the thinkers, writers and investigators, a man who was the first of the Florentines by birth and the first of the Italians by culture – such a man was to all intents and purposes already a prince. To Cosimo belongs the special glory of recognizing in the Platonic philosophy the fairest flower of the ancient world of thought, of inspiring his friends with the same belief, and thus of fostering within humanistic circles themselves another and a higher resuscitation of antiquity. The story is known to us minutely. It all hangs on the calling of the learned Johannes Argyropulos, and on the personal enthusiasm of Cosimo himself in his last years, which was such that the great Marsilio Ficino could style himself, as far as Platonism was concerned, the spiritual son of Cosimo. Under Pietro Medici, Ficino was already at the head of a school; to him Pietro's son and Cosimo's grandson, the illustrious Lorenzo, came over from the Peripatetics. Among his most distinguished fellow-scholars were Bartolommeo Valori, Donato Acciaiuoli and Pierfilippo Pandolfini. The enthusiastic teacher declares in several passages of his writings that Lorenzo had sounded all the depths of the Platonic philosophy, and had uttered his conviction that without Plato it would be hard to be a good Christian or a good citizen. The famous band of scholars which surrounded Lorenzo was united together, and distinguished from all other circles of the kind, by this passion for a higher and idealistic philosophy. Only in such a world could a man like Pico della Mirandola feel happy. But perhaps the best thing of all that can be said about it is that, with all this worship of antiquity, Italian poetry found here a sacred refuge, and that of all the rays of light which streamed from the circle of which Lorenzo was the centre, none was more powerful than this. As a statesman, let each man judge him as he pleases; a foreigner will hesitate to pronounce what was due to human guilt and what to circumstances in the fate of Florence, but no more unjust charge was ever made than that in the field of culture Lorenzo was the protector of mediocrity, that through his fault Leonardo da Vinci and the mathematician Fra Luca Paciolo lived abroad, and that Toscanella, Vespucci and others at least remained unsupported. He was not, indeed, a man of universal mind; but of all the great men who have striven to favour and promote spiritual interests, few certainly have been so many-sided, and in none probably was the inward need to do so equally deep.

The age in which we live is loud enough in proclaiming the worth of culture, and especially of the culture of antiquity. But the enthusiastic devotion to it, the recognition that the need of it is the first and greatest of all needs, is nowhere to be found in such a degree as among the Florentines of the fifteenth and the early part of the sixteenth centuries. On this point we have indirect proof which precludes all doubt. It would not have been so common to give the daughters of the house a share in the same studies, had they not been held to be the noblest of earthly pursuits; exile would not have been turned into a happy retreat, as was done by Palla Strozzi; nor would men who indulged in every conceivable excess have retained the strength and the spirit to write critical treatises on the *Natural History* of Pliny like Filippo Strozzi. Our business here is not to deal out either praise or blame, but to understand the spirit of the age in all its vigorous individuality.

Besides Florence, there were many cities of Italy where individuals and social circles devoted all their energies to the support of humanism and the protection of the scholars who lived among them. The correspondence of that period is full of references to personal relations of this kind. The feeling of the instructed classes set strongly and almost exclusively in this direction.

But it is now time to speak of humanism at the Italian courts. The natural alliance between the despot and the scholar, each relying solely on his personal talent, has already been touched upon; that the latter should avowedly prefer the princely courts to the free cities was only to be expected from the higher pay which they there received. At a time when the great Alfonso of Aragon seemed likely to become master of all Italy, Aeneas Sylvius wrote to another citizen of Siena: 'I had rather that Italy attained peace under his rule than under that of the free cities, for kingly generosity rewards excellence of every kind.' Too much stress has latterly been laid on the unworthy side of this relation, and the mercenary flattery to which it gave rise, just as formerly the eulogies of the humanists led to a too favourable judgement on their patrons. Taking all things together, it is greatly to the honour of the latter that they felt bound to place themselves at the head of the culture of their age and country, one-sided though this culture was. In some of the popes, the fearlessness of the consequences to which the new learning might lead strikes us as something truly, but unconsciously, imposing. Nicholas V was confident of the future of the Church, since thousands of learned men supported her. Pius II was far from making such splendid sacrifices for humanism as were made by Nicholas, and the poets who frequented his court were few in number; but he himself was much more the personal head of the republic of letters than his predecessor, and enjoyed his position without the least misgiving. Paul II was the first to dread and mistrust the culture of his secretaries, and his three successors, Sixtus, Innocent and Alexander, accepted dedications and allowed themselves to be sung to the hearts' content of the poets – there even existed a *Borgiad*, probably in hexameters – but were too busy elsewhere, and too occupied in seeking other foundations for their power, to trouble themselves much about the poet-scholars. Julius II found poets to eulogize him, because he himself was no mean subject for poetry, but he does not seem to have troubled himself much about them. He was followed by Leo X, 'as Romulus by Numa' – in other words, after the warlike turmoil of the first pontificate, a new one was hoped for wholly given to the muses. The enjoyment of elegant Latin prose and melodious verse was part of the programme of Leo's life, and his patronage certainly had the result that his Latin poets have left us a living picture of that joyous and brilliant spirit of the Leonine days, with which the biography of Jovius is filled, in countless epigrams, elegies, odes and orations. Probably in all European history there is no prince who, in proportion to the few striking events of his life, has received such manifold homage. The poets had access to him chiefly about noon, when the musicians had ceased playing; but one of the best among them tells us how they also pursued him when he walked in his garden or withdrew to the privacy of his chamber, and if they failed to catch him there, would try to win him with a mendicant ode or elegy, filled, as usual, with the whole population of Olympus. For Leo, prodigal of his money, and disliking to be surrounded by any but cheerful faces, displayed a generosity in his gifts which was fabulously exaggerated in the hard times that followed. His reorganization of the Sapienza has already been spoken of. In order not to underrate Leo's influence on humanism we must guard against being misled by the toy-work that was mixed up with it, and must not allow ourselves to be deceived by the apparent irony with which he himself sometimes treated these matters. Our judgement must rather dwell on the countless spiritual possibilities which are included in the word 'stimulus', and which, although they cannot be measured as a whole, can still, on closer study, be actually followed out in particular cases. Whatever influence in Europe the Italian humanists have had since 1520 depends in some way or other on the impulse which was given by Leo. He was the pope who, in granting permission to print the newly found Tacitus, could say that the great writers were a rule of life and a consolation in misfortune; that helping learned men and obtaining excellent books had ever been one of his highest aims; and that he now thanked heaven that he could benefit the human race by furthering the publication of this book.

The sack of Rome in the year 1527 scattered the scholars no less than the artists in every direction, and spread the fame of the great departed Maecenas to the farthest boundaries of Italy.

Among the secular princes of the fifteenth century, none displayed such enthusiasm for antiquity as Alfonso the Great of Aragon, King of Naples. It appears that his zeal was thoroughly unaffected, and that the monuments and writings of the ancient world made upon him, from the time of his arrival in Italy, an impression deep and powerful enough to reshape his life. With strange readiness he surrendered the stubborn Aragon to his brother, and devoted himself wholly to his new possessions. He had in his service, either successively or together, George of Trebizond, the younger Chrysoloras, Lorenzo Valla, Bartolommeo Facio and Antonio Panormita, of whom the two latter were his historians; Panormita daily instructed the king and his court in Livy, even during military expeditions. These men cost him yearly 20,000 gold florins. He gave Panormita 1,000 for his work: Facio received for the *Historia Alfonsi*, besides a yearly income of 500 ducats, a present of 1,500 more when it was finished, with the words, 'It is not given to pay you, for your work would not be paid for if I gave you the fairest of my cities; but in time I hope to satisfy you.' When he took Giannozzo Manetti as his secretary on the most brilliant conditions, he said to him, 'My last crust I will share with you.' When Giannozzo first came to bring the congratulations of the Florentine government on the marriage of Prince Ferrante, the impression he made was so great that the king sat motionless on the throne, 'like a brazen statue, and did not even brush away a fly, which had settled on his nose at the beginning of the oration'. His favourite haunt seems to have been the library of the castle at Naples, where he would sit at a window overlooking the bay, and listen to learned debates on the Trinity. For he was profoundly religious, and had the Bible, as well as Livy and Seneca, read to him, till after fourteen perusals he knew it almost by heart. Who can fully understand the feeling with which he regarded the supposititious remains of Livy at Padua? When, by dint of great entreaties, he obtained an arm-bone of the skeleton from the Venetians, and received it with solemn pomp at Naples, how strangely Christian and pagan sentiment must have been blended in his heart! During a campaign in the Abruzzi, when the distant Sulmona, the birthplace of Ovid, was pointed out to him, he saluted the spot and returned thanks to its tutelary genius. It gladdened him to make good the prophecy of the great poet as to his future fame. Once indeed, at his famous entry into the conquered city of Naples (1443), he himself chose to appear before the world in ancient style. Not far from the market a breach forty ells wide was made in the wall, and through this he drove in a gilded chariot like a Roman *triumphator*.[61] The memory of the scene is preserved by a noble triumphal arch of marble in the Castel Nuovo. His Neapolitan successors inherited as little of this passion for antiquity as of his other good qualities.

Alfonso was far surpassed in learning by Federigo of Urbino, who had but few courtiers around him, squandered nothing, and in his appropriation of antiquity, as in all other things, went to work considerately. It was for him and for Nicholas V that most of the translations from the Greek, and a number of the best commentaries and other such works, were written. He spent much on the scholars whose services he used, but spent it to good purpose. There were no traces of the official poet at Urbino, where the duke himself was the most learned in the whole court. Classical antiquity, indeed, only formed a part of his culture. An accomplished ruler, captain and gentleman, he had mastered the greater part of the science of the day, and this with a view to its practical application. As a theologian, he was able to compare Scotus with Aquinas, and was familiar with the writings of the old fathers of the Eastern and Western Churches, the former in Latin translations. In philosophy, he seems to have left Plato altogether to his contemporary Cosimo, but he knew thoroughly not only the *Ethics* and *Politics* of Aristotle but the *Physics* and some other works. The rest of his reading lay chiefly among the ancient historians, all of whom he possessed; these, and not the poets, 'he was always reading and having read to him'.

The Sforza, too, were all of them men of more or less learning and patrons of literature; they have been already referred to in passing. Duke Francesco probably looked on humanistic culture as a matter of course in the education of his children, if only for political reasons. It was felt universally to be an advantage if the prince could mix with the most instructed men of his time on an equal footing. Lodovico il Moro, himself an excellent Latin scholar, showed an interest in intellectual matters which extended far beyond classical antiquity.

Even the petty despots strove after similar distinctions, and we do them injustice by thinking that they only supported the scholars at their courts as a means of diffusing their own fame. A ruler like Borso of Ferrara, with all his vanity, seems by no means to have looked for immortality from the poets, eager as they were to propitiate him with a *Borseid* and the like. He had far too proud a sense of his own position as a ruler for that. But intercourse with learned men, interest in antiquarian matters, and the passion for elegant Latin correspondence were necessities for the princes of that age. What bitter complaints are those of Duke Alfonso, competent as he was in practical matters, that his weakliness in youth had forced him to seek recreation in manual pursuits only! Or was this merely an excuse to keep the humanists at a distance? A nature like his was not intelligible even to contemporaries.

Even the most insignificant despots of Romagna found it hard to do without one or two men of letters about them. The tutor and secretary were often one and the same person, who sometimes, indeed, acted as a kind of court factotum. We are apt to treat the small scale of these courts as a reason for dismissing them with a too ready contempt, forgetting that the highest spiritual things are not precisely matters of measurement.

Life and manners at the court of Rimini must have been a singular spectacle under the bold pagan *condottiere* Sigismondo Malatesta. He had a number of scholars around him, some of whom he provided for liberally, even giving them landed estates, while others earned at least a livelihood as officers in his army. In his citadel – *arx Sismundea* – they used to hold discussions, often of a very venomous kind, in the presence of the '*rex*', as they termed him. In their Latin poems they sing his praises and celebrate his amour with the fair Isotta, in whose honour and as whose monument the famous rebuilding of San Francesco at Rimini took place – '*Divae Isottae Sacrum*'. When the humanists themselves came to die, they were laid in or under the sarcophagi with which the niches of the outside walls of the church were adorned, with an inscription testifying that they were laid here at the time when Sigismundus, the son of Pandulfus, ruled.[62] It is hard for us nowadays to believe that a monster like this prince felt learning and the friendship of cultivated people to be a necessity of life; and yet the man who excommunicated him, made war upon him and burnt him in effigy, Pope Pius II, says: 'Sigismund knew history and had a great store of philosophy; he seemed born to all that he undertook.'

REPRODUCTION OF ANTIQUITY:
LETTER-WRITING AND LATIN SPEECHES

There were two purposes, however, for which the humanist was as indispensable to the republics as to princes or popes, namely, the official correspondence of the state, and the making of speeches on public and solemn occasions.

Not only was the secretary required to be a competent Latinist, but conversely, only a humanist was credited with the knowledge and ability necessary for the post of secretary. And thus the greatest men in the sphere of science during the fifteenth century mostly devoted a considerable part of their lives to serve the state in this capacity. No importance was attached to a man's home or origin. Of the four great Florentine secretaries who filled the office between 1427 and 1465, three belonged to the subject city of Arezzo, namely, Leonardo (Bruni), Carlo (Marzuppini) and Benedetto Accolti; Poggio was from Terra Nuova, also in Florentine territory. For a long period, indeed, many of the highest offices of state were on principle given to foreigners. Leonardo, Poggio and Giannozzo Manetti were at one time or another private secretaries to the popes, and Carlo Aretino was to have been so. Blondus of Forlì, and, in spite of everything, at last even Lorenzo Valla,[63] filled the same office. From the time of Nicholas V and Pius II onwards, the papal chancery continued more and more to attract the ablest men, and this was still the case even under the last popes of the fifteenth century, little as they cared for letters. In Platina's *History of the Popes*, the life of Paul II is a charming piece of vengeance taken by a humanist on the one pope who did not know how to behave to his chancery -- to that circle 'of poets and orators who bestowed on the papal court as much glory as they received from it'. It is delightful to see the indignation of these haughty gentlemen, when some squabble about precedence happened, when, for instance, the *advocati consistoriales* claimed equal or superior rank to theirs. The Apostle John, to whom the *secreta coelestia* were revealed; the secretary of Porsenna, whom Mucius Scaevola mistook for the king; Maecenas, who was private secretary to Augustus; the archbishops, who in Germany were called chancellors – are all appealed to in turn.

> The apostolic secretaries have the most weighty business of the world in their hands. For who but they decide on matters of the Catholic faith, who else combat heresy, re-establish peace, and mediate between great monarchs; who but they write the statistical accounts of Christendom? It is they who astonish kings, princes and nations by what comes forth from the pope. They write commands and instructions for the legates, and receive their orders only from the pope, on whom they wait day and night.

But the highest summit of glory was only attained by the two famous secretaries and stylists of Leo X: Pietro Bembo and Jacopo Sadoleto.

All the chanceries did not turn out equally elegant documents. A leathern official style, in the impurest of Latin, was very common. In the Milanese documents preserved by Corio there is a remarkable contrast between this sort of composition and the few letters written by members of the princely house, which must have been written, too, in moments of critical importance. They are models of pure Latinity. To maintain a faultless style under all circumstances was a rule of good breeding, and a result of habit.

The letters of Cicero, Pliny and others were at this time diligently studied as models. As early as the fifteenth century a mass of forms and instructions for Latin correspondence had appeared, as accessory to the great grammatical and lexicographic works, the mass of which is astounding to us even now when we look at them in the libraries. But just as the existence of these helps tempted many to undertake a task to which they had no vocation, so were the really capable men stimulated to a more faultless excellence, till at length the letters of Politian, and at the beginning of the sixteenth century those of Pietro Bembo, appeared, and took their place as unrivalled masterpieces, not only of Latin style in general, but also of the more special art of letter-writing.

Together with these there appeared in the sixteenth century the classical style of Italian correspondence, at the head of which stands Bembo again. Its form is wholly modern, and deliberately kept free from Latin influence, and yet its spirit is thoroughly penetrated and possessed by the ideas of antiquity.

But, at a time and among a people where 'listening' was among the chief pleasures of life, and where every imagination was filled with the memory of the Roman senate and its great speakers, the orator occupied a far more brilliant place than the letter-writer. Eloquence had shaken off the influence of the Church, in which it had found a refuge during the Middle Ages, and now became an indispensable element and ornament of all elevated lives. Many of the social hours which are now filled with music were then given to Latin or Italian oratory, with results which every reader can imagine.

The social position of the speaker was a matter of perfect indifference; what was desired was simply the most cultivated humanistic talent. At the court of Borso of Ferrara, the duke's physician, Jeronimo da Castello, was chosen to deliver the congratulatory address on the visits of Frederick III and of Pius II. Married laymen ascended the pulpits of the churches at any scene of festivity or mourning, and even on the feast-days of the saints. It struck the non-Italian members of the Council of Basel as something strange that the Archbishop of Milan should summon Aeneas Sylvius, who was then unordained, to deliver a public discourse at the feast of St Ambrogius; but they suffered it in spite of the murmurs of the theologians, and listened to the speaker with the greatest curiosity.

Let us glance for a moment at the most frequent and important occasions of public speaking.

It was not for nothing, in the first place, that the ambassadors from one state to another received the title of orators. Whatever else might be done in the way of secret negotiation, the envoy never failed to make a public appearance and deliver a public speech, under circumstances of the greatest possible pomp and ceremony. As a rule, however numerous the embassy might be, one individual spoke for all; but it happened to Pius II, a critic before whom all were glad to be heard, to be forced to sit and listen to a whole deputation, one after another. Learned princes who had the gift of speech were themselves fond of discoursing in Latin or Italian. The children of the House of Sforza were trained to this exercise. The boy Galeazzo Maria delivered in 1455 a fluent speech before the Great Council at Venice, and his sister Ippolita saluted Pope Pius II with a graceful address at the Congress of Mantua (1459). Pius himself through all his life did much by his oratory to prepare the way for his final elevation to the papal chair. Great as he was both as scholar and diplomatist, he would probably never have become pope without the fame and the charm of his eloquence. 'For nothing was more lofty than the dignity of his oratory.' Without doubt this was a reason why multitudes held him to be the fittest man for the office, even before his election.

Princes were also commonly received on public occasions with speeches, which sometimes lasted for hours. This happened of course only when the prince was known as a lover of eloquence,[64] or wished to pass for such, and when a competent speaker was present, whether university professor, official, ecclesiastic, physician or court-scholar.

Every other political opportunity was seized with the same eagerness, and according to the reputation of the speaker, the concourse of the lovers of culture was great or small. At the yearly change of public officers, and even at the consecration of new bishops, a humanist was sure to come forward, and sometimes addressed his audience in hexameters or Sapphic verses. Often a newly appointed official was himself forced to deliver a speech more or less relevant to his department, as, for instance, on justice; and lucky for him if he were well up in his part! At Florence even the *condottieri*, whatever their origin or education might be, were compelled to accommodate themselves to the popular sentiment, and on receiving the insignia of their office, were harangued before the assembled people by the most learned secretary of state. It seems that beneath or close to the Loggia dei Lanzi – the porch where the government was wont to appear solemnly before the people – a tribune or platform (*rostra, ringhiera*) was erected for such purposes.

Anniversaries, especially those of the death of princes, were commonly celebrated by memorial speeches. Even the funeral oration strictly so-called was generally entrusted to a humanist, who delivered it in church, clothed in a secular dress; nor was it only princes, but officials, or persons otherwise distinguished, to whom this honour was paid.[65] This was also the case with the speeches delivered at weddings or betrothals, with the difference that they seem to have been made in the palace, instead of in church, like that of Filelfo at the betrothal of Anna Sforza to Alfonso of Este in the castle of Milan. It is still possible that the ceremony may have taken place in the chapel of the castle. Private families of distinction no doubt also employed such wedding orators as one of the luxuries of high life. At Ferrara, Guarino was requested on these occasions to send some one or other of his pupils. The church simply took charge of the religious ceremonies at weddings and funerals.

The academical speeches, both those made at the installation of a new teacher and at the opening of a new course of lectures, were delivered by the professor himself, and treated as occasions of great rhetorical display. The ordinary university lectures also usually had an oratorical character.

With regard to forensic eloquence, the quality of the audience determined the form of speech. In case of need it was enriched with all sorts of philosophical and antiquarian learning.

As a special class of speeches we may mention the address made in Italian on the battlefield, either before or after the combat. Frederick of Urbino was esteemed a classic in this style; he used to pass round among his squadrons as they stood drawn up in order of battle, inspiring them in turn with pride and enthusiasm. Many of the speeches in the military historians of the fifteenth century, as for instance in Porcellius (p. 80), may be, in fact at least, imaginary, but may be also in part faithful representations of words actually spoken. The addresses again which were delivered to the Florentine militia, organized in 1506 chiefly through the influence of Machiavelli, and which were spoken first at reviews, and afterwards at special annual festivals, were of another kind. They were simply general appeals to the patriotism of the hearers, and were addressed to the assembled troops in the church of each quarter of the city by a citizen in armour, sword in hand.

Finally, the oratory of the pulpit began in the fifteenth century to lose its distinctive peculiarities. Many of the clergy had entered into the circle of classical culture and were ambitious of success in it. The street-preacher Bernardino da Siena, who even in his lifetime passed for a saint and who was worshipped by the populace, was not above taking lessons in rhetoric from the famous Guarino, although he had only to preach in Italian. Never indeed was more expected from preachers than at that time – especially from the Lenten preachers; and there were not a few audiences which could not only tolerate, but which demanded a strong dose of philosophy from the pulpit. But we have here especially to speak of the distinguished occasional preachers in Latin. Many of their opportunities had been taken away from them, as has been observed, by learned laymen. Speeches on particular saints' days, at weddings and funerals, or at the installation of a bishop, and even the introductory speech at the first mass of a clerical friend, or the address at the festival of some religious order, were all left to laymen. But at all events at the papal court in the fifteenth century, whatever the occasion might be, the preachers were generally monks. Under Sixtus IV, Giacomo da Volterra regularly enumerates these preachers, and criticizes them according to the rules of the art. Fedra Inghirami, famous as an orator under Julius II, had at least received holy orders and was canon at St John Lateran; and besides him, elegant Latinists were now common enough among the prelates. In this matter, as in others, the exaggerated privileges of the profane humanists appear lessened in the sixteenth century – on which point we shall presently speak more fully.

What now was the subject and general character of these speeches? The national gift of eloquence was not wanting to the Italians of the

Middle Ages, and a so-called 'rhetoric' belonged from the first to the seven liberal arts; but so far as the revival of the ancient methods is concerned, this merit must be ascribed, according to Filippo Villani, to the Florentine Bruno Casini, who died of the plague in 1348. With the practical purpose of fitting his countrymen to speak with ease and effect in public, he treated, after the pattern of the ancients, invention, declamation, bearing and gesticulation, each in its proper connection. Elsewhere too we read of an oratorical training directed solely to practical application. No accomplishment was more highly esteemed than the power of elegant improvisation in Latin. The growing study of Cicero's speeches and theoretical writings, of Quintilian and of the imperial panegyrists, the appearance of new and original treatises, the general progress of antiquarian learning, and the stores of ancient matter and thought which now could and must be drawn upon – all combined to shape the character of the new eloquence.

This character nevertheless differed widely according to the individual. Many speeches breathe a spirit of true eloquence, especially those which keep to the matter treated of; of this kind is the mass of what is left to us of Pius II. The miraculous effects produced by Giannozzo Manetti point to an orator the like of whom has not been often seen. His great audiences as envoy before Nicholas V and before the doge and Council of Venice were events not to be soon forgotten. Many orators, on the contrary, would seize the opportunity, not only to flatter the vanity of distinguished hearers, but to load their speeches with an enormous mass of antiquarian rubbish. How it was possible to endure this infliction for two and even three hours can only be understood when we take into account the intense interest then felt in everything connected with antiquity, and the rarity and defectiveness of treatises on the subject at a time when printing was but little diffused. Such orations had at least the value which we have claimed (p. 137) for many of Petrarch's letters. But some speakers went too far. Most of Filelfo's speeches are an atrocious patchwork of classical and biblical quotations, tacked on to a string of commonplaces, among which the great people he wishes to flatter are arranged under the head of the cardinal virtues, or some such category, and it is only with the greatest trouble, in his case and in that of many others, that we can extricate the few historical notices of value which they really contain. The speech, for instance, of a scholar and professor of Piacenza at the reception of the Duke Galeazzo Maria, in 1467, begins with Julius

Caesar, then proceeds to mix up a mass of classical quotations with a number from an allegorical work by the speaker himself, and concludes with some exceedingly indiscreet advice to the ruler. Fortunately it was late at night, and the orator had to be satisfied with handing his written panegyric to the prince. Filelfo begins a speech at a betrothal with the words: 'Aristotle, the peripatetic'. Others start with P. Cornelius Scipio, and the like, as though neither they nor their hearers could wait a moment for a quotation. At the end of the fifteenth century public taste suddenly improved, chiefly through Florentine influence, and the practice of quotation was restricted within due limits. Many works of reference were now in existence, in which the first comer could find as much as he wanted of what had hitherto been the admiration of princes and people.

As most of the speeches were written out beforehand in the study, the manuscripts served as a means of further publicity afterwards. The great extemporaneous speakers, on the other hand, were attended by shorthand writers. We must further remember that not all the orations which have come down to us were intended to be actually delivered. The panegyric, for example, of the elder Beroaldus on Lodovico il Moro was presented to him in manuscript. In fact, just as letters were written addressed to all conceivable persons and parts of the world as exercises, as formularies, or even to serve a controversial end, so there were speeches for imaginary occasions to be used as models for the reception of princes, bishops and other dignitaries.

For oratory, as for the other arts, the death of Leo X (1521) and the sack of Rome (1527) mark the epoch of decadence. Giovio, just escaped from the desolation of the eternal city, describes, not exhaustively, but on the whole truly, the causes of this decline.

The plays of Plautus and Terence, once a school of Latin style for the educated Romans, are banished to make room for Italian comedies. Graceful speakers no longer find the recognition and reward which they once did. The consistorial advocates no longer prepare anything but the introductions to their speeches, and deliver the rest – a confused muddle – on the inspiration of the moment. Sermons and occasional speeches have sunk to the same level. If a funeral oration is wanted for a cardinal or other great personage, the executors do not apply to the best orators in the city, to whom they would have to pay a hundred pieces of gold, but they hire for a trifle the first impudent pendant whom they come across, and who only wants to be talked of whether for good or

ill. The dead, they say, is none the wiser if an ape stands in a black dress
in the pulpit, and beginning with a hoarse, whimpering mumble, passes
little by little into a loud howling. Even the sermons preached at great
papal ceremonies are no longer profitable, as they used to be. Monks of
all orders have again got them into their hands, and preach as if they
were speaking to the mob. Only a few years ago a sermon at mass
before the pope might easily lead the way to a bishopric.

THE TREATISE, AND HISTORY IN LATIN

From the oratory and the epistolary writings of the humanists we shall
here pass on to their other creations, which were all, to a greater or less
extent, reproductions of antiquity.

Among these must be placed the treatise, which often took the
shape of a dialogue. In this case it was borrowed directly from Cicero.
In order to do anything like justice to this class of literature – in order
not to throw it aside at first sight as a bore – two things must be taken
into consideration. The century which escaped from the influence of
the Middle Ages felt the need of something to mediate between itself
and antiquity in many questions of morals and philosophy; and this
need was met by the writer of treatises and dialogues. Much which
appears to us as mere commonplace in their writings was for them and
their contemporaries a new and hardly won view of things upon
which mankind had been silent since the days of antiquity. The
language too, in this form of writing, whether Italian or Latin, moved
more freely and flexibly than in historical narrative, in letters or in
oratory, and thus became in itself the source of a special pleasure.
Several Italian compositions of this kind still hold their place as
patterns of style. Many of these works have been or will be mentioned
on account of their contents; we here refer to them as a class. From the
time of Petrarch's letters and treatises down to near the end of the
fifteenth century, the heaping up of learned quotations, as in the case
of the orators, is the main business of most of these writers. The whole
style, especially in Italian, was then suddenly clarified, till, in the
Asolani of Bembo, and the *Vita Sobria* of Luigi Cornaro, a classical
perfection was reached. Here too the decisive fact was that antiquarian
matter of every kind had meantime begun to be deposited in
encyclopedic works (now printed), and no longer stood in the way of
the essayist.

It was inevitable too that the humanistic spirit should control the writing of history. A superficial comparison of the histories of this period with the earlier chronicles, especially with works so full of life, colour and brilliancy as those of the Villani, will lead us loudly to deplore the change. How insipid and conventional appear by their side the best of the humanists, and particularly their immediate and most famous successors among the historians of Florence, Leonardo, Aretino and Poggio! The enjoyment of the reader is incessantly marred by the sense that, in the classical phrases of Facius, Sabellicus, Folieta, Senarega, Platina in the chronicles of Mantua, Bembo in the annals of Venice, and even of Giovio in his histories, the best local and individual colouring and the full sincerity of interest in the truth of events have been lost. Our mistrust is increased when we hear that Livy, the pattern of this school of writers, was copied just where he is least worthy of imitation – on the ground, namely, 'that he turned a dry and naked tradition into grace and richness'. In the same place we meet with the suspicious declaration that it is the function of the historian – just as if he were one with the poet – to excite, charm or overwhelm the reader. We ask ourselves, finally, whether the contempt for modern things, which these same humanists sometimes avowed openly, must not necessarily have had an unfortunate influence on their treatment of them. Unconsciously the reader finds himself looking with more interest and confidence on the unpretending Latin and Italian annalists, like those of Bologna and Ferrara, who remained true to the old style, and still more grateful does he feel to the best of the genuine chroniclers who wrote in Italian – to Marin Sanudo, Corio and Infessura – who were followed at the beginning of the sixteenth century by that new and illustrious band of great national historians who wrote in their mother tongue.

Contemporary history, no doubt, was written far better in the language of the day than when forced into Latin. Whether Italian was also more suitable for the narrative of events long past, or for historical research, is a question which admits, for that period, of more answers than one. Latin was, at that time, the lingua franca of instructed people, not only in an international sense, as a means of intercourse between Englishmen, Frenchmen and Italians, but also in an inter-provincial sense. The Lombard, the Venetian and the Neapolitan modes of writing, though long modelled on the Tuscan, and bearing but slight traces of the dialect, were still not recognized by the

Florentines. This was of less consequence in local contemporary histories, which were sure of readers at the place where they were written, than in the narratives of the past, for which a larger public was desired. In these the local interests of the people had to be sacrificed to the general interests of the learned. How far would the influence of a man like Blondus of Forlì have reached if he had written his great monuments of learning in the dialect of the Romagna? They would have assuredly sunk into neglect, if only through the contempt of the Florentines, while written in Latin they exercised the profoundest influence on the whole European world of learning. And even the Florentines in the fifteenth century wrote Latin, not only because their minds were imbued with humanism, but in order to be more widely read.

Finally, there exist certain Latin essays in contemporary history, which stand on a level with the best Italian works of the kind. When the continuous narrative after the manner of Livy – that Procrustean bed of so many writers – is abandoned, the change is marvellous. The same Platina and Giovio, whose great histories we only read because and so far as we must, suddenly come forward as masters in the biographical style. We have already spoken of Tristan Caracciolo, of the biographical works of Facius and of the Venetian topography of Sabellico, and others will be mentioned in the sequel.

The Latin treatises on past history were naturally concerned, for the most part, with classical antiquity. What we are most surprised to find among these humanists are some considerable works on the history of the Middle Ages. The first of this kind was the chronicle of Matteo Palmieri (449–1449), beginning where Prosper Aquitanus ceases. On opening the *Decades* of Blondus of Forlì, we are surprised to find a universal history, '*ab inclinatione Romanorum imperii*', as in Gibbon, full of original studies on the authors of each century, and occupied, through the first 300 folio pages, with early medieval history down to the death of Frederick II. And this when in northern countries nothing more was wanted than chronicles of the popes and emperors, and the *fasciculus temporum*. We cannot here stay to show what writings Blondus made use of, and where he found his materials, though this justice will some day be done to him by the historians of literature. This book alone would entitle us to say that it was the study of antiquity which made the study of the Middle Ages possible, by first training the mind to habits of impartial historical criticism. To this must be added that the Middle Ages were now over for Italy, and that the Italian mind could the better appreciate them, because it stood outside them. It cannot, nevertheless, be said that it at once judged them fairly, and still less that it judged them with piety. In art a fixed prejudice showed itself against all that those centuries had created, and the humanists date the new era from the time of their own appearance. 'I begin,' says Boccaccio, 'to hope and believe that God has had mercy on the Italian name, since I see that His infinite goodness puts souls into the breasts of the Italians like those of the ancients – souls which seek fame by other means than robbery and violence, but rather on the path of poetry, which makes men immortal.' But this narrow and unjust temper did not preclude investigation in the minds of the more gifted men, at a time, too, when elsewhere in Europe any such investigation would have been out of the question. A historical criticism of the Middle Ages was practicable just because the rational treatment of all subjects by the humanists had trained the historical spirit. In the fifteenth century this spirit had so far penetrated the history even of the individual cities of Italy that the stupid fairy tales about the origin of Florence, Venice and Milan vanished, while at the same time, and long after, the chronicles of the North were stuffed with this fantastic rubbish, destitute for the most part of all poetical value, and invented as late as the fourteenth century.

The close connection between local history and the sentiment of glory has already been touched on in reference to Florence. Venice would not be behindhand. Just as a great rhetorical triumph of the Florentines would cause a Venetian embassy to write home post-haste for an orator to be sent after them, so too the Venetians felt the need of a history which would bear comparison with those of Leonardo, Aretino and Poggio. And it was to satisfy this feeling that, in the fifteenth century, the *Decades* of Sabellico appeared, and in the sixteenth the *Historia rerum Venetarum* of Pietro Bembo, both written at the express charge of the republic, the latter a continuation of the former.

The great Florentine historians at the beginning of the sixteenth century were men of a wholly different kind from the Latinists Bembo and Giovio. They wrote Italian, not only because they could not vie with the Ciceronian elegance of the philologists, but because, like Machiavelli, they could only record in a living tongue the living results of their own immediate observations – and we may add in the case of Machiavelli, of his observation of the past – and because, as in the case of Guicciardini, Varchi and many others, what they most desired was that their view of the course of events should have as wide and deep a practical effect as possible. Even when they only write for a few friends, like Francesco Vettori, they feel an inward need to utter their testimony on men and events, and to explain and justify their share in the latter.

And yet, with all that is characteristic in their language and style, they were powerfully affected by antiquity, and, without its influence, would be inconceivable. They were not humanists, but they had passed through the school of humanism, and they have in them more of the spirit of the ancient historians than most of the imitators of Livy. Like the ancients, they were citizens who wrote for citizens.

ANTIQUITY AS THE COMMON SOURCE

We cannot attempt to trace the influence of humanism in the special sciences. Each has its own history, in which the Italian investigators of this period, chiefly through their rediscovery of the results attained by antiquity, mark a new epoch, with which the modern period of the science in question begins with more or less distinctness. With regard to philosophy, too, we must refer the reader to the special historical works on the subject. The influence of the old philosophers on Italian culture will appear at times immense, at times inconsiderable; the former, when we consider how the doctrines of Aristotle, chiefly drawn from the *Ethics* and *Politics* – both widely diffused at an early period – became the common property of educated Italians, and how the whole method of abstract thought was governed by him; the latter, when we remember how slight was the dogmatic influence of the old philosophies, and even of the enthusiastic Florentine Platonists, on the spirit of the people at large. What looks like such an influence is generally no more than a consequence of the new culture in general, and of the special growth and development of the Italian mind. When we come to speak of religion, we shall have more to say on this head. But in by far the greater number of cases, we have to do, not with the general culture of the people, but with the utterances of individuals or of learned circles; and here, too, a distinction must be drawn between the true assimilation of ancient doctrines and fashionable make-believe. For with many antiquity was only a fashion, even among very learned people.

Nevertheless, all that looks like affectation to our age need not then have actually been so. The giving of Greek and Latin names to children, for example, is better and more respectable than the present practice of taking them, especially the female names, from novels. When the enthusiasm for the ancient world was greater than for the saints, it was simple and natural enough that noble families called their sons Agamemnon, Tydeus and Achilles, and that a painter named his son Apelles and his daughter Minerva.[66] Nor will it appear unreasonable that, instead of a family name, which people were often glad to get rid of, a well-sounding ancient name was chosen. A local name, shared by all residents in the place, and not yet transformed into a family name, was willingly given up, especially when its religious associations made it inconvenient; Filippo da San Gimignano called himself Callimachus. The man, misunderstood and insulted by his family, who made his fortune as a scholar in foreign cities, could afford, even if he were a Sanseverino, to change his name to Julius Pomponius Laetus. Even the simple translation of a name into Latin or Greek, as was almost uniformly the custom in Germany, may be excused to a generation which spoke and wrote Latin, and which needed names that could be not only declined, but used with facility in verse and prose. What was blameworthy and ridiculous was the change of half a name, baptismal or family, to give it a classical sound and a new sense. Thus Giovanni was turned into Jovianus or Janus, Pietro to Petreius or Pierius, Antonio to Aonius, Sannazaro to Syncerus, Luca Grasso to Lucius Crassus. Ariosto, who speaks with such derision of all this, lived to see children called after his own heroes and heroines.

Nor must we judge too severely the Latinization of many usages of social life, such as the titles of officials, of ceremonies and the like, in the writers of the period. As long as people were satisfied with a simple, fluent Latin style, as was the case with most writers from Petrarch to Aeneas Sylvius, this practice was not so frequent and striking; it became inevitable when a faultless, Ciceronian Latin was demanded. Modern names and things no longer harmonized with the style, unless they were first artificially changed. Pedants found a pleasure in addressing municipal counsellors as 'patres conscripti', nuns as 'virgines vestales', and entitling every saint 'divus' or 'deus'; but men of better taste, such as Paolo Giovio, only did so when and because they could not help it. But as Giovio does it naturally, and lays no special stress upon it, we are not offended if, in his melodious language, the cardinals appear as *senatores*, their dean as *princeps senatus*, excommunication as *dirae*, and the carnival as *lupercalia*. This example of this author alone is enough to warn us against drawing a hasty inference from these peculiarities of style as to the writer's whole mode of thinking.

The history of Latin composition cannot here be traced in detail. For fully two centuries the humanists acted as if Latin were, and must remain, the only language worthy to be written. Poggio deplores that Dante wrote his great poem in Italian; and Dante, as is well known, actually made the attempt in Latin, and wrote the beginning of the *Inferno* first in hexameters. The whole future of Italian poetry hung on his not continuing in the same style, but even Petrarch relied more on his Latin poetry than on the Sonnets and *Canzoni*, and Ariosto himself was desired by some to write his poem in Latin. A stronger coercion never existed in literature; but poetry shook it off for the most part, and it may be said, without the risk of too great optimism, that it was well for Italian poetry to have had both means of expressing itself. In both something great and characteristic was achieved, and in each we can see the reason why Latin or Italian was chosen. Perhaps the same may be said of prose. The position and influence of Italian culture throughout the world depended on the fact that certain subjects were treated in Latin – *urbi et orbi* – while Italian prose was written best of all by those to whom it cost an inward struggle not to write in Latin.

From the fourteenth century Cicero was recognized universally as the purest model of prose. This was by no means due solely to a dispassionate opinion in favour of his choice of language, of the structure of his sentences and of his style of composition, but rather to the fact that the Italian spirit responded fully and instinctively to the amiability of the letter-writer, to the brilliancy of the orator, and to the lucid exposition of the philosophical thinker. Even Petrarch recognized clearly the weakness of Cicero as a man and a statesman, though he respected him too much to rejoice over them. After Petrarch's time, the epistolary style was formed entirely on the pattern of Cicero; and the rest, with the exception of the narrative style, followed the same influence. Yet the true Ciceronianism, which rejected every phrase which could not be justified out of the great authority, did not appear till the end of the fifteenth century, when the grammatical writings of Lorenzo Valla had begun to tell on all Italy, and when the opinions of the Roman historians of literature had been sifted and compared. Then every shade of difference in the style of the ancients was studied with closer and closer attention till the consoling conclusion was at last reached that in Cicero alone was the perfect model to be found, or, if all forms of literature were to be embraced, in 'that immortal and almost heavenly age of Cicero'. Men like Pietro Bembo and Pierio Valeriano now turned all their energies to this one object. Even those who had long resisted the tendency, and had formed for themselves an archaic style from the earlier authors, yielded at last, and joined in the worship of Cicero. Longolius, at Bembo's advice, determined to read nothing but Cicero for five years long, and finally took an oath to use no word which did not occur in this author. It was this temper which broke out at last in the great war among the scholars, in which Erasmus and the elder Scaliger led the battle.

For all the admirers of Cicero were by no means so one-sided as to consider him the only source of language. In the fifteenth century, Politian and Ermolao Barbaro made a conscious and deliberate effort to form a style of their own, naturally on the basis of their 'overflowing' learning, and our informant of this fact, Paolo Giovio, pursued the same end. He first attempted, not always successfully, but often with remarkable power and elegance, and at no small cost of effort, to reproduce in Latin a number of modern, particularly aesthetic, ideas. His Latin characteristics of the great painters and sculptors of his time contain a mixture of the most intelligent and the most blundering interpretation.[67] Even Leo X, who placed his glory in the fact, '*ut lingua latina nostro pontificatu dicatur facta auctior*', was inclined to a liberal and not too exclusive Latinity, which, indeed, was in harmony with his pleasure-loving nature. He was satisfied when the Latin which he had to read and hear was lively, elegant and idiomatic. Then, too, Cicero offered no model for Latin conversation, so that here other gods had to be worshipped beside him. The want was supplied by representations of the comedies of Plautus and Terence, frequent both in and out of Rome, which for the actors were an incomparable exercise in Latin as the language of daily life. A few years later, in the pontificate of Paul II, the learned Cardinal of Teano (probably Niccolò Forteguerra of Pistoia) became famous for his critical labours in this branch of scholarship. He set to work upon the most defective plays of Plautus, which were destitute even of the list of the characters, and went carefully through the whole remains of this author, chiefly with an eye to the language. Possibly it was he who gave the first impulse for the public representations of these plays. Afterwards Pomponius Laetus took up the same subject, and acted as manager when Plautus was put on the stage in the houses of great churchmen. That these representations became less common after 1520 is mentioned by Giovio, as we have seen, among the causes of the decline of eloquence.

We may mention, in conclusion, the analogy between Ciceronianism in literature and the revival of Vitruvius[68] by the architects in the sphere of art. And here, too, the law holds good which prevails elsewhere in the history of the Renaissance, that each artistic movement is preceded by a corresponding movement in the general culture of the age. In this case, the interval is not more than about twenty years, if we reckon from Cardinal Adrian of Corneto (1505?) to the first avowed Vitruvians.

NEO-LATIN POETRY

The chief pride of the humanists is, however, their modern Latin poetry. It lies within the limits of our task to treat of it, at least in so far as it serves to characterize the humanist movement.

How favourable public opinion was to that form of poetry, and how nearly it supplanted all others, has been already shown. We may be very sure that the most gifted and highly developed nation then existing in the world did not renounce the use of a language such as the Italian out of mere folly and without knowing what they were doing. It must have been a weighty reason which led them to do so.

This cause was the devotion to antiquity. Like all ardent and genuine devotion it necessarily prompted men to imitation. At other times and among other nations we find many isolated attempts of the same kind. But only in Italy were the two chief conditions present which were needful for the continuance and development of neo-Latin poetry: a general interest in the subject among the instructed classes, and a partial re-awakening of the old Italian genius among the poets themselves – the wondrous echo of a far-off strain. The best of what is produced under these conditions is not imitation, but free production. If we decline to tolerate any borrowed forms in art, if we either set no value on antiquity at all, or attribute to it some magical and unapproachable virtue, or if we will pardon no slips in poets who were forced, for instance, to guess or to discover a multitude of syllabic quantities, then we had better let this class of literature alone. Its best works were not created in order to defy criticism, but to give pleasure to the poet and to thousands of his contemporaries.

The least success of all was attained by the epic narratives drawn from the history or legends of antiquity. The essential conditions of a living epic poetry were denied, not only to the Romans who now served as models, but even to the Greeks after Homer. They could not be looked for among the Latins of the Renaissance. And yet the *Africa* of Petrarch probably found as many and as enthusiastic readers and hearers as any epos of modern times. The purpose and origin of the poem are not without interest. The fourteenth century recognized with sound historical tact the time of the second Punic war as the noonday of Roman greatness; and Petrarch could not resist writing of this time. Had Silius Italicus been then discovered, Petrarch would probably have chosen another subject; but, as it was, the glorification of Scipio Africanus the Elder was so much in accordance with the spirit of the fourteenth century that another poet, Zanobi di Strada, also proposed to himself the same task, and only from respect for Petrarch withdrew the poem with which he had already made great progress. If any justification were needed for the *Africa*, it lies in the fact that in Petrarch's time and afterwards Scipio was as much an object of public interest as if he were then alive, and that he was held by many to be a greater man than Alexander, Pompey and Caesar. How many modern epics treat of a subject at once so popular, so historical in its basis, and so striking to the imagination? For us, it is true, the poem is unreadable. For other themes of the same kind the reader may be referred to the histories of literature.

A richer and more fruitful vein was discovered in expanding and completing the Greco-Roman mythology. In this too Italian poetry began early to take a part, beginning with the *Teseide* of Boccaccio, which passes for his best poetical work. Under Martin V, Maffeo Vegio wrote in Latin a thirteenth book to the *Aeneid*; besides which we meet with many less considerable attempts, especially in the style of Claudian – a *Meleagris*, a *Hesperis*, and so forth. Still more curious were the newly invented myths, which peopled the fairest regions of Italy with a primeval race of gods, nymphs, genii and even shepherds, the epic and bucolic styles here passing into one another. In the narrative or conversational eclogue after the time of Petrarch, pastoral life was treated in a purely conventional manner, as a vehicle of all possible feelings and fancies; and this point will be touched on again in the sequel. For the moment, we have only to do with the new myths. In them, more clearly than anywhere else, we see the double significance of the old gods to the men of the Renaissance. On the one hand they replace abstract terms in poetry, and render allegorical figures superfluous; and, on the other, they serve as free and independent elements in art, as forms of beauty which can be turned to some account in any and every poem. The example was boldly set by Boccaccio, with his fanciful world of gods and shepherds who people the country round Florence in his *Ninfale d'Ameto* and *Ninfale Fiesolano*. Both these poems were written in Italian. But the masterpiece in this style was the *Sarca* of Pietro Bembo, which tells how the river-god of that name wooed the nymph Garda; of the brilliant marriage feast in a cave of Monte Baldo; of the prophecies of Manto, daughter of Tiresias; of the birth of the child Mincius; of the founding of Mantua, and of the future glory of Virgil, son of Mincius and of Maia, nymph of Andes. This humanistic rococo is set forth by Bembo in verses of great beauty, concluding with an address to Virgil, which any poet might envy him. Such works are often slighted as mere declamation. This is a matter of taste on which we are all free to form our own opinion.

Further, we find long epic poems in hexameters on biblical or ecclesiastical subjects. The authors were by no means always in search of preferment or of papal favour. With the best of them, and even with less gifted writers, like Battista Mantovano, the author of the *Parthenice*, there was probably an honest desire to serve religion by their Latin verses – a desire with which their half-pagan conception of Catholicism harmonized well enough. Gyraldus goes through a list of these poets, among whom Vida, with his *Christiad,* and Sannazaro, with his three books, *De partu virginis,* hold the first place. Sannazaro (b. 1458, d. 1530) is impressive by the steady and powerful flow of his verse, in which Christian and pagan elements are mingled without scruple, by the plastic vigour of his description, and by the perfection of his workmanship. He could venture to introduce Virgil's fourth eclogue into his song of the shepherds at the manger without fearing a comparison. In treating of the unseen world, he sometimes gives proofs of a boldness worthy of Dante, as when King David in the Limbo of the Patriarchs rises up to sing and prophesy, or when the Eternal, sitting on the throne clad in a mantle shining with pictures of all the elements, addresses the heavenly host. At other times he does not hesitate to weave the whole classical mythology into his subject, yet without spoiling the harmony of the whole, since the pagan deities are only accessory figures, and play no important part in the story. To appreciate the artistic genius of that age in all its bearings, we must not refuse to notice such works as these. The merit of Sannazaro will appear the greater, when we consider that the mixture of Christian and pagan elements is apt to disturb us much more in poetry than in the plastic arts. The latter can still satisfy the eye by beauty of form and colour, and in general are much more independent of the signifi-cance of the subject than poetry. With them, the imagination is interested chiefly in the form, with poetry, in the matter. Honest Battista Mantovano in his calendar of the festivals tried another expedi-ent. Instead of making the gods and demigods serve the purposes of sacred history, he put them, as the fathers of the Church did, in active opposition to it. When the angel Gabriel salutes the Virgin at Nazareth, Mercury flies after him from Carmel, and listens at the door. He then announces the result of his eavesdropping to the assembled gods, and stimulates them thereby to desperate resolutions. Elsewhere, it is true, in his writings, Thetis, Ceres, Aeolus and other pagan deities pay willing homage to the glory of the Madonna.

The fame of Sannazaro, the number of his imitators, the enthusiastic homage which was paid to him by the greatest men, all show how dear and necessary he was to his age. On the threshold of the Reforma-tion he solved for the Church the problem of whether it were possible for a poet to be a Christian as well as a classic; and both Leo and Clement were loud in their thanks for his achievements.

And, finally, contemporary history was now treated in hexameters or distichs, sometimes in a narrative and sometimes in a panegyrical style, but most commonly to the honour of some prince or princely family. We thus meet with a *Sforziad*, a *Borseid*, a *Laurentiad*, a *Borgiad*, a *Trivulziad* and the like. The object sought after was certainly not attained; for those who became famous and are now immortal owe it to anything rather than to this sort of poem, for which the world has always had an ineradicable dislike, even when they happen to be written by good poets. A wholly different effect is produced by smaller, simpler and more unpretentious scenes from the lives of distinguished men, such as the beautiful poem on Leo X's 'Hunt at Palo', or the 'Journey of Julius II' by Adrian of Corneto. Brilliant descriptions of hunting-parties are found in Ercole Strozzi, in the above-mentioned Adrian, and in others; and it is a pity that the modern reader should allow himself to be irritated or repelled by the adulation with which they are doubtless filled. The masterly treatment and the considerable historical value of many of these most graceful poems, guarantee to them a longer existence than many popular works of our own day are likely to attain.

In general, these poems are good in proportion to the sparing use of the sentimental and the general. Some of the smaller epic poems, even of recognized masters, unintentionally produce, by the ill-timed introduction of mythological elements, an impression that is indescribably ludicrous. Such, for instance, is the lament of Ercole Strozzi on Cesare Borgia. We there listen to the complaint of Rome, who had set all her hopes on the Spanish popes, Calixtus III and Alexander VI, and who saw her promised deliverer in Cesare. His history is related down to the catastrophe of 1503. The poet then asks the muse what were the counsels of the gods at that moment, and Erato tells how, upon Olympus, Pallas took the part of the Spaniards, Venus of the Italians, how both then embrace the knees of Jupiter, how thereupon he kisses them, soothes them, and explains to them that he can do nothing against the fate woven by the Parcae, but that the divine promises will be fulfilled by the child of the House of Este-Borgia. After relating the fabulous origin of both families, he declares that he can confer immortality on Cesare as little as he could once, in spite of all entreaties, on Memnon or Achilles; and concludes with the consoling assurance that Cesare, before his own death, will destroy many people in war. Mars then hastens to Naples to stir up war and confusion, while Pallas goes to Nepi, and there appears to the dying Cesare under the form of Alexander VI. After giving him the good advice to submit to his fate and be satisfied with the glory of his name, the papal goddess vanishes 'like a bird'.

Yet we should needlessly deprive ourselves of an enjoyment, which is sometimes very great, if we threw aside everything in which classical mythology plays a more or less appropriate part. Here, as in painting and sculpture, art has often ennobled what is in itself purely conventional. The beginnings of parody are also to be found by lovers of that class of literature, e.g. in the *Macaroneid* – to which the comic *Feast of the Gods*, by Giovanni Bellini, forms an early parallel.

Many, too, of the narrative poems in hexameters are merely exercises, or adaptations of histories in prose, which latter the reader will prefer, where he can find them. At last, everything – every quarrel and every ceremony – came to be put into verse, and this even by the German humanists of the Reformation. And yet it would be unfair to attribute this to mere want of occupation, or to an excessive facility in stringing verses together. In Italy, at all events, it was rather due to an abundant sense of style, as is further proved by the mass of contemporary reports, histories, and even pamphlets, in the *terza rima*. Just as Niccolò da Uzzano published his scheme for a new constitution, Machiavelli his view of the history of his own time, a third, the life of Savonarola, and a fourth, the siege of Piombino by Alfonso the Great, in this difficult metre, in order to produce a stronger effect, so did many others feel the need of hexameters in order to win their special public. What was then tolerated and demanded, in this shape, is best shown by the didactic poetry of the time. Its popularity in the fifteenth century is something astounding. The most distinguished humanists were ready to celebrate in Latin hexameters the most commonplace, ridiculous or disgusting themes, such as the making of gold, the game of chess, the management of silkworms, astrology, and venereal diseases (*morbus gallicus*), to say nothing of many long Italian poems of the same kind. Nowadays this class of poem is condemned unread, and how far, as a matter of fact, they are really worth the reading, we are unable to say. One thing is certain, the epochs far above our own in the sense of beauty – the Renaissance and the Greco-Roman world – could not dispense with this form of poetry. It may be urged in reply that it is not the lack of a sense of beauty, but the greater seriousness and the altered method of scientific treatment which renders the poetical form inappropriate, on which point it is unnecessary to enter.

One of these didactic works has of late years been occasionally republished – the *Zodiac of Life*, by Marcellus Palingenius (Pier Angelo Manzolli), a secret adherent of Protestantism at Ferrara, written about 1528. With the loftiest speculations on God, virtue and immortality, the writer connects the discussion of many questions of practical life, and is, on this account, an authority of some weight in the history of morals. On the whole, however, his work must be considered as lying outside the boundaries of the Renaissance, as is further indicated by the fact that, in harmony with the serious didactic purpose of the poem, allegory tends to supplant mythology.

But it was in lyric, and more particularly in elegiac, poetry that the poet-scholar came nearest to antiquity; and next to this, in epigram.

In the lighter style, Catullus exercised a perfect fascination over the Italians. Not a few elegant Latin madrigals, not a few little satires and malicious epistles are mere adaptations from him; and the death of parrots and lapdogs is bewailed, even where there is no verbal imitation, in precisely the tone and style of the verses on Lesbia's sparrow. There are short poems of this sort, the date of which even a critic would be unable to fix, in the absence of positive evidence that they are works of the fifteenth and sixteenth centuries.

On the other hand, we can find scarcely an ode in the Sapphic or Alcaic metre which does not clearly betray its modern origin. This is shown mostly by a rhetorical verbosity, rare in antiquity before the time of Statius, and by a singular want of the lyrical concentration which is indispensable to this style of poetry. Single passages in an ode, sometimes two or three strophes together, may look like an ancient fragment; but a longer extract will seldom keep this character throughout. And where it does so, as, for instance, in the fine 'Ode to Venus', by Andrea Navagero, it is easy to detect a simple paraphrase of ancient masterpieces. Some of the ode-writers take the saints for their subject, and invoke them in verses tastefully modelled after the pattern of analogous odes of Horace and Catullus. This is the manner of Navagero, in the 'Ode to the Archangel Gabriel', and particularly of Sannazaro (p. 170), who goes still further in his appropriation of pagan sentiment. He celebrates above all his patron saint, whose chapel was attached to his lovely villa on the shores of Posillipo, 'there where the waves of the sea drink up the stream from the rocks, and surge against the walls of the little sanctuary'. His delight is in the annual feast of St Nazzaro, and the branches and garlands with which the chapel is hung on this day seem to him like sacrificial gifts. Full of sorrow, and far off in exile, at St Nazaire, on the banks of the Loire, with the banished Federigo of Aragon, he brings wreaths of box and oak leaves to his patron saint on the same anniversary, thinking of former years, when all the youth of Posillipo used to come forth to greet him on flower-hung boats, and praying that he may return home.

Perhaps the most deceptive likeness to the classical style is borne by a class of poems in elegiacs or hexameters, whose subject ranges from elegy, strictly so-called, to epigram. As the humanists dealt most freely of all with the text of the Roman elegiac poets, so they felt themselves most at home in imitating them. The elegy of Navagero addressed to the night, like other poems of the same age and kind, is full of points which remind us of his model; but it has the finest antique ring about it. Indeed Navagero always begins by choosing a truly poetical subject, which he then treats, not with servile imitation, but with masterly freedom, in the style of the Anthology, of Ovid, of Catullus, or of the Virgilian eclogues. He makes a sparing use of mythology, only, for instance, to introduce a sketch of country life, in a prayer to Ceres and other rural divinities. An address to his country, on his return from an embassy to Spain, though left unfinished, might have been worthy of a place beside the 'Bella Italia, amate sponde' of Vincenzo Monti, if the rest had been equal to this beginning:

> Salve cura Deûm, mundi felicior ora,
> Formosae Veneris dulces salvete recessus;
> Ut vos post tantos animi mentisque labores
> Aspicio lustroque libens, ut munere vestro
> Sollicitas toto depello e pectore curas!

The elegiac or hexametral form was that in which all higher sentiment found expression, both the noblest patriotic enthusiasm and the most elaborate eulogies on the ruling houses, as well as the tender melancholy of a Tibullus. Francesco Mario Molza, who rivals Statius and Martial in his flattery of Clement VII and the Farnesi, gives us in his elegy to his 'comrades', written from a sick-bed, thoughts on death as beautiful and genuinely antique as can be found in any of the poets of antiquity, and this without borrowing anything worth speaking of from them. The spirit and range of the Roman elegy were best understood and reproduced by Sannazaro, and no other writer of his time offers us so varied a choice of good poems in this style as he. We shall have occasion now and then to speak of some of these elegies in reference to the matter they treat of.

The Latin epigram finally became in those days an affair of serious importance, since a few clever lines, engraved on a monument or quoted with laughter in society, could lay the foundation of a scholar's celebrity. This tendency showed itself early in Italy. When it was known that Guido da Polenta wished to erect a monument at Dante's grave, epitaphs poured in from all directions, 'written by such as wished to *show themselves*, or to honour the dead poet, or to win the favour of Polenta'. On the tomb of the Archbishop Giovanni Visconti (d. 1354) in the cathedral at Milan, we read at the foot of thirty-six hexameters: 'Master Gabrius de Zamoreis of Parma, Doctor of Laws, wrote these verses.' In course of time, chiefly under the influence of Martial, and partly of Catullus, an extensive literature of this sort was formed. It was held the greatest of all triumphs when an epigram was mistaken for a genuine copy from some old marble, or when it was so good that all Italy learned it by heart, as happened in the case of some of Bembo's. When the Venetian government paid Sannazaro 600 ducats for a eulogy in three distichs, no one thought it an act of generous prodigality. The epigram was prized for what it was, in truth, to all the educated classes of that age – the concentrated essence of fame. Nor, on the other hand, was any man then so powerful as to be above the reach of a satirical epigram, and even the most powerful needed, for every inscription which they set before the public eye, the aid of careful and learned scholars, lest some blunder or other should qualify it for a place in the collections of ludicrous epitaphs. The epigraph and the epigram were branches of the same pursuit; the reproduction of the former was based on a diligent study of ancient monuments.

The city of epigrams and inscriptions was, above all others, Rome. In this state without hereditary honours, each man had to look after his own immortality, and at the same time found the epigram an effective weapon against his competitors. Pius II counts with satisfaction the distichs which his chief poet Campanus wrote on any event of his government which could be turned to poetical account. Under the following popes satirical epigrams came into fashion, and reached, in the opposition to Alexander VI and his family, the highest pitch of defiant invective. Sannazaro, it is true, wrote his verses in a place of comparative safety, but others in the immediate neighbourhood of the court ventured on the most reckless attacks. On one occasion when eight threatening distichs were found fastened to the doors of the library, Alexander strengthened his guard by 800 men; we can imagine what he would have done to the poet if he had caught him. Under Leo X, Latin epigrams were like daily bread. For complimenting or for reviling the pope, for punishing enemies and victims, named or unnamed, for real or imaginary subjects of wit, malice, grief or contemplation, no form was held more suitable. On the famous group of the *Virgin with St Anne and the Child*, which Andrea Sansovino carved for Sant' Agostino, no fewer than 120 persons wrote Latin verses, not so much, it is true, from devotion, as from regard for the patron who ordered the work. This man, Johann Goritz of

Luxemburg, papal referendary of petitions, not only held a religious service on the feast of St Anne, but gave a great literary dinner in his garden on the slopes of the Capitol. It was then worth while to pass in review, in a long poem *De poetis urbanis*, the whole crowd of singers who sought their fortune at the court of Leo. This was done by Franciscus Arsillus – a man who needed the patronage neither of pope nor prince, and who dared to speak his mind, even against his colleagues. The epigram survived the pontificate of Paul III only in a few rare echoes, while the epigraph continued to flourish till the seventeenth century, when it perished finally of bombast.

In Venice, also, this form of poetry had a history of its own, which we are able to trace with the help of the *Venezia* of Francesco Sansovino. A standing task for the epigram-writers was offered by the mottoes (*brievi*) on the pictures of the doges in the great hall of the ducal palace – two or four hexameters, setting forth the most noteworthy facts in the government of each. In addition to this, the tombs of the doges in the fourteenth century bore short inscriptions in prose, recording merely facts, and beside them turgid hexameters or leonine verses. In the fifteenth century more care was taken with the style; in the sixteenth century it is seen at its best; and then soon after came pointless antithesis, prosopopoeia, false pathos, praise of abstract qualities – in a word, affectation and bombast. A good many traces of satire can be detected, and veiled criticism of the living is implied in open praise of the dead. At a much later period we find a few instances of deliberate recurrence to the old, simple style.

Architectural works and decorative works in general were constructed with a view to receiving inscriptions, often in frequent repetition; while the northern Gothic seldom, and with difficulty, offered a suitable place for them, and in sepulchral monuments, for example, left free only the most exposed parts – namely the edges.

By what has been said hitherto we have, perhaps, failed to convince the reader of the characteristic value of this Latin poetry of the Italians. Our task was rather to indicate its position and necessity in the history of civilization. In its own day, a caricature of it appeared – the so-called macaronic poetry. The masterpiece of this style, the *opus macaronicorum*, was written by Merlinus Coccaius (Teofilo Folengo of Mantua). We shall now and then have occasion to refer to the matter of this poem. As to the form – hexameter and other verses, made up of Latin words and Italian words with Latin endings – its comic effect lies chiefly in the fact that these combinations sound like so many slips of the tongue, or the effusions of an over-hasty Latin *improvvisatore*. The German imitations do not give the smallest notion of this effect.

FALL OF THE HUMANISTS IN THE SIXTEENTH CENTURY

After a brilliant succession of poet-scholars had, since the beginning of the fourteenth century, filled Italy and the world with the worship of antiquity, had determined the forms of education and culture, had often taken the lead in political affairs and had, to no small extent, reproduced ancient literature – at length in the sixteenth century, before their doctrines and scholarship had lost hold of the public mind, the whole class fell into deep and general disgrace. Though they still served as models to the poets, historians and orators, personally no one would consent to be reckoned of their number. To the two chief accusations against them – that of malicious self-conceit, and that of abominable profligacy – a third charge of irreligion was now loudly added by the rising powers of the Counter-Reformation.

Why, it may be asked, were not these reproaches, whether true or false, heard sooner? As a matter of fact, they were heard at a very early period, but the effect they produced was insignificant, for the plain reason that men were far too dependent on the scholars for their knowledge of antiquity – that the scholars were personally the possessors and diffusers of ancient culture. But the spread of printed editions of the classics, and of large and well-arranged hand-books and dictionaries, went far to free the people from the necessity of personal intercourse with the humanists, and, as soon as they could be but partly dispensed with, the change in popular feeling became manifest. It was a change under which the good and bad suffered indiscriminately.

The first to make these charges were certainly the humanists themselves. Of all men who ever formed a class, they had the least sense of their common interests, and least respected what there was of this sense. All means were held lawful, if one of them saw a chance of supplanting another. From literary discussion they passed with astonishing suddenness to the fiercest and the most groundless vituperation. Not satisfied with refuting, they sought to annihilate an opponent. Something of this must be put to the account of their position and circumstances; we have seen how fiercely the age, whose loudest spokesmen they were, was borne to and fro by the passion for glory and the passion for satire. Their position, too, in practical life was one that they had continually to fight for. In such a temper they wrote and spoke and described one another. Poggio's works alone contain dirt enough to create a prejudice against the whole class – and these *Opere Poggii* were just those most often printed, on the north as well as on the south side of the Alps. We must take care not to rejoice too soon, when we meet among these men a figure which seems immaculate; on further inquiry there is always a danger of meeting with some foul charge, which, even when it is incredible, still discolours the picture. The mass of indecent Latin poems in circulation, and such things as ribaldry on the subject of his own family in Pontano's dialogue, *Antonius*, did the rest to discredit the class. The sixteenth century was not only familiar with all these ugly symptoms, but had also grown tired of the type of the humanist. These men had to pay both for the misdeeds they had done, and for the excess of honour which had hitherto fallen to their lot. Their evil fate willed it that the greatest poet of the nation wrote of them in a tone of calm and sovereign contempt.[69]

Of the reproaches which combined to excite so much hatred, many were only too well founded. Yet a clear and unmistakable tendency to strictness in matters of religion and morality was alive in many of the philologists, and it is a proof of small knowledge of the period, if the whole class is condemned. Yet many, and among them the loudest speakers, were guilty.

Three facts explain and perhaps diminish their guilt: the overflowing excess of favour and fortune, when the luck was on their side; the uncertainty of the future, in which luxury or misery depended on the caprice of a patron or the malice of an enemy; and finally, the misleading influence of antiquity. This undermined their morality, without giving them its own instead; and in religious matters, since they could never think of accepting the positive belief in the old gods, it affected them only on the negative and sceptical side. Just because they conceived of antiquity dogmatically – that is, took it as the model for all thought and action – its influence was here pernicious. But that an age existed which idolized the ancient world and its products with an exclusive devotion was not the fault of individuals. It was the work of an historical providence, and all the culture of the ages which have followed, and of the ages to come, rests upon the fact that it was so, and that all the ends of life but this one were then deliberately put aside.

The career of the humanists was, as a rule, of such a kind that only the strongest characters could pass through it unscathed. The first danger came, in some cases, from the parents, who sought to turn a precocious child into a miracle of learning, with an eye to his future position in that class which then was supreme. Youthful prodigies, however, seldom rise above a certain level; or, if they do, are forced to achieve their further progress and development at the cost of the bitterest trials. For an ambitious youth, the fame and the brilliant position of the humanists were a perilous temptation; it seemed to him that he too 'through inborn pride could no longer regard the low and common things of life'. He was thus led to plunge into a life of excitement and vicissitude, in which exhausting studies, tutorships, secretaryships, professorships, offices in princely households, mortal enmities and perils, luxury and beggary, boundless admiration and boundless contempt followed confusedly one upon the other, and in which the most solid worth and learning were often pushed aside by superficial impudence. But the worst of all was that the position of the humanist was almost incompatible with a fixed home, since it either made frequent changes of dwelling necessary for a livelihood, or so affected the mind of the individual that he could never be happy for long in one place. He grew tired of the people, and had no peace among the enmities which he excited, while the people themselves in their turn demanded something new. Much as this life reminds us of the Greek sophists of the Empire, as described to us by Philostratus, yet the position of the sophists was more favourable. They often had money, or could more easily do without it than the humanists, and as professional teachers of rhetoric, rather than men of learning, their life was freer and simpler. But the scholar of the Renaissance was forced to combine great learning with the power of resisting the influence of ever-changing pursuits and situations. Add to this the deadening effect of licentious excess and – since do what he might, the worst was believed of him – a total indifference to the moral laws recognized by others. Such men can hardly be conceived to exist without an inordinate pride. They needed it, if only to keep their heads above water, and were confirmed in it by the admiration which alternated with hatred in the treatment they received from the world. They are the most striking examples and victims of an unbridled subjectivity.

The attacks and the satirical pictures began, as we have said, at an early period. For all strongly marked individuality, for every kind of distinction, a corrective was at hand in the national taste for ridicule. And in this case the men themselves offered abundant and terrible materials which satire had but to make use of. In the fifteenth century, Battista Mantovano, in discoursing of the seven monsters, includes the humanists, with many others, under the head 'Superbia'. He describes how, fancying themselves children of Apollo, they walk along with affected solemnity and with sullen, malicious looks, now gazing at their own shadow, now brooding over the popular praise they hunted after, like cranes in search of food. But in the sixteenth century the indictment was presented in full. Besides Ariosto, their own historian Gyraldus gives evidence of this, whose treatise, written under Leo X, was probably revised about the year 1540. Warning examples from ancient and modern times of the moral disorder and the wretched existence of the scholars meet us in astonishing abundance, and along with these, accusations of the most serious nature are brought formally against them. Among these are anger, vanity, obstinacy, self-adoration, a dissolute private life, immorality of all descriptions, heresy, atheism; further, the habit of speaking without conviction, a sinister influence on government, pedantry of speech, thanklessness towards teachers, and abject flattery of the great, who first give the scholar a taste of their favours and then leave him to starve. The description is closed by a reference to the golden age, when no such thing as science existed on the earth. Of these charges, that of heresy soon became the most dangerous, and Gyraldus himself, when he afterwards republished a perfectly harmless youthful work, was compelled to take refuge beneath the mantle of Duke Hercules II of Ferrara, since men now had the upper hand who held that people had better spend their time on Christian themes than on mythological researches. He justifies himself on the ground that the latter, on the contrary, were at such a time almost the only harmless branches of study, as they deal with subjects of a perfectly neutral character.

But if it is the duty of the historian to seek for evidence in which moral judgement is tempered by human sympathy, he will find no authority comparable in value to the work so often quoted of Pierio Valeriano, *On the Infelicity of the Scholar*. It was written under the gloomy impressions left by the sack of Rome, which seems to the writer, not only the direct cause of untold misery to the men of learning, but, as it were, the fulfilment of an evil destiny which had long pursued them. Pierio is here led by a simple and, on the whole, just feeling. He does not introduce a special power, which plagued the men of genius on account of their genius, but he states facts, in which an unlucky chance often wears the aspect of fatality. Not wishing to write a tragedy or to refer events to the conflict of higher powers, he is content to lay before us the scenes of everyday life. We are introduced to men who, in times of trouble, lose first their incomes and then their places; to others who, in trying to get two appointments, miss both; to unsociable misers who carry about their money sewn into their clothes, and die mad when they are robbed of it; to others, who accept well-paid offices, and then sicken with a melancholy longing for their lost freedom. We read how some died young of a plague or fever, and how the writings which had cost them so much toil were burnt with their bed and clothes; how others lived in terror of the murderous threats of their colleagues; how one was slain by a covetous servant, and another caught by highwaymen on a journey, and left to pine in a dungeon, because unable to pay his ransom. Many died of unspoken grief for the insults they received and the prizes of which they were defrauded. We are told of the death of a Venetian, because his son, a youthful prodigy, had died; and the mother and brothers followed, as if the lost child drew them all after him. Many, especially Florentines, ended their lives by suicide; others through the secret justice of a tyrant. Who, after all, is happy? And by what means? By blunting all feeling for such misery? One of the speakers in the dialogue in which Pierio clothed his argument can give an answer to these questions – the illustrious Gasparo Contarini, at the mention of whose name we turn with the expectation to hear at last something of the truest and deepest which was then thought on such matters. As a type of the happy scholar, he mentions Fra Urbano Valeriano of Belluno, who was for years teacher of Greek at Venice, who visited Greece and the East, and towards the close of his life travelled, now through this country, now through that, without ever mounting a horse; who never had a penny of his own, rejected all honours and distinctions, and after a gay old age, died in his eighty-fourth year, without, if we except a fall from a ladder, having ever known an hour of sickness. And what was the difference between such a man and the humanists? The latter had more free will, more subjectivity, than they could turn to purposes of happiness. The mendicant friar, who had lived from his boyhood in the monastery, and never eaten or slept except by rule, ceased to feel the compulsion under which he lived. Through the power of this habit he led, amid all outward hardships, a life of inward peace, by which he impressed his hearers far more than by his teaching. Looking at him, they could believe that it depends on ourselves whether we bear up against misfortune or surrender to it. 'Amid want and toil he was happy, because he willed to be so, because he had contracted no evil habits, was not capricious, inconstant, immoderate; but was always contented with little or nothing.' If we heard Contarini himself, religious motives would no doubt play a part in the argument – but the practical philosopher in sandals speaks plainly enough. An allied character, but placed in other circumstances, is that of Fabio Calvi of Ravenna, the commentator of Hippocrates. He lived to a great age in Rome, eating only pulse 'like the Pythagoreans', and dwelt in a hovel little better than the tub of Diogenes. Of the pension which Pope Leo gave him, he spent enough to keep body and soul together, and gave the rest away. He was not a healthy man, like Fra Urbano, nor is it likely that, like him, he died with a smile on his lips. At the age of ninety, in the sack of Rome, he was dragged away by the Spaniards, who hoped for a ransom, and died of hunger in a hospital. But his name has passed into the kingdom of the immortals, for Raphael loved the old man like a father, and honoured him as a teacher, and came to him for advice in all things. Perhaps they discoursed chiefly of the projected restoration of ancient Rome,[70] perhaps of still higher matters. Who can tell what a share Fabio may have had in the conception of the *School of Athens*, and in other great works of the master?

We would gladly close this part of our essay with the picture of some pleasing and winning character. Pomponius Laetus, of whom we shall briefly speak, is known to us principally through the letter of his pupil Sabellicus, in which an antique colouring is purposely given to his character. Yet many of its features are clearly recognizable. He was a bastard of the House of the Neapolitan Sanseverini, princes of Salerno, whom he nevertheless refused to recognize, writing, in reply to an invitation to live with them, the famous letter: '*Pomponius Laetus cognatis et propinquis suis, salutem. Quod petitis fieri non potest. Valete.*' An insignificant little figure, with small, quick eyes, and quaint dress, he lived, during the last decades of the fifteenth century, as professor in the university of Rome, either in his cottage in a garden on the

Esquiline hill, or in his vineyard on the Quirinal. In the one he bred his ducks and fowls; the other he cultivated according to the strictest precepts of Cato, Varro and Columella. He spent his holidays in fishing or bird-catching in the Campagna, or in feasting by some shady spring or on the banks of the Tiber. Wealth and luxury he despised. Free himself from envy and uncharitable speech, he would not suffer them in others. It was only against the hierarchy that he gave his tongue free play, and passed, till his latter years, for a scorner of religion altogether. He was involved in the persecution of the humanists begun by Pope Paul II, and surrendered to this pontiff by the Venetians; but no means could be found to wring unworthy confessions from him. He was afterwards befriended and supported by popes and prelates, and when his house was plundered in the disturbances under Sixtus IV, more was collected for him than he had lost. No teacher was more conscientious. Before daybreak he was to be seen descending the Esquiline with his lantern, and on reaching his lecture-room found it always filled to overflowing. A stutter compelled him to speak with care, but his delivery was even and effective. His few works give evidence of careful writing. No scholar treated the text of ancient authors more soberly and accurately. The remains of antiquity which surrounded him in Rome touched him so deeply that he would stand before them as if entranced, or would suddenly burst into tears at the sight of them. As he was ready to lay aside his own studies in order to help others, he was much loved and had many friends; and at his death, even Alexander VI sent his courtiers to follow the corpse, which was carried by the most distinguished of his pupils. The funeral service in the Aracoeli was attended by forty bishops and by all the foreign ambassadors.

It was Laetus who introduced and conducted the representations of ancient, chiefly Plautine, plays in Rome. Every year, he celebrated the anniversary of the foundation of the city by a festival, at which his friends and pupils recited speeches and poems. Such meetings were the origin of what acquired, and long retained, the name of the Roman Academy. It was simply a free union of individuals, and was connected with no fixed institution. Besides the occasions mentioned, it met at the invitation of a patron, or to celebrate the memory of a deceased member, as of Platina. At such times, a prelate belonging to the academy would first say mass; Pomponio would then ascend the pulpit and deliver a speech; someone else would then follow him and recite an elegy. The customary banquet, with declamations and recitations, concluded the festival, whether joyous or serious, and the academicians, notably Platina himself, early acquired the reputation of epicures. At other times, the guests performed farces in the old Atellan style. As a free association of very varied elements, the academy lasted in its original form down to the sack of Rome, and included among its guests Angelus Coloccius, Joh. Corycius and others. Its precise value as an element in the intellectual life of the people is as hard to estimate as that of any other social union of the same kind; yet a man like Sadoleto reckoned it among the most precious memories of his youth. A large number of other academies appeared and passed away in many Italian cities, according to the number and significance of the humanists living in them, and to the patronage bestowed by the great and wealthy. Of these we may mention the Academy of Naples, of which Jovianus Pontanus was the centre, and which sent out a colony to Lecce, and that of Pordenone, which formed the court of the *condottiere* Alviano. The circle of Lodovico il Moro, and its peculiar importance for that prince, has been already spoken of.

About the middle of the sixteenth century, these associations seem to have undergone a complete change. The humanists, driven in other spheres from their commanding position, and viewed askance by the men of the Counter-Reformation, lost the control of the academies: and here, as elsewhere, Latin poetry was replaced by Italian. Before long every town of the least importance had its academy, with some strange, fantastic name, and its own endowment and subscriptions. Besides the recitation of verses, the new institutions inherited from their predecessors the regular banquets and the representation of plays, sometimes acted by the members themselves, sometimes under their direction by young amateurs, and sometimes by paid players. The fate of the Italian stage, and afterwards of the opera, was long in the hands of these associations.

PART IV

The Discovery of the World
and of Man

JOURNEYS OF THE ITALIANS

FREED FROM the countless bonds which elsewhere in Europe checked progress, having reached a high degree of individual development and been schooled by the teachings of antiquity, the Italian mind now turned to the discovery of the outward universe, and to the representation of it in speech and in form.

On the journeys of the Italians to distant parts of the world we can here make but a few general observations. The Crusades had opened unknown distances to the European mind, and awakened in all the passion for travel and adventure. It may be hard to indicate precisely the point where this passion allied itself with, or became the servant of, the thirst for knowledge; but it was in Italy that this was first and most completely the case. Even in the Crusades the interest of the Italians was wider than that of other nations, since they already were a naval power and had commercial relations with the East. From time immemorial the Mediterranean sea had given to the nations that dwelt on its shores mental impulses different from those which governed the peoples of the North; and never, from the very structure of their character, could the Italians be adventurers in the sense which the word bore among the Teutons. After they were once at home in all the eastern harbours of the Mediterranean, it was natural that the most enterprising among them should be led to join that vast international movement of the Muhammadans which there found its outlet. A new half of the world lay, as it were, freshly discovered before them. Or, like Polo of Venice, they were caught in the current of the Mongolian peoples, and carried on to the steps of the throne of the Great Khan. At an early period, we find Italians sharing in the discoveries made in the Atlantic ocean; it was the Genoese who, in the thirteenth century, found the Canary Islands. In the same year, 1291, when Ptolemais, the last remnant of the Christian East, was lost, it was again the Genoese who made the first known attempt to find a sea-passage to the East Indies. Columbus himself is but the greatest of a long list of Italians who, in the service of the Western nations, sailed into distant seas. The true discoverer, however, is not the man who first chances to stumble upon anything, but the man who finds what he has sought. Such a one alone stands in a link with the thoughts and interests of his predecessors, and this relationship will also determine the account he gives of his search. For which reason the Italians, although their claim to be the first comers on this or that shore may be disputed, will yet retain their title to be pre-eminently the nation of discoverers for the whole latter part of the Middle Ages. The fuller proof of this assertion belongs to the special history of discoveries. Yet ever and again we turn with admiration to the august figure of the great Genoese, by whom a new continent beyond the ocean was demanded, sought and found; and who was the first to be able to say: '*il mondo è poco*' – the world is not so large as men have thought. At the time when Spain gave Alexander VI to the Italians, Italy gave Columbus to the Spaniards. Only a few weeks before the death of that pope (7 July 1503), Columbus wrote from Jamaica his noble letter to the thankless Catholic kings, which the ages to come can never read without profound emotion. In a codicil to his will, dated Valladolid, 4 May 1506, he bequeathed to 'his beloved home, the republic of Genoa, the prayer-book which Pope Alexander had given him, and which in prison, in conflict and in every kind of adversity had been to him the greatest of comforts'. It seems as if these words cast upon the abhorred name of Borgia one last gleam of grace and mercy.

The development of geographical and allied sciences among the Italians must, like the history of their voyages, be touched upon but very briefly. A superficial comparison of their achievements with those of other nations shows an early and striking superiority on their part. Where, in the middle of the fifteenth century, could be found, anywhere but in Italy, such a union of geographical, statistical and historical knowledge as was found in Aeneas Sylvius? Not only in his great geographical work, but in his letters and commentaries, he describes with equal mastery landscapes, cities, manners, industries and products, political conditions and constitutions, wherever he can use his own observation or the evidence of eye-witnesses. What he takes from books is naturally of less moment. Even the short sketch of that valley in the Tyrolese Alps, where Frederick III had given him a benefice, and still more his description of Scotland, leaves untouched none of the relations of human life, and displays a power and method of unbiased observation and comparison impossible in any but a countryman of Columbus, trained in the school of the ancients. Thousands saw and, in part, knew what he did, but they felt no impulse to draw a picture of it, and were unconscious that the world desired such pictures.

In geography[71] as in other matters, it is vain to attempt to distinguish how much is to be attributed to the study of the ancients, and how much to the special genius of the Italians. They saw and treated the things of this world from an objective point of view, even before they were familiar with ancient literature, partly because they were themselves a half-ancient people, and partly because their political circumstances predisposed them to it; but they would not so rapidly have attained to such perfection had not the old geographers showed them the way. The influence of the existing Italian geographies on the spirit and tendencies of the travellers and discoverers was also inestimable. Even the simple dilettante of a science – if in the present case we should assign to Aeneas Sylvius so low a rank – can diffuse just that sort of general interest in the subject which prepares for new pioneers the indispensable groundwork of a favourable predisposition in the public mind. True discoverers in any science know well what they owe to such mediation.

THE NATURAL SCIENCES IN ITALY

For the position of the Italians in the sphere of the natural sciences, we must refer the reader to the special treatises on the subject, of which the only one with which we are familiar is the superficial and depreciatory work of Libri. The dispute as to the priority of particular discoveries concerns us all the less, since we hold that, at any time, and among any civilized people, a man may appear who, starting with very scanty preparation, is driven by an irresistible impulse into the paths of scientific investigation, and through his native gifts achieves the most astonishing success. Such men were Gerbert of Rheims and Roger Bacon. That they were masters of the whole knowledge of the age in their several departments was a natural consequence of the spirit in which they worked. When once the veil of illusion was torn asunder, when once the dread of nature and the slavery to books and tradition were overcome, countless problems lay before them for solution. It is another matter when a whole people takes a natural delight in the study and investigation of nature, at a time when other nations are indifferent, that is to say, when the discoverer is not threatened or wholly ignored, but can count on the friendly support of congenial spirits. That this was the case in Italy is unquestionable. The Italian students of nature trace with pride in the *Divine Comedy* the hints and proofs of Dante's scientific interest in nature. On his claim to priority in this or that discovery or reference we must leave the men of science to decide; but every layman must be struck by the wealth of his observations on the external world, shown merely in his pictures and comparisons. He, more than any other modern poet, takes them from reality, whether in nature or human life, and uses them, never as mere ornament, but in order to give the reader the fullest and most adequate sense of his meaning. It is in astronomy that he appears chiefly as a scientific specialist, though it must not be forgotten that many astronomical allusions in his great poem, which now appear to us learned, must then have been intelligible to the general reader. Dante, learning apart, appeals to a popular knowledge of the heavens, which the Italians of this day, from the mere fact that they were a nautical people, had in common with the ancients. This knowledge of the rising and setting of the constellations has been rendered superfluous to the modern world by calendars and clocks, and with it has gone whatever interest in astronomy the people may once have had. Nowadays, with our schools and handbooks, every child knows – what Dante did not know – that the earth moves round the sun; but the interest once taken in the subject itself has given place, except in the case of astronomical specialists, to the most absolute indifference.

The pseudo-science, which also dealt with the stars, proves nothing against the inductive spirit of the Italians of that day. That spirit was but crossed, and at times overcome, by the passionate desire to penetrate the future. We shall recur to the subject of astrology when we come to speak of the moral and religious character of the people.

The Church treated this and other pseudo-sciences nearly always with toleration; and showed itself actually hostile even to genuine science only when a charge of heresy together with necromancy was also in question – which certainly was often the case. A point which it would be interesting to decide is this: whether and in what cases the Dominican (and also the Franciscan) Inquisitors in Italy were conscious of the falsehood of the charges, and yet condemned the accused, either to oblige some enemy of the prisoner or from hatred to natural science, and particularly to experiments. The latter doubtless occurred, but it is not easy to prove the fact. What helped to cause such persecutions in the North, namely, the opposition made to the innovators by the upholders of the received official, scholastic system of nature, was of little or no weight in Italy. Pietro of Albano, at the beginning of the fourteenth century, is well known to have fallen a victim to the envy of another physician, who accused him before the Inquisition of heresy and magic; and something of the same kind may have happened in the case of his Paduan contemporary, Giovannino Sanguinacci, who was known as an innovator in medical practice. He escaped, however, with banishment. Nor must it be forgotten that the inquisitorial power of the Dominicans was exercised less uniformly in Italy than in the North. Tyrants and free cities in the fourteenth century treated the clergy at times with such sovereign contempt that very different matters from natural science went unpunished. But when, with the fifteenth century, antiquity became the leading power in Italy, the breach it made in the old system was turned to account by every branch of secular science. Humanism, nevertheless, attracted to itself the best strength of the nation, and thereby, no doubt, did injury to the inductive investigation of nature. Here and there the Inquisition suddenly started into life, and punished or burned physicians as blasphemers or magicians. In such cases it is hard to discover what was the true motive underlying the condemnation. And after all, Italy, at the close of the fifteenth century, with Paolo Toscanelli, Luca Pacioli and Leonardo da Vinci, held incomparably the highest place among European nations in mathematics and the natural sciences, and the learned men of every country, even Regiomontanus and Copernicus, confessed themselves its pupils. This glory survived the Counter-Reformation, and even today the Italians would occupy the first place in this respect if circumstances had not made it impossible for the greatest minds to devote themselves to tranquil research.

A significant proof of the widespread interest in natural history is found in the zeal which showed itself at an early period for the collection and comparative study of plants and animals. Italy claims to be the first creator of botanical gardens, though possibly they may have served a chiefly practical end, and the claim to priority may be itself disputed. It is of far greater importance that princes and wealthy men, in laying out their pleasure-gardens, instinctively made a point of collecting the greatest possible number of different plants in all their species and varieties. Thus in the fifteenth century the noble grounds of the Medicean Villa Careggi appear from the description we have of them to have been almost a botanical garden, with countless specimens of different trees and shrubs. Of the same kind was a villa of the Cardinal Trivulzio, at the beginning of the sixteenth century, in the Roman Campagna towards Tivoli, with hedges made up of various species of roses, with trees of every description – the fruit-trees especially showing an astonishing variety – with twenty different sorts of vines and a large kitchen-garden. This is evidently something very different from the score or two of familiar medicinal plants, which were to be found in the garden of any castle or monastery in Western Europe. Along with a careful cultivation of fruit for the purposes of the table, we find an interest in the plant for its own sake, on account of the pleasure it gives to the eye. We learn from the history of art at how late a period this passion for botanical collections was laid aside, and gave place to what was considered the picturesque style of landscape-gardening.

The collections, too, of foreign animals not only gratified curiosity, but served also the higher purposes of observation. The facility of transport from the southern and eastern harbours of the Mediterranean, and the mildness of the Italian climate, made it practicable to buy the largest animals of the south, or to accept them as presents from the sultans. The cities and princes were especially anxious to keep live lions, even when the lion was not, as in Florence, the emblem of the state. The lions' den was generally in or near the government palace, as in Perugia and Florence; in Rome, it lay on the slope of the Capitol. The beasts sometimes served as executioners of political judgements, and no doubt, apart from this, they kept alive a certain terror in the popular mind. Their condition was also held to be ominous of good or evil. Their fertility, especially, was considered a sign of public prosperity, and no less a man than Giovanni Villani thought it worth recording that he was present at the delivery of a lioness. The cubs were often given to allied states and princes, or to *condottieri* as a reward of valour. In addition to the lions, the Florentines began very early to keep leopards, for which a special keeper was appointed.

Borso of Ferrara used to set his lions to fight with bulls, bears and wild boars.

By the end of the fifteenth century, however, true menageries (*serragli*), now reckoned part of the suitable appointments of a court, were kept by many of the princes. 'It belongs to the position of the great,' says Matarazzo, 'to keep horses, dogs, mules, falcons and other birds, court-jesters, singers and foreign animals.' The menagerie at Naples, in the time of Ferrante and others, contained a giraffe and a zebra, presented, it seems, by the ruler of Baghdad. Filippo Maria Visconti possessed not only horses which each cost him 500 or 1,000 pieces of gold, and valuable English dogs, but a number of leopards brought from all parts of the East; the expense of his hunting-birds, which were collected from the countries of northern Europe, amounted to 3,000 pieces of gold a month. King Emanuel the Great of Portugal knew well what he was about when he presented Leo X with an elephant and a rhinoceros. It was under such circumstances that the foundations of a scientific zoology and botany were laid.

A practical fruit of these zoological studies was the establishment of studs, of which the Mantuan, under Francesco Gonzaga, was esteemed the first in Europe. All interest in and knowledge of the different breeds of horses is as old, no doubt, as riding itself, and the crossing of the European with the Asiatic must have been common from the time of the Crusades. In Italy, a special inducement to perfect the breed was offered by the prizes at the horse-races held in every considerable town in the peninsula. In the Mantuan stables were found the infallible winners in these contests, as well as the best military chargers, and the horses best suited by their stately appearance for presents to great people. Gonzaga kept stallions and mares from Spain, Ireland, Africa, Thrace and Cilicia, and for the sake of the last he cultivated the friendship of the sultans. All possible experiments were here tried in order to produce the most perfect animals.

Even human menageries were not wanting. The famous Cardinal Ippolito Medici, bastard of Giuliano, Duke of Nemours, kept at his strange court a troop of barbarians who talked no less than twenty different languages, and who were all of them perfect specimens of their races. Among them were incomparable *voltigeurs* of the best blood of the North African Moors, Tartar bowmen, Negro wrestlers, Indian divers, and Turks, who generally accompanied the cardinal on his hunting expeditions. When he was overtaken by an early death

(1535), this motley band carried the corpse on their shoulders from Itri to Rome, and mingled with the general mourning for the open-handed cardinal their medley of tongues and violent gesticulations.[72]

These scattered notices of the relations of the Italians to natural science, and their interest in the wealth and variety of the products of nature, are only fragments of a great subject. No one is more conscious than the author of the defects in his knowledge on this point. Of the multitude of special works in which the subject is adequately treated even the names are but imperfectly known to him.

DISCOVERY OF THE BEAUTY OF LANDSCAPE

But, outside the sphere of scientific investigation, there is another way to draw near to nature. The Italians are the first among modern peoples by whom the outward world was seen and felt as something beautiful.

The power to do so is always the result of a long and complicated development, and its origin is not easily detected, since a dim feeling of this kind may exist long before it shows itself in poetry and painting, and thereby becomes conscious of itself. Among the ancients, for example, art and poetry had gone through the whole circle of human interests, before they turned to the representation of nature, and even then the latter filled always a limited and subordinate place. And yet, from the time of Homer downwards, the powerful impression made by nature upon man is shown by countless verses and chance expressions. The Germanic races, which founded their states on the ruins of the Roman Empire, were thoroughly and specially fitted to understand the spirit of natural scenery; and though Christianity compelled them for a while to see in the springs and mountains, in the lakes and woods, which they had till then revered, the working of evil demons, yet this transitional conception was soon outgrown. By the year 1200, at the height of the Middle Ages, a genuine, hearty enjoyment of the external world was again in existence, and found lively expression in the minstrelsy of different nations, which gives evidence of the sympathy felt with all the simple phenomena of nature – spring with its flowers, the green fields and the woods. But these pictures are all foreground without perspective. Even the crusaders, who travelled so far and saw so much, are not recognizable as such in these poems. The epic poetry, which describes armour and costumes so fully, does not attempt more than a sketch of outward nature; and even the great Wolfram von Eschenbach scarcely anywhere gives us an adequate picture of the scene on which his heroes move. From these poems it would never be guessed that their noble authors in all countries inhabited or visited lofty castles, commanding distant prospects. Even in the Latin poems of the wandering clerks, we find no traces of a distant view – of landscape properly so called – but what lies near is sometimes described with a glow and splendour which none of the knightly minstrels can surpass. What picture of the Grove of Love can equal that of the Italian poet – for such we take him to be – of the twelfth century?

> *Immortalis fieret*
> *Ibi manens homo;*
> *Arbor ibi quaelibet*
> *Suo gaudet pomo;*
> *Viae myrrha, cinnamo*
> *Fragrant, et amomo –*
> *Conjectari poterat*
> *Dominus ex domo*, etc.

To the Italian mind, at all events, nature had by this time lost its taint of sin, and had shaken off all trace of demoniacal powers. St Francis of Assisi, in his Hymn to the Sun, frankly praises the Lord for creating the heavenly bodies and the four elements.

But the unmistakable proofs of a deepening effect of nature on the human spirit begin with Dante. Not only does he awaken in us by a few vigorous lines the sense of the morning air and the trembling light on the distant ocean, or of the grandeur of the storm-beaten forest, but he makes the ascent of lofty peaks, with the only possible object of enjoying the view – the first man, perhaps, since the days of antiquity who did so. In Boccaccio we can do little more than infer how country scenery affected him; yet his pastoral romances show his imagination to have been filled with it. But the significance of nature for a receptive spirit is fully and clearly displayed by Petrarch – one of the first truly modern men. That clear soul – who first collected from the literature of all countries evidence of the origin and progress of the sense of natural beauty, and himself, in his *Aspects of Nature*, achieved the noblest masterpiece of description – Alexander von Humboldt, has not done full justice to Petrarch; and, following in the steps of the great reaper, we may still hope to glean a few ears of interest and value.

Petrarch was not only a distinguished geographer – the first map of Italy is said to have been drawn by his direction – and not only a reproducer of the sayings of the ancients, but felt himself the influence of natural beauty. The enjoyment of nature is, for him, the favourite accompaniment of intellectual pursuits; it was to combine the two that he lived in learned retirement at Vaucluse and elsewhere, that he from time to time fled from the world and from his age. We should do him wrong by inferring from his weak and undeveloped power of describing natural scenery that he did not feel it deeply. His picture, for instance, of the lovely Gulf of Spezia and Porto Venere, which he inserts at the end of the sixth book at the *Africa*, for the reason that none of the ancients or moderns had sung of it, is no more than a simple enumeration, but Petrarch is also conscious of the beauty of rock scenery, and is perfectly able to distinguish the picturesqueness from the utility of nature. During his stay among the woods of Reggio, the sudden sight of an impressive landscape so affected him that he resumed a poem which he had long laid aside. But the deepest impression of all was made upon him by the ascent of Mont Ventoux, near Avignon. An indefinable longing for a distant panorama grew stronger and stronger in him, till at length the accidental sight of a passage in Livy, where King Philip, the enemy of Rome, ascends the Haemus, decided him. He thought that what was not blamed in a grey-headed monarch might well be *excused* in a young man of private station. The ascent of a mountain for its own sake was unheard of, and there could be no thought of the companionship of friends or acquaintances. Petrarch took with him only his younger brother and two country people from the last place where he halted. At the foot of the mountain an old herdsman besought him to turn back, saying that he himself had attempted to climb it fifty years before, and had brought home nothing but repentance, broken bones and torn clothes, and that neither before nor after had anyone ventured to do the same. Nevertheless, they struggled forward and upward, till the clouds lay beneath their feet, and at last they reached the top. A description of the view from the summit would be looked for in vain, not because the poet was insensible to it, but, on the contrary, because the impression was too overwhelming. His whole past life, with all its follies, rose before his mind; he remembered that ten years ago that day he had quitted

Bologna a young man, and turned a longing gaze towards his native country; he opened a book which then was his constant companion, the *Confessions* of St Augustine, and his eye fell on the passage in the tenth chapter, 'and men go forth, and admire lofty mountains and broad seas, and roaring torrents, and the ocean, and the course of the stars, and forget their own selves while doing so'. His brother, to whom he read these words, could not understand why he closed the book and said no more.

Some decades later, about 1360, Fazio degli Uberti describes, in his rhyming geography, the wide panorama from the mountains of Auvergne, with the interest, it is true, of the geographer and anti-quarian only, but still showing clearly that he himself had seen it. He must, however, have ascended far higher peaks, since he is familiar with facts which only occur at a height of 10,000 feet or more above the sea – mountain-sickness and its accompaniments – of which his imaginary comrade Solinus tries to cure him with a sponge dipped in an essence. The ascents of Parnassus and Olympus, of which he speaks, are perhaps only fictions.

In the fifteenth century, the great masters of the Flemish school, Hubert and Jan van Eyck, suddenly lifted the veil from nature. Their landscapes are not merely the fruit of an endeavour to reflect the real world in art, but have, even if expressed conventionally, a certain poetical meaning – in short, a soul. Their influence on the whole art of the West is undeniable, and extended to the landscape-painting of the Italians, but without preventing the characteristic interest of the Italian eye for nature from finding its own expression.

On this point, as in the scientific description of nature, Aeneas Sylvius is again one of the most weighty voices of his time. Even if we grant the justice of all that has been said against his character, we must nevertheless admit that in few other men was the picture of the age and its culture so fully reflected, and that few came nearer to the normal type of the men of the early Renaissance. It may be added parenthetically that even in respect to his moral character he will not be fairly judged if we listen solely to the complaints of the German Church, which his fickleness helped to balk of the Council it so ardently desired.

He here claims our attention as the first who not only enjoyed the magnificence of the Italian landscape, but described it with enthusiasm down to its minutest details. The ecclesiastical state and the south of

Tuscany – his native home – he knew thoroughly, and after he became pope he spent his leisure during the favourable season chiefly in excursions to the country. Then at last the gouty man was rich enough to have himself carried in a litter through the mountains and valleys; and when we compare his enjoyments with those of the popes who succeeded him, Pius, whose chief delight was in nature, antiquity and simple but noble architecture, appears almost a saint. In the elegant and flowing Latin of his *Commentaries* he freely tells us of his happiness.[73]

His eye seems as keen and practised as that of any modern observer. He enjoys with rapture the panoramic splendour of the view from the summit of the Alban Hills – from the Monte Cavo – whence he could see the shores of St Peter from Terracina and the promontory of Circe as far as Monte Argentaro, and the wide expanse of country round about, with the ruined cities of the past, and with the mountain-chains of central Italy beyond; and then his eye would turn to the green woods in the hollows beneath and the mountain-lakes among them. He feels the beauty of the position of Todi, crowning the vineyards and olive-clad slopes, looking down upon distant woods and upon the valley of the Tiber, where towns and castles rise above the winding river. The lovely hills about Siena, with villas and monasteries on every height, are his own home, and his descriptions of them are touched with a peculiar feeling. Single picturesque glimpses charm him too, like the little promontory of Capo di Monte that stretches out into the Lake of Bolsena. 'Rocky steps,' we read, 'shaded by vines, descend to the water's edge, where the evergreen oaks stand between the cliffs, alive with the song of thrushes.' On the path round the Lake of Nemi, beneath the chestnuts and fruit-trees, he feels that here, if anywhere, a poet's soul must awake – here in the hiding-place of Diana! He often held consistories or received ambassadors under huge old chestnut-trees, or beneath the olives on the greensward by some gurgling spring. A view like that of a narrowing gorge, with a bridge arched boldly over it, awakens at once his artistic sense. Even the smallest details give him delight through something beautiful, or perfect, or characteristic in them – the blue fields of waving flax, the yellow gorse which covers the hills, even tangled thickets, or single trees, or springs, which seem to him like wonders of nature.

The height of his enthusiasm for natural beauty was reached during his stay on Monte Amiata, in the summer of 1462, when plague and heat made the lowlands uninhabitable. Half-way up the mountain, in the old Lombard monastery of San Salvatore, he and his court took up their quarters. There, between the chestnuts which clothe the steep declivity, the eye may wander over all southern Tuscany, with the towers of Siena in the distance. The ascent of the highest peak he left to his companions, who were joined by the Venetian envoy; they found at the top two vast blocks of stone one upon the other – perhaps the sacrificial altar of a pre-historical people – and fancied that in the far distance they saw Corsica and Sardinia rising above the sea. In the cool air of the hills, among the old oaks and chestnuts, on the green meadows where there were no thorns to wound the feet, and no snakes or insects to hurt or to annoy, the pope passed days of unclouded happiness. For the *segnatura*, which took place on certain days of the week, he selected on each occasion some new shady retreat, '*novos in convallibus fontes et novas inveniens umbras, quae dubiam facerent electionem*'. At such times the dogs would perhaps start a great stag from his lair, who, after defending himself a while with hoofs and antlers, would fly at last up the mountain. In the evening the pope was accustomed to sit before the monastery on the spot from which the whole valley of the Paglia was visible, holding lively conversations with the cardinals. The courtiers who ventured down from the heights on their hunting expeditions found the heat below intolerable, and the scorched plains like a very hell, while the monastery, with its cool, shady woods, seemed like an abode of the blessed.

All this is genuine modern enjoyment, not a reflection of antiquity. As surely as the ancients themselves felt in the same manner, so surely, nevertheless, were the scanty expressions of the writers whom Pius knew insufficient to awaken in him such enthusiasm.

The second great age of Italian poetry, which now followed at the end of the fifteenth and the beginning of the sixteenth centuries, as well as the Latin poetry of the same period, is rich in proofs of the powerful effect of nature on the human mind. The first glance at the lyric poets of that time will suffice to convince us. Elaborate descriptions, it is true, of natural scenery, are very rare, for the reason that, in this energetic age, the novels and the lyric or epic poetry had something else to deal with. Boiardo and Ariosto paint nature vigorously, but as briefly as possible, and with no effort to appeal by their descriptions to the feelings of the reader, which they endeavour to reach solely by their narrative and characters. Letter-writers and the authors of philosophical dialogues are, in fact, better evidence of the growing love of nature than the poets. The novelist Bandello, for example, observes rigorously the rules of his department of literature; he gives us in his novels themselves not a word more than is necessary on the natural scenery amid which the action of his tales takes place, but in the dedications which always precede them we meet with charming descriptions of nature as the setting for his dialogues and social pictures. Among letter-writers, Aretino unfortunately must be named as the first who has fully painted in words the splendid effect of light and shadow in an Italian sunset.

We sometimes find the feeling of the poets, also, attaching itself with tenderness to graceful scenes of country life. Tito Strozzi, about the year 1480, describes in a Latin elegy the dwelling of his mistress. We are shown an old ivy-clad house, half hidden in trees, and adorned with weather-stained frescoes of the saints, and near it a chapel, much damaged by the violence of the river Po, which flowed hard by; not far off, the priest ploughs his few barren roods with borrowed cattle. This is no reminiscence of the Roman elegists, but true modern sentiment; and the parallel to it – a sincere, unartificial description of country life in general – will be found at the end of this part of our work.

It may be objected that the German painters at the beginning of the sixteenth century succeed in representing with perfect mastery these scenes of country life, as, for instance, Albrecht Dürer, in his engraving of the Prodigal Son. But it is one thing if a painter, brought up in a school of realism, introduces such scenes, and quite another thing if a poet, accustomed to an ideal or mythological framework, is driven by inward impulse into realism. Besides which, priority in point of time is here, as in the descriptions of country life, on the side of the Italian poets.

DISCOVERY OF MAN

To the discovery of the outward world the Renaissance added a still greater achievement, by first discerning and bringing to light the full, whole nature of man.

This period, as we have seen, first gave the highest development to individuality, and then led the individual to the most zealous and thorough study of himself in all forms and under all conditions.

Indeed, the development of personality is essentially involved in the recognition of it in oneself and in others. Between these two great processes our narrative has placed the influence of ancient literature because the mode of conceiving and representing both the individual and human nature in general was defined and coloured by that influence. But the power of conception and representation lay in the age and in the people.

The facts which we shall quote in evidence of our thesis will be few in number. Here, if anywhere in the course of this discussion, the author is conscious that he is treading on the perilous ground of conjecture, and that what seems to him a clear, if delicate and gradual, transition in the intellectual movement of the fourteenth and fifteenth centuries, may not be equally plain to others. The gradual awakening of the soul of a people is a phenomenon which may produce a different impression on each spectator. Time will judge which impression is the most faithful.

Happily the study of the intellectual side of human nature began, not with the search after a theoretical psychology – for that, Aristotle still sufficed – but with the endeavour to observe and to describe. The indispensable ballast of theory was limited to the popular doctrine of the four temperaments, in its then habitual union with the belief in the influence of the planets. Such conceptions may remain ineradicable in the minds of individuals without hindering the general progress of the age. It certainly makes on us a singular impression, when we meet them at a time when human nature in its deepest essence and in all its characteristic expressions was not only known by exact observation, but represented by an immortal poetry and art. It sounds almost ludicrous when an otherwise competent observer considers Clement VII to be of a melancholy temperament, but defers his judgement to that of the physicians, who declare the pope of a sanguine-choleric nature; or when we read that the same Gaston de Foix, the victor of Ravenna, whom Giorgione painted and Bambaia carved, and whom all the historians describe, had the saturnine temperament. No doubt those who use these expressions mean something by them; but the terms in which they tell us their meaning are strangely out of date in the Italy of the sixteenth century.

As examples of the free delineation of the human spirit, we shall first speak of the great poets of the fourteenth century.

If we were to collect the pearls from the courtly and knightly poetry of all the countries of the West during the two preceding centuries, we should have a mass of wonderful divinations and single pictures of the inward life, which at first sight would seem to rival the poetry of the Italians. Leaving lyrical poetry out of account, Godfrey of Strassburg gives us, in *Tristan und Isolde*, a representation of human passion, some features of which are immortal. But those pearls lie scattered in the ocean of artificial convention, and they are altogether something very different from a complete objective picture of the inward man and his spiritual wealth.

Italy, too, in the thirteenth century had, through the *trovatori*, its share in the poetry of the courts and of chivalry. To them is mainly due the *canzone*, whose construction is as difficult and artificial as that of the songs of any northern minstrel. Their subject and mode of thought represents simply the conventional tone of the courts, be the poet a burgher or a scholar.

But two new paths at length showed themselves, along which Italian poetry could advance to another and a characteristic future. They are not the less important for being concerned only with the formal and external side of the art.

To the same Brunetto Latini – the teacher of Dante – who, in his *Canzoni*, adopts the customary manner of the *trovatori*, we owe the first-known *versi sciolti*, or blank hendecasyllabic verses, and in his apparent absence of form, a true and genuine passion suddenly showed itself. The same voluntary renunciation of outward effect, through confidence in the power of the inward conception, can be observed some years later in fresco-painting, and later still in painting of all kinds, which began to cease to rely on colour for its effect, using simply a lighter or darker shade. For an age which laid so much stress on artificial form in poetry, these verses of Brunetto mark the beginning of a new epoch.

About the same time, or even in the first half of the thirteenth century, one of the many strictly balanced forms of metre, in which Europe was then so fruitful, became a normal and recognized form in Italy – the sonnet. The order of rhymes and even the number of lines varied for a whole century, till Petrarch fixed them permanently. In this form all higher lyrical or meditative subjects, and at a later time subjects of every possible description, were treated, and the madrigals, the *sestine* and even the *canzoni* were reduced to a subordinate place. Later Italian writers complain, half jestingly, half resentfully, of this inevitable mould, this Procrustean bed, to which they were compelled to make their thoughts and feelings fit. Others were, and still are, quite satisfied with this particular form of verse, which they freely use to express any personal reminiscence or idle sing-song without necessity or serious purpose. For which reason there are many more bad or insignificant sonnets than good ones.

Nevertheless, the sonnet must be held to have been an unspeakable blessing for Italian poetry. The clearness and beauty of its structure, the invitation it gave to elevate the thought in the second and more rapidly moving half, and the ease with which it could be learned by heart, made it valued even by the greatest masters. In fact, they would not have kept it in use down to our own century, had they not been penetrated with a sense of its singular worth. These masters could have given us the same thoughts in other and wholly different forms. But when once they had made the sonnet the normal type of lyrical poetry, many other writers of great, if not the highest, gifts, who otherwise would have lost themselves in a sea of diffusiveness, were forced to concentrate their feelings. The sonnet became for Italian literature a condenser of thoughts and emotions such as was possessed by the poetry of no other modern people.

Thus the world of Italian sentiment comes before us in a series of pictures, clear, concise, and most effective in their brevity. Had other nations possessed a form of expression of the same kind, we should perhaps have known more of their inward life; we might have had a number of pictures of inward and outward situations – reflections of the national character and temper – and should not be dependent for such knowledge on the so-called lyrical poets of the fourteenth and fifteenth centuries, who can hardly ever be read with any serious enjoyment. In Italy we can trace an undoubted progress from the time when the sonnet came into existence. In the second half of the thirteenth century the *trovatori della transizione*, as they have been recently named, mark the passage from the troubadours to the poets – that is, to those who wrote under the influence of antiquity. The simplicity and strength of their feeling, the vigorous delineation of fact, the precise expression and rounding off of their sonnets and other poems, herald the coming of a Dante. Some political sonnets of the Guelphs and Ghibellines (1260–70) have about them the ring of his passion, and others remind us of his sweetest lyrical notes.

Of his own theoretical view of the sonnet, we are unfortunately ignorant, since the last books of his work, *De vulgari eloquentia*, in which he proposed to treat of ballads and sonnets, either remained unwritten or have been lost. But, as a matter of fact, he has left us in his sonnets and *canzoni* a treasure of inward experience. And in what a framework he has set them! The prose of the *Vita nuova*, in which he gives an account of the origin of each poem, is as wonderful as the verses themselves, and forms with them a uniform whole, inspired with the deepest glow of passion. With unflinching frankness and sincerity he lays bare every shade of his joy and his sorrow, and moulds it resolutely into the strictest forms of art. Reading attentively these sonnets and *canzoni*, and the marvellous fragments of the diary of his youth which lie between them, we fancy that throughout the Middle Ages the poets have been purposely fleeing from themselves, and that he was the first to seek his own soul. Before his time we meet with many an artistic verse; but he is the first artist in the full sense of the word — the first who consciously cast immortal matter into an immortal form. Subjective feeling has here a full objective truth and greatness, and most of it is so set forth that all ages and peoples can make it their own. Where he writes in a thoroughly objective spirit, and lets the force of his sentiment be guessed at only by some outward fact, as in the magnificent sonnets '*Tanto gentile*', etc., and '*Vede perfettamente*', etc., he seems to feel the need to excuse himself. The most beautiful of these poems really belongs to this class — the '*Deh peregrini che pensosi andate*'.

Even apart from the *Divine Comedy*, Dante would have marked by these youthful poems the boundary between medievalism and modern times. The human spirit had taken a mighty step towards the consciousness of its own secret life.

The revelations in this matter which are contained in the *Divine Comedy* itself are simply immeasurable; and it would be necessary to go through the whole poem, one canto after another, in order to do justice to its value from this point of view. Happily we have no need to do this, as it has long been a daily food of all the countries of the West. Its plan, and the ideas on which it is based, belong to the Middle Ages, and appeal to our interest only historically; but it is nevertheless the beginning of all modern poetry, through the power and richness shown in the description of human nature in every shape and attitude.

From this time forward poetry may have experienced unequal fortunes, and may show, for half a century together, a so-called relapse. But its nobler and more vital principle was saved for ever; and whenever in the fourteenth, fifteenth and the beginning of the sixteenth centuries an original mind devotes himself to it, he represents a more advanced stage than any poet out of Italy, given – what is certainly not always easy to settle satisfactorily – an equality of natural gifts to start with.

Here, as in other things in Italy, culture – to which poetry belongs – precedes the plastic arts and, in fact, gives them their chief impulse. More than a century elapsed before the spiritual element in painting and sculpture attained a power of expression in any way analogous to that of the *Divine Comedy*. How far the same rule holds good for the artistic development of other nations, and of what importance the whole question may be, does not concern us here. For Italian civilization it is of decisive weight.

The position to be assigned to Petrarch in this respect must be settled by the many readers of the poet. Those who come to him in the spirit of a cross-examiner, and busy themselves in detecting the contradictions between the poet and the man, his infidelities in love, and the other weak sides of his character, may perhaps, after sufficient effort, end by losing all taste for his poetry. In place, then, of artistic enjoyment, we may acquire a knowledge of the man in his 'totality'. What a pity that Petrarch's letters from Avignon contain so little gossip to take hold of, and that the letters of his acquaintances and of the friends of these acquaintances have either been lost or never existed! Instead of Heaven being thanked when we are not forced to inquire how and through what struggles a poet has rescued something immortal from his own poor life and lot, a biography has been stitched together for Petrarch out of these so-called 'remains', which reads like an indictment. But the poet may take comfort. If the printing and editing of the correspondence of celebrated people goes on for another half-century as it has begun in England and Germany, he will have illustrious company enough sitting with him on the stool of repentance.

Without shutting our eyes to much that is forced and artificial in his poetry, where the writer is merely imitating himself and singing on in the old strain, we cannot fail to admire the marvellous abundance of pictures of the inmost soul – descriptions of moments of joy and sorrow which must have been thoroughly his own, since no one before him gives us anything of the kind, and on which his significance rests for his country and for the world. His verse is not in all places equally transparent; by the side of his most beautiful thoughts stands at times some allegorical conceit, or some sophistical trick of logic, altogether foreign to our present taste. But the balance is on the side of excellence.

Boccaccio, too, in his imperfectly known sonnets, succeeds some-times in giving a most powerful and effective picture of his feeling. The return to a spot consecrated by love (Son. 22), the melancholy of spring (Son. 33), the sadness of the poet who feels himself growing old (Son. 65), are admirably treated by him. And in the *Ameto* he has described the ennobling and transfiguring power of love in a manner which would hardly be expected from the author of the *Decameron*. In the *Fiammetta* we have another great and minutely painted picture of the human soul, full of the keenest observation, though executed with anything but uniform power, and in parts marred by the passion for high-sounding language and by an unlucky mixture of mythological allusions and learned quotations. The *Fiammetta*, if we are not mistaken, is a sort of feminine counterpart to the *Vita nuova* of Dante, or at any rate owes its origin to it.

That the ancient poets, particularly the elegists, and Virgil, in the fourth book of the *Aeneid*, were not without influence on the Italians of this and the following generation is beyond a doubt; but the spring of sentiment within the latter was nevertheless powerful and original. If we compare them in this respect with their contemporaries in other countries, we shall find in them the earliest complete expression of modern European feeling. The question, be it remembered, is not to know whether eminent men of other nations did not feel as deeply and as nobly, but who first gave documentary proof of the widest knowledge of the movements of the human heart.

Why did the Italians of the Renaissance do nothing above the second rank in tragedy? That was the field on which to display human character, intellect and passion in the thousand forms of their growth, their struggles and their decline. In other words: why did Italy produce no Shakespeare? For with the stage of other northern countries besides England the Italians of the sixteenth and seventeenth centuries had no reason to fear a comparison; and with the Spaniards they could not enter into competition, since Italy had long lost all traces of religious fanaticism, treated the chivalrous code of honour only as a form, and was both too proud and too intelligent to bow down before its tyrannical and illegitimate masters. We have therefore only to consider the English stage in the period of its brief splendour.

It is an obvious reply that all Europe produced but one Shakespeare, and that such a mind is the rarest of Heaven's gifts. It is further possible that the Italian stage was on the way to something great when the Counter-Reformation broke in upon it, and, aided by the Spanish rule over Naples and Milan, and indirectly over almost the whole peninsula, withered the best flowers of the Italian spirit. It would be hard to conceive of Shakespeare himself under a Spanish viceroy, or in the neighbourhood of the Holy Inquisition at Rome, or even in his own country a few decades later, at the time of the English Revolution. The stage, which in its perfection is a late product of every civilization, must wait for its own time and fortune.

We must not, however, quit this subject without mentioning certain circumstances which were of a character to hinder or retard a high development of the drama in Italy till the time for it had gone by.

As the most weighty of these causes we must mention without doubt that the scenic tastes of the people were occupied elsewhere, and chiefly in the mysteries and religious processions. Throughout all Europe dramatic representations of sacred history and legend form the origin of the secular drama; but Italy, as it will be shown more fully in the sequel, had spent on the mysteries such a wealth of decorative splendour as could not but be unfavourable to the dramatic element. Out of all the countless and costly representations, there sprang not even a branch of poetry like the *autos sacramentales* of Calderón and other Spanish poets, much less any advantage or foundation for the legitimate drama.

And when the latter did at length appear, it at once gave itself up to magnificence of scenic effects, to which the mysteries had already accustomed the public taste to far too great an extent. We learnt with astonishment how rich and splendid the scenes in Italy were, at a time when in the North the simplest indication of the place was thought sufficient. This alone might have had no such unfavourable effect on the drama if the attention of the audience had not been drawn away from the poetical conception of the play partly by the splendour of the costumes, partly and chiefly by fantastic interludes (*intermezzi*).

That in many places, particularly in Rome and Ferrara, Plautus and Terence, as well as pieces by the old tragedians, were given in Latin or in Italian, that the academies of which we have already spoken made this one of their chief objects, and that the poets of the Renaissance followed these models too servilely, were all untoward conditions for the Italian stage at the period in question. Yet I hold them to be of secondary importance. Had not the Counter-Reformation and the rule of foreigners intervened, these very disadvantages might have been turned into useful means of transition. At all events, by the year 1520 the victory of the mother-tongue in tragedy and comedy was, to the great disgust of the humanists, as good as won. On this side, then, no obstacle stood in the way of the most developed people in Europe to hinder them from raising the drama, in its noblest forms, to be a true reflection of human life and destiny. It was the Inquisitors and Spaniards who cowed the Italian spirit, and rendered impossible the representation of the greatest and most sublime themes, most of all when they were associated with patriotic memories. At the same time, there is no doubt that the distracting *intermezzi* did serious harm to the drama. We must now consider them a little more closely.

When the marriage of Alfonso of Ferrara with Lucrezia Borgia was celebrated, Duke Hercules in person showed his illustrious guests the 110 costumes which were to serve at the representation of five comedies of Plautus, in order that all might see that not one of them was used twice. But all this display of silk and camlet was nothing to the ballets and pantomimes which served as interludes between the acts of the Plautine dramas. That, in comparison, Plautus himself seemed mortally dull to a lively young lady like Isabella Gonzaga, and that while the play was going on everybody was longing for the interludes, is quite intelligible when we think of the picturesque brilliancy with which they were put on the stage. There were to be seen combats of Roman warriors, who brandished their weapons to the sound of music, torch-dances executed by Moors, a dance of savages with horns of plenty, out of which streamed waves of fire – all as the ballet of a pantomime in which a maiden was delivered from a dragon. Then came a dance of fools, got up as Punches, beating one another with pigs' bladders, with more of the same kind. At the court of Ferrara they never gave a comedy without 'its' ballet (*moresca*). In what style the *Amphitruo* of Plautus was there represented (1491, at the first marriage of Alfonso with Anna Sforza) is doubtful. Possibly it was given rather as a pantomime with music than as a drama. In any case, the accessories were more considerable than the play itself. There was a choral dance of ivy-clad youths, moving in intricate figures, done to the music of a

ringing orchestra; then came Apollo, striking the lyre with the plec-
trum, and singing an ode to the praise of the House of Este; then
followed, as an interlude within an interlude, a kind of rustic farce,
after which the stage was again occupied by classical mythology –
Venus, Bacchus and their followers – and by a pantomime representing
the judgement of Paris. Not till then was the second half of the fable of
Amphitruo performed, with unmistakable references to the future
birth of a Hercules of the House of Este. At a former representation of
the same piece in the courtyard of the palace (1487), 'a paradise with
stars and other wheels' was constantly burning, by which is probably
meant an illumination with fireworks, that, no doubt, absorbed most
of the attention of the spectators. It was certainly better when such
performances were given separately, as was the case at other courts.
We shall have to speak of the entertainments given by the Cardinal
Pietro Riario, by the Bentivogli at Bologna, and by others, when we
come to treat of the festivals in general.

This scenic magnificence, now become universal, had a disastrous
effect on Italian tragedy. 'In Venice formerly,' writes Francesco Sansovino, about 1570,

> besides comedies, tragedies by ancient and modern writers were put on
> the stage with great pomp. The fame of the scenic arrangements
> (*apparati*) brought spectators from far and near. Nowadays, perform-
> ances are given by private individuals in their own houses, and the
> custom has long been fixed of passing the carnival in comedies and
> other cheerful entertainments.

In other words, scenic display had helped to kill tragedy.

The various starts or attempts of these modern tragedians, among
which the *Sofonisba* of Trissino (1515) was the most celebrated, belong
to the history of literature. The same may be said of genteel comedy,
modelled on Plautus and Terence. Even Ariosto could do nothing of
the first order in this style. On the other hand, popular prose-comedy,
as treated by Machiavelli, Bibbiena and Aretino, might have had a
future, if its matter had not condemned it to destruction. This was, on
the one hand, licentious to the last degree, and on the other, aimed at
certain classes in society, which, after the middle of the sixteenth
century, ceased to afford a ground for public attacks. If in the *Sofonisba*
the portrayal of character gave place to brilliant declamation, the latter,
with its half-sister caricature, was used far too freely in comedy also.

The writing of tragedies and comedies, and the practice of putting both ancient and modern plays on the stage, continued without intermission; but they served only as occasions for display. The national genius turned elsewhere for living interest. When the opera and the pastoral fable came up, these attempts were at length wholly abandoned.

One form of comedy only was and remained national – the unwritten, improvised *commedia dell'arte*. It was of no great service in the delineation of character, since the masks used were few in number and familiar to everybody. But the talent of the nation had such an affinity for this style that often in the middle of written comedies the actors would throw themselves on their own inspiration, so that a new mixed form of comedy came into existence in some places. The plays given in Venice by Burchiello, and afterwards by the company of Armonio, Val. Zuccato, Lod. Dolce and others, were perhaps of this character. Of Burchiello we know expressly that he used to heighten the comic effect by mixing Greek and Slavonic words with the Venetian dialect. A complete *commedia dell'arte*, or very nearly so, was represented by Angelo Beolco, known as *il Ruzzante* (1502–42), whose customary masks were Paduan peasants, with the names Menato, Vezzo, Billora, etc. He studied their dialect when spending the summer at the villa of his patron Luigi Cornaro (Aloysius Cornelius) at Codevico. Gradually all the famous local masks made their appearance, whose remains still delight the Italian populace in our day: Pantalone, the Doctor, Brighella, Pulcinella, Arlecchino and the rest. Most of them are of great antiquity, and possibly are historically connected with the masks in the old Roman farces; but it was not till the sixteenth century that several of them were combined in one piece. At the present time this is less often the case; but every great city still keeps to its local mask – Naples to the Pulcinella, Florence to the Stentorello, Milan to its often so admirable Meneghino.

This is indeed scanty compensation for a people which possessed the power, perhaps to a greater degree than any other, to reflect and contemplate its own highest qualities in the mirror of the drama. But this power was destined to be marred for centuries by hostile forces, for whose predominance the Italians were only in part responsible. The universal talent for dramatic representation could not indeed be uprooted, and in music Italy long made good its claim to supremacy in Europe. Those who can find in this world of sound a compensation for the drama, to which all future was denied, have, at all events, no meagre source of consolation.

But perhaps we can find in epic poetry what the stage fails to offer us. Yet the chief reproach made against the heroic poetry of Italy is precisely on the score of the insignificance and imperfect representation of its characters.

Other merits are allowed to belong to it, among the rest, that for three centuries it has been actually read and constantly reprinted, while nearly the whole of the epic poetry of other nations has become a mere matter of literary or historical curiosity. Does this perhaps lie in the taste of the readers, who demand something different from what would satisfy a northern public? Certainly, without the power of entering to some degree into Italian sentiment, it is impossible to appreciate the characteristic excellence of these poems, and many distinguished men declare that they can make nothing of them. And in truth, if we criticize Pulci, Boiardo, Ariosto and Berni solely with an eye to their thought and matter, we shall fail to do them justice. They are artists of a peculiar kind, who write for a people which is distinctly and eminently artistic.

The medieval legends had lived on after the gradual extinction of the poetry of chivalry, in the form partly of rhyming adaptations and collections, and partly of novels in prose. The latter was the case in Italy during the fourteenth century; but the newly awakened memories of antiquity were rapidly growing up to a gigantic size, and soon cast into the shade all the fantastic creations of the Middle Ages. Boccaccio, for example, in his *Amorosa visione*, names among the heroes in his enchanted palace Tristram, Arthur, Galeotto and others, but briefly, as if he were ashamed to speak of them; and following writers either do not name them at all, or name them only for purposes of ridicule. But the people kept them in its memory, and from the people they passed into the hands of the poets of the fifteenth century. These were now able to conceive and represent their subjects in a wholly new manner. But they did more. They introduced into it a multitude of fresh elements, and in fact recast it from beginning to end. It must not be expected of them that they should treat such subjects with the respect once felt for them. All other countries must envy them the advantage of having a popular interest of this kind to appeal to; but they could not without hypocrisy treat these myths with any respect.

Instead of this, they moved with victorious freedom in the new field which poetry had won. What they chiefly aimed at seems to have been that their poems, when recited, should produce the most harmonious and exhilarating effect. These works indeed gain immensely when they are repeated, not as a whole, but piecemeal, and with a slight touch of comedy in voice and gesture. A deeper and more detailed portrayal of character would do little to enhance this effect; though the reader may desire it, the hearer, who sees the rhapsodist standing before him, and who hears only one piece at a time, does not think about it at all. With respect to the figures, which the poet found ready made for him, his feeling was of a double kind; his humanistic culture protested against their medieval character, and their combats as counterparts of the battles and tournaments of the poet's own age exercised all his knowledge and artistic power, while at the same time they called forth all the highest qualities in the reciter. Even in Pulci, accordingly, we find no parody, strictly speaking, of chivalry, nearly as the rough humour of his paladins at times approaches it. By their side stands the ideal of pugnacity – the droll and jovial Morgante – who masters whole armies with his bell-clapper, and who is himself thrown into relief by contrast with the grotesque and most interesting monster Margutte. Yet Pulci lays no special stress on these two rough and vigorous characters, and his story, long after they had disappeared from it, maintains its singular course. Boiardo treats his characters with the same mastery, using them for serious or comic purposes as he pleases; he has his fun even out of supernatural beings, whom he sometimes intentionally depicts as louts. But there is one artistic aim which he pursues as earnestly as Pulci, namely, the lively and exact description of all that goes forward. Pulci recited his poem, as one book after another was finished, before the society of Lorenzo il Magnifico, and in the same way Boiardo recited his at the court of Hercules of Ferrara. It may be easily imagined what sort of excellence such an audience demanded, and how little thanks a profound exposition of character would have earned for the poet. Under these circumstances the poems naturally formed no complete whole, and might just as well be half or twice as long as they now are. Their composition is not that of a great historical picture, but rather that of a frieze, or of some rich festoon entwined among groups of picturesque figures. And precisely as in the figures or tendrils of a frieze we do not look for minuteness of execution in the individual forms, or for distant perspectives and different planes, so we must as little expect anything of the kind from these poems.

The varied richness of invention which continually astonishes us, most of all in the case of Boiardo, turns to ridicule all our school definitions as to the essence of epic poetry. For that age, this form of literature was the most agreeable diversion from archeological studies, and, indeed, the only possible means of re-establishing an independent class of narrative poetry. For the versification of ancient history could only lead to the false tracks which were trodden by Petrarch in his *Africa*, written in Latin hexameters, and a hundred and fifty years later by Trissino in his *Italy Delivered from the Goths*, composed in *versi sciolti* – a never-ending poem of faultless language and versification, which only makes us doubt whether this unlucky alliance has been more disastrous to history or to poetry.

And whither did the example of Dante beguile those who imitated him? The visionary *Trionfi* of Petrarch were the last of the works written under this influence which satisfy our taste. The *Amorosa visione* of Boccaccio is at bottom no more than an enumeration of historical or fabulous characters, arranged under allegorical categories. Others preface what they have to tell with a baroque imitation of Dante's first canto, and provide themselves with some allegorical comparison, to take the place of Virgil. Uberti, for example, chose Solinus for his geographical poem, the *Dittamondo*, and Giovanni Santi, Plutarch for his encomium on Frederick of Urbino. The only salvation of the time from these false tendencies lay in the new epic poetry which was represented by Pulci and Boiardo. The admiration and curiosity with which it was received, and the like of which will perhaps never fall again to the lot of epic poetry to the end of time, is a brilliant proof of how great was the need of it. It is idle to ask whether that epic ideal which our own day has formed from Homer and the *Nibelungenlied* is or is not realized in these works; an ideal of their own age certainly was. By their endless descriptions of combats, which to us are the most fatiguing part of these poems, they satisfied, as we have already said, a practical interest of which it is hard for us to form a just conception – as hard, indeed, as of the esteem in which a lively and faithful reflection of the passing moment was then held.

Nor can a more inappropriate test be applied to Ariosto than the degree in which his *Orlando Furioso* serves for the representation of character. Characters, indeed, there are, and drawn with an affectionate care; but the poem does not depend on these for its effect, and would lose, rather than gain, if more stress were laid upon them. But the demand for them is part of a wider and more general desire which Ariosto fails to satisfy as our day would wish it satisfied. From a poet of such fame and such mighty gifts we would gladly receive something better than the adventures of Orlando. From him we might have hoped for a work expressing the deepest conflicts of the human soul, the highest thoughts of his time on human and divine things – in a word, one of those supreme syntheses like the *Divine Comedy* or *Faust*. Instead of which he goes to work like the plastic artists of his own day, not caring for originality in our sense of the word, simply reproducing a familiar circle of figures, and even, when it suits his purpose, making use of the details left him by his predecessors. The excellence which, in spite of all this, can nevertheless be attained, will be the more incomprehensible to people born without the artistic sense, the more learned and intelligent in other respects they are. The artistic aim of Ariosto is brilliant, living action, which he distributes equally through the whole of his great poem. For this end he needs to be excused, not only from all deeper expression of character, but also from maintaining any strict connection in his narrative. He must be allowed to take up lost and forgotten threads when and where he pleases; his heroes must come and go, not because their character, but because the story requires it. Yet in this apparently irrational and arbitrary style of composition he displays a harmonious beauty, never losing himself in description, but giving only such a sketch of scenes and persons as does not hinder the flowing movement of the narrative. Still less does he lose himself in conversation and monologue, but maintains the lofty privilege of the true epos, by transforming all into living narrative. His pathos does not lie in the words, not even in the famous twenty-third and following cantos, where Roland's madness is described. That the love-stories in the heroic poem are without all lyrical tenderness must be reckoned a merit, though from a moral point of view they cannot be always approved. Yet at times they are of such truth and reality, notwithstanding all the magic and romance which surrounds them, that we might think them personal affairs of the poet himself. In the full consciousness of his own genius, he does not scruple to interweave the events of his own day into the poem, and to celebrate the fame of the house of Este in visions and prophecies. The wonderful stream of his octaves bears it all forward in even and dignified movement.

With Teofilo Folengo, or, as he here calls himself, Limerno Pitocco, the parody of the whole system of chivalry attained the end it had so long desired. But here comedy, with its realism, demanded of necessity a stricter delineation of character. Exposed to all the rough usage of the half-savage street-lads in a Roman country town, Sutri, the little Orlando grows up before our eyes into the hero, the priest-hater and the disputant. The conventional world which had been recognized since the time of Pulci and had served as a framework for the epos, here falls to pieces. The origin and position of the paladins is openly ridiculed, as in the tournament of donkeys in the second book, where the knights appear with the most ludicrous armament. The poet utters his ironical regrets over the inexplicable faithlessness which seems implanted in the house of Gano of Mainz, over the toilsome acquisition of the sword Durindana, and so forth. Tradition, in fact, serves him only as a substratum for episodes, ludicrous fancies, allusions to events of the time (among which some, like the close of cap. vi., are exceedingly fine) and indecent jokes. Mixed with all this, a certain derision of Ariosto is unmistakable, and it was fortunate for the *Orlando Furioso* that the *Orlandino*, with its Lutheran heresies, was soon put out of the way by the Inquisition. The parody is evident when (cap. v. str. 28) the house of Gonzaga is deduced from the paladin Guidone, since the Colonna claimed Orlando, the Orsini Rinaldo, and the house of Este – according to Ariosto – Ruggiero as their ancestors. Perhaps Ferrante Gonzaga, the patron of the poet, was a party to this sarcasm on the house of Este.

That in the *Jerusalem Delivered* of Torquato Tasso the delineation of character is one of the chief tasks of the poet proves only how far his mode of thought differed from that prevalent half a century before. His admirable work is a true monument of the Counter-Reformation which had meanwhile been accomplished, and of the spirit and tendency of that movement.

BIOGRAPHY IN THE MIDDLE AGES AND IN THE RENAISSANCE

Outside the sphere of poetry also, the Italians were the first of all European nations who displayed any remarkable power and inclination accurately to describe man as shown in history, according to his inward and outward characteristics.

It is true that in the Middle Ages considerable attempts were made in the same direction; and the legends of the Church, as a kind of standing biographical task, must, to some extent, have kept alive the interest and the gift for such descriptions. In the annals of the monasteries and cathedrals, many of the churchmen, such as Meinwerk of Paderborn, Godehard of Hildesheim and others, are brought vividly before our eyes; and descriptions exist of several of the German emperors, modelled after old authors – particularly Suetonius – which contain admirable features. Indeed these and other profane *vitae* came in time to form a continuous counterpart to the sacred legends. Yet neither Einhard nor Wippo nor Radevicus can be named by the side of Joinville's picture of St Louis, which certainly stands almost alone as the first complete spiritual portrait of a modern European nature. Characters like St Louis are rare at all times, and his was favoured by the rare good fortune that a sincere and naïve observer caught the spirit of all the events and actions of his life, and represented it admirably. From what scanty sources are we left to guess at the inward nature of Frederick II or of Philip the Fair. Much of what, till the close of the Middle Ages, passed for biography, is properly speaking nothing but contemporary narrative, written without any sense of what is individual in the subject of the memoir.

Among the Italians, on the contrary, the search for the characteristic features of remarkable men was a prevailing tendency; and this it is which separates them from the other Western peoples, among whom the same thing happens but seldom, and in exceptional cases. This keen eye for individuality belongs only to those who have emerged from the half-conscious life of the race and become themselves individuals.

Under the influence of the prevailing conception of fame an art of comparative biography arose which no longer found it necessary, like Anastasius, Agnellus and their successors, or like the biographers of the Venetian doges, to adhere to a dynastic or ecclesiastical succession. It felt itself free to describe a man if and because he was remarkable. It took as models Suetonius, Nepos (the *viri illustres*) and Plutarch, so far as he was known and translated; for sketches of literary history, the lives of the grammarians, rhetoricians and poets, known to us as the 'Appendices' to Suetonius, seem to have served as patterns, as well as the widely read life of Virgil by Donatus.

It has been already mentioned that biographical collections – lives of famous men and famous women – began to appear in the fourteenth century. Where they do not describe contemporaries, they are naturally dependent on earlier narratives. The first great original effort is the life of Dante by Boccaccio. Lightly and rhetorically written, and full, as it is, of arbitrary fancies, this work nevertheless gives us a lively sense of the extraordinary features in Dante's nature. Then follow, at the end of the fourteenth century, the *vite* of illustrious Florentines, by Filippo Villani. They are men of every calling: poets, jurists, physicians, scholars, artists, statesmen and soldiers, some of them then still living. Florence is here treated like a gifted family, in which all the members are noticed in whom the spirit of the house expresses itself vigorously. The descriptions are brief, but show a remarkable eye for what is characteristic, and are noteworthy for including the inward and out-ward physiognomy in the same sketch. From that time forward, the Tuscans never ceased to consider the description of man as lying within their special competence, and to them we owe the most valuable portraits of the Italians of the fifteenth and sixteenth centuries. Giovanni Cavalcanti, in the appendices to his Florentine history, written before the year 1450, collects instances of civil virtue and abnegation, of political discernment and of military valour, all shown by Florentines. Pius II gives us in his *Commentaries* valuable portraits of famous contemporaries; and not long ago a separate work of his earlier years, which seems preparatory to these portraits, but which has colours and features that are very singular, was reprinted. To Jacob of Volterra we owe piquant sketches of members of the Curia in the time of Sixtus IV. Vespasiano Fiorentino has been often referred to already, and as a historical authority a high place must be assigned to him; but his gift as a painter of character is not to be compared with that of Machiavelli, Niccolò Valori, Guicciardini, Varchi, Francesco Vettori and others, by whom European historical literature has been probably as much influenced in this direction as by the ancients. It must not be forgotten that some of these authors soon found their way into north-ern countries by means of Latin translations. And without Giorgio Vasari of Arezzo and his all-important work, we should perhaps to this day have no history of northern art, or of the art of modern Europe, at all.

Among the biographers of North Italy in the fifteenth century, Bartolommeo Facio of Spezia holds a high rank. Platina, born in the territory of Cremona, gives us, in his *Life of Paul II*, examples of biographical caricatures. The description of the last Visconti, written by Piercandido Decembrio – an enlarged imitation of Suetonius – is of special importance. Sismondi regrets that so much trouble has been spent on so unworthy an object, but the author would hardly have been equal to deal with a greater man, while he was thoroughly competent to describe the mixed nature of Filippo Maria, and in and through it to represent with accuracy the conditions, the forms and the consequences of this particular kind of despotism. The picture of the fifteenth century would be incomplete without this unique biography, which is characteristic down to its minutest details. Milan afterwards possessed, in the historian Corio, an excellent portrait-painter; and after him came Paolo Giovio of Como, whose larger biographies and shorter *Elogia* have achieved a world-wide reputation, and become models for subsequent writers in all countries. It is easy to prove by a hundred passages how superficial and even dishonest he was; nor from a man like him can any high and serious purpose be expected. But the breath of the age moves in his pages, and his Leo, his Alfonso, his Pompeo Colonna, live and act before us with such perfect truth and reality that we seem admitted to the deepest recesses of their nature.

Among Neapolitan writers, Tristano Caracciolo, so far as we are able to judge, holds indisputably the first place in this respect, although his purpose was not strictly biographical. In the figures which he brings before us, guilt and destiny are wondrously mingled. He is a kind of unconscious tragedian. That genuine tragedy which then found no place on the stage, 'swept by' in the palace, the street and the public square. The *Words and Deeds of Alfonso the Great*, written by Antonio Panormita during the lifetime of the king, is remarkable as one of the first of such collections of anecdotes and of wise and witty sayings.

The rest of Europe followed the example of Italy in this respect but slowly, although great political and religious movements had broken so many bonds, and had awakened so many thousands to new spiritual life. Italians, whether scholars or diplomatists, still remained, on the whole, the best source of information for the characters of the leading men all over Europe. It is well known how speedily and unanimously in recent times the reports of the Venetian embassies in the sixteenth and seventeenth centuries have been recognized as authorities of the first order for personal description. Even autobiography takes here and there in Italy a bold and vigorous flight, and puts before us, together with the most varied incidents of external life, striking revelations of the inner man. Among other nations, even in Germany at the time of the Reformation, it deals only with outward experiences, and leaves us to guess at the spirit within from the style of the narrative. It seems as though Dante's *Vita nuova*, with the inexorable truthfulness which runs through it, had shown his people the way.

The beginnings of autobiography are to be traced in the family histories of the fourteenth and fifteenth centuries, which are said to be not uncommon as manuscripts in the Florentine libraries – unaffected narratives written for the sake of the individual or of his family, like that of Buonaccorso Pitti.

A profound self-analysis is not to be looked for in the *Commentaries* of Pius II. What we here learn of him as a man seems at first sight to be chiefly confined to the account which he gives of the various steps in his career. But further reflection will lead us to a different conclusion with regard to this remarkable book. There are men who are by nature mirrors of what surrounds them. It would be irrelevant to ask incessantly after their convictions, their spiritual struggles, their inmost victories and achievements. Aeneas Sylvius lived wholly in the interest which lay near, without troubling himself about the problems and contradictions of life. His Catholic orthodoxy gave him all the help of this kind which he needed. And at all events, after taking part in every intellectual movement which interested his age, and notably furthering some of them, he still at the close of his earthly course retained character enough to preach a crusade against the Turks, and to die of grief when it came to nothing.

Nor is the autobiography of Benvenuto Cellini, any more than that of Pius II, founded on introspection. And yet it describes the whole man – not always willingly – with marvellous truth and completeness. It is no small matter that Benvenuto, whose most important works have perished half-finished, and who, as an artist, is perfect only in his little decorative speciality, but in other respects, if judged by the works of his which remain, is surpassed by so many of his greater contemporaries – that Benvenuto as a man will interest mankind to the end of time. It does not spoil the impression when the reader often detects him bragging or lying; the stamp of a mighty, energetic and thoroughly developed nature remains. By his side our modern autobiographers, though their tendency and moral character may stand much higher, appear incomplete beings. He is a man who can do all and dares do all, and who carries his measure in himself. Whether we like him or not, he lives, such as he was, as a significant type of the modern spirit.

Another man deserves a brief mention in connection with this subject – a man who, like Benvenuto, was not a model of veracity: Girolamo Cardano of Milan (b. 1500). His little book, *De propria vita*, will outlive and eclipse his fame in philosophy and natural science, just as Benvenuto's life, though its value is of another kind, has thrown his works into the shade. Cardano is a physician who feels his own pulse, and describes his own physical, moral and intellectual nature, together with all the conditions under which it had developed, and this, to the best of his ability, honestly and sincerely. The work which he avowedly took as his model – the *Confessions* of Marcus Aurelius – he was able, hampered as he was by no stoical maxims, to surpass in this particular. He desires to spare neither himself nor others, and begins the narrative of his career with the statement that his mother tried, and failed, to procure abortion. It is worth remark that he attributes to the stars which presided over his birth only the events of his life and his intellectual gifts, but not his moral qualities; he confesses (cap. 10) that the astrological prediction that he would not live to the age of forty or fifty years did him much harm in his youth. But there is no need to quote from so well-known and accessible a book; whoever opens it will not lay it down till the last page. Cardano admits that he cheated at play, that he was vindictive, incapable of all compunction, purposely cruel in his speech. He confesses it without impudence and without feigned contrition, without even wishing to make himself an object of interest, but with the same simple and sincere love of fact which guided him in his scientific researches. And, what is to us the most repulsive of all, the old man, after the most shocking experiences and with his confidence in his fellow-men gone, finds himself after all tolerably happy and comfortable. He has still left him a grandson, immense learning, the fame of his works, money, rank and credit, powerful friends, the knowledge of many secrets and, best of all, belief in God. After this, he counts the teeth in his head, and finds that he has fifteen.

Yet when Cardano wrote, Inquisitors and Spaniards were already busy in Italy, either hindering the production of such natures, or, where they existed, by some means or other putting them out of the way. There lies a gulf between this book and the memoirs of Alfieri.

Yet it would be unjust to close this list of autobiographers without listening to a word from one man who was both worthy and happy. This is the well-known philosopher of practical life, Luigi Cornaro, whose dwelling at Padua, classical as an architectural work, was at the same time the home of all the muses. In his famous treatise *On the Sober Life*, he describes the strict regimen by which he succeeded, after a sickly youth, in reaching an advanced and healthy age, then of eighty-three years. He goes on to answer those who despise life after the age of sixty-five as a living death, showing them that his own life had nothing deadly about it.

Let them come and see, and wonder at my good health, how I mount on horseback without help, how I run upstairs and up hills, how cheerful, amusing and contented I am, how free from care and disagreeable thoughts. Peace and joy never quit me ... My friends are wise, learned and distinguished people of good position, and when they are not with me I read and write, and try thereby, as by all other means, to be useful to others. Each of these things I do at the proper time, and at my ease, in my dwelling, which is beautiful and lies in the best part of Padua, and is arranged both for summer and winter with all the resources of architecture, and provided with a garden by the running water. In the spring and autumn, I go for a while to my hill in the most beautiful part of the Euganean moun- tains, where I have fountains and gardens, and a comfortable dwell- ing; and there I amuse myself with some easy and pleasant chase, which is suitable to my years. At other times I go to my villa on the plain; there all the paths lead to an open space, in the middle of which stands a pretty church; an arm of the Brenta flows through the plantations – fruitful, well-cultivated fields, now fully peopled, which the marshes and the foul air once made fitter for snakes than for men. It was I who drained the country; then the air became good, and people settled there and multiplied, and the land became cultivated as it now is, so that I can truly say: 'On this spot I gave to God an altar and a temple, and souls to worship Him.' This is my consolation and my happiness whenever I come here. In the spring and autumn, I also visit the neighbouring towns, to see and converse with my friends, through whom I make the acquaintance of other distinguished men, architects, painters, sculptors, musicians and cul- tivators of the soil. I see what new things they have done, I look again at what I know already, and learn much that is of use to me. I see palaces, gardens, antiquities, public grounds, churches and fortifica- tions. But what most of all delights me when I travel is the beauty of the country and the places, lying now on the plain, now on the slopes of the hills, or on the banks of rivers and streams, surrounded by gardens and villas. And these enjoyments are not diminished through weakness of the eyes or the ears; all my senses (thank God!) are in the best condition, including the sense of taste; for I enjoy more the simple food which I now take in moderation, than all the delicacies which I ate in my years of disorder.

After mentioning the works he had undertaken on behalf of the republic for draining the marshes, and the projects which he had constantly advocated for preserving the lagoons, he thus concludes:

These are the true recreations of an old age which God has permitted to be healthy, and which is free from those mental and bodily sufferings to which so many young people and so many sickly older people succumb. And if it be allowable to add the little to the great, to add jest to earnest, it may be mentioned as a result of my moderate life that in my eighty-third year I have written a most amusing comedy, full of blameless wit. Such works are generally the business of youth, as tragedy is the business of old age. If it is reckoned to the credit of the famous Greek that he wrote a tragedy in his seventy-third year, must I not, with my ten years more, be more cheerful and healthy than he ever was? And that no consolation may be wanting in the overflowing cup of my old age, I see before my eyes a sort of bodily immortality in the persons of my descendants. When I come home I see before me, not one or two, but eleven grandchildren, between the ages of two and eighteen, all from the same father and mother, all healthy, and, so far as can already be judged, all gifted with the talent and disposition for learning and a good life. One of the younger I have as my playmate [*buffoncello*], since children from the third to the fifth year are born to tricks; the elder ones I treat as my companions, and, as they have admirable voices, I take delight in hearing them sing and play on different instruments. And I sing myself, and find my voice better, clearer and louder than ever. These are the pleasures of my last years. My life, therefore, is alive, and not dead; nor would I exchange my age for the youth of such as live in the service of their passions.

In the 'Exhortation' which Cornaro added at a much later time, in his ninety-fifth year, he reckons it among the elements of his happiness that his treatise had made many converts. He died at Padua in 1565, at the age of over a hundred years.

This national gift did not, however, confine itself to the criticism and description of individuals, but felt itself competent to deal with the qualities and characteristics of whole peoples. Throughout the Middle Ages the cities, families and nations of all Europe were in the habit of making insulting and derisive attacks on one another, which, with much caricature, contained commonly a kernel of truth. But from the first the Italians surpassed all others in their quick apprehension of the mental differences among cities and populations. Their local patriotism, stronger probably than in any other medieval people, soon found expression in literature, and allied itself with the current conception of 'fame'. Topography became the counterpart of biography; while all the more important cities began to celebrate their own praises in prose and verse, writers appeared who made the chief towns and districts the subject partly of a serious comparative description, partly of satire, and sometimes of notices in which jest and earnest are not easy to distinguish. After this, next to some famous passages in the *Divine Comedy*, comes the *Dittamondo* of Uberti (about 1360). As a rule, only single remarkable facts and characteristics are here mentioned: the Feast of the Crows at Sant' Apollinare in Ravenna, the springs at Treviso, the great cellar near Vicenza, the high duties at Mantua, the forest of towers at Lucca. Yet mixed up with all this we find laudatory and satirical criticisms of every kind. Arezzo figures with the crafty disposition of its citizens, Genoa with the artificially blackened eyes and teeth (?) of its women, Bologna with its prodigality, Bergamo with its coarse dialect and hard-headed people. In the fifteenth century the fashion was to belaud one's own city even at the expense of others. Michele Savonarola allows that, in comparison with his native Padua, only Rome and Venice are more splendid, and Florence perhaps more joyous – by which our knowledge is naturally not much extended. At the end of the century, Jovianus Pontanus, in his *Antonius*, writes an imaginary journey through Italy, simply as a vehicle for malicious observations. But in the sixteenth century we meet with a series of exact and profound studies of national characteristics, such as no other people of that time could rival. Machiavelli sets forth in some of his valuable essays the character and the political condition of the Germans and French in such a way that the born northerner, familiar with the history of his own country, is grateful to the Florentine thinker for his flashes of insight. The Florentines begin to take pleasure in describing themselves; and basking in the well-earned sunshine of their intellectual glory, their pride seems to attain its height when they derive the artistic pre-eminence of Tuscany among Italians, not from any special gifts of nature, but from hard, patient work. The homage of famous men from other parts of Italy, of which the sixteenth *capitolo* of Ariosto is a splendid example, they accepted as a merited tribute to their excellence.

Of an admirable description of the Italians, with their various pursuits and characteristics, though in few words and with special stress laid on the Lucchese, to whom the work was dedicated, we can give only the title: *Forcianae Questiones*. Leandro Alberti is not so fruitful as might be expected in his description of the character of the different cities. An anonymous *Commentario* contains among many absurdities some valuable information on the unfortunate conditions prevailing about the middle of the century.

To what extent this comparative study of national and local characteristics may, by means of Italian humanism, have influenced the rest of Europe, we cannot say with precision. To Italy, at all events, belongs the priority in this respect, as in the description of the world in general.

DESCRIPTION OF THE OUTWARD MAN

But the discoveries made with regard to man were not confined to the spiritual characteristics of individuals and nations; his outward appearance was in Italy the subject of an entirely different interest from that shown in it by northern peoples.

Of the position held by the great Italian physicians with respect to the progress of physiology we cannot venture to speak; and the artistic study of the human figure belongs, not to a work like the present, but to the history of art. But something must here be said of that universal education of the eye, which rendered the judgement of the Italians as to bodily beauty or ugliness perfect and final.

On reading the Italian authors of that period attentively, we are astounded at the keenness and accuracy with which outward features are seized, and at the completeness with which personal appearance in general is described. Even today the Italians, and especially the Romans, have the art of sketching a man's picture in a couple of words. This rapid apprehension of what is characteristic is an essential condition for detecting and representing the beautiful. In poetry, it is true, circumstantial description may be a fault, not a merit, since a single feature, suggested by deep passion or insight, will often awaken in the reader a far more powerful impression of the figure described. Dante gives us nowhere a more splendid idea of his Beatrice than where he only describes the influence which goes forth from her upon all around. But here we have not to treat particularly of poetry, which follows its own laws and pursues its own ends, but rather of the general capacity to paint in words real or imaginary forms.

In this Boccaccio is a master – not in the *Decameron*, where the character of the tales forbids lengthy description, but in the romances, where he is free to take his time. In his *Ameto* he describes a blonde and a brunette much as an artist a hundred years later would have painted them – for here, too, culture long precedes art. In the account of the brunette – or, strictly speaking, of the less blonde of the two – there are touches which deserve to be called classical. In the words '*la spaziosa testa e distesa*' lies the feeling for grander forms, which go beyond a graceful prettiness; the eyebrows with him no longer resemble two bows, as in the Byzantine ideal, but a single wavy line; the nose seems to have been meant to be aquiline; the broad, full breast, the arms of moderate length, the effect of the beautiful hand as it lies on the purple mantle – all both foretells the sense of beauty of a coming time, and unconsciously approaches that of classical antiquity. In other descriptions Boccaccio mentions a flat (not medievally rounded) brow, a long, earnest, brown eye and round, not hollowed neck, as well as – in a very modern tone – the 'little feet' and the 'two roguish eyes' of a black-haired nymph.

Whether the fifteenth century has left any written account of its ideal of beauty, I am not able to say. The works of the painters and sculptors do not render such an account as unnecessary as might appear at first sight, since possibly, as opposed to their realism, a more ideal type might have been favoured and preserved by the writers. In the sixteenth century Firenzuola came forward with his remarkable work on female beauty. We must clearly distinguish in it what he had learned from old authors or from artists, such as the fixing of proportions according to the length of the head, and certain abstract conceptions. What remains is his own genuine observation, illustrated with examples of women and girls from Prato. As his little work is a kind of lecture, delivered before the women of this city – that is to say, before very severe critics – he must have kept pretty closely to the truth. His principle is avowedly that of Zeuxis and of Lucian – to piece together an ideal beauty out of a number of beautiful parts. He defines the shades of colour which occur in the hair and skin, and gives to the *biondo* the preference, as the most beautiful colour for the hair, understanding by it a soft yellow, inclining to brown. He requires that the hair should be thick, long and locky; the forehead serene, and twice as broad as high; the skin bright and clear (*candida*), but not of a dead white (*bianchezza*); the eyebrows dark, silky, most strongly marked in the middle, and shading off towards the ears and the nose; the white of the eye faintly touched with blue, the iris not actually black, though all the poets praise *occhi neri* as a gift of Venus, despite that even goddesses were known for their eyes of heavenly blue, and that soft, joyous, brown eyes were admired by everybody. The eye itself should be large and full, and brought well forward; the lids white, and marked with almost invisible tiny red veins; the lashes neither too long, nor too thick, nor too dark. The hollow round the eye should have the same colour as the cheek. The ear, neither too large nor too small, firmly and neatly fitted on, should show a stronger colour in the winding that in the even parts, with an edge of the transparent ruddiness of the pomegranate. The temples must be white and even, and for the most perfect beauty ought not to be too narrow. The red should grow deeper as the cheek gets rounder. The nose, which chiefly determines the value of the profile, must recede gently and uniformly in the direction of the eyes; where the cartilage ceases, there may be a slight elevation, but not so marked as to make the nose aquiline, which is not pleasing in women; the lower part must be less strongly coloured than the ears, but not of a chilly whiteness, and the middle partition above the lips lightly tinted with red. The mouth, our author would have rather small, and neither projecting to a point, nor quite flat, with the lips not too thin, and fitting neatly together; an accidental opening, that is, when the woman is neither speaking nor laughing, should not display more than six upper teeth. As delicacies of detail, he mentions a dimple in the upper lip, a certain fullness of the under lip, and a tempting smile in the left corner of the mouth – and so on. The teeth should not be too small, regular, well marked off from one another, and of the colour of ivory; and the gums must not be too dark or even like red velvet. The chin is to be round, neither pointed nor curved outwards, and growing slightly red as it rises; its glory is the dimple. The neck should be white and round and rather long than short, with the hollow and the Adam's apple but faintly marked; and the skin at every movement must show pleasing lines. The shoulders he desires broad, and in the breadth of the bosom sees the first condition of its beauty. No bone may be visible upon it, its fall and swell must be gentle and gradual, its colour *candidissimo*. The leg should be long and not too hard in the lower parts, but still not without flesh on the shin, which must be provided with white, full calves. He likes the foot small, but not bony, the instep (it seems) high, and the colour white as alabaster. The arms are to be white, and in the upper parts tinted with red; in their consistence fleshy and muscular, but still soft as those of Pallas, when she stood before the shepherd on Mount Ida – in a word, ripe, fresh and firm. The hand should be white, especially towards the wrist, but large and plump, feeling soft as silk, the rosy palm marked with a few, but distinct and not intricate lines; the elevations in it should be not too great, the space between thumb and forefinger brightly coloured and without wrinkles, the fingers long, delicate and scarcely at all thinner towards the tips, with nails clear, even, not too long nor too square, and cut so as to show a white margin about the breadth of a knife's back.

Aesthetic principles of a general character occupy a very subordinate place to these particulars. The ultimate principles of beauty, according to which the eye judges '*senza appello*', are for Firenzuola a secret, as he frankly confesses; and his definitions of *leggiadria*, *grazia*, *vaghezza*, *venustà*, *aria*, *maestà* are partly, as has been remarked, philological, and partly vain attempts to utter the unutterable. Laughter he prettily defines, probably following some old author, as a radiance of the soul.

The literature of all countries can, at the close of the Middle Ages, show single attempts to lay down theoretic principles of beauty; but no other work can be compared to that of Firenzuola. Brantôme, who came a good half-century later, is a bungling critic by his side, because governed by lasciviousness and not by a sense of beauty.

DESCRIPTION OF HUMAN LIFE

Among the new discoveries made with regard to man, we must reckon, in conclusion, the interest taken in descriptions of the daily course of human life.

The comical and satirical literature of the Middle Ages could not dispense with pictures of everyday events. But it is another thing when the Italians of the Renaissance dwelt on this picture for its own sake – for its inherent interest – and because it forms part of that great, universal life of the world whose magic breath they felt everywhere around them. Instead of and together with the satirical comedy, which wanders through houses, villages and streets, seeking food for its derision in parson, peasant and burgher, we now see in literature the beginnings of a true *genre*, long before it found any expression in painting. That *genre* and satire are often met with in union does not prevent them from being wholly different things.

How much of earthly business must Dante have watched with attentive interest before he was able to make us see with our own eyes all that happened in his spiritual world. The famous pictures of the busy movement in the arsenal at Venice, of the blind men laid side by side before the church door, and the like, are by no means the only instances of this kind: for the art, in which he is a master, of expressing the inmost soul by the outward gesture cannot exist without a close and incessant study of human life.

The poets who followed rarely came near him in this respect, and the novelists were forbidden by the first laws of their literary style to linger over details. Their prefaces and narratives might be as long as they pleased, but what we understand by *genre* was outside their province. The taste for this class of description was not fully awakened till the time of the revival of antiquity.

And here we are again met by the man who had a heart for everything – Aeneas Sylvius. Not only natural beauty, not only that which has an antiquarian or a geographical interest, finds a place in his descriptions, but any living scene of daily life. Among the numerous passage in his memoirs in which scenes are described which hardly one of his contemporaries would have thought worth a line of notice, we will here only mention the boat-race on the Lake of Bolsena. We are not able to detect from what old letter-writer or story-teller the impulse was derived to which we owe such lifelike pictures. Indeed, the whole spiritual communion between antiquity and the Renaissance is full of delicacy and of mystery.

To this class belong those descriptive Latin poems of which we have already spoken – hunting-scenes, journeys, ceremonies and so forth. In Italian we also find something of the same kind, as, for example, the descriptions of the famous Medicean tournament by Politian and Luca Pulci. The true epic poets, Luigi Pulci, Boiardo and Ariosto, are carried on more rapidly by the stream of their narrative; yet in all of them we must recognize the lightness and precision of their descriptive touch, as one of the chief elements of their greatness. Franco Sacchetti amuses himself with repeating the short speeches of a troop of pretty women caught in the woods by a shower of rain.

Other scenes of moving life are to be looked for in the military historians. In a lengthy poem, dating from an earlier period, we find a faithful picture of a combat of mercenary soldiers in the fourteenth century, chiefly in the shape of the orders, cries of battle and dialogue with which it is accompanied.

But the most remarkable productions of this kind are the realistic descriptions of country life, which are found most abundantly in Lorenzo il Magnifico and the poets of his circle.

Since the time of Petrarch, an unreal and unconventional style of bucolic poetry had been in vogue, which, whether written in Latin or Italian, was essentially a copy of Virgil. Parallel to this, we find the pastoral novel of Boccaccio and other works of the same kind down to the *Arcadia* of Sannazaro, and later still, the pastoral comedy of Tasso and Guarini. They are works whose style, whether poetry or prose, is admirably finished and perfect, but in which pastoral life is only an ideal dress for sentiments which belong to a wholly different sphere of culture.

But by the side of all this there appeared in Italian poetry, towards the close of the fifteenth century, signs of a more realistic treatment of rustic life. This was not possible out of Italy; for here only did the peasant, whether labourer or proprietor, possess human dignity, personal freedom and the right of settlement, hard as his lot might sometimes be in other respects. The difference between town and country is far from being so marked here as in northern countries. Many of the smaller towns are peopled almost exclusively by peasants who, on coming home at nightfall from their work, are transformed into townfolk. The masons of Como wandered over nearly all Italy; the child Giotto was free to leave his sheep and join a guild at Florence; everywhere there was a human stream flowing from the country into the cities, and some mountain populations seemed born to supply this current. It is true that the pride and local conceit supplied poets and novelists with abundant motives for making game of the *villano*, and what they left undone was taken charge of by the comic improvisers. But nowhere do we find a trace of that brutal and contemptuous class-hatred against the *vilains* which inspired the aristocratic poets of Provence, and often, too, the French chroniclers. On the contrary, Italian authors of every sort gladly recognize and accentuate what is great or remarkable in the life of the peasant. Gioviano Pontano mentions with admiration instances of the fortitude of the savage inhabitants of the Abruzzi; in the biographical collections and in the novelists we meet with the figure of the heroic peasant-maiden who hazards her life to defend her family and her honour.

Such conditions made the poetical treatment of country life possible. The first instance we shall mention is that of Battista Mantovano, whose eclogues, once much read and still worth reading, appeared among his earliest works about 1480. They are a mixture of real and conventional rusticity, but the former tends to prevail. They represent the mode of thought of a well-meaning village clergyman, not without a certain leaning to liberal ideas. As a Carmelite monk, the writer may have had occasion to mix freely with the peasantry.

But it is with a power of a wholly different kind that Lorenzo il Magnifico transports himself into the peasant's world. His *Nencia di Barberino* reads like a crowd of genuine extracts from the popular songs of the Florentine country, fused into a great stream of octaves. The objectivity of the writer is such that we are in doubt whether the speaker – the young peasant Vallera, who declares his love to Nencia – awakens his sympathy or ridicule. The deliberate contrast to the conventional eclogue is unmistakable. Lorenzo surrenders himself purposely to the realism of simple, rough country life, and yet his work makes upon us the impression of true poetry.

The *Beca da Dicomano* of Luigi Pulci is an admitted counterpart to the *Nencia* of Lorenzo. But the deeper purpose is wanting. The *Beca* is written not so much from the inward need to give a picture of popular life, as from the desire to win the approbation of the educated Florentine world by a successful poem. Hence the greater and more deliberate coarseness of the scenes, and the indecent jokes. Nevertheless, the point of view of the rustic lover is admirably maintained.

Third in this company of poets comes Angelo Poliziano, with his *Rusticus* in Latin hexameters. Keeping clear of all imitation of Virgil's *Georgics*, he describes the year of the Tuscan peasant, beginning with the late autumn, when the countryman gets ready his new plough and prepares the seed for the winter. The picture of the meadows in spring is full and beautiful, and the 'Summer' has fine passages; but the vintage-feast in autumn is one of the gems of modern Latin poetry. Politian wrote poems in Italian as well as Latin, from which we may infer that in Lorenzo's circle it was possible to give a realistic picture of the passionate life of the lower classes. His gipsy's love-song is one of the earliest products of that wholly modern tendency to put oneself with poetic consciousness into the position of another class. This had probably been attempted for ages with a view to satire, and the opportunity for it was offered in Florence at every carnival by the songs of the maskers. But the sympathetic understanding of the feelings of another class was new; and with it the *Nencia* and this *Canzone zingaresca* mark a new starting-point in the history of poetry.

Here, too, we must briefly indicate how culture prepared the way for artistic development. From the time of the *Nencia*, a period of eighty years elapses to the rustic genre-painting of Jacopo Bassano and his school.

In the next part of this work we shall show how differences of birth had lost their significance in Italy. Much of this was doubtless owing to the fact that men and mankind were here first thoroughly and profoundly understood. This one single result of the Renaissance is enough to fill us with everlasting thankfulness. The logical notion of humanity was old enough – but here the notion became a fact.

The loftiest conceptions on this subject were uttered by Pico della Mirandola in his speech on the dignity of man,[74] which may justly be called one of the noblest of that great age. God, he tells us, made man at the close of the creation, to know the laws of the universe, to love its beauty, to admire its greatness. He bound him to no fixed place, to no prescribed form of work, and by no iron necessity, but gave him freedom to will and to love. 'I have set thee,' says the Creator to Adam,

> in the midst of the world, that thou mayst the more easily behold and see all that is therein. I created thee a being neither heavenly nor earthly, neither mortal nor immortal only, that thou mightest be free to shape and to overcome thyself. Thou mayst sink into a beast, and be born anew to the divine likeness. The brutes bring from their mother's body what they will carry with them as long as they live; the higher spirits are from the beginning, or soon after, what they will be for ever. To thee alone is given a growth and a development depending on thine own free will. Thou bearest in thee the germs of a universal life.

PART V

Society and Festivals

EQUALITY OF CLASSES

EVERY PERIOD of civilization which forms a complete and consistent whole manifests itself not only in political life, in religion, art and science, but also sets its characteristic stamp on social life. Thus the Middle Ages had their courtly and aristocratic manners and etiquette, differing but little in the various countries of Europe, as well as their peculiar forms of middle-class life.

Italian customs at the time of the Renaissance offer in these respects the sharpest contrast to medievalism. The foundation on which they rest is wholly different. Social intercourse in its highest and most perfect form now ignored all distinctions of caste, and was based simply on the existence of an educated class as we now understand the word. Birth and origin were without influence, unless combined with leisure and inherited wealth. Yet this assertion must not be taken in an absolute and unqualified sense, since medieval distinctions still sometimes made themselves felt to a greater or less degree, if only as a means of maintaining equality with the aristocratic pretensions of the less advanced countries of Europe. But the main current of the time went steadily towards the fusion of classes in the modern sense of the phrase.

The fact was of vital importance that, from certainly the twelfth century onwards, the nobles and the burghers dwelt together within the walls of the cities. The interests and pleasures of both classes were thus identified, and the feudal lord learned to look at society from another point of view than that of his mountain castle. The Church, too, in Italy never suffered itself, as in northern countries, to be used as a means of providing for the younger sons of noble families. Bishoprics, abbacies and canonries were often given from the most unworthy motives, but still not according to the pedigrees of the applicants; and if the bishops in Italy were more numerous, poorer and, as a rule, destitute of all sovereign rights, they still lived in the cities where their cathedrals stood, and formed, together with their chapters, an important element in the cultivated society of the place. In the age of despots and absolute princes which followed, the nobility in most of the cities had the motives and the leisure to give themselves up to a private life free from the political danger and adorned with all that was elegant and enjoyable, but at the same time hardly distinguishable from that of the wealthy burgher. And after the time of Dante, when the new poetry and literature were in the hands of all Italy, when to this was added the revival of ancient culture and the new interest in man as such, when the successful *condottiere* became a prince, and not only good birth, but legitimate birth, ceased to be indispensable for a throne, it might well seem that the age of equality had dawned, and the belief in nobility vanished for ever.

From a theoretical point of view, when the appeal was made to antiquity, the conception of nobility could be both justified and condemned from Aristotle alone. Dante, for example, adapts from Aristotelian definition, 'Nobility rests on excellence and inherited wealth', his own saying, 'Nobility rests on personal excellence or on that of predecessors'. But elsewhere he is not satisfied with this conclusion. He blames himself, because even in Paradise, while talking with his ancestor Cacciaguida, he made mention of his noble origin, which is but a mantle from which time is ever cutting something away, unless we ourselves add daily fresh worth to it. And in the *Convito* he disconnects '*nobile*' and '*nobiltà*' from every condition of birth, and identifies the idea with the capacity for moral and intellectual eminence, laying a special stress on high culture by calling *nobiltà* the sister of *filosofia*.

And as time went on, the greater the influence of humanism on the Italian mind, the firmer and more widespread became the conviction that birth decides nothing as to the goodness or badness of a man. In the fifteenth century this was the prevailing opinion. Poggio, in his dialogue *On Nobility*, agrees with his interlocutors – Niccolò Niccoli and Lorenzo Medici, brother of the great Cosimo – that there is no other nobility than that of personal merit. The keenest shafts of his ridicule are directed against much of what vulgar prejudice thinks indispensable to an aristocratic life.

A man is all the farther removed from true nobility, the longer his forefathers have plied the trade of brigands. The taste for hawking and hunting savours no more of nobility than the nests and lairs of the hunted creatures of spikenard. The cultivation of the soil, as practised by the ancients, would be much nobler than this senseless wandering through the hills and woods, by which men make themselves liker to the brutes than to the reasonable creatures. It may serve well enough as a recreation, but not as the business of a lifetime.

The life of the English and French chivalry in the country or in the woody fastnesses seems to him thoroughly ignoble, and worst of all the doings of the robber-knights of Germany. Lorenzo here begins to take the part of the nobility, but not — which is characteristic — appealing to any natural sentiment in its favour, but because Aristotle in the fifth book of the *Politics* recognizes the nobility as existent, and defines it as resting on excellence and inherited wealth. To this Niccoli retorts that Aristotle gives this not as his own conviction, but as the popular impression; in his *Ethics*, where he speaks as he thinks, he calls him noble who strives after that which is truly good. Lorenzo urges upon him vainly that the Greek word for nobility (*eugeneia*) means good birth; Niccoli thinks the Roman word *nobilis* (i.e. remarkable) a better one, since it makes nobility depend on a man's deeds. Together with these discussions, we find a sketch of the conditions of the nobles in various parts of Italy. In Naples they will not work, and busy themselves neither with their own estates nor with trade and commerce, which they hold to be discreditable; they either loiter at home or ride about on horseback. The Roman nobility also despise trade, but farm their own property; the cultivation of the land even opens the way to a title; 'it is a respectable but boorish nobility'. In Lombardy the nobles live upon the rent of their inherited estates; descent and the abstinence from any regular calling constitute nobility. In Venice, the *nobili*, the ruling caste, were all merchants. Similarly in Genoa the nobles and non-nobles were alike merchants and sailors, and only separated by their birth; some few of the former, it is true, still lurked as brigands in their mountain castles. In Florence a part of the old nobility had devoted themselves to trade; another, and certainly by far the smaller part, enjoyed the satisfaction of their titles, and spent their time, either in nothing at all, or else in hunting and hawking.

The decisive fact was that, nearly everywhere in Italy, even those who might be disposed to pride themselves on their birth could not make good the claims against the power of culture and of wealth, and that their privileges in politics and at court were not sufficient to encourage any strong feeling of caste. Venice offers only an apparent exception to this rule, for there the *nobili* led the same life as their fellow-citizens, and were distinguished by few honorary privileges. The case was certainly different at Naples, where the strict isolation and the ostentatious vanity of its nobility excluded it, above all other causes, from the spiritual movement of the Renaissance. The traditions of medieval Lombardy and Normandy, and the French aristocratic influences which followed, all tended in this direction; and the Aragonese government, which was established by the middle of the fifteenth century, completed the work, and accomplished in Naples what followed a hundred years later in the rest of Italy – a social transformation in obedience to Spanish ideas, of which the chief features were the contempt for work and the passion for titles. The effect of this new influence was evident, even in the smaller towns, before the year 1500. We hear complaints from La Cava that the place had been proverbially rich, as long as it was filled with masons and weavers; whilst now, since instead of looms and trowels nothing but spurs, stirrups and gilded belts was to be seen, since everybody was trying to become a doctor of laws or of medicine, notary, officer or knight, the most intolerable poverty prevailed. In Florence an analogous change appears to have taken place by the time of Cosimo, the first grand duke; he is thanked for adopting the young people, who now despise trade and commerce, as knights of his order of St Stephen. This goes straight in the teeth of the good old Florentine custom, by which fathers left property to their children on the condition that they should have some occupation. But a mania for titles of a curious and ludicrous sort sometimes crossed and thwarted, especially among the Florentines, the levelling influence of art and culture. This was the passion for knighthood, which became one of the most striking follies of the day, at a time when the dignity itself had lost every shadow of significance.

'A few years ago,' writes Franco Sacchetti, towards the end of the fourteenth century,

> everybody saw how all the workpeople down to the bakers, how all the wool-carders, usurers, money-changers and blackguards of all descriptions, became knights. Why should an official need knighthood when he goes to preside over some little provincial town? What has this title to do with any ordinary bread-winning pursuit? How art thou sunken, unhappy dignity! Of all the long list of knightly duties, what

single one do these knights of ours discharge? I wished to speak of these things that the reader might see that knighthood is dead. And as we have gone so far as to confer the honour upon dead men, why not upon figures of wood and stone, and why not upon an ox?

The stories which Sacchetti tells by way of illustration speak plainly enough. There we read how Bernabò Visconti knighted the victor in a drunken brawl, and then did the same derisively to the vanquished; how German knights with their decorated helmets and devices were ridiculed – and more of the same kind. At a later period Poggio makes merry over the many knights of his day without a horse and without military training. Those who wished to assert the privilege of the order, and ride out with lance and colours, found in Florence that they might have to face the government as well as the jokers.

On considering the matter more closely, we shall find that this belated chivalry, independent of all nobility of birth, though partly the fruit of an insane passion for titles, had nevertheless another and a better side. Tournaments had not yet ceased to be practised, and no one could take part in them who was not a knight. But the combat in the lists, and especially the difficult and perilous tilting with the lance, offered a favourable opportunity for the display of strength, skill and courage, which no one, whatever might be his origin, would willingly neglect in an age which laid such stress on personal merit.

It was in vain that from the time of Petrarch downwards the tournament was denounced as a dangerous folly. No one was converted by the pathetic appeal of the poet: 'In what book do we read that Scipio and Caesar were skilled at the joust?' The practice became more and more popular in Florence. Every honest citizen came to consider his tournament – now, no doubt, less dangerous than formerly – as a fashionable sport. Franco Sacchetti has left us a ludicrous picture of one of these holiday cavaliers – a notary seventy years old. He rides out on horseback to Peretola, where the tournament was cheap, on a jade hired from a dyer. A thistle is stuck by some wag under the tail of the steed, who takes fright, runs away and carries the helmeted rider, bruised and shaken, back into the city. The inevitable conclusion of the story is a severe curtain-lecture from the wife, who is not a little enraged at these break-neck follies of her husband.

It may be mentioned in conclusion that a passionate interest in this sport was displayed by the Medici, as if they wished to show – private citizens as they were, without noble blood in their veins – that the society

which surrounded them was in no respect inferior to a court. Even under
Cosimo (1459), and afterwards under the elder Pietro, brilliant tournaments were held at Florence. The younger Pietro neglected the duties of
government for these amusements and would never suffer himself to be
painted except clad in armour. The same practice prevailed at the court
of Alexander VI, and when the Cardinal Ascanio Sforza asked the
Turkish Prince Djem how he liked the spectacle, the barbarian replied
with much discretion that such combats in his country only took place
among slaves, since then, in the case of accident, nobody was the worse
for it. The Oriental was unconsciously in accord with the old Romans in
condemning the manners of the Middle Ages.

Apart, however, from this particular prop of knighthood, we find
here and there in Italy, for example at Ferrara, orders of court servants,
whose members had a right to the title.

But, great as were individual ambitions, and the vanities of nobles
and knights, it remains a fact that the Italian nobility took its place in
the centre of social life, and not at the extremity. We find it habitually
mixing with other classes on a footing of perfect equality, and seeking
its natural allies in culture and intelligence. It is true that for the
courtier a certain rank of nobility was required, but this exigence is
expressly declared to be caused by a prejudice rooted in the public
mind – *per l'opinion'universale* – and never was held to imply the belief
that the personal worth of one who was not of noble blood was in any
degree lessened thereby, nor did it follow from this rule that the prince
was limited to the nobility for his society. It meant simply that the
perfect man – the true courtier – should not be wanting in any
conceivable advantage, and therefore not in this. If in all the relations
of life he was specially bound to maintain a dignified and reserved
demeanour, the reason was not found in the blood which flowed in his
veins, but in the perfection of manner which was demanded from
him. We are here in the presence of a modern distinction, based on
culture and on wealth, but on the latter solely because it enables men to
devote their life to the former, and effectually to promote its interests
and advancement.

COSTUMES AND FASHIONS

But in proportion as distinctions of birth ceased to confer any special
privilege, the individual himself was compelled to make the most of

his personal qualities, and society to find its worth and charm in itself. The demeanour of individuals, and all the higher forms of social intercourse, became ends pursued with a deliberate and artistic purpose.

Even the outward appearance of men and women and the habits of daily life were more perfect, more beautiful and more polished than among the other nations of Europe. The dwellings of the upper classes fall rather within the province of the history of art; but we may note how far the castle and the city mansion in Italy surpassed in comfort, order and harmony the dwellings of the northern noble. The style of dress varied so continually that it is impossible to make any complete comparison with the fashions of other countries, all the more because since the close of the fifteenth century imitations of the latter were frequent. The costumes of the time, as given us by the Italian painters, are the most convenient, and the most pleasing to the eye which were then to be found in Europe; but we cannot be sure if they represent the prevalent fashion, or if they are faithfully reproduced by the artist. It is nevertheless beyond a doubt that nowhere was so much importance attached to dress as in Italy. The nation was, and is, vain; and even serious men among it looked on a handsome and becoming costume as an element in the perfection of the individual. At Florence, indeed, there was a brief period when dress was a purely personal matter, and every man set the fashion for himself, and till far into the sixteenth century there were exceptional people who still had the courage to do so; and the majority at all events showed themselves capable of varying the fashion according to their individual tastes. It is a symptom of decline when Giovanni della Casa warns his readers not to be singular or to depart from existing fashions. Our own age, which, in men's dress at any rate, treats uniformity as the supreme law, gives up by so doing far more than it is itself aware of. But it saves itself much time, and this, according to our notions of business, outweighs all other disadvantages.

In Venice and Florence at the time of the Renaissance there were rules and regulations prescribing the dress of the men and restraining the luxury of the women. Where the fashions were more free, as in Naples, the moralists confess with regret that no difference can be observed between noble and burgher. They further deplore the rapid changes of fashion, and – if we rightly understand their words – the senseless idolatry of whatever comes from France, though in many cases the fashions which were received back from the French were originally Italian. It does not further concern us how far these frequent changes, and the adoption of French and Spanish ways, contributed to the national passion for external display; but we find in them additional evidence of the rapid movement of life in Italy in the decades before and after the year 1500.

We may note in particular the efforts of the women to alter their appearance by all the means which the toilette could afford. In no country of Europe since the fall of the Roman Empire was so much trouble taken to modify the face, the colour of the skin and the growth of the hair, as in Italy at this time. All tended to the formation of a conventional type, at the cost of the most striking and transparent deceptions. Leaving out of account costume in general, which in the fourteenth century was in the highest degree varied in colour and loaded with ornament, and at a later period assumed a character of more harmonious richness, we here limit ourselves more particularly to the toilette in the narrower sense.

No sort of ornament was more in use than false hair, often made of white or yellow silk. The law denounced and forbade it in vain, till some preacher of repentance touched the worldly minds of the wearers. Then was seen, in the middle of the public square, a lofty pyre (*talamo*), on which, besides lutes, dice-boxes, masks, magical charms, song-books and other vanities, lay masses of false hair, which the purging fires soon turned into a heap of ashes. The ideal colour sought for both natural and artificial hair was blond. And as the sun was supposed to have the power of making the hair this colour,[75] many ladies would pass their whole time in the open air on sunshiny days. Dyes and other mixtures were also used freely for the same purpose. Besides all these, we meet with an endless list of beautifying waters, plasters and paints for every single part of the face – even for the teeth and eyelids – of which in our day we can form no conception. The ridicule of the poets, the invectives of the preachers and the experience of the baneful effects of these cosmetics on the skin were powerless to hinder women from giving their faces an unnatural form and colour. It is possible that the frequent and splendid representations of mysteries, at which hundreds of people appeared painted and masked, helped to further this practice in daily life. It is certain that it was widely spread, and that the countrywomen vied in this respect with their sisters in the towns. It was vain to preach that such decorations were the mark of the courtesan; the most honourable matrons, who all the year round never touched paint, used it nevertheless on holidays when they showed themselves in public. But whether we look on this bad habit as a remnant of barbarism, to which the painting of savages is a parallel, or as a consequence of the desire for perfect youthful beauty in feature and in colour, as the art and complexity of the toilette would lead us to think – in either case there was no lack of good advice on the part of the men.

The use of perfumes, too, went beyond all reasonable limits. They were applied to everything with which human beings came into contact. At festivals even the mules were treated with scents and ointments. Pietro Aretino thanks Cosimo I for a perfumed roll of money.

The Italians of that day lived in the belief that they were more cleanly than other nations. There are in fact general reasons which speak rather for than against this claim. Cleanliness is indispensable to our modern notion of social perfection, which was developed in Italy earlier than elsewhere. That the Italians were one of the richest of existing peoples is another presumption in their favour. Proof, either for or against these pretensions, can of course never be forthcoming, and if the question were one of priority in establishing rules of cleanliness, the chivalrous poetry of the Middle Ages is perhaps in advance of anything that Italy can produce. It is nevertheless certain that the singular neatness and cleanliness of some distinguished representatives of the Renaissance, especially in their behaviour at meals, was noticed expressly, and that 'German' was the synonym in Italy for all that is filthy. The dirty habits which Massimiliano Sforza picked up in the course of his German education, and the notice they attracted on his return to Italy, are recorded by Giovio. It is at the same time very curious that, at least in the fifteenth century, the inns and hotels were left chiefly in the hands of Germans, who probably, however, made their profit mostly out of the pilgrims journeying to Rome. Yet the statements on this point may refer rather to the country districts, since it is notorious that in the great cities Italian hotels held the first place. The want of decent inns in the country may also be explained by the general insecurity of life and property.

To the first half of the sixteenth century belongs the manual of politeness which Giovanni della Casa, a Florentine by birth, published under the title *Il Galateo*.[76] Not only cleanliness in the strict sense of the word, but the dropping of all the tricks and habits which we consider unbecoming, is here prescribed with the same unfailing tact with which the moralist discerns the highest ethical truths. In the literature of other countries the same lessons are taught, though less systematically, by the indirect influence of repulsive descriptions.

In other respects also, the *Galateo* is a graceful and intelligent guide to good manners – a school of tact and delicacy. Even now it may be read with no small profit by people of all classes, and the politeness of European nations is not likely to outgrow its precepts. So far as tact is an affair of the heart, it has been inborn in some men from the dawn of civilization, and acquired through force of will by others; but the Italian first recognized it as a universal social duty and a mark of culture and education. And Italy itself had altered much in the course of two centuries. We feel at their close that the time for practical jokes between friends and acquaintances – for *burle* and *beffe* – was over in good society, that the people had emerged from the walls of the cities and had learned a cosmopolitan politeness and consideration. We shall speak later on of the intercourse of society in the narrower sense.

Outward life, indeed, in the fifteenth and the early part of the sixteenth centuries, was polished and ennobled as among no other people in the world. A countless number of those small things and great things which combine to make up what we mean by comfort we know to have first appeared in Italy. In the well-paved streets of the Italian cities, driving was universal, while elsewhere in Europe walking or riding was the custom, and at all events no one drove for amusement. We read in the novelists of soft, elastic beds, of costly carpets and bedroom furniture, of which we hear nothing in other countries. We often hear especially of the abundance and beauty of the linen. Much of all this is drawn within the sphere of art. We note with admiration the thousand ways in which art ennobles luxury, not only adorning the massive sideboard or the light brackets with noble vases, clothing the walls with the moving splendour of tapestry, and covering the toilet-table with numberless graceful trifles, but absorbing whole branches of mechanical work – especially carpentering – into its province. All Western Europe, as soon as its wealth enabled it to do so, set to work in the same way at the close of the Middle Ages. But its efforts produced either childish and fantastic toy-work, or were bound by the chains of a narrow and purely Gothic art, while the Renaissance moved freely, entering into the spirit of every task it undertook and working for a far larger circle of patrons and admirers than the northern artists. The rapid victory of Italian decorative art over north-ern in the course of the sixteenth century is due partly to this fact, though partly the result of wider and more general causes.

LANGUAGE AND SOCIETY

The higher forms of social intercourse, which here meet us as a work of art – as a conscious product and one of the highest products of national life – have no more important foundation and condition than language. In the most flourishing period of the Middle Ages, the nobility of Western Europe had sought to establish a 'courtly' speech for social intercourse as well as for poetry. In Italy, too, where the dialects differed so greatly from one another, we find in the thirteenth century a so-called *curiale*, which was common to the courts and to the poets. It is of decisive importance for Italy that the attempt was there seriously and deliberately made to turn this into the language of literature and society. The introduction to the *Cento novelle antiche*, which were put into their present shape before 1300, avows this object openly. Language is here considered apart from its uses in poetry; its highest function is clear, simple, intelligent utterance in short speeches, epigrams and answers. This faculty was admired in Italy as nowhere else but among the Greeks and Arabs: 'how many in the course of a long life have scarcely produced a single *bel parlare*?'

But the matter was rendered more difficult by the diversity of the aspects under which it was considered. The writings of Dante transport us into the midst of the struggle. His work on the Italian language is not only of the utmost importance for the subject itself, but is also the first complete treatise on any modern language. His method and results belong to the history of linguistic science, in which they will always hold a high place. We must here content ourselves with the remark that long before the appearance of this book the subject must have been one of daily and pressing importance, that the various dialects of Italy had long been the objects of eager study and dispute, and that the birth of the one classical language was not accomplished without many throes.

Nothing certainly contributed so much to this end as the great poem of Dante. The Tuscan dialect became the basis of the new national speech. If this assertion may seem to some to go too far, as foreigners we may be excused, in a matter on which much difference of opinion prevails, for following the general belief.

Literature and poetry probably lost more than they gained by the contentious purism which was long prevalent in Italy, and which marred the freshness and vigour of many an able writer. Others, again, who felt themselves masters of this magnificent language, were tempted to rely upon its harmony and flow, apart from the thought which it expressed. A very insignificant melody, played upon such an instrument, can produce a very great effect. But however this may be, it is certain that socially the language had great value. It was, as it were, the crown of a noble and dignified behaviour, and compelled the gentleman, both in his ordinary bearing and in exceptional moments, to observe external propriety. No doubt this classical garment, like the language of Attic society, served to drape much that was foul and malicious; but it was also the adequate expression of all that is noblest and most refined. But politically and nationally it was of supreme importance, serving as an ideal home for the educated classes in all the states of the divided peninsula. Nor was it the special property of the nobles or of any one class, but the poorest and humblest might learn it if they would. Even now – and perhaps more than ever – in those parts of Italy where, as a rule, the most unintelligible dialect prevails, the stranger is often astonished at hearing pure and well-spoken Italian from the mouths of peasants or artisans, and looks in vain for anything analogous in France or in Germany, where even the educated classes retain traces of a provincial speech. There is certainly a larger number of people able to read in Italy than we should be led to expect from the condition of many parts of the country – as for instance, the States of the Church – in other respects; but what is more important is the general and undisputed respect for pure language and pronunciation as something precious and sacred. One part of the country after another came to adopt the classical dialect officially. Venice, Milan and Naples did so at the noontime of Italian literature, and partly through its influences. It was not till the present century that Piedmont became of its own free will a genuine Italian province by sharing in this chief treasure of the people – pure speech. The dialects were from the beginning of the sixteenth century purposely left to deal with a certain class of subjects, serious as well as comic, and the style which was thus developed proved equal to all its tasks. Among other nations a conscious separation of this kind did not occur till a much later period.

The opinion of educated people as to the social value of language is fully set forth in the *Cortigiano*. There were then persons, at the beginning of the sixteenth century, who purposely kept to the anti-quated expressions of Dante and the other Tuscan writers of his time, simply because they were old. Our author forbids the use of them altogether in speech, and is unwilling to permit them even in writing, which he considers a form of speech. Upon this follows the admission that the best style of speech is that which most resembles good writing. We can clearly recognize the author's feeling that people who have anything of importance to say must shape their own speech, and that language is something flexible and changing because it is some-thing living. It is allowable to make use of any expression, however ornate, as long as it is used by the people; nor are non-Tuscan words, or even French and Spanish words, forbidden, if custom has once applied them to definite purposes.[77] Thus care and intelligence will produce a language, which, if not the pure old Tuscan, is still Italian, rich in flowers and fruit like a well-kept garden. It belongs to the completeness of the *cortigiano* that his wit, his polished manners and his poetry must be clothed in this perfect dress.

When style and language had once become the property of a living society, all the efforts of purists and archaists failed to secure their end. Tuscany itself was rich in writers and talkers of the first order, who ignored and ridiculed these endeavours. Ridicule in abundance awaited the foreign scholar who explained to the Tuscans how little they understood their own language. The life and influence of a writer like Machiavelli was enough to sweep away all these cobwebs. His vigorous thoughts, his clear and simple mode of expression, wore a form which had any merit but that of the *trecentisti*. And on the other hand there were too many North Italians, Romans and Neapolitans who were thankful if the demand for purity of style in literature and conversa-tion was not pressed too far. They repudiated, indeed, the forms and idioms of their dialect; and Bandello, with what a foreigner might suspect to be false modesty, is never tired of declaring: 'I have no style; I do not write like a Florentine, but like a barbarian; I am not ambitious of giving new graces to my language; I am a Lombard, and from the Ligurian border into the bargain.' But the claims of the purists were most successfully met by the express renunciation of the higher qualities of style, and the adoption of a vigorous, popular language in their stead. Few could hope to rival Pietro Bembo who, though born in Venice, nevertheless wrote the purest Tuscan, which to him was a foreign language, or the Neapolitan Sannazaro, who did the same. But the essential point was that language, whether spoken or written, was held to be an object of respect. As long as this feeling was prevalent, the fanaticism of the purists – their linguistic congresses and the rest of it – did little harm. Their bad influence was not felt till much later, when the original power of Italian literature relaxed and yielded to other and far worse influences. At last it became possible for the Accademia della Crusca to treat Italian like a dead language. But this association proved so helpless that it could not even hinder the invasion of Gallicism in the eighteenth century.

This language – loved, tended and trained to every use – now served as the basis of social intercourse. In northern countries, the nobles and the princes passed their leisure either in solitude, or in hunting, fighting, drinking and the like; the burghers in games and bodily exercises, with a mixture of literary or festive amusements. In Italy there existed a neutral ground, where people of every origin, if they had the needful talent and culture, spent their time in conversation and the polished interchange of jest and earnest. As eating and drinking formed a small part of such entertainments, it was not difficult to keep at a distance those who sought society for these objects. If we are to take the writers of dialogues literally, the loftiest problems of human existence were not excluded from the conversation of thinking men, and the production of noble thoughts was not, as was commonly the case in the North, the work of solitude, but of society. But we must here limit ourselves to the less serious side of social intercourse – to the side which existed only for the sake of amusement.

SOCIAL ETIQUETTE

This society, at all events at the beginning of the sixteenth century, was a matter of art; and had, and rested on, tacit or avowed rules of good sense and propriety, which are the exact reverse of all mere etiquette. In less polished circles, where society took the form of a permanent corporation, we meet with a system of formal rules and a prescribed mode of entrance, as was the case with those wild sets of Florentine artists of whom Vasari tells us that they were capable of giving representations of the best comedies of the day. In the easier intercourse of society it was not unusual to select some distinguished lady as president, whose word was law for the evening. Everybody knows the introduction to Boccaccio's *Decameron*, and looks on the presidency of Pampinea as a graceful fiction. That it was so in this particular case is a matter of course; but the fiction was nevertheless based on a practice which often occurred in reality. Firenzuola, who nearly two centuries later (1523) prefaces his collection of tales in a similar manner, with express reference to Boccaccio, comes assuredly nearer to the truth when he puts into the mouth of the queen of the society a formal speech on the mode of spending the hours during the stay which the company proposed to make in the country. The day was to begin with a stroll among the hills passed in philosophical talk; then followed breakfast, with music and singing, after which came the recitation, in some cool, shady spot, of a new poem, the subject of which had been given the night before; in the evening the whole party walked to a spring of water where they all sat down and each one told a tale; last of all came supper and lively conversation 'of such a kind that the women might listen to it without shame and the men might not seem to be speaking under the influence of wine'. Bandello, in the introductions and dedications to single novels, does not give us, it is true, such inaugural discourses as this, since the circles before which the stories are told are represented as already formed; but he gives us to understand in other ways how rich, how manifold and how charming the conditions of society must have been. Some readers may be of opinion that no good was to be got from a world which was willing to be amused by such immoral literature. It would be juster to wonder at the secure foundations of a society which, notwithstanding these tales, still observed the rules of order and decency, and which knew how to vary such pastimes with serious and solid discussion. The need of noble forms of social intercourse was felt to be stronger than all others. To convince ourselves of it, we are not obliged to take as our standard the idealized society which Castiglione depicts as discussing the loftiest sentiments and aims of human life at the court of Guido-baldo of Urbino, and Pietro Bembo at the castle of Asolo. The society described by Bandello, with all the frivolities which may be laid to its charge, enables us to form the best notion of the easy and polished dignity, of the urbane kindliness, of the intellectual freedom, of the wit and the graceful dilettantism, which distinguished these circles. A significant proof of the value of such circles lies in the fact that the women who were the centres of them could become famous and illustrious without in any way compromising their reputation. Among the patronesses of Bandello, for example, Isabella Gonzaga (born an Este) was talked of unfavourably not through any fault of her own, but on account of the too free-lived young ladies who filled her court. Giulia Gonzaga Colonna, Ippolita Sforza married to a Bentivoglio, Bianca Rangona, Cecilia Gallerana, Camilla Scarampa and others were either altogether irreproachable, or their social fame threw into the shade whatever they may have done amiss. The most famous woman of Italy, Vittoria Colonna (b. 1490, d. 1547), the friend of Castiglione and Michelangelo, enjoyed the reputation of a saint. It is hard to give such a picture of the unconstrained intercourse of these circles in the city, at the baths or in the country, as will furnish literal proof of the superiority of Italy in this respect over the rest of Europe. But let us read Bandello, and then ask ourselves if anything of the same kind would have been possible, say, in France, before this kind of society was there introduced by people like himself. No doubt the supreme achievements of the human mind were then produced independently of the help of the drawing-room. Yet it would be unjust to rate the influence of the latter on art and poetry too low, if only for the reason that society helped to shape that which existed in no other country – a widespread interest in artistic production and an intelligent and critical public opinion. And apart from this, society of the kind we have described was in itself a natural flower of that life and culture which was then purely Italian, and which since then has extended to the rest of Europe.

In Florence society was powerfully affected by literature and politics. Lorenzo the Magnificent was supreme over his circle, not, as we might be led to believe, through the princely position which he occupied, but rather through the wonderful tact he displayed in giving perfect freedom of action to the many and varied natures which surrounded him. We see how gently he dealt with his great tutor Politian, and how the sovereignty of the poet and scholar was reconciled, though not without difficulty, with the inevitable reserve prescribed by the approaching change in the position of the house of Medici and by consideration for the sensitiveness of the wife. In return for the treatment he received, Politian became the herald and the living symbol of Medicean glory. Lorenzo, after the fashion of a true Medici, delighted in giving an outward and artistic expression to his social amusements. In his brilliant improvisation – 'The Hawking Party' –

he gives us a humorous description of his comrades, and in the 'Symposium' a burlesque of them, but in both cases in such a manner that we clearly feel his capacity for more serious companionship. Of this intercourse his correspondence and the records of his literary and philosophical conversation give ample proof. Some of the social unions which were afterwards formed in Florence were in part political clubs, though not without a certain poetical and philosophical character. Of this kind was the so-called Platonic Academy which met after Lorenzo's death in the gardens of the Rucellai.

At the courts of the princes, society naturally depended on the character of the ruler. After the beginning of the sixteenth century they became few in number, and these few soon lost their importance. Rome, however, possessed in the unique court of Leo X a society to which the history of the world offers no parallel.

EDUCATION OF THE *CORTIGIANO*

It was for this society – or rather for his own sake – that the *cortigiano*, as described to us by Castiglione, educated himself. He was the ideal man of society, and was regarded by the civilization of that age as its choicest flower; and the court existed for him rather than he for the court. Indeed, such a man would have been out of place at any court, since he himself possessed all the gifts and the bearing of an accomplished ruler, and because his calm supremacy in all things, both outward and spiritual, implied a too independent nature. The inner impulse which inspired him was directed, though our author does not acknowledge the fact, not to the service of the prince, but to his own perfection. One instance will make this clear. In time of war the courtier refuses even useful and perilous tasks, if they are not beautiful and dignified in themselves, such as for instance the capture of a herd of cattle; what urges him to take part in war is not duty but *l'onore*. The moral relation to the prince, as described in the fourth book, is singularly free and independent. The theory of well-bred love-making, set forth in the third book, is full of delicate psychological observation, which perhaps would be more in place in a treatise on human nature generally; and the magnificent praise of ideal love, which occurs at the end of the fourth book, and which rises to a lyrical elevation of feeling, has no connection whatever with the special object of the work. Yet here, as in the *Asolani* of Bembo, the culture of the time shows itself in the delicacy with which this sentiment is represented and analysed. It is true that these writers are not in all cases to be taken literally; but that the discourses they give us were actually frequent in good society cannot be doubted, and that it was no affectation, but genuine passion, which appeared in this dress we shall see further on.

Among outward accomplishments, the so-called knightly exercises were expected in thorough perfection from the courtier, and besides these much that could only exist at courts highly organized and based on personal emulation, such as were not to be found out of Italy. Other points obviously rest on an abstract notion of individual perfection. The courtier must be at home in all noble sports, among them running, leaping, swimming and wrestling; he must, above all things, be a good dancer and, as a matter of course, an accomplished rider. He must be master of several languages, at all events of Latin and Italian; he must be familiar with literature and have some knowledge of the fine arts. In music a certain practical skill was expected of him, which he was bound, nevertheless, to keep as secret as possible. All this is not to be taken too seriously, except what relates to the use of arms. The mutual interaction of these gifts and accomplishments results in the perfect man, in whom no one quality usurps the place of the rest.

So much is certain, that in the sixteenth century the Italians had all Europe for their pupils both theoretically and practically in every noble bodily exercise and in the habits and manners of good society. Their instructions and their illustrated books on riding, fencing and dancing served as the model to other countries. Gymnastics as an art, apart both from military training and from mere amusement, was probably first taught by Vittorino da Feltre and after his time became essential to a complete education. The important fact is that they were taught systematically, though what exercises were most in favour, and whether they resembled those now in use, we are unable to say. But we may infer, not only from the general character of the people, but from positive evidence which has been left for us, that not only strength and skill, but grace of movement was one of the main objects of physical training. It is enough to remind the reader of the great Federigo of Urbino directing the evening games of the young people committed to his care.

The games and contests of the popular classes did not differ essentially from those which prevailed elsewhere in Europe. In the maritime cities boat-racing was among the number, and the Venetian regattas

were famous at an early period. The classical game of Italy was and is
the ball;[78] and this was probably played at the time of the Renaissance
with more zeal and brilliancy than elsewhere. But on this point no
distinct evidence is forthcoming.

MUSIC

A few words on music will not be out of place in this part of our
work. Musical composition down to the year 1500 was chiefly in the
hands of the Flemish school, whose originality and artistic dexterity
were greatly admired. Side by side with this, there nevertheless existed
an Italian school, which probably stood nearer to our present taste.
Half a century later came Palestrina, whose genius still works powerfully among us. We learn among other facts that he was a great
innovator; but whether he or others took the decisive part in shaping
the musical language of the modern world lies beyond the judgement
of the unprofessional critic. Leaving on one side the history of musical
composition, we shall confine ourselves to the position which music
held in the social life of the day.

A fact most characteristic of the Renaissance and of Italy is the
specialization of the orchestra, the search for new instruments and
modes of sound, and, in close connection with this tendency, the
formation of a class of *virtuosi*, who devoted their whole attention to
particular instruments or particular branches of music.

Of the more complex instruments which were perfected and widely
diffused at a very early period, we find not only the organ, but a
corresponding string instrument, the *gravicembalo* or *clavicembalo*. Fragments of these, dating from the beginning of the fourteenth century,
have come down to our own days, adorned with paintings from the
hands of the greatest masters. Among other instruments the first place
was held by the violin, which even then conferred great celebrity on
the successful player. At the court of Leo X, who, when cardinal, had
filled his house with singers and musicians, and who enjoyed the
reputation of a critic and performer, the Jew Giovan Maria and Jacopo
Sansecondo were among the most famous. The former received from
Leo the title of count and a small town; the latter has been taken to be
the Apollo in the *Parnassus* of Raphael. In the course of the sixteenth
century, celebrities in every branch of music appeared in abundance,
and Lomazzo (about the year 1580) names the then most distinguished

masters of the art of singing, of the organ, the lute, the lyre, the *viola da gamba*, the harp, the cithern, the horn and the trumpet, and wishes that their portraits might be painted on the instruments themselves. Such many-sided comparative criticism would have been impossible anywhere but in Italy, although the same instruments were to be found in other countries.

The number and variety of these instruments is shown by the fact that collections of them were now made from curiosity. In Venice, which was one of the most musical cities of Italy, there were several such collections, and when a sufficient number of performers happened to be on the spot, a concert was at once improvised. In one of these museums there was a large number of instruments, made after ancient pictures and descriptions, but we are not told if anybody could play them, or how they sounded. It must not be forgotten that such instruments were often beautifully decorated, and could be arranged in a manner pleasing to the eye. We thus meet with them in collections of other rarities and works of art.

The players, apart from the professional performers, were either single amateurs, or whole orchestras of them, organized into a corporate academy. Many artists in other branches were at home in music, and often masters of the art. People of position were averse to wind instruments, for the same reason which made them distasteful to Alcibiades and Pallas Athene. In good society singing, either alone or accompanied with the violin, was usual; but quartettes of string instruments were also common, and the *clavicembalo* was liked on account of its varied effects. In singing the solo only was permitted, 'for a single voice is heard, enjoyed and judged far better'. In other words, as singing, notwithstanding all conventional modesty, is an exhibition of the individual man of society, it is better that each should be seen and heard separately. The tender feelings produced in the fair listeners are taken for granted, and elderly people are therefore recommended to abstain from such forms of art, even though they excel in them. It was held important that the effect of the song should be enhanced by the impression made on the sight. We hear nothing, however, of the treatment in these circles of musical composition as an independent branch of art. On the other hand it happened sometimes that the subject of the song was some terrible event which had befallen the singer himself.

This dilettantism, which pervaded the middle as well as the upper classes, was in Italy both more widespread and more genuinely artistic than in any other country of Europe. Wherever we meet with a description of social intercourse, there music and singing are always and expressly mentioned. Hundreds of portraits show us men and women, often several together, playing or holding some musical instrument, and the angelic concerts represented in the ecclesiastical pictures prove how familiar the painters were with the living effects of music. We read of the lute-player Antonio Rota, at Padua (d. 1549), who became a rich man by his lessons, and published a handbook on the practice of the lute.

At a time when there was no opera to concentrate and monopolize musical talent, this general cultivation of the art must have been something wonderfully varied, intelligent and original. It is another question how much we should find to satisfy us in these forms of music, could they now be reproduced for us.

EQUALITY OF MEN AND WOMEN

To understand the higher forms of social intercourse at this period, we must keep before our minds the fact that women stood on a footing of perfect equality with men. We must not suffer ourselves to be misled by the sophistical and often malicious talk about the assumed inferiority of the female sex, which we meet with now and then in the dialogues of this time, nor by such satires as the third of Ariosto, who treats woman as a dangerous grown-up child, whom a man must learn how to manage, in spite of the great gulf between them. There is, indeed, a certain amount of truth in what he says. Just because the educated woman was on a level with the man, that communion of mind and heart which comes from the sense of mutual dependence and completion could not be developed in marriage at this time, as it has been developed later in the cultivated society of the North.

The education given to women in the upper classes was essentially the same as that given to men. The Italian, at the time of the Renaissance, felt no scruple in putting sons and daughters alike under the same course of literary and even philological instruction. Indeed, looking at this ancient culture as the chief treasure of life, he was glad that his girls should have a share in it. We have seen what perfection was attained by the daughters of princely houses in writing and speaking Latin. Many others must at least have been able to read it, in order to follow the conversation of the day, which turned largely on classical subjects. An active interest was taken by many in Italian poetry, in which, whether prepared or improvised, a large number of Italian women, from the time of the Venetian Cassandra Fedele onwards (about the close of the fifteenth century), made themselves famous. One, indeed, Vittoria Colonna, may be called immortal. If any proof were needed of the assertion made above, it would be found in the manly tone of this poetry. Even the love-sonnets and religious poems are so precise and definite in their character, and so far removed from the tender twilight of sentiment, and from all the dilettantism which we commonly find in the poetry of women, that we should not hesitate to attribute them to male authors, if we had not clear external evidence to prove the contrary.

For, with education, the individuality of women in the upper classes was developed in the same way as that of men. Till the time of the Reformation, the personality of women out of Italy, even of the highest rank, comes forward but little. Exceptions like Isabella of Bavaria, Margaret of Anjou and Isabella of Castille are the forced result of very unusual circumstances. In Italy, throughout the whole of the fifteenth century, the wives of the rulers, and still more those of the *condottieri*, have nearly all a distinct, recognizable personality, and take their share of notoriety and glory. To these came gradually to be added a crowd of famous women of the most varied kind; among them those whose distinction consisted in the fact that their beauty, disposition, education, virtue and piety combined to render them harmonious human beings. There was no question of 'woman's rights' or female emancipation, simply because the thing itself was a matter of course. The educated woman, no less than the man, strove naturally after a characteristic and complete individuality. The same intellectual and emotional development which perfected the man was demanded for the perfection of the woman. Active literary work, nevertheless, was not expected from her, and if she were a poet, some powerful utterance of feeling, rather than the confidences of the novel or the diary, was looked for. These women had no thought of the public; their function was to influence distinguished men, and to moderate male impulse and caprice.

The highest praise which could then be given to the great Italian women was that they had the mind and the courage of men. We have only to observe the thoroughly manly bearing of most of the women in the heroic poems, especially those of Boiardo and Ariosto, to convince ourselves that we have before us the ideal of the time. The title *virago*, which is an equivocal compliment in the present day, then implied nothing but praise. It was borne in all its glory by Caterina Sforza, wife and afterwards widow of Girolamo Riario, whose hereditary possession, Forlì, she gallantly defended first against his murderers, and then against Cesare Borgia. Though finally vanquished, she retained the admiration of her countrymen and the title *prima donna d'Italia*. This heroic vein can be detected in many of the women of the Renaissance, though none found the same opportunity of showing their heroism to the world. In Isabella Gonzaga this type is clearly recognizable.

Women of this stamp could listen to novels like those of Bandello, without social intercourse suffering from it. The ruling genius of society was not, as now, womanhood, or the respect for certain presuppositions, mysteries and susceptibilities, but the consciousness of energy, of beauty, and of a social state full of danger and opportunity. And for this reason we find, side by side with the most measured and polished social forms, something our age would call immodesty, forgetting that by which it was corrected and counterbalanced – the powerful characters of the women who were exposed to it.

That in all the dialogues and treatises together we can find no absolute evidence on these points is only natural, however freely the nature of love and the position and capacities of women were discussed.

What seems to have been wanting in this society were the young girls, who, even when not brought up in the monasteries, were still carefully kept away from it. It is not easy to say whether their absence was the cause of the greater freedom of conversation, or whether they were removed on account of it.

Even the intercourse with courtesans seems to have assumed a more elevated character, reminding us of the position of the hetaerae in classical Athens. The famous Roman courtesan Imperia was a woman of intelligence and culture, had learned from a certain Domenico Campana the art of making sonnets, and was not without musical accomplishments. The beautiful Isabella de Luna, of Spanish extraction, who was reckoned amusing company, seems to have been an odd compound of a kind heart with a shockingly foul tongue, which latter sometimes brought her into trouble. At Milan, Bandello knew the majestic Caterina di San Celso, who played and sang and recited superbly. It is clear from all we read on the subject that the distinguished people who visited these women, and from time to time lived with them, demanded from them a considerable degree of intelligence and instruction, and that the famous courtesans were treated with no slight respect and consideration. Even when relations with them were broken off, their good opinion was still desired, which shows that departed passion had left permanent traces behind. But on the whole this intellectual intercourse is not worth mentioning by the side of that sanctioned by the recognized forms of social life, and the traces which it has left in poetry and literature are for the most part of a scandalous nature. We may well be astonished that among the 6,800 persons of this class who were to be found in Rome in 1490 – that is, before the appearance of syphilis – scarcely a single woman seems to have been remarkable for any higher gifts. Those whom we have mentioned all belong to the period which immediately followed. The mode of life, the morals and the philosophy of the public women, who with all their sensuality and greed were not always incapable of deeper passions, as well as the hypocrisy and devilish malice shown by some in their later years, are best set forth by Giraldi, in the novels which form the introduction to the *Hecatom-mithi*. Pietro Aretino, in his *Ragionamenti*, gives us rather a picture of his own depraved character than of this unhappy class of women as they really were.

The mistresses of the princes, as has already been pointed out, were sung by poets and painted by artists, and thus have become personally familiar to their contemporaries and to posterity. We hardly know more than the name of Alice Perries; and of Clara Dettin, the mistress of Frederick the Victorious, and of Agnes Sorel, we have only a half-legendary story. With the monarchs of the age of the Renaissance – Francis I and Henry II – the case is different.

DOMESTIC LIFE

After treating of the intercourse of society, let us glance for a moment at the domestic life of this period. We are commonly disposed to look on the family life of the Italians at this time as hopelessly ruined by the national immorality, and this side of the question will be more fully discussed in the sequel. For the moment we must content ourselves with pointing out that conjugal infidelity has by no means so disastrous an influence on family life in Italy as in the North, so long at least as certain limits are not overstepped.

The domestic life of the Middle Ages was a product of popular morals, or if we prefer to put it otherwise, a result of the inborn tendencies of national life, modified by the varied circumstances which affected them. Chivalry at the time of its splendour left domestic economy untouched. The knight wandered from court to court, and from one battlefield to another. His homage was given systematically to some other woman than his own wife, and things went how they might at home in the castle. The spirit of the Renaissance first brought order into domestic life, treating it as a work of deliberate contrivance. Intelligent economical views and a rational style of domestic architecture served to promote this end. But the chief cause of the change was the thoughtful study of all questions relating to social intercourse, to education, to domestic service and organization.

The most precious document on this subject is the treatise on the management of the home by Agnolo Pandolfini (actually written by L. B. Alberti, in 1472).[79] He represents a father speaking to his grown-up sons, and initiating them into his method of administration. We are introduced into a large and wealthy household, which, if governed with moderation and reasonable economy, promises happiness and prosperity for generations to come. A considerable landed estate, whose produce furnishes the table of the house and serves as the basis of the family fortune, is combined with some industrial pursuit, such as the weaving of wool or silk. The dwelling is solid and the food good. All that has to do with the plan and arrangement of the house is great, durable and costly, but the daily life within it is as simple as possible. All other expenses, from the largest in which the family honour is at stake, down to the pocket-money of the younger sons, stand to one another in a rational, not a conventional relation. Nothing is considered of so much importance as education, which the head of the house gives not only to the children, but to the whole household. He first develops his wife from a shy girl, brought up in careful seclusion, to the true woman of the house, capable of commanding and guiding the servants. The sons are brought up without any undue severity, carefully watched and counselled, and controlled 'rather by authority than by force'. And finally the servants are chosen and treated on such principles that they gladly and faithfully hold by the family.

One feature of this book must be referred to, which is by no means peculiar to it, but which it treats with special warmth – the love of the educated Italian for country life. In northern countries the nobles lived in the country in their castles, and the monks of the higher orders in their well-guarded monasteries, while the wealthiest burghers dwelt from one year's end to another in the cities. But in Italy, so far as the neighbourhood of certain towns at all events was concerned, the security of life and property was so great, and the passion for a country residence was so strong, that men were willing to risk a loss in time of war. Thus arose the villa, the country-house of the well-to-do citizen. This precious inheritance of the old Roman world was thus revived, as soon as the wealth and culture of the people were sufficiently advanced.

Pandolfini (Alberti) finds at his villa a peace and happiness for an account of which the reader must hear him speak himself. The economical side of the matter is that one and the same property must, if possible, contain everything – corn, wine, oil, pasture-land and woods – and that in such cases the property was paid for well, since nothing needed then to be got from the market. But the higher enjoyment derived from the villa is shown by some words of the introduction:

> Round about Florence lie many villas in a transparent atmosphere, amid cheerful scenery, and with a splendid view; there is little fog, and no injurious winds; all is good, and the water pure and healthy. Of the numerous buildings many are like palaces, many like castles costly and beautiful to behold.

He is speaking of those unrivalled villas, of which the greater number were sacrificed, though vainly, by the Florentines themselves in the defence of their city in the year 1529.

In these villas, as in those on the Brenta, on the Lombard hills, at Posillipo and on the Vomero, social life assumes a freer and more rural character than in the palaces within the city. We meet with charming descriptions of the intercourse of the guests, the hunting-parties, and all the open-air pursuits and amusements. But the noblest achievements of poetry and thought are sometimes also dated from these scenes of rural peace.

FESTIVALS

It is by no arbitrary choice that in discussing the social life of this period we are led to treat of the processions and shows which formed part of the popular festivals. The artistic power of which the Italians of the Renaissance gave proof on such occasions was attained only by means of that free intercourse of all classes which formed the basis of Italian society. In northern Europe the monasteries, the courts and the burghers had their special feasts and shows as in Italy; but in the one case the form and substance of these displays differed according to the class which took part in them, in the other an art and culture common to the whole nation stamped them with both a higher and a more popular character. The decorative architecture, which served to aid in these festivals, deserves a chapter to itself in the history of art, although our imagination can only form a picture of it from the descriptions which have been left to us. We are here more especially concerned with the festival as a higher phase in the life of the people, in which its religious, moral and poetical ideas took visible shape. The Italian festivals in their best form mark the point of transition from real life into the world of art.

The two chief forms of festal display were originally here, as elsewhere in the West, the mystery, or the dramatization of sacred history and legend, and the procession, the motive and character of which was also purely ecclesiastical.

The performances of the mysteries in Italy were from the first more frequent and splendid than elsewhere, and were most favourably affected by the progress of poetry and of the other arts. In the course of time not only did the farce and the secular drama branch off from the mystery, as in other countries of Europe, but the pantomime also, with its accompaniments of singing and dancing, the effect of which depended on the richness and beauty of the spectacle.

The procession, in the broad, level and well-paved streets of the Italian cities, was soon developed into the *trionfo*, or train of masked figures on foot and in chariots, the ecclesiastical character of which gradually gave way to the secular. The processions at the carnival and at the feast of Corpus Christi were alike in the pomp and brilliancy with which they were conducted, and set the pattern afterwards followed by the royal or princely progresses. Other nations were willing to spend vast sums of money on these shows, but in Italy alone do we find an artistic method of treatment which arranged the processions as a harmonious and significative whole.

What is left of these festivals is but a poor remnant of what once existed. Both religious and secular displays of this kind have abandoned the dramatic element – the costumes – partly from dread of ridicule, and partly because the cultivated classes, who formerly gave their whole energies to these things, have for several reasons lost their interest in them. Even at the carnival, the great procession of masks is out of fashion. What still remains, such as the costumes adopted in imitation of certain religious confraternities, or even the brilliant festival of Santa Rosalia at Palermo, shows clearly how far the higher culture of the country has withdrawn from such interests.

The festivals did not reach their full development till after the decisive victory of the modern spirit in the fifteenth century, unless perhaps Florence was here, as in other things, in advance of the rest of Italy. In Florence, the several quarters of the city were, in early times, organized with a view to such exhibitions, which demanded no small expenditure of artistic effort. Of this kind was the representation of hell, with a scaffold and boats in the Arno, on 1 May 1304, when the Ponte alla Carraia broke down under the weight of the spectators. That at a later time Florentines used to travel through Italy as directors of festivals (*festaiuoli*) shows that the art was early perfected at home.

In setting forth the chief points of superiority in the Italian festivals over those of other countries, the first that we shall have to remark is the developed sense of individual characteristics, in other words, the capacity to invent a given mask, and to act the part with dramatic propriety. Painters and sculptors not merely did their part towards the decoration of the place where the festival was held, but helped in getting up the characters themselves, and prescribed the dress, the paints and the other ornaments to be used. The second fact to be pointed out is the universal familiarity of the people with the poetical basis of the show. The mysteries, indeed, were equally well understood all over Europe, since the biblical story and the legends of the saints were the common property of Christendom; but in all other respects the advantage was on the side of Italy. For the recitations, whether of religious or secular heroes, she possessed a lyrical poetry so rich and harmonious that none could resist its charm. The majority, too, of the spectators – at least in the cities – understood the meaning of mythological figures, and could guess without much difficulty at the allegorical and historical, which were drawn from sources familiar to the mass of Italians.

This point needs to be more fully discussed. The Middle Ages were essentially the ages of allegory. Theology and philosophy treated their categories as independent beings, and poetry and art had but little to add, in order to give them personality. Here all the countries of the West were on the same level. Their world of ideas was rich enough in types and figures, but when these were put into concrete shape, the costume and attributes were likely to be unintelligible and unsuited to the popular taste. This, even in Italy, was often the case, and not only so during the whole period of the Renaissance, but down to a still later time. To produce the confusion, it was enough if a predicate of the allegorical figures was wrongly translated by an attribute. Even Dante is not wholly free from such errors, and, indeed, he prides himself on the obscurity of his allegories in general. Petrarch, in his *Trionfi*, attempts to give clear, if short, descriptions of at all events the figures of Love, of Chastity, of Death and of Fame. Others again load their allegories with inappropriate attributes. In the *Satires* of Vinciguerra, for example, Envy is depicted with rough, iron teeth; Gluttony as biting its own lips, and with a shock of tangled hair, the latter probably to show its indifference to all that is not meat and drink. We cannot here discuss the bad influence of these misunderstandings on the plastic arts. They, like poetry, might think themselves fortunate if allegory could be expressed by a mythological figure – by a figure which antiquity saved from absurdity – if Mars might stand for war, and Diana for the love of the chase.

Nevertheless art and poetry had better allegories than these to offer, and we may assume with regard to such figures of this kind as appeared in the Italian festivals, that the public required them to be clearly and vividly characteristic, since its previous training had fitted it to be a competent critic. Elsewhere, particularly at the Burgundian court, the most inexpressive figures, and even mere symbols, were allowed to pass, since to understand, or to seem to understand them, was a part of aristocratic breeding. On the occasion of the famous 'Oath of the Pheasant' in the year 1454, the beautiful young horsewoman, who appears as 'Queen of Pleasure', is the only pleasing allegory. The huge dishes, with automatic or even living figures within them, are either mere curiosities or are intended to convey some clumsy moral lesson. A naked female statue guarding a live lion was supposed to represent Constantinople and its future saviour, the Duke of Burgundy. The rest, with the exception of a pantomime – *Jason in Colchis* – seems either too recondite to be understood or to have no sense at all. Olivier himself, to whom we owe the description of the scene, appeared costumed as 'The Church', in a tower on the back of an elephant, and sang a long elegy on the victory of the unbelievers.

But although the allegorical element in the poetry, the art and the festivals of Italy is superior both in good taste and in unity of conception to what we find in other countries, yet it is not in these qualities that it is most characteristic and unique. The decisive point of superiority lay rather in the fact that, besides the personifications of abstract qualities, historical representatives of them were introduced in great number – that both poetry and plastic art were accustomed to represent famous men and women. The *Divine Comedy*, the *Trionfi* of Petrarch, the *Amorosa visione* of Boccaccio – all of them works constructed on this principle – and the great diffusion of culture which took place under the influence of antiquity, had made the nation familiar with this historical element. These figures now appeared at festivals, either individualized, as definite masks, or in groups, as characteristic attendants on some leading allegorical figure. The art of grouping and composition was thus learnt in Italy at a time when the most splendid exhibitions in other countries were made up of unintelligible symbolism or unmeaning puerilities.

Let us begin with that kind of festival which is perhaps the oldest of all – the mysteries. They resembled in their main features those performed in the rest of Europe. In the public squares, in the churches and in the cloisters, extensive scaffolds were constructed, the upper storey of which served as a paradise to open and shut at will, and the ground-floor often as a hell, while between the two lay the stage properly so called, representing the scene of all the earthly events of the drama. In Italy, as elsewhere, the biblical or legendary play often began with an introductory dialogue between Apostles, Prophets, Sibyls, Virtues and Fathers of the Church, and sometimes ended with a dance. As a matter of course the half-comic *intermezzi* of secondary characters were not wanting in Italy, yet this feature was hardly so broadly marked as in northern countries. The artificial means by which figures were made to rise and float in the air – one of the chief delights of these representations – were probably much better understood in Italy than elsewhere; and at Florence in the fourteenth century the hitches in these performances were a stock subject of ridicule. Soon after Brunellesco invented for the Feast of the Annunciation in the Piazza San Felice a marvellous apparatus consisting of a heavenly globe surrounded by two circles of angels, out of which Gabriel flew down in a machine shaped like an almond. Cecca, too, devised the mechanism for such displays. The spiritual corporations or the quarters of the city which undertook the charge and in part the performance of these plays spared, at all events in the larger towns, no trouble and expense to render them as perfect and artistic as possible. The same was no doubt the case at the great court festivals, when mysteries were acted as well as pantomimes and secular dramas. The court of Pietro Riario and that of Ferrara were assuredly not wanting in all that human invention could produce. When we picture to ourselves the theatrical talent and the splendid costumes of the actors, the scenes constructed in the style of the architecture of the period, and hung with garlands and tapestry, and in the background the noble buildings of an Italian piazza, or the slender columns of some great courtyard or cloister, the effect is one of great brilliance. But just as the secular drama suffered from this passion for display, so the higher poetical development of the mystery was arrested by the same cause. In the texts which are left we find for the most part the poorest dramatic groundwork, relieved now and then by a fine lyrical or rhetorical passage, but no trace of the grand symbolic enthusiasm which distinguishes the *autos sacramentales* of Calderón.

In the smaller towns, where the scenic display was less, the effect of these spiritual plays on the character of the spectators may have been greater. We read that one of the great preachers of repentance, of whom more will be said later on, Roberto da Lecce, closed his Lenten sermons during the plague of 1448, at Perugia, with a representation of the Passion. The piece followed the New Testament closely. The actors were few, but the whole people wept aloud. It is true that on such occasions emotional stimulants were resorted to which were borrowed from the crudest realism. We are reminded of the pictures of Matteo da Siena, or of the groups of clay-figures by Guido Mazzoni, when we read that the actor who took the part of Christ appeared covered with weals and apparently sweating blood, and even bleeding from a wound in the side.

The special occasions on which these mysteries were performed, apart from the great festivals of the Church, princely weddings and the like, were of various kinds. When, for example, St Bernardino of Siena was canonized by the pope (1450), a sort of dramatic imitation of the ceremony took place (*rappresentazione*), probably on the great square of his native city, and for two days there was feasting with meat and drink for all comers. We are told that a learned monk celebrated his promotion to the degree of doctor of theology by giving a representation of the legend about the patron saint of the city. Charles VIII had scarcely entered Italy before he was welcomed at Turin by the widowed Duchess Bianca of Savoy with a sort of half-religious pantomime, in which a pastoral scene first symbolized the Law of Nature, and then a procession of patriarchs the Law of Grace. Afterwards followed the story of Lancelot of the Lake, and that 'of Athens'. And no sooner had the king reached Chieri than he was received with another pantomime, in which a woman in childbed was shown, surrounded by distinguished visitors.

If any church festival was held by universal consent to call for exceptional efforts, it was the feast of Corpus Christi, which in Spain gave rise to a special class of poetry. We possess a splendid description of the manner in which that feast was celebrated at Viterbo by Pius II in 1462. The procession itself, which advanced from a vast and gorgeous tent in front of San Francesco along the main street to the cathedral, was the least part of the ceremony. The cardinals and wealthy prelates had divided the whole distance into parts, over which they severally presided, and which they decorated with curtains, tapestry and garlands. Each of them had also erected a stage of his own, on which, as the procession passed by, short historical and allegorical scenes were represented. It is not clear from the account whether all the characters were living beings or some merely draped figures; the expense was certainly very great. There was a suffering Christ amid singing cherubs, the Last Supper with a figure of St Thomas Aquinas, the combat between the Archangel Michael and the devils, fountains of wine and orchestras of angels, the grave of Christ with all the scene of the Resurrection, and finally, on the square before the cathedral, the tomb of the Virgin. It opened after high mass and the benediction, and the Mother of God ascended singing to paradise, where she was crowned by her Son, and led into the presence of the Eternal Father.

Among these representations in the public street, that given by the Cardinal Vice-Chancellor Roderigo Borgia, afterwards Pope

Alexander VI, was remarkable for its splendour and obscure symbolism. It offers an early instance of the fondness for salvos of artillery which was characteristic of the house of Borgia.

The account is briefer which Pius II gives us of the procession held the same year in Rome on the arrival of the skull of St Andrew from Greece. There, too, Roderigo Borgia distinguished himself by his magnificence; but this festival has a more secular character than the other, as, besides the customary choirs of angels, other masks were exhibited, as well as 'strong men', who seemed to have performed various feats of muscular prowess.

Such representations as were wholly or chiefly secular in their character were arranged, especially at the more important princely courts, mainly with a view to splendid and striking scenic effects. The subjects were mythological or allegorical, and the interpretation commonly lay on the surface. Extravagances, indeed, were not wanting – gigantic animals from which a crowd of masked figures suddenly emerged, as at Siena in the year 1465, when at a public reception a ballet of twelve persons came out of a golden wolf; living table ornaments, not always, however, showing the tasteless exaggeration of the Burgundian court – and the like. Most of them showed some artistic or poetical feeling. The mixture of pantomime and the drama at the court of Ferrara has been already referred to in the treating of poetry. The entertainments given in 1473 by the Cardinal Pietro Riario at Rome when Leonora of Aragon, the destined bride of Prince Hercules of Ferrara, was passing through the city were famous far beyond the limits of Italy. The plays acted were mysteries on some ecclesiastical subject; the pantomimes, on the contrary, were mythological. There were represented Orpheus with the beasts, Perseus and Andromeda, Ceres drawn by dragons, Bacchus and Ariadne by panthers, and finally the education of Achilles. Then followed a ballet of the famous lovers of ancient times, with a troop of nymphs, which was interrupted by an attack of predatory centaurs, who in their turn were vanquished and put to flight by Hercules. The fact, in itself a trifle, may be mentioned, as characteristic of the taste of the time, that the human beings who at all festivals appeared as statues in niches or on pillars and triumphal arches, and then showed themselves to be alive by singing or speaking, wore their natural complexion and a natural costume, and thus the sense of incongruity was removed; while in the house of Riario there was exhibited a living child, gilt from head to foot, who showered water round him from a spring.[80]

Brilliant pantomimes of the same kind were given at Bologna, at the marriage of Annibale Bentivoglio with Lucrezia of Este. Instead of the orchestra, choral songs were sung, while the fairest of Diana's nymphs flew over to the Juno Pronuba, and while Venus walked with a lion – which in this case was a disguised man – among a troop of savages. The decorations were a faithful representation of a forest. At Venice, in 1491, the princesses of the house of Este were met and welcomed by the Bucentaur, and entertained by boat-races and a splendid pantomime, called *Meleager*, in the court of the ducal palace. At Milan Leonardo da Vinci directed the festivals of the duke and of some leading citizens. One of his machines, which must have rivalled that of Brunellesco, represented the heavenly bodies with all their movements on a colossal scale. Whenever a planet approached Isabella, the bride of the young duke, the divinity whose name it bore stepped forth from the globe, and sang some verses written by the court-poet Bellincioni (1489). At another festival (1493) the model of the equestrian statue of Francesco Sforza appeared with other objects under a triumphal arch on the square before the castle. We read in Vasari of the ingenious automata which Leonardo invented to welcome the French kings as masters of Milan. Even in the smaller cities great efforts were sometimes made on these occasions. When Duke Borso came in 1453 to Reggio, to receive the homage of the city, he was met at the gate by a great machine, on which St Prospero, the patron saint of the town, appeared to float, shaded by a baldachin held by angels, while below him was a revolving disk with eight singing cherubs, two of whom received from the saint the sceptre and keys of the city, which they then delivered to the duke, while saints and angels held forth in his praise. A chariot drawn by concealed horses now advanced, bearing an empty throne, behind which stood a figure of Justice attended by a genius. At the corners of the chariot sat four grey-headed lawgivers, encircled by angels with banners; by its side rode standard-bearers in complete armour. It need hardly be added that the goddess and the genius did not suffer the duke to pass by without an address. A second car, drawn by a unicorn, bore a Caritas with a burning torch; between the two came the classical spectacle of a car in the form of a ship, moved by men concealed within it. The whole procession now advanced before the duke. In front of the church of San Pietro, a halt was again made. The saint, attended by two angels, descended in an aureole from the façade, placed a wreath of laurel on the head of the duke, and then floated back to his former position. The clergy provided another allegory of a purely religious kind. Idolatry and Faith stood on two lofty pillars, and after Faith, represented by a beautiful girl, had uttered her welcome, the other column fell to pieces with the lay figure upon it. Further on, Borso was met by Caesar with seven beautiful women, who were presented to him as the seven Virtues which he was exhorted to pursue. At last the cathedral was reached, but after the service the duke again took his seat on a lofty golden throne, and a second time received the homage of some of the masks already mentioned. To conclude all, three angels flew down from an adjacent building, and, amid songs of joy, delivered to him branches of palm, as symbols of peace.

Let us now give a glance at those festivals the chief feature of which was the procession itself.

There is no doubt that from an early period of the Middle Ages the religious processions gave rise to the use of masks. Little angels accompanied the sacrament or the sacred pictures and reliques on their way through the streets; or characters in the Passion – such as Christ with the Cross, the thieves and the soldiers, or the faithful women – were represented for public edification. But the great feasts of the Church were from an early time accompanied by a civic procession, and the *naïveté* of the Middle Ages found nothing unfitting in the many secular elements which it contained. We may mention especially the naval car (*carrus navalis*), which had been inherited from pagan times, and which, as an instance already quoted shows, was admissible at festivals of very various kinds, and is associated with one of them in particular – the carnival. Such ships, decorated with all possible splendour, delighted the eyes of spectators long after the original meaning of them was forgotten. When Isabella of England met her bridegroom, the Emperor Frederick II, at Cologne, she was met by a number of such chariots, drawn by invisible horses, and filled with a crowd of priests who welcomed her with music and singing.

But the religious processions were not only mingled with secular accessories of all kinds, but were often replaced by processions of clerical masks. Their origin is perhaps to be found in the parties of actors who wound their way through the streets of the city to the place where they were about to act the mystery; but it is possible that at an early period the clerical procession may have constituted itself as a distinct species. Dante describes the *trionfo* of Beatrice, with the twenty-four Elders of the Apocalypse, with the four mystical Beasts, with the three Christian and four Cardinal Virtues, and with St Luke, St Paul and other Apostles, in a way which almost forces us to conclude that such processions actually occurred before his time. We are chiefly led to this conclusion by the chariot in which Beatrice drives, and which in the miraculous forest of the vision would have been unnecessary or rather out of place. It is possible, on the other hand, that Dante looked on the chariot as a symbol of victory and triumph, and that his poem rather served to give rise to these processions, the form of which was borrowed from the triumph of the Roman emperors. However this may be, poetry and theology continued to make free use of the symbol. Savonarola in his *Triumph of the Cross* represents Christ on a chariot of victory, above his head the shining sphere of the Trinity, in his left hand the Cross, in his right the Old and New Testaments; below him the Virgin Mary; on both sides the Martyrs and Doctors of the Church with open books; behind him all the multitude of the saved; and in the distance the countless host of his enemies – emperors, princes, philosophers, heretics – all vanquished, their idols broken and their books burned. A great picture of Titian, which is known only as a woodcut,[81] has a good deal in common with this description. The ninth and tenth of Sabellico's thirteen elegies on the Mother of God contain a minute account of her triumph, richly adorned with allegories, and especially interesting from that matter-of-fact air which also characterizes the realistic painting of the fifteenth century.

Nevertheless, the secular *trionfi* were far more frequent than the religious. They were modelled on the procession of the Roman Imperator, as it was known from the old reliefs and from the writings of ancient authors. The historical conceptions then prevalent in Italy, with which these shows were closely connected, have already been discussed.

We now and then read of the actual triumphal entrance of a victorious general, which was organized as far as possible on the ancient pattern, even against the will of the hero himself. Francesco Sforza had the courage (1450) to refuse the triumphal chariot which had been prepared for his return to Milan, on the ground that such things were monarchial superstitions. Alfonso the Great, on his entrance into Naples (1443), declined the wreath of laurel, which Napoleon did not disdain to wear at his coronation in Notre-Dame.

For the rest, Alfonso's procession, which passed by a breach in the wall through the city to the cathedral, was a strange mixture of antique, allegorical and purely comic elements. The car, drawn by four white horses, on which he sat enthroned, was lofty and covered with gilding; twenty patricians carried the poles of the canopy of cloth of gold which shaded his head. The part of the procession which the Florentines then present in Naples had undertaken was composed of elegant young cavaliers, skilfully brandishing their lances, of a chariot with the figure of Fortune, and of seven Virtues on horseback. The goddess herself, in accordance with the inexorable logic of allegory to which even the painters at that time conformed, wore hair only on the front part of her head, while the back part was bald, and the genius who sat on the lower steps of the car, and who symbolized the fugitive character of fortune, had his feet immersed in a basin of water. Then followed, equipped by the same Florentines, a troop of horsemen in the costumes of various nations, dressed as foreign princes and nobles, and then, crowned with laurel and standing above a revolving globe, a Julius Caesar, who explained to the king in Italian verse the meaning of the allegories, and then took his place in the procession. Sixty Florentines, all in purple and scarlet, closed this splendid display of what their home could achieve. Then a band of Catalans advanced on foot, with lay figures of horses fastened on to them before and behind, and engaged in a mock combat with a body of Turks, as though in derision of the Florentine sentimentalism. Last of all came a gigantic tower, the door of which was guarded by an angel with a drawn sword; on it stood four Virtues, who each addressed the king with a song. The rest of the show had nothing specially characteristic about it.

At the entrance of Louis XII into Milan in the year 1507 we find, besides the inevitable chariot with Virtues, a living group representing Jupiter, Mars and a figure of Italy caught in a net. After which came a car laden with trophies, and so forth.

And when there were in reality no triumphs to celebrate, the poets found a compensation for themselves and their patrons. Petrarch and Boccaccio had described the representation of every sort of fame as attendants each of an allegorical figure; the celebrities of past ages were now made attendants of the prince. The poetess Cleofe Gabrielli of Gubbio paid this honour to Borso of Ferrara. She gave him seven queens – the seven liberal arts – as his handmaids, with whom he mounted a chariot; further, a crowd of heroes, distinguished by names written on their foreheads; then followed all the famous poets; and after them the gods driving in their chariots. There is, in fact, at this time simply no end to the mythological and allegorical charioteering, and the most important work of art of Borso's time – the frescoes in the Palazzo Schifanoia – shows us a whole frieze filled with these motives. Raphael, when he had to paint the Camera della Segnatura, found this mode of artistic thought completely vulgarized and worn out. The new and final consecration which he gave to it will remain a wonder to all ages.

The triumphal processions, strictly speaking, of victorious generals formed the exception. But all the festive processions, whether they celebrated any special event or were mainly held for their own sakes, assumed more or less the character and nearly always the name of a *trionfo*. It is a wonder that funerals were not also treated in the same way.

It was the practice, both at the carnival and on other occasions, to represent the triumphs of ancient Roman commanders, such as that of Paulus Aemilius under Lorenzo the Magnificent at Florence, and that of Camillus on the visit of Leo X. Both were conducted by the painter Francesco Granacci. In Rome, the first complete exhibition of this kind was the triumph of Augustus after the victory over Cleopatra, under Paul II, where, besides the comic and mythological masks, which, as a matter of fact, were not wanting in the ancient triumphs, all the other requisites were to be found – kings in chains, tablets with decrees of the senate and people, a senate clothed in the ancient costume, praetors, aediles and quaestors, four chariots filled with singing masks and, doubtless, cars laden with trophies. Other processions rather aimed at setting forth, in a general way, the universal empire of ancient Rome; and in answer to the very real danger which threatened Europe from the side of the Turks, a cavalcade of camels bearing masks representing Ottoman prisoners appeared before the people. Later, at the carnival of the year 1500, Cesare Borgia, with a bold allusion to himself, celebrated the triumph of Julius Caesar, with a procession of eleven magnificent chariots, doubtless to the scandal of the pilgrims who had come for the jubilee. Two *trionfi*, famous for their taste and beauty, were given by rival companies in Florence, on the election of Leo X to the papacy. One of them represented the three Ages of Man, the other the Ages of the World, ingeniously set forth in five scenes of Roman history, and in two allegories of the golden age of Saturn and of its final return. The imagination displayed in the adornment of the chariots, when the great Florentine artists undertook the work, made the scene so impressive that such representations became in time a permanent element in the popular life. Hitherto the subject cities had been satisfied merely to present their symbolical gifts – costly stuffs and wax-candles – on the day when they annually did homage. The guild of merchants now built ten chariots, to which others were afterwards to be added, not so much to carry as to symbolize the tribute, and Andrea del Sarto, who painted some of them, no doubt did his work to perfection. These cars, whether used to hold tribute or trophies, now formed part of all such celebrations, even when there was not much money to be laid out. The Sienese announced, in 1477, the alliance between Ferrante and Sixtus IV, with which they themselves were associated, by driving a chariot round the city, with 'one clad as the goddess of peace standing on a hauberk and other arms'.

At the Venetian festivals the processions, not on land but on water, were marvellous in their fantastic splendour. The sailing of the *Bucentaur* to meet the princesses of Ferrara in the year 1491 seems to have been something belonging to fairyland. Countless vessels with garlands and hangings, filled with the richly dressed youth of the city, moved in front; genii with attributes symbolizing the various gods floated on machines hung in the air; below stood others grouped as tritons and nymphs; the air was filled with music, sweet odours and the fluttering of embroidered banners. The *Bucentaur* was followed by such a crowd of boats of every sort that for a mile all round (*octo stadia*) the water could not be seen. With regard to the rest of the festivities, besides the pantomime mentioned above, we may notice as something new a boat-race of fifty powerful girls. In the sixteenth century the nobility were divided into corporations with a view to these festivals, whose most noteworthy feature was some extraordinary machine placed on a ship. So, for instance, in the year 1541, at the festival of the *Sempiterni*, a round 'universe' floated along the Grand Canal, and a splendid ball was given inside it. The carnival, too, in this city was famous for its dances, processions and exhibitions of every kind. The Square of St Mark was found to give space enough not only for tournaments but for *trionfi*, similar to those common on the mainland. At a festival held on the conclusion of peace, the pious brotherhoods (*scuole*) took each its part in the procession. There, among golden chandeliers with red candles, among crowds of musicians and winged boys with golden bowls and horns of plenty, was seen a car on which Noah and David sat together enthroned; then came Abigail, leading a camel laden with treasures, and a second car with a group of political figures – Italy sitting between Venice and Liguria – and on a raised step three female symbolical figures with the arms of the allied princes. This was followed by a great globe with the constellations, as it seems, round it. The princes themselves, or rather their bodily representatives, appeared on other chariots with their servants and their coats of arms, if we have rightly interpreted our author.

The carnival, properly so called, apart from these great triumphal marches, had nowhere, perhaps, in the fifteenth century so varied a character as in Rome. There were races of every kind – of horses, asses, buffaloes, old men, young men, Jews and so on. Paul II entertained the people in crowds before the Palazzo di Venezia, in which he lived. The games in the Piazza Navona, which had probably never altogether ceased since the classical times, were remarkable for their warlike splendour. We read of a sham fight of cavalry, and a review of all the citizens in arms. The greatest freedom existed with regard to the use of masks, which were sometimes allowed for several months together. Sixtus IV ventured, in the most populous part of the city – at the Campofiore and near the Banchi – to make his way through crowds of masks, though he declined to receive them as visitors in the Vatican. Under Innocent VIII, a discreditable usage, which had already appeared among the cardinals, attained its height. In the carnival of 1491, they sent one another chariots full of splendid masks, of singers and of buffoons, chanting scandalous verses. They were accompanied by men on horseback. Apart from the carnival, the Romans seem to have been the first to discover the effect of a great procession by torchlight. When Pius II came back from the Congress of Mantua in 1459, the people waited on him with a squadron of horsemen bearing torches, who rode in shining circles before his palace. Sixtus IV, however, thought it better to decline a nocturnal visit of the people, who proposed to wait on him with torches and olive-branches.

But the Florentine carnival surpassed the Roman in a certain class of processions, which have left their mark even in literature.[82] Among a crowd of masks on foot and on horseback appeared some huge, fantastic chariots, and upon each an allegorical figure or group of figures with the proper accompaniments, such as Jealousy with four spectacled faces on one head; the four temperaments with the planets belonging to them; the three Fates; Prudence enthroned above Hope and Fear, which lay bound before her; the four Elements, Ages, Winds, Seasons and so on; as well as the famous chariot of death with the coffins, which presently opened. Sometimes we meet with a splendid scene from classical mythology – Bacchus and Ariadne, Paris and Helen, and others. Or else a chorus of figures forming some single class or category, as the beggars, the hunters and nymphs, the lost souls, who in their lifetime were hard-hearted women, the hermits, the astrologers, the vagabonds, the devils, the sellers of various kinds of wares, and even on one occasion *il popolo*, the people as such, who all reviled one another in their songs. The songs, which still remain and have been collected, give the explanation of the masquerade sometimes in a pathetic, sometimes in a humorous, and sometimes in an excessively indecent tone. Some of the worst in this respect are attributed to Lorenzo the Magnificent, probably because the real author did not venture to declare himself. However this may be, we must certainly ascribe to him the beautiful song which accompanied the masque of Bacchus and Ariadne, whose refrain still echoes to us from the fifteenth century, like a regretful presentiment of the brief splendour of the Renaissance itself:

> *Quanto è bella giovinezza,*
> *Che si fugge tuttavia!*
> *Chi vuol esser lieto, sia:*
> *Di doman non c'è certezza.*

PART VI

Morality and Religion[83]

MORALITY AND JUDGEMENT

THE RELATION of the various peoples of the earth to the supreme interests of life, to God, virtue and immortality, may be investigated up to a certain point, but can never be compared to one another with absolute strictness and certainty. The more plainly in these matters our evidence seems to speak, the more carefully must we refrain from unqualified assumptions and rash generalizations.

This remark is especially true with regard to our judgement on questions of morality. It may be possible to indicate many contrasts and shades of difference among different nations, but to strike the balance of the whole is not given to human insight. The ultimate truth with respect to the character, the conscience and the guilt of a people remains for ever a secret; if only for the reason that its defects have another side, where they reappear as peculiarities or even as virtues. We must leave those who find pleasure in passing sweeping censures on whole nations to do so as they like. The people of Europe can maltreat, but happily not judge, one another. A great nation, interwoven by its civilization, its achievements and its fortunes with the whole life of the modern world, can afford to ignore both its advocates and its accusers. It lives on with or without the approval of theorists.

Accordingly, what here follows is no judgement, but rather a string of marginal notes, suggested by a study of the Italian Renaissance extending over some years. The value to be attached to them is all the more qualified as they mostly touch on the life of the upper classes, with respect to which we are far better informed in Italy than in any other country in Europe at that period. But though both fame and infamy sound louder here than elsewhere, we are not helped thereby in forming an adequate moral estimate of the people.

What eye can pierce the depths in which the character and fate of nations are determined? – in which that which is inborn and that which has been experienced combine to form a new whole and a fresh nature? – in which even those intellectual capacities, which at first

sight we should take to be most original, are in fact evolved late and
slowly? Who can tell if the Italian before the thirteenth century
possessed that flexible activity and certainty in his whole being – that
play of power in shaping whatever subject he dealt with in word or in
form – which was peculiar to him later? And if no answer can be
found to these questions, how can we possibly judge of the infinite and
infinitely intricate channels through which character and intellect are
incessantly pouring their influence one upon the other. A tribunal
there is for each one of us, whose voice is our conscience; but let us
have done with these generalities about nations. For the people that
seems to be most sick the cure may be at hand; and one that appears to
be healthy may bear within it the ripening germs of death, which the
hour of danger will bring forth from their hiding-place.

MORALITY AND IMMORALITY

At the beginning of the sixteenth century, when the civilization of the
Renaissance had reached its highest pitch, and at the same time the
political ruin of the nation seemed inevitable, there were not wanting
serious thinkers who saw a connection between this ruin and the
prevalent immorality. It was not one of those methodistical moralists
who in every age think themselves called to declaim against the
wickedness of the time, but it was Machiavelli, who, in one of his
most well-considered works, said openly: 'We Italians are irreligious
and corrupt above others.' Another man would have perhaps said,
'We are individually highly developed; we have outgrown the limits
of morality and religion which were natural to us in our undeveloped
state, and we despise outward law, because our rulers are illegitimate,
and their judges and officers wicked men.' Machiavelli adds, 'because
the Church and her representatives set us the worst example'.

Shall we add also, 'because the influence exercised by antiquity was
in this respect unfavourable'? The statement can only be received with
many qualifications. It may possibly be true of the humanists, especially
as regards the profligacy of their lives. Of the rest it may perhaps be
said, with some approach to accuracy, that, after they became familiar
with antiquity, they substituted for holiness – the Christian ideal of life
– the cult of historical greatness. We can understand, therefore, how
easily they would be tempted to consider those faults and vices to be
matters of indifference, in spite of which their heroes were great. They

were probably scarcely conscious of this themselves, for if we are summoned to quote any statement of doctrine on this subject, we are again forced to appeal to humanists like Paolo Giovio, who excuses the perjury of Giangaleazzo Visconti, through which he was enabled to found an empire, by the example of Julius Caesar. The great Florentine historians and statesmen never stoop to these slavish quotations, and what seems antique in their deeds and their judgements is so because the nature of their political life necessarily fostered in them a mode of thought which has some analogy with that of antiquity.

Nevertheless, it cannot be denied that Italy at the beginning of the sixteenth century found itself in the midst of a grave moral crisis, out of which the best men saw hardly any escape.

Let us begin by saying a few words about that moral force which was then the strongest bulwark against evil. The highly gifted man of that day thought to find it in the sentiment of honour. This is that enigmatic mixture of conscience and egotism which often survives in the modern man after he has lost, whether by his own fault or not, faith, love and hope. This sense of honour is compatible with much selfishness and great vices, and may be the victim of astonishing illusions; yet, nevertheless, all the noble elements that are left in the wreck of a character may gather around it, and from this fountain may draw new strength. It has become, in a far wider sense than is commonly believed, a decisive test of conduct in the minds of the cultivated Europeans of our own day, and many of those who yet hold faithfully by religion and morality are unconsciously guided by this feeling in the gravest decisions of their lives.

It lies without the limits of our task to show how the men of antiquity also experienced this feeling in a peculiar form, and how, afterwards, in the Middle Ages, a special sense of honour became the mark of a particular class. Nor can we here dispute with those who hold that conscience, rather than honour, is the motive power. It would indeed be better and nobler if it were so; but since it must be granted that even our worthier resolutions result from 'a conscience more or less dimmed by selfishness', it is better to call the mixture by its right name. It is certainly not always easy, in treating of the Italian of this period, to distinguish this sense of honour from the passion for fame, into which, indeed, it easily passes. Yet the two sentiments are essentially different.

There is no lack of witnesses on this subject. One who speaks plainly may here be quoted as a representative of the rest. We read in the recently published *Aphorisms* of Guicciardini: 'He who esteems honour highly succeeds in all that he undertakes, since he fears neither trouble, danger, nor expense; I have found it so in my own case, and may say it and write it; vain and dead are the deeds of men which have not this as their motive.' It is necessary to add that, from what is known of the life of the writer, he can here be only speaking of honour, and not of fame. Rabelais has put the matter more clearly than perhaps any Italian. We quote him, indeed, unwillingly in these pages. What the great, baroque Frenchman gives us is a picture of what the Renaissance would be without form and without beauty. But his description of an ideal state of things in the Thelemite monastery is decisive as historical evidence. In speaking of his gentlemen and ladies of the Order of Free Will, he tells us as follows:

> *En leur reigle n'estoit que ceste clause: Fay ce que vouldras. Parce que gens liberes, bien nez, bien instruictz, conversans en compaignies honnestes, ont par nature ung instinct et aguillon qui toujours les poulse à faitz vertueux, et retire de vice; lequel ilz nommoyent honneur.*

This is that same faith in the goodness of human nature which inspired the men of the second half of the eighteenth century, and helped to prepare the way for the French Revolution. Among the Italians, too, each man appeals to this noble instinct within him, and though with regard to the people as a whole – chiefly in consequence of the national disasters – judgements of a more pessimistic sort became prevalent, the importance of this sense of honour must still be rated highly. If the boundless development of individuality, stronger than the will of the individual, be the work of a historical providence, not less so is the opposing force which then manifested itself in Italy. How often, and against what passionate attacks of selfishness it won the day, we cannot tell, and therefore no human judgement can estimate with certainty the absolute moral value of the nation.

A force which we must constantly take into account in judging of the morality of the more highly developed Italian of this period is that of the imagination. It gives to his virtues and vices a peculiar colour, and under its influence his unbridled egotism shows itself in its most terrible shape.

The force of his imagination explains, for example, the fact that he was the first gambler on a large scale in modern times. Pictures of future wealth and enjoyment rose in such lifelike colours before his eyes that he was ready to hazard everything to reach them. The Muhammadan nations would doubtless have anticipated him in this respect, had not the Koran, from the beginning, set up the prohibition against gambling as a chief safeguard of public morals, and directed the imagination of its followers to the search after buried treasures. In Italy, the passion for play reached an intensity which often threatened or altogether broke up the existence of the gambler. Florence had already, at the end of the fourteenth century, its Casanova — a certain Buonaccorso Pitti,[84] who, in the course of his incessant journeys as merchant, political agent, diplomatist and professional gambler, won and lost sums so enormous that none but princes like the dukes of Brabant, Bavaria and Savoy were able to compete with him. That great lottery-bank, which was called the court of Rome, accustomed people to a need of excitement, which found its satisfaction in games of hazard during the intervals between one intrigue and another. We read, for example, how Franceschetto Cibò, in two games with the Cardinal Raffaello Riario, lost no less than 14,000 ducats, and after-wards complained to the pope that his opponent had cheated him. Italy has since that time been the home of the lottery.

It was to the imagination of the Italians that the peculiar character of their vengeance was due. The sense of justice was, indeed, one and the same throughout Europe, and any violation of it, so long as no punishment was inflicted, must have been felt in the same manner. But other nations, though they found it no easier to forgive, nevertheless forgot more easily, while the Italian imagination kept the picture of the wrong alive with frightful vividness. The fact that, according to the popular morality, the avenging of blood is a duty — a duty often performed in a way to make us shudder — gives to this passion a peculiar and still firmer basis. The government and the tribunals recognize its existence and justification, and only attempt to keep it within certain limits. Even among the peasantry, we read of Thyestean banquets and mutual assassination on the widest scale. Let us look at an instance.

In the district of Acquapendente three boys were watching cattle, and one of them said, 'Let us find out the way in which people are hanged.' While one was sitting on the shoulders of the other, and the third, after fastening the rope round the neck of the first, was tying it to an oak, a wolf came, and the two who were free ran away and left the other hanging. Afterwards they found him dead, and buried him. On the Sunday his father came to bring him bread, and one of the two confessed what had happened, and showed him the grave. The old man then killed him with a knife, cut him up, brought away the liver, and entertained the boy's father with it at home. After dinner, he told him whose liver it was. Hereupon began a series of reciprocal murders between the two families, and within a month 36 persons were killed, women as well as men.

And such vendettas, handed down from father to son, and extending to friends and distant relations, were not limited to the lower classes, but reached to the highest. The chronicles and novels of the period are full of such instances, especially of vengeance taken for the violation of women. The classic land for these feuds was Romagna, where the vendetta was interwoven with intrigues and party divisions of every conceivable sort. The popular legends present an awful picture of the savagery into which this brave and energetic people had relapsed. We are told, for instance, of a nobleman at Ravenna who had got all his enemies together in a tower, and might have burned them; instead of which he let them out, embraced them and entertained them sumptuously; whereupon shame drove them mad, and they conspired against him. Pious and saintly monks exhorted unceasingly to reconciliation, but they can scarcely have done more than restrain to a certain extent the feuds already established; their influence hardly prevented the growth of new ones. The novelists sometimes describe to us this effect of religion – how sentiments of generosity and forgiveness were suddenly awakened, and then again paralysed by the force of what had once been done and could never be undone. The pope himself was not always lucky as a peacemaker.

> Pope Paul II desired that the quarrel between Antonio Caffarello and the family of Alberino should cease, and ordered Giovanni Alberino and Antonio Caffarello to come before him, and bade them kiss one another, and promised them a fine of 2,000 ducats in case they renewed this strife, and two days after Antonio was stabbed by the same Giacomo Alberino, son of Giovanni, who had wounded him once before; and the pope was full of anger, and confiscated the goods of Alberino, and destroyed his houses, and banished father and son from Rome.

The oaths and ceremonies by which reconciled enemies attempted to guard themselves against a relapse are sometimes utterly horrible. When the parties of the *Nove* and the *Popolari* met and kissed one another by twos in the cathedral at Siena on New Year's Eve 1494, an oath was read by which all salvation in time and eternity was denied to the future violator of the treaty – 'an oath more astonishing and dreadful than had ever yet been heard'. The last consolations of religion in the hour of death were to turn to the damnation of the man who should break it. It is clear, however, that such a ceremony rather represents the despairing mood of the mediators than offers any real guarantee of peace, inasmuch as the truest reconciliation is just that one which has least need of it.

This personal need of vengeance felt by the cultivated and highly placed Italian, resting on the solid basis of an analogous popular custom, naturally displays itself under a thousand different aspects, and receives the unqualified approval of public opinion, as reflected in the works of the novelists. All are at one on the point that, in the case of those injuries and insults for which Italian justice offered no redress, and all the more in the case of those against which no human law can ever adequately provide, each man is free to take the law into his own hands. Only there must be art in the vengeance, and the satisfaction must be compounded of the material injury and moral humiliation of the offender. A mere brutal, clumsy triumph of force was held by public opinion to be no satisfaction. The whole man with his sense of fame and of scorn, not only his fist, must be victorious.

The Italian of that time shrank, it is true, from no dissimulation in order to attain his ends, but was wholly free from hypocrisy in matters of principle. In these he attempted to deceive neither himself nor others. Accordingly, revenge was declared with perfect frankness to be a necessity of human nature. Cool-headed people declared that it was then most worthy of praise when it was disengaged from passion, and worked simply from motives of expedience, 'in order that other men may learn to leave us unharmed'. Yet such instances must have formed only a small minority in comparison with those in which passion sought an outlet. This sort of revenge differs clearly from the avenging of blood, which has already been spoken of; while the latter keeps more or less within the limits of retaliation – the *jus talionis* – the former necessarily goes much further, not only requiring the sanction of the sense of justice, but craving admiration, and even striving to get the laugh on its own side.

Here lies the reason why men were willing to wait so long for their revenge. A *bella vendetta* demanded as a rule a combination of circumstances for which it was necessary to wait patiently. The gradual ripening of such opportunities is described by the novelists with heartfelt delight.

There is no need to discuss the morality of actions in which plaintiff and judge are one and the same person. If this Italian thirst for vengeance is to be palliated at all, it must be by proving the existence of a corresponding national virtue, namely gratitude. The same force of imagination which retains and magnifies wrong once suffered might be expected also to keep alive the memory of kindness received. It is not possible, however, to prove this with regard to the nation as a whole, though traces of it may be seen in the Italian character of today. The gratitude shown by the inferior classes for kind treatment, and the good memory of the upper for politeness in social life, are instances of this.

This connection between the imagination and the moral qualities of the Italian repeats itself continually. If, nevertheless, we find more cold calculation in cases where the northerner rather follows his impulses, the reason is that individual development in Italy was not only more marked and earlier in point of time, but also far more frequent. Where this is the case in other countries, the results are also analogous. We find, for example, that the early emancipation of the young from domestic and paternal authority is common to North America and Italy. Later on, in the more generous natures, a tie of freer affection grows up between parents and children.

It is in fact a matter of extreme difficulty to judge fairly of other nations in the sphere of character and feeling. In these respects a people may be developed highly, and yet in a manner so strange that a foreigner is utterly unable to understand it. Perhaps all the nations of the West are in this point equally favoured.

But where the imagination has exercised the most powerful and despotic influence on morals is in the illicit intercourse of the two sexes. It is well known that prostitution was freely practised in the Middle Ages, before the appearance of syphilis. A discussion, however, on these questions does not belong to our present work. What seems characteristic of Italy at this time is that here marriage and its rights were more often and more deliberately trampled underfoot than anywhere else. The girls of the higher classes were carefully secluded, and of them we do not speak. All passion was directed to the married women.

Under these circumstances it is remarkable that, so far as we know, there was no diminution in the number of marriages, and that family life by no means underwent that disorganization which a similar state of things would have produced in the North. Men wished to live as they pleased, but by no means to renounce the family, even when they were not sure that it was all their own. Nor did the race sink, either physically or mentally, on this account; for that apparent intellectual decline which showed itself towards the middle of the sixteenth century may be certainly accounted for by political and ecclesiastical causes, even if we are not to assume that the circle of achievements possible to the Renaissance had been completed. Notwithstanding their profligacy, the Italians continued to be, physically and mentally, one of the healthiest and best-born populations in Europe, and have retained this position, with improved morals, down to our own time.

When we come to look more closely at the ethics of love at the time of the Renaissance, we are struck by a remarkable contrast. The novelists and comic poets give us to understand that love consists only in sensual enjoyment, and that to win this, all means, tragic or comic, are not only permitted, but are interesting in proportion to their audacity and unscrupulousness. But if we turn to the best of the lyric poets and writers of dialogues, we find in them a deep and spiritual passion of the noblest kind, whose last and highest expression is a revival of the ancient belief in an original unity of souls in the Divine Being. And both modes of feeling were then genuine, and could co-exist in the same individual. It is not exactly a matter of glory, but it is a fact that, in the cultivated man of modern times, this sentiment can be not merely unconsciously present in both its highest and lowest stages, but may thus manifest itself openly, and even artistically. The modern man, like the man of antiquity, is in this respect too a microcosm, which the medieval man was not and could not be.

To begin with the morality of the novelists. They treat chiefly, as we have said, of married women, and consequently of adultery.

The opinion mentioned above of the equality of the two sexes is of great importance in relation to this subject. The highly developed and cultivated woman disposes of herself with a freedom unknown in northern countries; and her unfaithfulness does not break up her life in the same terrible manner, so long as no outward consequences follow

from it. The husband's claim on her fidelity has not that firm foundation which it acquires in the North through the poetry and passion of
courtship and betrothal. After the briefest acquaintance with her
future husband, the young wife quits the convent or the paternal roof
to enter upon a world in which her character begins rapidly to
develop. The rights of the husband are for this reason conditional, and
even the man who regards them in the light of a *jus quaesitum* thinks
only of the outward conditions of the contract, not of the affections.
The beautiful young wife of an old man sends back the presents and
letters of a youthful lover, in the firm resolve to keep her honour
(*honestà*). But she rejoices in the love of the youth for his great
excellence; and she perceives that a noble woman may love a man of
merit without loss to her honour. But the way is short from such a
distinction to a complete surrender.

The latter seems indeed as good as justified when there is unfaithfulness on the part of the husband. The woman, conscious of her own
dignity, feels this not only as a pain, but also as a humiliation and deceit,
and sets to work, often with the calmest consciousness of what she is
about, to devise the vengeance which the husband deserves. Her tact
must decide as to the measure of punishment which is suited to the
particular case. The deepest wound, for example, may prepare the
way for a reconciliation and a peaceful life in the future, if only it
remain secret. The novelists, who themselves undergo such experiences
or invent them according to the spirit of the age, are full of admiration
when the vengeance is skilfully adapted to the particular case; in fact,
when it is a work of art. As a matter of course, the husband never at
bottom recognizes this right of retaliation, and only submits to it from
fear or prudence. Where these motives are absent, where his wife's
unfaithfulness exposes him or may expose him to the derision of
outsiders, the affair becomes tragical, and not seldom ends in murder
or other vengeance of a violent sort. It is characteristic of the real
motive from which these deeds arise that not only the husband but the
brothers and the father of the woman feel themselves not only justified
in taking vengeance, but bound to take it. Jealousy, therefore, has
nothing to do with the matter, moral reprobation but little; the real
reason is the wish to spoil the triumph of others. 'Nowadays,' says
Bandello,

we see a woman poison her husband to gratify her lusts, thinking that a

widow may do whatever she desires. Another, fearing the discovery of
an illicit amour, has her husband murdered by her lover. And though
fathers, brothers and husbands arise to extirpate the shame with poison,
with the sword and by every other means, women still continue to
follow their passions, careless of their honour and their lives.

Another time, in milder strain, he exclaims:

Would that we were not daily forced to hear that one man has
murdered his wife because he suspected her of infidelity; that another
has killed his daughter, on account of a secret marriage; that a third has
caused his sister to be murdered, because she would not marry as he
wished! It is great cruelty that we claim the right to do whatever we
list, and will not suffer women to do the same. If they do anything
which does not please us, there we are at once with cords and daggers
and poison. What folly it is of men to suppose their own and their
house's honour depend on the appetite of a woman!

The tragedy in which such affairs commonly ended was so well
known that the novelist looked on the threatened gallant as a dead
man, even while he went about alive and merry. The physician and
lute-player Antonio Bologna had made a secret marriage with the
widowed Duchess of Amalfi, of the house of Aragon. Soon afterwards
her brother succeeded in securing both her and her children, and
murdered them in a castle. Antonio, ignorant of their fate, and still
cherishing the hope of seeing them again, was staying at Milan, closely
watched by hired assassins, and one day in the society of Ippolita
Sforza sang to the lute the story of his misfortunes. A friend of the
house, Delio, 'told the story up to this point to Scipione Atellano, and
added that he would make it the subject of a novel, as he was sure that
Antonio would be murdered'. The manner in which this took place,
almost under the eyes of Delio and Atellano, is thrillingly described by
Bandello.

Nevertheless, the novelists habitually show a sympathy for all the
ingenious, comic and cunning features which may happen to attend
adultery. They describe with delight how the lover manages to hide
himself in the house, all the means and devices by which he communi-
cates with his mistress, the boxes with cushions and sweetmeats in
which he can be hidden and carried out of danger. The deceived
husband is described sometimes as a fool to be laughed at, sometimes
as a bloodthirsty avenger of his honour; there is no third situation

except when the woman is painted as wicked and cruel, and the husband or lover is the innocent victim. It may be remarked, however, that narratives of the latter kind are not strictly speaking novels, but rather warning examples taken from real life.

When in the course of the sixteenth century Italian life fell more and more under Spanish influence, the violence of the means to which jealousy had recourse perhaps increased. But this new phase must be distinguished from the punishment of infidelity which existed before, and which was founded in the spirit of the Renaissance itself. As the influence of Spain declined, these excesses of jealousy declined also, till towards the close of the seventeenth century they had wholly disappeared, and their place was taken by that indifference which regarded the *cicisbeo* as an indispensable figure in every household, and took no offence at one or two contemporary lovers (*patiti*).

But who can undertake to compare the vast sum of wickedness which all these facts imply with what happened in other countries? Was the marriage-tie, for instance, really more sacred in France during the fifteenth century than in Italy? The *fabliaux* and farces would lead us to doubt it, and rather incline us to think that unfaithfulness was equally common, though its tragic consequences were less frequent, because the individual was less developed and his claims were less consciously felt than in Italy. More evidence, however, in favour of the Germanic peoples lies in the fact of the social freedom enjoyed among them by girls and women, which impressed Italian travellers so pleasantly in England and in the Netherlands. And yet we must not attach too much importance to this fact. Unfaithfulness was doubtless very frequent, and in certain cases led to a sanguinary vengeance. We have only to remember how the northern princes of that time dealt with their wives on the first suspicion of infidelity.

But it was not merely the sensual desire, not merely the vulgar appetite of the ordinary man, which trespassed upon forbidden ground among the Italians of that day, but also the passion of the best and noblest; and this, not only because the unmarried girl did not appear in society, but also because the man, in proportion to the completeness of his own nature, felt himself most strongly attracted by the woman whom marriage had developed. These are the men who struck the loftiest notes of lyrical poetry, and who have attempted in their treatises and dialogues to give us an idealized image of the devouring passion — *l'amor divino*. When they complain of the cruelty of the winged god, they are not only thinking of the coyness or hard-heartedness of the beloved one, but also of the unlawfulness of the passion itself. They seek to raise themselves above this painful conscious-ness by that spiritualization of love which found a support in the Platonic doctrine of the soul, and of which Pietro Bembo is the most famous representative. His thoughts on this subject are set forth by himself in the third book of the *Asolani*, and indirectly by Castiglione, who puts in his mouth the splendid speech with which the fourth book of the *Cortigiano* concludes: neither of these writers was a stoic in his conduct, but at that time it meant something to be at once a famous and a good man, and this praise must be accorded to both of them; their contemporaries took what these men said to be a true expression of their feeling, and we have not the right to despise it as affectation. Those who take the trouble to study the speech in the *Cortigiano* will see how poor an idea of it can be given by an extract. There were then living in Italy several distinguished women, who owed their celebrity chiefly to relations of this kind, such as Giulia Gonzaga, Veronica da Correggio and, above all, Vittoria Colonna. The land of profligates and scoffers respected these women and this sort of love – and what more can be said in their favour? We cannot tell how far vanity had to do with the matter, how far Vittoria was flattered to hear around her the sublimated utterances of hopeless love from the most famous men in Italy. If the thing was here and there a fashion, it was still no trifling praise for Vittoria that she, at least, never went out of fashion, and in her latest years produced the most profound impressions. It was long before other countries had anything similar to show.

In the imagination then, which governed this people more than any other, lies one general reason why the course of every passion was violent, and why the means used for the gratification of passion were often criminal. There is a violence which cannot control itself because it is born of weakness; but in Italy we find what is the corruption of powerful natures. Sometimes this corruption assumes a colossal shape, and crime seems to acquire almost a personal existence of its own.

The restraints of which men were conscious were but few. Each individual, even among the lowest of the people, felt himself inwardly emancipated from the control of the state and its police, whose title to respect was illegitimate, and itself founded on violence; and no man believed any longer in the justice of the law. When a murder was committed, the sympathies of the people, before the circumstances of the case were known, ranged themselves instinctively on the side of the murderer. A proud, manly bearing before and at the execution excited such admiration that the narrator often forgets to tell us for what offence the criminal was put to death. But when we add to this inward contempt of law and to the countless grudges and enmities which called for satisfaction, the impunity which crime enjoyed during times of political disturbance, we can only wonder that the state and society were not utterly dissolved. Crises of this kind occurred at Naples, during the transition from the Aragonese to the French and Spanish rule, and at Milan, on the repeated expulsions and returns of the Sforzas; at such times those men who have never in their hearts recognized the bonds of law and society come forward and give free play to their instincts of murder and rapine. Let us take, by way of example, a picture drawn from a humbler sphere.

When the duchy of Milan was suffering from the disorders which followed the death of Galeazzo Maria Sforza, about the year 1480, all safety came to an end in the provincial cities. This was the case in Parma, where the Milanese governor, terrified by threats of murder, consented to throw open the gaols and let loose the most abandoned criminals. Burglary, the demolition of houses, public assassination and murders were events of everyday occurrence. At first the authors of these deeds prowled about singly, and masked; soon large gangs of armed men went to work every night without disguise. Threatening letters, satires and scandalous jests circulated freely; and a sonnet in ridicule of the government seems to have roused its indignation far more than the frightful condition of the city. In many churches the sacred vessels with the host were stolen, and this fact is characteristic of the temper which prompted these outrages. It is impossible to say what would happen now in any country of the world if the government and police ceased to act, and yet hindered by their presence the establishment of a provisional authority; but what then occurred in Italy wears a character of its own, through the great share which the personal hatred and revenge had in it. The impression, indeed, which Italy at this period makes on us is that even in quiet times great crimes were commoner than in other countries. We may, it is true, be misled by the fact that we have far fuller details on such matters here than elsewhere, and that the same force of imagination, which gives a special character to crimes actually committed, causes much to be invented which never really happened. The amount of violence was perhaps as great elsewhere. It is hard to say for certain whether in the year 1500 men were any safer, whether human life was after all better protected, in powerful, wealthy Germany, with its robber knights, extortionate beggars and daring highwaymen. But one thing is certain, that premeditated crimes, committed professionally and for hire by third parties, occurred in Italy with great and appalling frequency.

So far as regards brigandage, Italy, especially in the more fortunate provinces, such as Tuscany, was certainly not more, and probably less, troubled than the countries of the North. But the figures which do meet us are characteristic of the country. It would be hard, for instance, to find elsewhere the case of a priest gradually driven by passion from one excess to another, till at last he came to head a band of robbers. That age offers us this example among others. On 12 August 1495, the priest Don Niccolò de' Pelegati of Figarolo was shut up in an iron cage outside the tower of San Giuliano at Ferrara. He had twice celebrated his first mass; the first time he had the same day committed murder, but afterwards received absolution at Rome; he then killed four people and married two wives, with whom he travelled about. He afterwards took part in many assassinations, violated women, carried others away by force, plundered far and wide, and infested the territory of Ferrara with a band of followers in uniform, extorting food and shelter by every sort of violence. When we think of what all this implies, the mass of guilt on the head of this one man is something tremendous. The clergy and monks had many privileges and little supervision, and among them were doubtless plenty of murderers and other malefactors – but hardly a second Pelegati. It is another matter, though by no means creditable, when ruined characters sheltered themselves in the cowl in order to escape the arm of the law, like the corsair whom Masuccio knew in a convent at Naples. What the real truth was with regard to Pope John XXIII in this respect is not known with certainty.[85]

The age of the famous brigand chief did not begin till later, in the seventeenth century, when the political strife of Guelph and Ghibelline, of Frenchman and Spaniard, no longer agitated the country. The robber then took the place of the partisan.

In certain districts of Italy, where civilization had made little progress, the country people were disposed to murder any stranger who fell into their hands. This was especially the case in the more remote parts of the kingdom of Naples, where the barbarism dated probably from the days of the Roman *latifundia*, and when the stranger and the enemy (*hospes* and *hostis*) were in all good faith held to be one and the same. These people were far from being irreligious. A herdsman once appeared in great trouble at the confessional, avowing that, while making cheese during Lent, a few drops of milk had found their way into his mouth. The confessor, skilled in the customs of the country, discovered in the course of his examination that the penitent and his friends were in the practice of robbing and murdering travellers, but that, through the force of habit, this usage gave rise to no twinges of conscience within them. We have already mentioned to what a degree of barbarism the peasants elsewhere could sink in times of political confusion.

A worse symptom than brigandage of the morality of that time was the frequency of paid assassination. In that respect Naples was admitted to stand at the head of all the cities of Italy. 'Nothing,' says Pontano, 'is cheaper here than human life.' But other districts could also show a terrible list of these crimes. It is hard, of course, to classify them according to the motives by which they were prompted, since political expediency, personal hatred, party hostility, fear and revenge all play into one another. It is no small honour to the Florentines, the most highly developed people of Italy, that offences of this kind occurred more rarely among them than anywhere else, perhaps because there was a justice at hand for legitimate grievances which was recognized by all, or because the higher culture of the individual gave him different views as to the right of men to interfere with the decrees of fate. In Florence, if anywhere, men were able to feel the incalculable consequences of a deed of blood, and to understand how uncertain the author of a so-called profitable crime is of any true and lasting gain. After the fall of Florentine liberty, assassination, especially by hired agents, seems to have rapidly increased, and continued till the government of Cosimo I had attained such strength that the police were at last able to repress it.

Elsewhere in Italy paid crimes were probably more or less frequent in proportion to the number of powerful and solvent buyers. Imposs-ible as it is to make any statistical estimate of their amount, yet if only a fraction of the deaths which public report attributed to violence were really murders, the crime must have been terribly frequent. The worst example of all was set by princes and governments, who without the faintest scruple reckoned murder as one of the instruments of their power. And this, without being in the same category with Cesare Borgia. The Sforzas, the Aragonese monarchs and, later on, the agents of Charles V resorted to it whenever it suited their purpose. The imagination of the people at last became so accustomed to facts of this kind that the death of any powerful man was seldom or never attributed to natural causes. There were certainly absurd notions current with regard to the effect of various poisons. There may be some truth in the story of that terrible white powder used by the Borgias, which did its work at the end of a definite period, and it is possible that it was really a *venenum atterminatum* which the Prince of Salerno handed to the Cardinal of Aragon, with the words: 'In a few days you will die, because your father, King Ferrante, wished to trample upon us all.' But the poisoned letter which Caterina Riario sent to Pope Alexander VI would hardly have caused his death even if he had read it; and when Alfonso the Great was warned by his physicians not to read in the Livy which Cosimo de' Medici had presented to him, he told them with justice not to talk like fools. Nor can that poison with which the secretary of Piccinino wished to anoint the sedan-chair of Pius II have affected any other organ than the imagination. The proportion which mineral and vegetable poisons bore to one another cannot be ascertained precisely. The poison with which the painter Rosso Fiorentino destroyed himself (1541) was evidently a powerful acid, which it would have been impossible to administer to another person without his knowledge. The secret use of weapons, especially of the dagger, in the service of powerful individuals was habitual in Milan, Naples and other cities. Indeed, among the crowds of armed retainers who were necessary for the personal safety of the great, and who lived in idleness, it was natural that outbreaks of this mania for blood should from time to time occur. Many a deed of horror would never have been committed, had not the master known that he needed but to give a sign to one or other of his followers.

Among the means used for the secret destruction of others – so far, that is, as the intention goes – we find magic, practised, however, sparingly. Where *maleficii, malie* and so forth are mentioned, they appear rather as a means of heaping up additional terror on the head of some hated enemy. At the courts of France and England in the fourteenth and fifteenth centuries, magic, practised with a view to the death of an opponent, plays a far more important part than in Italy.

In this country, finally, where individuality of every sort attained its highest development, we find instances of that ideal and absolute wickedness which delights in crimes for their own sake, and not as means to an end, or at any rate as means to ends for which our psychology has no measure.

Among these appalling figures we may first notice certain of the *condottieri*, such as Braccio da Montone, Tiberto Brandolino and that Werner von Urslingen whose silver hauberk bore the inscription: 'The enemy of God, of pity and of mercy'. This class of men offers us some of the earliest instances of criminals deliberately repudiating every moral restraint. Yet we shall be more reserved in our judgement of them when we remember that the worst part of their guilt – in the estimate of those who record it – lay in their defiance of spiritual threats and penalties, and that to this fact is due that air of horror with which they are represented as surrounded. In the case of Braccio, the hatred of the Church went so far that he was infuriated at the sight of monks at their psalms, and had them thrown down from the top of a tower; but at the same time 'he was loyal to his soldiers and a great general'. As a rule, the crimes of the *condottieri* were committed for the sake of some definite advantage, and must be attributed to a position in which men could not fail to be demoralized. Even their apparently gratuitous cruelty had commonly a purpose, if it were only to strike terror. The barbarities of the House of Aragon, as we have seen, were mainly due to fear and to the desire for vengeance. The thirst for blood on its own account, the devilish delight in destruction, is most clearly exemplified in the case of the Spaniard Cesare Borgia, whose cruelties were certainly out of all proportion to the end which he had in view. In Sigismondo Malatesta, tyrant of Rimini, the same disinterested love of evil may also be detected. It is not only the court of Rome, but the verdict of history, which convicts him of murder, rape, adultery, incest, sacrilege, perjury and treason, committed not once but often. The most shocking crime of all – the unnatural attempt on his own son Roberto, who frustrated it with his drawn dagger – may have been the result, not merely of moral corruption, but perhaps of some magical or astrological superstition. The same conjecture has been made to account for the rape of the Bishop of Fano by Pierluigi Farnese of Parma, son of Paul III.

If we now attempt to sum up the principal features in the Italian character of that time, as we know it from a study of the life of the upper classes, we shall obtain something like the following result. The fundamental vice of this character was at the same time a condition of its greatness, namely, excessive individualism. The individual first inwardly casts off the authority of a state which, as a fact, is in most cases tyrannical and illegitimate, and what he thinks and does is, rightly or wrongly, now called treason. The sight of victorious egotism in others drives him to defend his own right by his own arm. And, while thinking to restore his inward equilibrium, he falls, through the vengeance which he executes, into the hands of the powers of darkness. His love, too, turns mostly for satisfaction to another individuality equally developed, namely, to his neighbour's wife. In face of all objective facts, of laws and restraints of whatever kind, he retains the feeling of his own sovereignty, and in each single instance forms his decision independently, according as honour or interest, passion or calculation, revenge or renunciation, gain the upper hand in his own mind.

If therefore egotism in its wider as well as narrower sense is the root and fountain of all evil, the more highly developed Italian was for this reason more inclined to wickedness than the members of other nations of that time.

But this individual development did not come upon him through any fault of his own, but rather through an historical necessity. It did not come upon him alone, but also, and chiefly, by means of Italian culture, upon the other nations of Europe, and has constituted since then the higher atmosphere which they breathe. In itself it is neither good nor bad, but necessary; within it has grown up a modern standard of good and evil – a sense of moral responsibility – which is essentially different from that which was familiar to the Middle Ages.

But the Italian of the Renaissance had to bear the first mighty surging of a new age. Through his gifts and his passions, he has become the most characteristic representative of all the heights and all the depths of his time. By the side of profound corruption appeared human personalities of the noblest harmony, and an artistic splendour which shed upon the life of man a lustre which neither antiquity nor medievalism either could or would bestow upon it.

RELIGION IN DAILY LIFE

The morality of a people stands in the closest connection with its consciousness of God, that is to say, with its firmer or weaker faith in the divine government of the world, whether this faith looks on the world as destined to happiness or to misery and speedy destruction. The infidelity then prevalent in Italy is notorious, and whoever takes the trouble to look about for proofs, will find them by the hundred. Our present task, here as elsewhere, is to separate and discriminate; refraining from an absolute and final verdict.

The belief in God at earlier times had its source and chief support in Christianity and the outward symbol of Christianity, the Church. When the Church became corrupt, men ought to have drawn a distinction, and kept their religion in spite of all. But this is more easily said than done. It is not every people which is calm enough, or dull enough, to tolerate a lasting contradiction between a principle and its outward expression. But history does not record a heavier responsibility than that which rests upon the decaying Church. She set up as absolute truth, and by the most violent means, a doctrine which she had distorted to serve her own aggrandizement. Safe in the sense of her inviolability, she abandoned herself to the most scandalous profligacy, and, in order to maintain herself in this state, she levelled mortal blows against the conscience and the intellect of nations, and drove multitudes of the noblest spirits, whom she had inwardly estranged, into the arms of unbelief and despair.

Here we are met by the question, why did not Italy, intellectually so great, react more energetically against the hierarchy; why did she not accomplish a reformation like that which occurred in Germany, and accomplish it at an earlier date?

A plausible answer has been given to this question. The Italian mind, we are told, never went further than the denial of the hierarchy, while the origin and the vigour of the German Reformation was due to its positive religious doctrines, most of all to the doctrines of justification by faith and of the inefficacy of good works.

It is certain that these doctrines only worked upon Italy through Germany, and this not till the power of Spain was sufficiently great to root them out without difficulty, partly by itself and partly by means of the papacy and its instruments. Nevertheless, in the earlier religious movements of Italy, from the mystics of the thirteenth century down to Savonarola, there was a large amount of positive religious doctrine which, like the very definite Christianity of the Huguenots, failed to achieve success only because circumstances were against it. Mighty events like the Reformation elude, as respects their details, their outbreak and their development, the deductions of the philosophers, however clearly the necessity of them as a whole may be demonstrated. The movements of the human spirit, its sudden flashes, its expansions and its pauses, must for ever remain a mystery to our eyes, since we can but know this or that of the forces at work in it, never all of them together.

The feeling of the upper and middle classes in Italy with regard to the Church at the time when the Renaissance culminated was compounded of deep and contemptuous aversion, of acquiescence in the outward ecclesiastical customs which entered into daily life, and of a sense of dependence on sacraments and ceremonies. The great personal influence of religious preachers may be added as a fact characteristic of Italy.

That hostility to the hierarchy which displays itself more especially from the time of Dante onwards in Italian literature and history has been fully treated by several writers. We have already (p. 147) said something of the attitude of public opinion with regard to the papacy. Those who wish for the strongest evidence which the best authorities offer us can find it in the famous passages of Machiavelli's *Discorsi*, and in the unmutilated edition of Guicciardini. Outside the Roman Curia, some respect seems to have been felt for the best men among the bishops, and for many of the parochial clergy. On the other hand, the mere holders of benefices, the canons and the monks were held in almost universal suspicion, and were often the objects of the most scandalous aspersions, extending to the whole of their order.

It has been said that the monks were made the scapegoats for the whole clergy, for the reason that none but they could be ridiculed without danger. But this is certainly incorrect. They are introduced so frequently in the novels and comedies because these forms of literature need fixed and well-known types where the imagination of the reader can easily fill up an outline. Besides which, the novelists do not as a fact spare the secular clergy. In the third place, we have abundant proof in the rest of Italian literature that men could speak boldly enough about the papacy and the court of Rome. In works of imagination we cannot expect to find criticism of this kind. Fourthly, the monks, when attacked, were sometimes able to take a terrible vengeance.

It is nevertheless true that the monks were the most unpopular class of all, and that they were reckoned a living proof of the worthlessness of conventual life, of the whole ecclesiastical organization, of the system of dogma, and of religion altogether, according as men pleased, rightly or wrongly, to draw their conclusions. We may also assume that Italy retained a clearer recollection of the origin of the two great mendicant orders than other countries, and had not forgotten that they were the chief agents in the reaction against what is called the heresy of the thirteenth century, that is to say, against an early and vigorous movement of the modern Italian spirit. And that spiritual police which was permanently entrusted to the Dominicans certainly never excited any other feeling than secret hatred and contempt.

After reading the *Decameron* and the novels of Franco Sacchetti, we might imagine that the vocabulary of abuse directed at the monks and nuns was exhausted. But towards the time of the Reformation this abuse became still fiercer. To say nothing of Aretino, who in the *Ragionamenti* uses conventual life merely as a pretext for giving free play to his own poisonous nature, we may quote one author as typical of the rest – Masuccio, in the first ten of his fifty novels. They are written in a tone of the deepest indignation, and with the purpose to make this indignation general; and are dedicated to men in the highest position, such as King Ferrante and Prince Alfonso of Naples. The stories are many of them old, and some of them familiar to readers of Boccaccio. But others reflect, with a frightful realism, the actual state of things at Naples. The way in which the priests befool and plunder the people by means of spurious miracles, added to their own scandalous lives, is enough to drive any thoughtful observer to despair. We read of the Minorite friars who travelled to collect alms: 'They cheat, steal and fornicate, and when they are at the end of their resources, they set up as saints and work miracles, one displaying the cloak of St Vincent, another the handwriting of St Bernardino,[86] a third the bridle of Capistrano's donkey.' Others 'bring with them confederates who pretend to be blind or afflicted with some mortal disease, and after touching the hem of the monk's cowl, or the relics which he carries, are healed before the eyes of the multitude. All then shout "*Misericordia!*", the bells are rung, and the miracle is recorded in a solemn protocol.' Or else the monk in the pulpit is denounced as a liar by another who stands below among the audience; the accuser is immediately possessed by the devil, and then healed by the preacher. The whole thing was a pre-arranged comedy, in which, however, the principal with his assistant made so much money that he was able to buy a bishopric from a cardinal, on which the two confederates lived comfortably to the end of their days. Masuccio makes no great distinction between Franciscans and Dominicans, finding the one worth as much as the other. 'And yet the foolish people lets itself be drawn into their hatreds and divisions, and quarrels about them in public places, and calls itself *franceschino* or *domenichino*.' The nuns are the exclusive property of the monks. Those of the former who have anything to do with the laity are prosecuted and put in prison, while others are wedded in due form to the monks, with the accompaniments of mass, a marriage-contract and a liberal indulgence in food and wine. 'I myself,' says the author, 'have been there not once, but several times, and seen it all with my own eyes. The nuns afterwards bring forth pretty little monks or else use means to hinder that result. And if anyone charges me with falsehood, let him search the nunneries well, and he will find there as many little bones as in Bethlehem at Herod's time.' These things, and the like, are among the secrets of monastic life. The monks are by no means too strict with one another in the confessional, and impose a paternoster in cases where they would refuse all absolution to a layman as if he were a heretic. 'Therefore may the earth open and swallow up the wretches alive, with those who protect them!' In another place Masuccio, speaking of the fact that the influence of the monks depends chiefly on the dread of another world, utters the following remarkable wish: 'The best punishment for them would be for God to abolish purgatory; they would then receive no more alms, and would be forced to go back to their spades.'

If men were free to write, in the time of Ferrante, and to him, in this strain, the reason is perhaps to be found in the fact that the king himself had been incensed by a false miracle which had been palmed off on him. An attempt had been made to urge him to a persecution of the Jews, like that carried out in Spain and imitated by the popes, by producing a tablet with an inscription bearing the name of St Cataldus, said to have been buried at Taranto, and afterwards dug up again. When he discovered the fraud, the monks defied him. He had also managed to detect and expose a pretended instance of fasting, as his father Alfonso had done before him. The court, certainly, was no accomplice in maintaining these blind superstitions.

We have been quoting from an author who wrote in earnest, and who by no means stands alone in his judgement. All the Italian literature of that time is full of ridicule and invective aimed at the begging friars. It can hardly be doubted that the Renaissance would soon have destroyed these two orders, had it not been for the German Reformation, and the Counter-Reformation which that provoked. Their saints and popular preachers could hardly have saved them. It would only have been necessary to come to an understanding at a favourable moment with a pope like Leo X, who despised the mendicant orders. If the spirit of the age found them ridiculous or repulsive, they could no longer be anything but an embarrassment to the Church. And who can say what fate was in store for the papacy itself, if the Reformation had not saved it?

The influence which the Father Inquisitor of a Dominican monastery was able habitually to exercise in the city where it was situated was in the latter part of the fifteenth century just considerable enough to hamper and irritate cultivated people, but not strong enough to extort any lasting fear or obedience. It was no longer possible to punish men for their thoughts, as it once was, and those whose tongues wagged most impudently against the clergy could easily keep clear of heretical doctrine. Except when some powerful party had an end to serve, as in the case of Savonarola, or when there was a question of the use of magical arts, as was often the case in the cities of North Italy, we seldom read at this time of men being burnt at the stake. The Inquisitors were in some instances satisfied with the most superficial retraction, in others it even happened that the victim was saved out of their hands on the way to the place of execution. In Bologna (1452) the priest Niccolò da Verona had been publicly degraded on a wooden scaffold in front of San Domenico as a wizard and profaner of the sacraments, and was about to be led away to the stake when he was set free by a gang of armed men, sent by Achille Malvezzi, a noted friend of heretics and violator of nuns. The legate, Cardinal Bessarion, was only able to catch and hang one of the party; Malvezzi lived on in peace.

It deserves to be noticed that the higher monastic orders – e.g. Benedictines, with their many branches – were, notwithstanding their great wealth and easy lives, far less disliked than the mendicant friars. For ten novels which treat of *frati*, hardly one can be found in which a *monaco* is the subject and the victim. It was no small advantage to these orders that they were founded earlier, and not as an instrument of police, and that they did not interfere with private life. They contained

men of learning, wit and piety, but the average has been described by
a member of it, Firenzuola, who says:

> These well-fed gentlemen with the capacious cowls do not pass their
> time in barefooted journeys and in sermons, but sit in elegant slippers
> with their hands crossed over their paunches, in charming cells wains-
> coted with cyprus-wood. And when they are obliged to quit the house,
> they ride comfortably, as if for their amusement, on mules and sleek,
> quiet horses. They do not overstrain their minds with the study of
> many books, for fear lest knowledge might put the pride of Lucifer in
> the place of monkish simplicity.

Those who are familiar with the literature of the time will see that
we have only brought forward what is absolutely necessary for the
understanding of the subject. That the reputation attaching to the
monks and the secular clergy must have shattered the faith of multitudes in all that is sacred is, of course, obvious.

And some of the judgements which we read are terrible; we will
quote one of them in conclusion, which has been published only lately
and is but little known. The historian Guicciardini, who was for many
years in the service of the Medicean popes, says (1529) in his
Aphorisms:[87]

> No man is more disgusted than I am with the ambition, the avarice and
> the profligacy of the priests, not only because each of these vices is
> hateful in itself, but because each and all of them are most unbecoming
> in those who declare themselves to be men in special relations with
> God, and also because they are vices so opposed to one another that
> they can only co-exist in very singular natures. Nevertheless, my
> position at the court of several popes forced me to desire their greatness
> for the sake of my own interest. But, had it not been for this, I should
> have loved Martin Luther as myself, not in order to free myself from
> the laws which Christianity, as generally understood and explained,
> lays upon us, but in order to see this swarm of scoundrels [*questa caterva
> di scellerati*] put back into their proper place, so that they may be forced
> to live either without vices or without power.

The same Guicciardini is of opinion that we are in the dark as to all
that is supernatural, that philosophers and theologians have nothing
but nonsense to tell us about it, that miracles occur in every religion
and prove the truth of none in particular, and that all of them may be
explained as unknown phenomena of nature. The faith which moves

mountains, then common among the followers of Savonarola, is mentioned by Guicciardini as a curious fact, but without any bitter remark.

Notwithstanding this hostile public opinion, the clergy and the monks had the great advantage that the people were used to them, and that their existence was interwoven with the everyday existence of all. This is the advantage which every old and powerful institution possesses. Everybody had some cowled or frocked relative, some prospect of assistance or future gain from the treasure of the Church; and in the centre of Italy stood the court of Rome, where men sometimes became rich in a moment. Yet it must never be forgotten that all this did not hinder people from writing and speaking freely. The authors of the most scandalous satires were themselves mostly monks or beneficed priests. Poggio, who wrote the *Facetiae*, was a clergyman; Francesco Berni, the satirist, held a canonry; Teofilo Folengo, the author of the *Orlandino*, was a Benedictine, certainly by no means a faithful one; Matteo Bandello, who held up his own order to ridicule, was a Dominican, and nephew of a general of this order. Were they encouraged to write by the sense that they ran no risk? Or did they feel an inward need to clear themselves personally from the infamy which attached to their order? Or were they moved by that selfish pessimism which takes for its maxim, 'it will last our time'? Perhaps all of these motives were more or less at work. In the case of Folengo, the unmistakable influence of Lutheranism must be added.

The sense of dependence on rites and sacraments, which we have already touched upon in speaking of the papacy (p. 81ff), is not surprising among that part of the people which still believed in the Church. Among those who were more emancipated, it testifies to the strength of youthful impressions, and to the magical force of traditional symbols. The universal desire of dying men for priestly absolution shows that the last remnants of the dread of hell had not, even in the case of one like Vitellozzo, been altogether extinguished. It would hardly be possible to find a more instructive instance than this. The doctrine taught by the Church of the *character indelibilis* of the priesthood, independently of the personality of the priest, had so far borne fruit that it was possible to loathe the individual and still desire his spiritual gifts. It is true, nevertheless, that there were defiant natures like Galeotto of Mirandola, who died unabsolved in 1499, after living for sixteen years under the ban of the Church. All this time the city lay under an interdict on his account, so that no mass was celebrated and no Christian burial took place.

A splendid contrast to all this is offered by the power exercised over the nation by its great preachers of repentance. Other countries of Europe were from time to time moved by the words of saintly monks, but only superficially, in comparison with the periodical upheaval of the Italian conscience. The only man, in fact, who produced a similar effect in Germany during the fifteenth century was an Italian, born in the Abruzzi, named Giovanni Capistrano. Those natures which bear within them this religious vocation and this commanding earnestness wore then in northern countries an intuitive and mystical aspect. In the South they were practical and expansive, and shared in the national gift of language and oratorical skill. The North produced an 'Imitation of Christ', which worked silently, at first only within the walls of the monastery, but worked for the ages; the South produced men who made on their fellows a mighty but passing impression.

This impression consisted chiefly in the awakening of the conscience. The sermons were moral exhortations, free from abstract notions and full of practical application, rendered more impressive by the saintly and ascetic character of the preacher, and by the miracles which, even against his will, the inflamed imagination of the people attributed to him. The most powerful argument used was not the threat of hell and purgatory, but rather the living results of the *maledizione*, the temporal ruin wrought on the individual by the curse which clings to wrong-doing. The grieving of Christ and the saints has its consequences in this life. And only thus could men, sunk in passion and guilt, be brought to repentance and amendment – which was the chief object of these sermons.

Among these preachers were Bernardino da Siena, Alberto da Sarzana, Jacopo della Marca, Giovanni Capistrano, Roberto da Lecce and others; and finally, Girolamo Savonarola. No prejudice of the day was stronger than that against the mendicant friar, and this they overcame. They were criticized and ridiculed by a scornful humanism; but when they raised their voices, no one gave heed to the humanists. The thing was no novelty, and the scoffing Florentines had already in the fourteenth century learned to caricature it whenever it appeared in the pulpit. But no sooner did Savonarola come forward than he carried the people so triumphantly with him that soon all their beloved art and culture melted away in the furnace which he lighted.

Even the grossest profanation done to the cause by hypocritical monks, who got up an effect in the audience by means of confederates, could not bring the thing itself into discredit. Men kept on laughing at the ordinary monkish sermons, with their spurious miracles and manufactured relics; but did not cease to honour the great and genuine preachers. These are a true speciality of the fifteenth century.

The order – generally that of St Francis, and more particularly the so-called Observantines – sent them out according as they were wanted. This was commonly the case when there was some important public or private feud in a city, or some alarming outbreak of violence, immorality or disease. When once the reputation of a preacher was made, the cities were all anxious to hear him even without any special occasion. He went wherever his superiors sent him. A special form of this work was the preaching of a crusade against the Turks; but here we have to speak more particularly of the exhortations to repentance.

The order of these, when they were treated methodically, seems to have followed the customary list of the deadly sins. The more pressing, however, the occasion is, the more directly does the preacher make for his main point. He begins perhaps in one of the great churches of the order, or in the cathedral. Soon the largest piazza is too small for the crowds which throng from every side to hear him, and he himself can hardly move without risking his life. The sermon is commonly followed by a great procession; but the first magistrates of the city, who take him in their midst, can hardly save him from the multitude of women who throng to kiss his hands and feet, and cut off fragments from his cowl.

The most immediate consequences which follow from the preacher's denunciations of usury, luxury and scandalous fashions are the opening of the gaols – which meant no more than the discharge of the poorer debtors – and the burning of various instruments of luxury and amusement, whether innocent or not. Among these are dice, cards, games of all kinds, written incantations, masks, musical instruments, song-books, false hair and so forth. All these would then be gracefully arranged on a scaffold (*talamo*), a figure of the devil fastened to the top, and then the whole set on fire.

Then came the turn of the more hardened consciences. Men who had long never been near the confessional now acknowledged their sins. Ill-gotten gains were restored, and insults which might have borne fruit in blood retracted. Orators like Bernardino of Siena entered diligently into all the details of the daily life of men, and the moral laws which are involved in it. Few theologians nowadays would feel tempted to give a morning sermon 'on contracts, restitutions, the public debt [*monte*] and the portioning of daughters', like that which he once delivered in the cathedral at Florence. Imprudent speakers easily fell into the mistake of attacking particular classes, professions or offices, with such energy that the enraged hearers proceeded to violence against those whom the preacher had denounced. A sermon which Bernardino once preached in Rome (1424) had another consequence besides a bonfire of vanities on the Capitol: 'After this,' we read, 'the witch Finicella was burnt, because by her diabolical arts she had killed many children and bewitched many other persons; and all Rome went to see the sight.'

But the most important aim of the preacher was, as has been already said, to reconcile enemies and persuade them to give up thoughts of vengeance. Probably this end was seldom attained till towards the close of a course of sermons, when the tide of penitence flooded the city, and when the air resounded with the cry of the whole people: '*Misericordia!*' Then followed those solemn embracings and treaties of peace which even previous bloodshed on both sides could not hinder. Banished men were recalled to the city to take part in these sacred transactions. It appears that these *paci* were on the whole faithfully observed, even after the mood which prompted them was over; and then the memory of the monk was blessed from generation to generation. But there were sometimes terrible crises like those in the families della Valle and Croce in Rome (1482), where even the great Roberto da Lecce raised his voice in vain. Shortly before Holy Week he had preached to immense crowds in the square before the Minerva. But on the night before Maundy Thursday a terrible combat took place in front of the Palazzo della Valle, near the Ghetto. In the morning Pope Sixtus gave orders for its destruction, and then performed the customary ceremonies of the day. On Good Friday Roberto preached again with a crucifix in his hand; but he and his hearers could do nothing but weep.

Violent natures, which had fallen into contradiction with themselves, often resolved to enter a convent, under the impression made by these men. Among such were not only brigands and criminals of every sort, but soldiers without employment. This resolve was stimulated by their admiration of the holy man, and by the desire to copy at least his outward position.

The concluding sermon is a general benediction, summed up in the words '*la pace sia con voi!*' Throngs of hearers accompany the preacher to the next city, and there listen for a second time to the whole course of sermons.

The enormous influence exercised by these preachers made it important, both for the clergy and for the government, at least not to have them as opponents; one means to this end was to permit only monks or priests who had received at all events the lesser consecration to enter the pulpit, so that the order or corporation to which they belonged was, to some extent, responsible for them. But it was not easy to make the rule absolute, since the Church and pulpit had long been used as a means of publicity in many ways, judicial, educational and others, and since even sermons were sometimes delivered by humanists and other laymen. There existed, too, in Italy a dubious class of persons, who were neither monks nor priests, and who yet had renounced the world – that is to say, the numerous class of hermits who appeared from time to time in the pulpit on their own authority, and often carried the people with them. A case of this kind occurred at Milan in 1516, after the second French conquest, certainly at a time when public order was much disturbed. A Tuscan hermit, Hieronymus of Siena, possibly an adherent of Savonarola, maintained his place for months together in the pulpit of the cathedral, denounced the hierarchy with great violence, caused a new chandelier and a new altar to be set up in the church, worked miracles, and only abandoned the field after a long and desperate struggle. During the decades in which the fate of Italy was decided, the spirit of prophecy was unusually active, and nowhere where it displayed itself was it confined to any one particular class. We know with what a tone of true prophetic defiance the hermits came forward before the sack of Rome. In default of any eloquence of their own, these men made use of messengers with symbols of one kind or another, like the ascetic near Siena (1429), who sent a 'little hermit', that is a pupil, into the terrified city with a skull upon a pole, to which was attached a paper with a threatening text from the Bible.

Nor did the monks themselves scruple to attack princes, governments, the clergy, or even their own order. A direct exhortation to overthrow a despotic house, like that uttered by Jacopo Bussolaro at Pavia in the fourteenth century, hardly occurs again in the following period: but there is no want of courageous reproofs, addressed even to the pope in his own chapel, and of naïve political advice given in the presence of rulers who by no means held themselves in need of it. In the Piazza del Castello at Milan, a blind preacher from the Incoronata – consequently an Augustinian – ventured in 1494 to exhort Lodovico il Moro from the pulpit: 'My lord, beware of showing the French the way, else you will repent it.' There were further prophetic monks who, without exactly preaching political sermons, drew such appalling pictures of the future that the hearers almost lost their senses. After the election of Leo X, in the year 1513, a whole association of these men, twelve Franciscan monks in all, journeyed through the various districts of Italy, of which one or other was assigned to each preacher. The one who appeared in Florence, Fra Francesco da Montepulciano, struck terror into the whole people. The alarm was not diminished by the exaggerated reports of his prophecies which reached those who were too far off to hear him. After one of his sermons he suddenly died 'of pain in the chest'. The people thronged in such numbers to kiss the feet of the corpse that it had to be secretly buried in the night. But the newly awakened spirit of prophecy, which seized upon even women and peasants, could not be controlled without great difficulty.

In order to restore to the people their cheerful humour, the Medici – Giuliano, Leo's brother, and Lorenzo – gave on St John's Day, 1514, those splendid festivals, tournaments, processions and hunting-parties which were attended by many distinguished persons from Rome, and among them, though disguised, by no less than six cardinals.

But the greatest of the prophets and apostles had already been burnt in Florence in the year 1498 – Fra Girolamo Savonarola of Ferrara. We must content ourselves with saying a few words respecting him.[88]

The instrument by means of which he transformed and ruled the city of Florence (1494–8) was his eloquence. Of this the meagre reports that are left to us, which were taken down mostly on the spot, give us evidently a very imperfect notion. It was not that he possessed any striking outward advantages, for voice, accent and rhetorical skill constituted precisely his weakest side; and those who required the preacher to be a stylist went to his rival Fra Mariano da Genazzano. The eloquence of Savonarola was the expression of a lofty and commanding personality, the like of which was not seen again till the time of Luther. He himself held his own influence to be the result of a divine illumination, and could therefore, without presumption, assign a very high place to the office of the preacher, who, in the great hierarchy of spirits, occupies, according to him, the next place below the angels.

This man, whose nature seemed made of fire, worked another and greater miracle than any of his oratorical triumphs. His own Dominican monastery of San Marco, and then all the Dominican monasteries of Tuscany, became like-minded with himself, and undertook voluntarily the work of inward reform. When we reflect what the monasteries then were, and what measureless difficulty attends the least change where monks are concerned, we are doubly astonished at so complete a revolution. While the reform was still in progress large numbers of Savonarola's followers entered the order, and thereby greatly facilitated his plans. Sons of the first houses in Florence entered San Marco as novices.

This reform of the order in a particular province was the first step to a national Church, in which, had the reformer himself lived longer, it must infallibly have ended. Savonarola, indeed, desired the regeneration of the whole Church, and near the end of his career sent pressing exhortations to the great potentates urging them to call together a Council. But in Tuscany his order and party were the only organs of his spirit – the salt of the earth – while the neighbouring provinces remained in their old condition. Fancy and asceticism tended more and more to produce in him a state of mind to which Florence appeared as the scene of the kingdom of God upon earth.

The prophecies, whose partial fulfilment conferred on Savonarola a supernatural credit, were the means by which the ever-active Italian imagination seized control of the soundest and most cautious natures. At first the Franciscans of the Osservanza, trusting in the reputation which had been bequeathed to them by St Bernardino of Siena, fancied that they could compete with the great Dominican. They put one of their own men into the cathedral pulpit, and outbid the Jeremiads of Savonarola by still more terrible warnings, till Pietro de' Medici, who then still ruled over Florence, forced them both to be silent. Soon after, when Charles VIII came to Italy and the Medici were expelled, as Savonarola had clearly foretold, he alone was believed in.

It must be frankly confessed that he never judged his own premonitions and visions critically, as he did those of others. In the funeral oration on Pico della Mirandola, he deals somewhat harshly with his dead friend. Since Pico, notwithstanding an inner voice which came from God, would not enter the order, he had himself prayed to God to chasten him for his disobedience. He certainly had not desired his death, and alms and prayers had obtained the favour that Pico's soul was safe in purgatory. With regard to a comforting vision which Pico had upon his sick-bed, in which the Virgin appeared and promised him that he should not die, Savonarola confessed that he had long regarded it as a deceit of the Devil, till it was revealed to him that the Madonna meant the second and eternal death. If these things and the like are proofs of presumption, it must be admitted that this great soul at all events paid a bitter penalty for his fault. In his last days Savonarola seems to have recognized the vanity of his visions and prophecies. And yet enough inward peace was left to him to enable him to meet death like a Christian. His partisans held to his doctrine and predictions for thirty years longer.

He only undertook the reorganization of the state for the reason that otherwise his enemies would have got the government into their own hands. It is unfair to judge him by the semi-democratic constitution of the beginning of the year 1495. Nor is it either better or worse than other Florentine constitutions.

He was at bottom the most unsuitable man who could be found for such a work. His ideal was a theocracy, in which all men were to bow in blessed humility before the Unseen, and all conflicts of passion were not even to be able to arise. His whole mind is written in that inscription on the Palazzo della Signoria, the substance of which was his maxim as early as 1495, and which was solemnly renewed by his partisans in 1527: '*Jesus Christus Rex populi Florentini S.P.Q. decreto creatus*'. He stood in no more relation to mundane affairs and their actual conditions than any other inhabitant of a monastery. Man, according to him, has only to attend to those things which make directly for his salvation.

This temper comes out clearly in his opinions on ancient literature:

The only good thing which we owe to Plato and Aristotle is that they brought forward many arguments which we can use against the heretics. Yet they and other philosophers are now in hell. An old woman knows more about the Faith than Plato. It would be good for religion if many books that seem useful were destroyed. When there were not so many books and not so many arguments [*ragioni naturali*] and disputes, religion grew more quickly than it has done since.

He wished to limit the classical instruction of the schools to Homer, Virgil and Cicero, and to supply the rest from Jerome and Augustine. Not only Ovid and Catullus, but Terence and Tibullus, were to be banished. This may be no more than the expressions of a nervous morality, but elsewhere in a special work he admits that science as a whole is harmful. He holds that only a few people should have to do with it, in order that the tradition of human knowledge may not perish, and particularly that there may be no want of intellectual athletes to confute the sophisms of the heretics. For all others, grammar, morals and religious teaching (*litterae sacrae*) suffice. Culture and education would thus return wholly into the charge of the monks, and as, in his opinion, the 'most learned and the most pious' are to rule over the states and empires, these rulers would also be monks. Whether he really foresaw this conclusion, we need not inquire.

A more childish method of reasoning cannot be imagined. The simple reflection that the new-born antiquity and the boundless enlargement of human thought and knowledge which was due to it might give splendid confirmation to a religion able to adapt itself thereto seems never even to have occurred to the good man. He wanted to forbid what he could not deal with by any other means. In fact, he was anything but liberal, and was ready, for example, to send the astrologers to the same stake at which he afterwards himself died.

How mighty must have been the soul which dwelt side by side with this narrow intellect! And what a flame must have glowed within him before he could constrain the Florentines, possessed as they were by the passion for culture, to surrender themselves to a man who could thus reason!

How much of their heart and their worldliness they were ready to sacrifice for his sake is shown by those famous bonfires by the side of which all the *talami* of Bernardino da Siena and others were certainly of small account.

All this could not, however, be effected without the agency of a tyrannical police. He did not shrink from the most vexatious interferences with the much-prized freedom of Italian private life, using the espionage of servants on their masters as a means of carrying out his moral reforms. That transformation of public and private life which the iron Calvin was but just able to effect at Geneva, with the aid of a permanent state of siege, necessarily proved impossible at Florence, and the attempt only served to drive the enemies of Savonarola to a more implacable hostility. Among his most unpopular measures may be mentioned those organized parties of boys who forced their way into the houses and laid violent hands on any objects which seemed suitable for the bonfire. As it happened that they were sometimes sent away with a beating, they were afterwards attended, in order to keep up the figment of a pious 'rising generation', by a bodyguard of grown-up persons.

On the last day of the carnival in the year 1497, and on the same day the year after, the great *auto-da-fé* took place on the Piazza della Signoria. In the centre of it rose a great pyramidal flight of stairs, like the *rogus* on which the Roman emperors were commonly burned. On the lowest tier were arranged false beards, masks and carnival disguises; above came volumes of the Latin and Italian poets, among others Boccaccio, the *Morgante* of Pulci, and Petrarch, partly in the form of valuable printed parchments and illuminated manuscripts; then women's ornaments and toilet articles, scents, mirrors, veils and false hair; higher up, lutes, harps, chess-boards, playing-cards; and finally, on the two uppermost tiers, paintings only, especially of female beauties, partly fancy-pictures, bearing the classical names of Lucretia, Cleopatra or Faustina, partly portraits of the beautiful Bencina, Lena Norella, Bina and Maria de' Lenzi. On the first occasion a Venetian merchant who happened to be present offered the Signoria 22,000 gold florins for the objects on the pyramid; but the only answer he received was that his portrait, too, was painted, and burned along with the rest. While the pile was lighted, the Signoria appeared on the balcony, and the air echoed with song, the sound of trumpets and the pealing of bells. The people then adjourned to the Piazza di San Marco, where they danced round in three concentric circles. The innermost was composed of monks of the monastery, alternating with boys, dressed as angels; then came young laymen and ecclesiastics; and on the outside old men, citizens and priests, the latter crowned with wreaths of olive.

All the ridicule of his victorious enemies, who in truth had no lack of justification or of talent for ridicule, was unable to discredit the memory of Savonarola. The more tragic the fortunes of Italy became, the brighter grew the halo which in the recollection of the survivors surrounded the figure of the great monk and prophet. Though his predictions may not have been confirmed in detail, the great and general calamity which he foretold was fulfilled with appalling truth.

Great, however, as the influence of all these preachers may have been, and brilliantly as Savonarola justified the claim of the monks to this office, nevertheless the order as a whole could not escape the contempt and condemnation of the people. Italy showed that she could give her enthusiasm only to individuals.

STRENGTH OF THE OLD FAITH

If, apart from all that concerns the priests and the monks, we attempt to measure the strength of the old faith, it will be found great or small according to the light in which it is considered. We have spoken already of the need felt for the sacraments as something indispensable. Let us now glance for a moment at the position of faith and worship in daily life. Both were determined partly by the habits of the people and partly by the policy and example of the rulers.

All that has to do with penitence and the attainment of salvation by means of good works was in much the same stage of development or corruption as in the North of Europe, both among the peasantry and among the poorer inhabitants of the cities. The instructed classes were here and there influenced by the same motives. Those sides of popular Catholicism which had their origin in the old pagan ways of addressing, rewarding and reconciling the gods have fixed themselves ineradicably in the consciousness of the people. The eighth eclogue of Battista Mantovano, which has already been quoted elsewhere, contains the prayer of a peasant to the Madonna, in which she is called upon as the special patroness of all rustic and agricultural interests. And what conceptions they were which the people formed of their protectress in heaven! What was in the mind of the Florentine woman who gave *ex voto* a keg of wax to the Annunziata, because her lover, a monk, had gradually emptied a barrel of wine without her absent husband finding it out! Then, too, as still in our own days, different departments of human life were presided over by their respective patrons. The attempt has often been made to explain a number of the commonest rites of the Catholic Church as remnants of pagan ceremonies, and no one doubts that many local and popular usages, which are associated with religious festivals, are forgotten fragments of the old pre-Christian faiths of Europe. In Italy, on the contrary, we find instances in which the affiliation of the new faith to the old seems consciously recognized. So, for example, the custom of setting out food for the dead four days before the feast of the Chair of St Peter, that is to say, on 18 February, the date of the ancient Feralia. Many other practices of this kind may then have prevailed and have since then been extirpated. Perhaps the paradox is only apparent if we say that the popular faith in Italy had a solid foundation just in proportion as it was pagan.

The extent to which this form of belief prevailed in the upper classes can to a certain point be shown in detail. It had, as we have said in speaking of the influence of the clergy, the power of custom and early impressions on its side. The love for ecclesiastical pomp and display helped to confirm it, and now and then there came one of those epidemics of revivalism, which few even among the scoffers and the sceptics were able to withstand.

But in questions of this kind it is perilous to grasp too hastily at absolute results. We might fancy, for example, that the feeling of educated men towards the relics of the saints would be a key by which some chambers of their religious consciousness might be opened. And in fact, some difference of degree may be demonstrable, though by no means as clearly as might be wished. The government of Venice in the fifteenth century seems to have fully shared in the reverence felt throughout the rest of Europe for the remains of the bodies of the saints. Even strangers who lived in Venice found it well to adapt themselves to this superstition. If we can judge of scholarly Padua from the testimony of its topographer Michele Savonarola, things must have been much the same there. With a mixture of pride and pious awe, Michele tells us how in times of great danger the saints were heard to sigh at night along the streets of the city, how the hair and nails on the corpse of a holy nun in Santa Chiara kept on continually growing, and how the same corpse, when any disaster was impending, used to make a noise and lift up the arms. When he sets to work to describe the chapel of St Anthony in the Santo, the writer loses himself in ejaculations and fantastic dreams. In Milan the people at least showed a fanatical devotion to relics; and when once, in the year 1517, the monks of San Simpliciano were careless enough to expose six holy corpses during certain alterations of the high altar, which event was followed by heavy floods of rain, the people attributed the visitation to this sacrilege, and gave the monks a sound beating whenever they met them in the street. In other parts of Italy, and even in the case of the popes themselves, the sincerity of this feeling is much more dubious, though here, too, a positive conclusion is hardly attainable. It is well known amid what general enthusiasm Pius II solemnly deposited the head of the Apostle Andrew, which had been brought from Greece, and then from San Mauro, in the Church of St Peter (1462); but we gather from his own narrative that he only did it from a kind of shame, as so many princes were competing for the relic. It was not till afterwards that the idea struck him of making Rome the common refuge for all the remains of the saints which had been driven from their own churches. Under Sixtus IV, the population of the city was still more zealous in this cause than the pope himself, and the magistracy (1483) complained bitterly that Sixtus had sent to Louis XI, the dying King of France, some specimens of the Lateran relics. A courageous voice was raised about this time at Bologna, advising the sale of the skull of St Dominic to the King of Spain, and the application of the money to some useful public object. But those who had the least reverence of all for the relics were the Florentines. Between the decision to honour their saint, St Zanobi, with a new sarcophagus and the final execution of the project by Ghiberti nineteen years elapsed (1409–28), and then it only happened by chance, because the master had executed a smaller order of the same kind with great skill.

Perhaps through being tricked by a cunning Neapolitan abbess (1352), who sent them a spurious arm of the patroness of the cathedral, Santa Reparata, made of wood and plaster, they began to get tired of relics. Or perhaps it would be truer to say that their aesthetic sense turned them away in disgust from dismembered corpses and mouldy clothes. Or perhaps their feeling was rather due to that sense of glory which thought Dante and Petrarch worthier of a splendid grave than all the twelve apostles put together. It is probable that throughout Italy, apart from Venice and from Rome, the condition of which latter city was exceptional, the worship of relics had long been giving way to the adoration of the Madonna,[89] at all events to a greater extent than elsewhere in Europe; and in this fact lies indirect evidence of an early development of the aesthetic sense.

It may be questioned whether in the North, where the vastest cathedrals are nearly all dedicated to Our Lady, and where an extensive branch of Latin and indigenous poetry sang the praises of the Mother of God, a greater devotion to her was possible. In Italy, however, the number of miraculous pictures of the Virgin was far greater, and the part they played in the daily life of the people much more important. Every town of any size contained a quantity of them, from the ancient, or ostensibly ancient, paintings by St Luke, down to the works of contemporaries, who not seldom lived to see the miracles wrought by their own handiwork. The work of art was in these cases by no means as harmless as Battista Mantovano thinks; sometimes it suddenly acquired a magical virtue. The popular craving for the miraculous, especially strong in women, may have been fully satisfied by these pictures, and for this reason the relics been less regarded. It cannot be said with certainty how far the respect for genuine relics suffered from the ridicule which the novelists aimed at the spurious.

The attitude of the educated classes towards Mariolatry is more clearly recognizable than towards the worship of images. One cannot but be struck with the fact that in Italian literature Dante's *Paradiso* is the last poem in honour of the Virgin, while among the people hymns in her praise have been constantly produced down to our own day. The names of Sannazaro and Sabellico and other writers of Latin poems prove little on the other side, since the object with which they wrote was chiefly literary. The poems written in Italian in the fifteenth and at the beginning of the sixteenth centuries, in which we meet with genuine religious feeling, such as the hymns of Lorenzo the Magnificent, and the sonnets of Vittoria Colonna and of Michelangelo, might have been just as well composed by Protestants. Besides the lyrical expression of faith in God, we chiefly notice in them the sense of sin, the consciousness of deliverance through the death of Christ, the longing for a better world. The intercession of the Mother of God is only mentioned by the way. The same phenomenon is repeated in the classical literature of the French at the time of Louis XIV. Not till the time of the Counter-Reformation did Mariolatry reappear in the higher Italian poetry. Meanwhile the plastic arts had certainly done their utmost to glorify the Madonna. It may be added that the worship of the saints among the educated classes often took an essentially pagan form.

We might thus critically examine the various sides of Italian Catholicism at this period, and so establish with a certain degree of probability the attitude of the instructed classes towards popular faith. Yet an absolute and positive result cannot be reached. We meet with contrasts hard to explain. While architects, painters and sculptors were working with restless activity in and for the churches, we hear at the beginning of the sixteenth century the bitterest complaints of the neglect of public worship and of these churches themselves.

It is well known how Luther was scandalized by the irreverence with which the priests in Rome said mass. And at the same time the feasts of the Church were celebrated with a taste and magnificence of which northern countries had no conception. It looks as if this most imaginative of nations was easily tempted to neglect everyday things, and as easily captivated by anything extraordinary.

It is to this excess of imagination that we must attribute the epidemic of religious revivals, upon which we shall again say a few words. They must be clearly distinguished from the excitement called forth by the great preachers. They were rather due to general public calamities, or to the dread of such.

In the Middle Ages all Europe was from time to time flooded by these great tides, which carried away whole peoples in their waves. The Crusades and the Flagellant revival are instances. Italy took part in both of these movements. The first great companies of Flagellants appeared, immediately after the fall of Ezzelino and his house, in the neighbourhood of the same Perugia which has been already spoken of as the headquarters of the revivalist preachers. Then followed the Flagellants of 1310 and 1334, and then the great pilgrimage without scourging in the year 1399, which Corio has recorded. It is not impossible that the jubilees were founded partly in order to regulate and render harmless this sinister passion for vagabondage which seized on the whole population at times of religious excitement. The great sanctuaries of Italy, such as Loreto and others, had meantime become famous, and no doubt diverted a certain part of this enthusiasm.

But terrible crises had still at a much later time the power to reawaken the glow of medieval penitence, and the conscience-stricken people, often still further appalled by signs and wonders, sought to move the pity of Heaven by wailing and scourgings. So it was at Bologna when the plague came in 1457, so in 1496 at a time of internal discord at Siena, to mention two only out of countless instances. No more moving scene can be imagined than that we read of at Milan in 1529, when famine, plague and war conspired with Spanish extortion to reduce the city to the lowest depths of despair. It chanced that the monk who had the ear of the people, Fra Tommaso Nieto, was himself a Spaniard. The Host was borne along in a novel fashion, amid barefooted crowds of old and young. It was placed on a decorated bier, which rested on the shoulders of four priests in linen garments – an imitation of the Ark of the Covenant which the children of Israel once carried round the walls of Jericho. Thus did the afflicted people of Milan remind their ancient God of His old covenant with man; and when the procession again entered the cathedral, and it seemed as if the vast building must fall in with the agonized cry of '*Misericordia!*', many who stood there may have believed that the Almighty would indeed subvert the laws of nature and of history, and send down upon them a miraculous deliverance.

There was one government in Italy, that of Duke Ercole I of Ferrara, which assumed the direction of public feeling, and compelled the popular revivals to move in regular channels. At the time when Savonarola was powerful in Florence, and the movement which he began spread far and wide among the population of central Italy, the people of Ferrara voluntarily entered on a general fast (at the beginning of 1496). A Lazarist announced from the pulpit the approach of a season of war and famine such as the world had never seen; but the Madonna had assured some pious people that these evils might be avoided by fasting. Upon this, the court itself had no choice but to fast, but it took the conduct of the public devotions into its own hands. On Easter Day, 3 April, a proclamation on morals and religion was published, forbidding blasphemy, prohibiting games, sodomy, concubinage, the letting of houses to prostitutes or panders, and the opening of all shops on feast-days, excepting those of the bakers and greengrocers. The Jews and Moors, who had taken refuge from the Spaniards at Ferrara, were now compelled to again wear the yellow O upon the breast. Contraveners were threatened not only with the punishments already provided by law, but also 'with such severer penalties as the duke might think good to inflict'. After this, the duke and the court went several days in succession to hear sermons in church, and on 10 April all the Jews in Ferrara were compelled to do the same. On 3 May the director of police, Zampante, sent the crier to announce that whoever had given money to the police-officers in order not to be denounced as a blasphemer, might, if he came forward, have it back with a further indemnification. These wicked officers, he said, had extorted as much as two or three ducats from innocent persons by threatening to lodge an information against them. They had then mutually informed against one another, and so had all found their way into prison. But as the money had been paid precisely in order not to have to do with Zampante, it is probable that his proclamation induced few people to come forward. In the year 1500, after the fall of Lodovico il Moro, when a similar outbreak of popular feeling took place, Ercole ordered a series of nine processions, in which there were 4,000 children dressed in white, bearing the standard of Jesus. He himself rode on horseback, as he could not walk without difficulty. An edict was afterwards published of the same kind as that of 1496. It is well known how many churches and monasteries were built by this ruler. He even sent for a live saint, the Suor Colomba, shortly before he married his son Alfonso to Lucrezia Borgia (1502). A special messenger fetched the saint with fifteen other nuns from Viterbo, and the duke himself conducted her on her arrival at Ferrara into a convent prepared for her reception. We shall probably do him no injustice if we attribute all these measures very largely to political calculation. To the conception of government formed by the House of Este, this employment of religion for the ends of statecraft belongs by a kind of logical necessity.

RELIGION AND THE SPIRIT OF THE RENAISSANCE

But in order to reach a definite conclusion with regard to the religious sense of the men of this period, we must adopt a different method. From their intellectual attitude in general, we can infer their relation both to the divine idea and to the existing religion of their age.

These modern men, the representatives of the culture of Italy, were born with the same religious instincts as other medieval Europeans. But their powerful individuality made them in religion, as in other matters, altogether subjective, and the intense charm which the discovery of the inner and outer universe exercised upon them rendered them markedly worldly. In the rest of Europe religion remained, till a much later period, something given from without, and in practical life egotism and sensuality alternated with devotion and repentance. The latter had no spiritual competitors, as in Italy, or only to a far smaller extent.

Further, the close and frequent relations of Italy with Byzantium and the Muhammadan peoples had produced a dispassionate tolerance which weakened the ethnographical conception of a privileged Christendom. And when classical antiquity with its men and institutions became an ideal of life, as well as the greatest of historical memories, ancient speculation and scepticism obtained in many cases a complete mastery over the minds of Italians.

Since, again, the Italians were the first modern people of Europe who gave themselves boldly to speculations on freedom and necessity, and since they did so under violent and lawless political circumstances, in which evil seemed often to win a splendid and lasting victory, their belief in God began to waver, and their view of the government of the world became fatalistic. And when their passionate natures refused to rest in the sense of uncertainty, they made a shift to help themselves out with ancient, oriental or medieval superstition. They took to astrology and magic.

Finally, these intellectual giants, these representatives of the Renaissance, show, in respect to religion, a quality which is common in youthful natures. Distinguishing keenly between good and evil, they yet are conscious of no sin. Every disturbance of their inward harmony they feel themselves able to make good out of the plastic resources of their own nature, and therefore they feel no repentance. The need of salvation thus becomes felt more and more dimly, while the ambitions and the intellectual activity of the present either shut out altogether every thought of a world to come, or else caused it to assume a poetic instead of a dogmatic form.

When we look on all this as pervaded and often perverted by the all-powerful Italian imagination, we obtain a picture of that time which is certainly more in accordance with truth than are vague declamations against modern paganism. And closer investigation often reveals to us that underneath this outward shell much genuine religion could still survive.

The fuller discussion of these points must be limited to a few of the most essential explanations.

That religion should again become an affair of the individual and of his own personal feeling was inevitable when the Church became corrupt in doctrine and tyrannous in practice, and is a proof that the European mind was still alive. It is true that this showed itself in many different ways. While the mystical and ascetical sects of the North lost no time in creating new outward forms for their new modes of thought and feeling, each individual in Italy went his own way, and thousands wandered on the sea of life without any religious guidance whatever. All the more must we admire those who attained and held fast to a personal religion. They were not to blame for being unable to have any part or lot in the old Church, as she then was; nor would it be reasonable to expect that they should all of them go through that mighty spiritual labour which was appointed to the German reformers. The form and aim of this personal faith, as it showed itself in the better minds, will be set forth at the close of our work.

The worldliness, through which the Renaissance seems to offer so striking a contrast to the Middle Ages, owed its first origin to the flood of new thoughts, purposes and views which transformed the medieval conception of nature and man. The spirit is not in itself more hostile to religion than that 'culture' which now holds its place, but which can give us only a feeble notion of the universal ferment which the discovery of a new world of greatness then called forth. This worldliness was not frivolous, but earnest, and was ennobled by art and poetry. It is a lofty necessity of the modern spirit that this attitude, once gained, can never again be lost, that an irresistible impulse forces us to the investigation of men and things, and that we must hold this inquiry to be our proper end and work. How soon and by what paths this search will lead us back to God, and in what ways the religious temper of the individual will be affected by it, are questions which cannot be met by any general answer. The Middle Ages, which spared themselves the trouble of induction and free inquiry, can have no right to impose upon us their dogmatical verdict in a matter of such vast importance.

To the study of man, among many other causes, was due the tolerance and indifference with which the Muhammadan religion was regarded. The knowledge and admiration of the remarkable civilization which Islam, particularly before the Mongol inundation, had attained, was peculiar to Italy from the time of the Crusades. This sympathy was fostered by the half-Muhammadan government of some Italian princes, by dislike and even contempt for the existing Church, and by constant commercial intercourse with the harbours of the eastern and southern Mediterranean. It can be shown that in the thirteenth century the Italians recognized a Muhammadan ideal of nobleness, dignity and pride, which they loved to connect with the person of a sultan. A Mameluke sultan is commonly meant; if any name is mentioned, it is the name of Saladin. Even the Osmanli Turks, whose destructive tendencies were no secret, gave the Italians only half a fright, and a peaceable accord with them was looked upon as no impossibility.

The truest and most characteristic expression of this religious indifference is the famous story of the Three Rings, which Lessing has put into the mouth of his Nathan, after it had been already told centuries earlier, though with some reserve, in *The Hundred Old Tales* (nov. 72 or 73), and more boldly in Boccaccio (*Decameron*, i, nov. 3). In what language and in what corner of the Mediterranean it was first told, can never be known; most likely the original was much more plain-spoken than the two Italian adaptations. The religious postulate on which it rests, namely deism, will be discussed later on in its wider significance for this period. The same idea is repeated, though in a clumsy caricature, in the famous proverb of the 'three who have deceived the world, that is, Moses, Christ and Muhammad'. If the Emperor Frederick II, in whom this saying is said to have originated, really thought so, he probably expressed himself with more wit. Ideas of the same kind were also current in Islam.

At the height of the Renaissance, towards the close of the fifteenth century, Luigi Pulci offers us an example of the same mode of thought in the *Morgante Maggiore*. The imaginary world of which his story treats is divided, as in all heroic poems of romance, into a Christian and a Muhammadan camp. In accordance with the medieval temper, the victory of the Christian and the final reconciliation among the combatants was attended by the baptism of the defeated Islamites, and the *improvisatori*, who preceded Pulci in the treatment of these subjects, must have made free use of this stock incident. It was Pulci's object to parody his predecessors, particularly the worst among them, and this he does by those appeals to God, Christ and the Madonna with which each canto begins; and still more clearly by the sudden conversions and baptisms, the utter senselessness of which must have struck every reader or hearer. This ridicule leads him further to the confession of his faith in the relative goodness of all religions, which faith, notwithstanding his profession of orthodoxy, rests on an essentially theistic basic. In another point too he departs widely from medieval conceptions. The alternatives in past centuries were: Christian, or else pagan and Muhammadan; orthodox believer or heretic. Pulci draws a picture of the Giant Margutte who, disregarding each and every religion, jovially confesses to every form of vice and sensuality, and only reserves to himself the merit of having never broken faith. Perhaps the poet intended to make something of this – in his way – honest monster, possibly to have led him into virtuous paths by Morgante, but he soon got tired of his own creation, and in the next canto brought him to a comic end. Margutte has been brought forward as a proof of Pulci's frivolity; but he is needed to complete the picture of the poetry of the fifteenth century. It was natural that it should somewhere present in grotesque proportions the figure of an untamed egotism, insensible to all established rule, and yet with a remnant of honourable feeling left. In other poems sentiments are put into the mouths of giants, fiends, infidels and Muhammadans which no Christian knight would venture to utter.

Antiquity exercised an influence of another kind than that of Islam, and this not through its religion, which was but too much like the Catholicism of this period, but through its philosophy. Ancient literature, now worshipped as something incomparable, is full of the victory of philosophy over religious tradition. An endless number of systems and fragments of systems were suddenly presented to the Italian mind, not as curiosities or even as heresies, but almost with the authority of dogmas, which had now to be reconciled rather than discriminated. In nearly all these various opinions and doctrines a certain kind of belief in God was implied; but taken altogether they formed a marked contrast to the Christian faith in a divine government of the world. And there was one central question, which medieval theology had striven in vain to solve, and which now urgently demanded an answer from the wisdom of the ancients, namely, the relation of providence to the freedom or necessity of the human will. To write the history of this question even superficially from the fourteenth century onwards would require a whole volume. A few hints must here suffice.

If we take Dante and his contemporaries as evidence, we shall find that ancient philosophy first came into contact with Italian life in the form which offered the most marked contrast to Christianity, that is to say, Epicureanism. The writings of Epicurus were no longer preserved, and even at the close of the classical age a more or less one-sided conception had been formed of his philosophy. Nevertheless, that phase of Epicureanism which can be studied in Lucretius, and especially in Cicero, is quite sufficient to make men familiar with a godless universe. To what extent his teaching was actually understood, and whether the name of the problematic Greek sage was not rather a catchword for the multitude, it is hard to say. It is probable that the Dominican Inquisition used it against men who could not be reached by a more definite accusation. In the case of sceptics born before the

time was ripe, whom it was yet hard to convict of positive heretical
utterances, a moderate degree of luxurious living may have sufficed to
provoke the charge. The word is used in this conventional sense by
Giovanni Villani, when he explains the Florentine fires of 1115 and
1117 as a divine judgement on heresies, among others, 'on the luxurious
and gluttonous sect of Epicureans'. The same writer says of Manfred,
'His life was Epicurean, since he believed neither in God, nor in the
saints, but only in bodily pleasure.'

Dante speaks still more clearly in the ninth and tenth cantos of the
Inferno. That terrible fiery field covered with half-opened tombs, from
which issued cries of hopeless agony, was peopled by the two great
classes of those whom the Church had vanquished or expelled in the
thirteenth century. The one were heretics who opposed the Church by
deliberately spreading false doctrine; the other were Epicureans, and
their sin against the Church lay in their general disposition, which was
summed up in the belief that the soul dies with the body. The Church
was well aware that this one doctrine, if it gained ground, must be
more ruinous to her authority than all the teachings of the Manichaeans
and Paterines, since it took away all reason for her interference in the
affairs of men after death. That the means which she used in her
struggles were precisely what had driven the most gifted natures to
unbelief and despair was what she naturally would not herself admit.

Dante's loathing of Epicurus, or of what he took to be his doctrine,
was certainly sincere. The poet of the life to come could not but detest
the denier of immortality; and a world neither made nor ruled by
God, no less than the vulgar objects of earthly life which the system
appeared to countenance, could not but be intensely repugnant to a
nature like his. But if we look closer, we find that certain doctrines of
the ancients made even on him an impression which forced the biblical
doctrine of the divine government into the background, unless, indeed,
it was his own reflection, the influence of opinions then prevalent, or
loathing for the injustice that seemed to rule this world, which made
him give up the belief in a special providence. His God leaves all the
details of the world's government to a deputy, Fortune, whose sole
work it is to change and change again all earthly things, and who can
disregard the wailings of men in unalterable beatitude. Nevertheless,
Dante does not for a moment loose his hold on the moral responsibility
of man; he believes in free will.

The belief in the freedom of the will, in the popular sense of the words, has always prevailed in Western countries. At all times men have been held responsible for their actions, as though this freedom were a matter of course. The case is otherwise with the religious and philosophical doctrine which labours under the difficulty of harmonizing the nature of the will with the laws of the universe at large. We have here to do with a question of more or less, which every moral estimate must take into account. Dante is not wholly free from those astrological superstitions which illumined the horizon of his time with deceptive light, but they do not hinder him from rising to a worthy conception of human nature. 'The stars,' he makes his Marco Lombardo say (*Purgatorio*, xvi, 73), 'the stars give the first impulse to your actions,' but 'a light is given you to know good and evil, and Freewill, which, if it endure the strain in its first battlings with the heavens, at length gains the whole victory, if it be well nurtured.'

Others might seek the necessity which annulled human freedom in another power than the stars, but the question was henceforth an open and inevitable one. So far as it was a question for the schools or the pursuit of isolated thinkers, its treatment belongs to the historian of philosophy. But inasmuch as it entered into the consciousness of a wider public, it is necessary for us to say a few words respecting it.

The fourteenth century was chiefly stimulated by the writings of Cicero, who, though in fact an eclectic, yet, by his habit of setting forth the opinions of different schools, without coming to a decision between them, exercised the influence of a sceptic. Next in importance came Seneca, and the few works of Aristotle which had been translated into Latin. The immediate fruit of these studies was the capacity to reflect on great subjects, if not in direct opposition to the authority of the Church, at all events independently of it.

In the course of the fifteenth century the works of antiquity were discovered and diffused with extraordinary rapidity. All the writings of the Greek philosophers which we ourselves possess were now, at least in the form of Latin translations, in everybody's hands. It is a curious fact that some of the most zealous apostles of this new culture were men of the strictest piety, or even ascetics. Fra Ambrogio Camaldolese, as a spiritual dignitary chiefly occupied with ecclesiastical affairs, and as a literary man with the translation of the Greek fathers of the Church, could not repress the humanistic impulse, and at the request of Cosimo de' Medici, undertook to translate Diogenes Laertius into Latin. His contemporaries, Niccolò Nicoli, Giannozzo Manetti,

Donato Acciaiuoli and Pope Nicholas V, united to a many-sided humanism profound biblical scholarship and deep piety. In Vittorino da Feltre the same temper has been already noticed. The same Matthew Vegio, who added a thirteenth book to the *Aeneid*, had an enthusiasm for the memory of St Augustine and his mother Monica which cannot have been without a deeper influence upon him. The result of all these tendencies was that the Platonic Academy at Florence deliberately chose for its object the reconciliation of the spirit of antiquity with that of Christianity. It was a remarkable oasis in the humanism of the period.

This humanism was in fact pagan, and became more and more so as its sphere widened in the fifteenth century. Its representatives, whom we have already described as the advance guard of an unbridled individualism, display as a rule such a character that even their religion, which is sometimes professed very definitely, becomes a matter of indifference to us. They easily got the name of atheists, if they showed themselves indifferent to religion, and spoke freely against the Church; but not one of them ever professed, or dared to profess, a formal, philosophical atheism. If they sought for any leading principle, it must have been a kind of superficial rationalism – a careless inference from the many and contradictory opinions of antiquity with which they busied themselves, and from the discredit into which the Church and her doctrines had fallen. This was the sort of reasoning which was near bringing Galeottus Martius to the stake, had not his former pupil, Pope Sixtus IV, perhaps at the request of Lorenzo de' Medici, saved him from the hands of the Inquisition. Galeotto had ventured to write that the man who walked uprightly, and acted according to the natural law born within him, would go to heaven, whatever nation he belonged to.

Let us take, by way of example, the religious attitude of one of the smaller men in the great army. Codrus Urceus was first the tutor of the last Ordelaffo, Prince of Forlì, and afterwards for many years professor at Bologna. Against the Church and the monks his language is as abusive as that of the rest. His tone in general is reckless to the last degree, and he constantly introduces himself in all his local history and gossip. But he knows how to speak to the edification of the true God-Man, Jesus Christ, and to commend himself by letter to the prayers of a saintly priest. On one occasion, after enumerating the follies of the pagan religions, he thus goes on: 'Our theologians, too, fight and quarrel *de lana caprina*, about the immaculate conception, antichrist, sacraments, predestination and other things, which were better let alone than talked of publicly.' Once, when he was not at home, his room and manuscripts were burnt. When he heard the news he stood opposite a figure of the Madonna in the street, and cried to it: 'Listen to what I tell you; I am not mad, I am saying what I mean. If I ever call upon you in the hour of my death, you need not hear me or take me among your own, for I will go and spend eternity with the Devil.' After which speech he found it desirable to spend six months in retirement at the home of a woodcutter. With all this, he was so superstitious that prodigies and omens gave him incessant frights, leaving him no belief to spare for the immortality of the soul. When his hearers questioned him on the matter, he answered that no one knew what became of a man, of his soul or his body, after death, and the talk about another life was only fit to frighten old women. But when he came to die, he commended in his will his soul or his spirit to Almighty God, exhorted his weeping pupils to fear the Lord, and especially to believe in immortality and future retribution, and received the sacrament with much fervour. We have no guarantee that more famous men in the same calling, however significant their opinions may be, were in practical life any more consistent. It is probable that most of them wavered inwardly between incredulity and a remnant of the faith in which they were brought up, and outwardly held for prudential reasons to the Church.

Through the connection of rationalism with the newly born science of historical investigation, some timid attempts at biblical criticism may here and there have been made. A saying of Pius II has been recorded, which seems intended to prepare the way for such criticism: 'Even if Christianity were not confirmed by miracles, it ought still to be accepted on account of its morality.' The legends of the Church, in so far as they contained arbitrary versions of the biblical miracles, were freely ridiculed, and this reacted on the religious sense of the people. Where Judaizing heretics are mentioned, we must understand chiefly those who denied the divinity of Christ, which was probably the offence for which Giorgio da Novara was burnt at Bologna about the year 1500. But again at Bologna in the year 1497 the Dominican Inquisitor was forced to let the physician Gabriele da Salò, who had powerful patrons, escape with a simple expression of penitence, although he was in the habit of maintaining that Christ was not God,

but son of Joseph and Mary, and conceived in the usual way; that by
his cunning he had deceived the world to its ruin; that he may have
died on the Cross on account of crimes which he had committed; that
his religion would soon come to an end; that his body was not really
contained in the sacrament, and that he performed his miracles, not
through any divine power, but through the influence of the heavenly
bodies. This latter statement is most characteristic of the time. Faith is
gone, but magic still holds its ground.

With respect to the moral government of the world, the humanists
seldom get beyond a cold and resigned consideration of the prevalent
violence and misrule. In this mood the many works *On Fate*, or
whatever name they bear, are written. They tell of the turning of the
wheel of fortune, and of the instability of earthly, especially political,
things. Providence is only brought in because the writers would still
be ashamed of undisguised fatalism, of the avowal of their ignorance,
or of useless complaints. Gioviano Pontano ingeniously illustrates the
nature of that mysterious something which men call fortune by a
hundred incidents, most of which belonged to his own experience.
The subject is treated more humorously by Aeneas Sylvius, in the
form of a vision seen in a dream. The aim of Poggio, on the other
hand, in a work written in his old age, is to represent the world as a
vale of tears, and to fix the happiness of various classes as low as
possible. This tone became in future the prevalent one. Distinguished
men drew up a debit and credit of the happiness and unhappiness of
their lives, and generally found that the latter outweighed the former.
The fate of Italy and the Italians, so far as it could be told in the year
1510, has been described with dignity and almost elegiac pathos by
Tristan Caracciolo. Applying this general tone of feeling to the humanists themselves, Pierio Valeriano afterwards composed his famous
treatise. Some of these themes, such as the fortunes of Leo, were most
suggestive. All the good that can be said of him politically has been
briefly and admirably summed up by Francesco Vettori; the picture
of Leo's pleasures is given by Paolo Giovio and in the anonymous
biography; and the shadows which attended his prosperity are drawn
with inexorable truth by the same Pierio Valeriano.

We cannot, on the other hand, read without a kind of awe how men
sometimes boasted of their fortune in public inscriptions. Giovanni II
Bentivoglio, ruler of Bologna, ventured to carve in stone on the
newly built tower by his palace that his merit and his fortune had

given him richly of all that could be desired – and this a few years before his expulsion. The ancients, when they spoke in this tone, had nevertheless a sense of the envy of the gods. In Italy it was probably the *condottieri* who first ventured to boast so loudly of their fortune.

But the way in which resuscitated antiquity affected religion most powerfully was not through any doctrines or philosophical system, but through a general tendency which it fostered. The men, and in some respects the institutions, of antiquity were preferred to those of the Middle Ages, and in the eager attempt to imitate and reproduce them, religion was left to take care of itself. All was absorbed in the admiration for historical greatness. To this the philologians added many special follies of their own, by which they became the mark for general attention. How far Paul II was justified in calling his Abbreviators and their friends to account for their paganism is certainly a matter of great doubt, as his biographer and chief victim, Platina, has shown a masterly skill in explaining his vindictiveness on other grounds, and especially in making him play a ludicrous figure. The charges of infidelity, paganism, denial of immortality and so forth were not made against the accused till the charge of high treason had broken down. Paul, indeed, if we are correctly informed about him, was by no means the man to judge of intellectual things. It was he who exhorted the Romans to teach their children nothing beyond reading and writing. His priestly narrowness of views reminds us of Savonarola, with the difference that Paul might fairly have been told that he and his like were in great part to blame if culture made men hostile to religion. It cannot, nevertheless, be doubted that he felt a real anxiety about the pagan tendencies which surrounded him. And what, in truth, may not the humanists have allowed themselves at the court of the profligate pagan, Sigismondo Malatesta? How far these men, destitute for the most part of fixed principle, ventured to go, depended assuredly on the sort of influences they were exposed to. Nor could they treat of Christianity without paganizing it. It is curious, for instance, to notice how far Gioviano Pontano carried this confusion. He speaks of a saint not only as '*divus*', but as '*deus*'; the angels he holds to be identical with the genii of antiquity;[90] and his notion of immortality reminds us of the old kingdom of the shades. This spirit occasionally appears in the most extravagant shapes. In 1526, when Siena was attacked by the exiled party, the worthy canon Tizio, who tells us the story himself, rose from his bed on 22 July, called to mind what is written in the third book of Macrobius, celebrated mass and then pronounced against the enemy the curse with which his author had supplied him, only altering '*Tellus mater teque Juppiter obtestor*' into '*Tellus teque Christe Deus obtestor*'. After he had done this for three days, the enemy retreated. On the one side, these things strike us as an affair of mere style and fashion; on the other, as a symptom of religious decadence.

INFLUENCE OF ANCIENT SUPERSTITION

But in another way, and that dogmatically, antiquity exercised a perilous influence. It imparted to the Renaissance its own forms of superstition. Some fragments of this had survived in Italy all through the Middle Ages, and the resuscitation of the whole was thereby made so much the more easy. The part played by the imagination in the process need not be dwelt upon. This only could have silenced the critical intellect of the Italians.

The belief in a divine government of the world was in many minds destroyed by the spectacle of so much injustice and misery. Others, like Dante, surrendered at all events this life to the caprices of chance, and if they nevertheless retained a sturdy faith, it was because they held that the higher destiny of man would be accomplished in the life to come. But when the belief in immortality began to waver, then fatalism got the upper hand, or sometimes the latter came first and had the former as its consequence.

The gap thus opened was in the first place filled by the astrology of antiquity, or even of the Arabs. From the relations of the planets among themselves and to the signs of the zodiac, future events and the course of whole lives were inferred, and the most weighty decisions were taken in consequence. In many cases the line of action thus adopted at the suggestion of the stars may not have been more immoral than that which would otherwise have been followed. But too often the decision must have been made at the cost of honour and conscience. It is profoundly instructive to observe how powerless culture and enlightenment were against this delusion, since the latter had its support in the ardent imagination of the people, in the passionate wish to penetrate and determine the future. Antiquity, too, was on the side of astrology.

At the beginning of the thirteenth century this superstition suddenly appeared in the foreground of Italian life. The Emperor Frederick II always travelled with his astrologer Theodorus; and Ezzelino da Romano with a large, well-paid court of such people, among them the famous Guido Bonatto and the long-bearded Saracen, Paul of Baghdad. In all important undertakings they fixed for him the day and the hour, and the gigantic atrocities of which he was guilty may have been in part practical inferences from their prophecies. Soon all scruples about consulting the stars ceased. Not only princes, but free cities, had their regular astrologers, and at the universities, from the fourteenth to the sixteenth century, professors of this pseudo-science were appointed, and lectured side by side with the astronomers. The popes commonly made no secret of their star-gazing, though Pius II, who also despised magic, omens and the interpretation of dreams, is an honourable exception. Even Leo X seems to have thought the flourishing condition of astrology a credit to his pontificate, and Paul III never held a consistory till the star-gazers had fixed the hour.

It may fairly be assumed that the better natures did not allow their actions to be determined by the stars beyond a certain point, and that there was a limit where conscience and religion made them pause. In fact, not only did pious and excellent people share the delusion, but they actually came forward to profess it publicly. One of these was Maestro Pagolo of Florence, in whom we can detect the same desire to turn astrology to moral account which meets us in the late Roman Firmicus Maternus. His life was that of a saintly ascetic. He ate almost nothing, despised all temporal goods, and only collected books. A skilled physician, he only practised among his friends, and made it a condition of his treatment that they should confess their sins. He frequented the small but famous circle which assembled in the Monastery of the Angeli around Fra Ambrogio Camaldolese. He also saw much of Cosimo the Elder, especially in his last years; for Cosimo accepted and used astrology, though probably only for objects of lesser importance. As a rule, however, Pagolo only interpreted the stars to his most confidential friends. But even without this severity of morals, the astrologers might be highly respected and show themselves everywhere. There were also far more of them in Italy than in other European countries, where they only appeared at the great courts, and there not always. All the great householders in Italy, when the fashion was once established, kept an astrologer, who, it must be added, was not always sure of his dinner. Through the literature of this science, which was widely diffused even before the invention of printing, a dilettantism also grew up which as far as possible followed in the steps of the masters. The worst class of astrologers were those who used the stars either as an aid or a cloak to magical arts.

Yet apart from the latter, astrology is a miserable feature in the life of that time. What a figure do all these highly gifted, many-sided, original characters play when the blind passion for knowing and determining the future dethrones their powerful will and resolution! Now and then, when the stars send them too cruel a message, they manage to brace themselves up, act for themselves, and say boldly, 'Vir sapiens dominabitur astris' – the wise man is master of the stars – then again relapse into the old delusion.

In all the better families the horoscope of the children was drawn as a matter of course, and it sometimes happened that for half a lifetime men were haunted by the idle expectation of events which never occurred. The stars were questioned whenever a great man had to come to any important decision, and even consulted as to the hour at which any undertaking was to be begun. The journeys of princes, the reception of foreign ambassadors, the laying of the foundation-stones of public buildings, depended on the answer. A striking instance of the latter occurs in the life of the aforenamed Guido Bonatto, who by his personal activity and by his great systematic work on the subject deserves to be called the restorer of astrology in the thirteenth century. In order to put an end to the struggle of the Guelphs and Ghibellines at Forlì, he persuaded the inhabitants to rebuild the city walls and to begin the works under a constellation indicated by himself. If then two men, one from each party, at the same moment put a stone into the foundation, there would henceforth and for ever be no more party divisions in Forlì. A Guelph and a Ghibelline were selected for this office; the solemn moment arrived, each held the stone in his hands, the workmen stood ready with their implements. Bonatto gave the signal, and the Ghibelline threw down his stone on to the foundation. But the Guelph hesitated, and at last refused to do anything at all, on the ground that Bonatto himself had the reputation of a Ghibelline and might be devising some mysterious mischief against the Guelphs. Upon which the astrologer addressed him: 'God damn thee and the Guelph party, with your distrustful malice! This constellation will not appear above our city for 500 years to come.' In fact God soon afterwards did destroy the Guelphs of Forlì, but now, writes the chronicler about 1480, the two parties are thoroughly reconciled, and their very names are heard no longer.

Nothing that depended upon the stars was more important than decisions in time of war. The same Bonatto procured for the great Ghibelline leader Guido da Montefeltro a series of victories by telling him the propitious hour for marching. When Montefeltro was no longer accompanied by him he lost the courage to maintain his despotism, and entered a Minorite monastery, where he lived as a monk for many years till his death. In the war with Pisa in 1362, the Florentines commissioned their astrologer to fix the hour for the march, and almost came too late through suddenly receiving orders to take a circuitous route through the city. On former occasions they had marched out by the Via di Borgo Santi Apostoli, and the campaign had been unsuccessful. It was clear that there was some bad omen connected with the exit through this street against Pisa, and conse-quently the army was now led out by the Porta Rossa. But as the tents stretched out there to dry had not been taken away, the flags – another bad omen – had to be lowered. The influence of astrology in war was confirmed by the fact that nearly all the *condottieri* believed in it. Jacopo Caldora was cheerful in the most serious illness, knowing that he was fated to fall in battle, which in fact happened. Bartolommeo Alviano was convinced that his wounds in the head were as much a gift of the stars as his military command. Niccolò Orsini-Pitigliano asked the physicist and astrologer Alessandro Benedetto to fix a favourable hour for the conclusion of his bargain with Venice (1495). When the Florentines on 1 June 1498 solemnly invested their new *condottiere* Paolo Vitelli with his office, the marshal's staff which they handed him was, at his own wish, decorated with pictures of the constellations.

Sometimes it is not easy to make out whether in important political events the stars were questioned beforehand, or whether the astrologers were simply impelled afterwards by curiosity to find out the constella-tion which decided the result. When Giangaleazzo Visconti by a master-stroke of policy took prisoner his uncle Bernabò, with the latter's family (1385), we are told by a contemporary that Jupiter, Saturn and Mars stood in the house of the Twins, but we cannot say if the deed was resolved on in consequence. It is also probable that the advice of the astrologers was often determined by political calculation not less than by the course of the planets.

All Europe, through the latter part of the Middle Ages, had allowed itself to be terrified by predictions of plagues, wars, floods and earthquakes, and in this respect Italy was by no means behind other countries. The unlucky year 1494, which for ever opened the gates of Italy to the stranger, was undeniably ushered in by many prophecies of misfortune – only we cannot say whether such prophecies were not ready for each and every year.

This mode of thought was extended with thorough consistency into regions where we should hardly expect to meet with it. If the whole outward and spiritual life of the individual is determined by the facts of his birth, the same law also governs groups of individuals and historical products – that is to say, nations and religions; and as the constellation of these things changes, so do the things themselves. The idea that each religion has its day first came into Italian culture in connection with these astrological beliefs. The conjunction of Jupiter with Saturn brought forth, we are told, the faith of Israel; that of Jupiter and Mars, the Chaldean; with the Sun, the Egyptian; with Venus, the Muhammadan; with Mercury, the Christian; and the conjunction of Jupiter with the Moon will one day bring forth the religion of Antichrist. Cecco d'Ascoli had already blasphemously calculated the nativity of Christ, and deduced from it his death upon the cross. For this he was burnt at the stake in 1327, at Florence. Doctrines of this sort ended by simply darkening men's whole perceptions of spiritual things.

So much more worthy then of recognition is the warfare which the clear Italian spirit waged against this army of delusions. Notwithstanding the great monumental glorification of astrology, as in the frescoes in the Salone at Padua, and those in Borso's summer palace (Schifanoia) at Ferrara, notwithstanding the shameless praises of even such a man as the elder Beroaldus, there was no want of thoughtful and independent minds to protest against it. Here, too, the way had been prepared by antiquity, but it was their own common sense and observation which taught them what to say. Petrarch's attitude towards the astrologers, whom he knew by personal intercourse, is one of bitter contempt; and no one saw through their system of lies more clearly than he. The novels, from the time when they first began to appear – from the time of the *Cento novelle antiche* – are almost always hostile to the astrologers. The Florentine chroniclers bravely keep themselves free from the delusions which, as part of historical tradition, they are compelled to record. Giovanni Villani says more than once, 'No constellation can subjugate either the free will of man, or the counsels of God.' Matteo Villani declares astrology to be a vice which the Florentines had inherited, along with other superstitions, from their pagan ancestors, the Romans. The question, however, did not remain one for mere literary discussion, but the parties for and against disputed publicly. After the terrible floods of 1333, and again in 1345, astrologers and theologians discussed with great minuteness the influence of the stars, the will of God and the justice of his punishments. These struggles never ceased throughout the whole time of the Renaissance, and we may conclude that the protestors were in earnest, since it was easier for them to recommend themselves to the great by defending than by opposing astrology.

In the circle of Lorenzo the Magnificent, among his most distinguished Platonists, opinions were divided on this question. Marsilio Ficino defended astrology, and drew the horoscope of the children of the house, promising the little Giovanni, afterwards Leo X, that he would one day be pope. Pico della Mirandola, on the other hand, made an epoch in the subject by his famous refutation. He detects in this belief the root of all impiety and immorality. If the astrologer, he maintains, believes in anything at all, he must worship not God, but the planets, from which all good and evil are derived. All other superstitions find a ready instrument in astrology, which serves as handmaid to geomancy, chiromancy and magic of every kind. As to morality, he maintains that nothing can more foster evil than the opinion that heaven itself is the cause of it, in which case the faith in eternal happiness and punishment must also disappear. Pico even took the trouble to check off the astrologers inductively, and found that in the course of a month three-fourths of their weather prophecies turned out false. But his main achievement was to set forth, in the *Fourth Book*, a positive Christian doctrine of the freedom of the will and the government of the universe which seems to have made a greater impression on the educated classes throughout Italy than all the revivalist preachers put together. The latter, in fact, often failed to reach these classes.

The first result of his book was that the astrologers ceased to publish their doctrines, and those who had already printed them were more or less ashamed of what they had done. Gioviano Pontano, for example, in his book on fate, had recognized the science, and in a great work of his had expounded the whole theory of it in the style of the old Firmicus, ascribing to the stars the growth of every bodily and spiritual quality. He now in his dialogue *Aegidius* surrendered, if not astrology, at least certain astrologers, and sounded the praises of free will, by which man is enabled to know God. Astrology remained more or less in fashion, but seems not to have governed human life in the way it formerly had done. The art of painting, which in the fifteenth century had done its best to foster the delusion, now expressed the altered tone of thought. Raphael, in the cupola of the Cappella Chigi, represents the gods of the different planets and the starry firmament, watched, however, and guided by beautiful angel-figures, and receiving from above the blessing of the Eternal Father. There was also another cause which now began to tell against astrology in Italy. The Spaniards took no interest in it, not even the generals, and those who wished to gain their favour declared open war against the half-heretical, half-Muhammadan science. It is true that Guicciardini writes in the year 1529: 'How happy are the astrologers, who are believed if they tell one truth to a hundred lies, while other people lose all credit if they tell one lie to a hundred truths.' But the contempt for astrology did not necessarily lead to a return to the belief in providence. It could as easily lead to an indefinite fatalism.

In this respect, as in others, Italy was unable to make its own way healthily through the ferment of the Renaissance, because the foreign invasion and the Counter-Reformation came upon it in the middle. Without such interfering causes its own strength would have enabled it thoroughly to get rid of these fantastic illusions. Those who hold that the onslaught of the strangers and the Catholic reactions were necessities for which the Italian people was itself solely responsible will look on the spiritual bankruptcy which they produced as a just retribution. But it is a pity that the rest of Europe had indirectly to pay so large a part of the penalty.

The belief in omens seems a much more innocent matter than astrology. The Middle Ages had everywhere inherited them in abundance from the various pagan religions; and Italy did not differ in this respect from other countries. What is characteristic of Italy is the support lent by humanism to the popular superstition. The pagan inheritance was here backed up by a pagan literary development.

The popular superstition of the Italians rested largely on premonitions and inferences drawn from ominous occurrences, with which a good deal of magic, mostly of an innocent sort, was connected. There was, however, no lack of learned humanists who boldly ridiculed these delusions, and to whose attacks we partly owe the knowledge of them. Gioviano Pontano, the author of the great astrological work already mentioned above, enumerates with pity in his *Charon* a long string of Neapolitan superstitions -- the grief of the women when a fowl or goose caught the pip; the deep anxiety of the nobility if a hunting falcon did not come home, or if a horse sprained its foot; the magical formulae of the Apulian peasants, recited on three Saturday evenings, when mad dogs were at large. The animal kingdom, as in antiquity, was regarded as specially significant in this respect, and the behaviour of the lions, leopards and other beasts kept by the state gave the people all the more food for reflection, because they had come to be considered as living symbols of the state. During the siege of Florence, in 1529, an eagle which had been shot at fled into the city, and the Signoria gave the bearer four ducats, because the omen was good. Certain times and places were favourable or unfavourable, or even decisive one way or the other, for certain actions. The Florentines, so Varchi tells us, held Saturday to be the fateful day on which all important events, good as well as bad, commonly happened. Their prejudice against marching out to war through a particular street has been already mentioned. At Perugia one of the gates, the Porta Eburnea, was thought lucky, and the Baglioni always went out to fight through it. Meteors and the appearance of the heavens were as significant in Italy as elsewhere in the Middle Ages, and the popular imagination saw warring armies in an unusual formation of clouds, and heard the clash of their collision high in the air. The superstition became a more serious matter when it attached itself to sacred things, when figures of the Virgin wept or moved the eyes, or when public calamities were associated with some alleged act of impiety, for which the people demanded expiation. In 1478, when Piacenza was visited with a violent and prolonged rainfall, it was said that there would be no dry weather till a certain usurer, who had been lately buried in San Francesco, had ceased to rest in consecrated earth. As the bishop was not obliging enough to have the corpse dug up, the young fellows of the town took it by force, dragged it round the streets amid frightful confusion, and at last threw it into the Po. Even Politian accepted this point of view in speaking of Giacomo Pazzi, one of the chiefs of the conspiracy of 1478, in Florence, which is called after his family. When he was put to death, he devoted his soul to Satan with fearful words. Here, too, rain followed and threatened to ruin the harvest; here, too, a party of men, mostly peasants, dug up the body in the church, and immediately the clouds departed and the sun shone – 'so gracious was fortune to the opinion of the people', adds the great scholar. The corpse was first cast into unhallowed ground, the next day dug up, and after a horrible procession through the city thrown into the Arno.

These facts and the like bear a popular character, and might have occurred in the tenth, just as well as in the sixteenth century. But now comes the literary influence of antiquity. We know positively that the humanists were peculiarly accessible to prodigies and auguries, and instances of this have been already quoted. If further evidence were needed, it would be found in Poggio. The same radical thinker who denied the rights of noble birth and the inequality of men, not only believed in all the medieval stories of ghosts and devils, but also in prodigies after the ancient pattern, like those said to have occurred on the last visit of Eugenius IV to Florence. 'Near Como there were seen one evening four thousand dogs, who took the road to Germany; these were followed by a great herd of cattle, and these by an army on foot and horseback, some with no heads and some with almost invisible heads, and then a gigantic horseman with another herd of cattle behind him.' Poggio also believes in a battle of magpies and jackdaws. He even relates, perhaps without being aware of it, a well-preserved piece of ancient mythology. On the Dalmatian coast a Triton had appeared, bearded and horned, a genuine sea-satyr, ending in fins and a tail; he carried away women and children from the shore, till five stout-hearted washer-women killed him with sticks and stones. A wooden model of the monster, which was exhibited at Ferrara, makes the whole story credible to Poggio. Though there were no more oracles, and it was no longer possible to take counsel of the gods, yet it became again the fashion to open Virgil at hazard, and take the passage hit upon as an omen (*sortes Virgilianae*). Nor can the belief in demons current in the later period of antiquity have been without influence on the Renaissance. The work of Jamblichus or Abammon on the mysteries of the Egyptians, which may have contributed to this result, was printed in a Latin translation at the end of the fifteenth century. The Platonic Academy at Florence was not free from these and other neoplatonic dreams of the Roman decadence. A few words must here be given to the belief in demons and to the magic which was connected with this belief.

The popular faith in what is called the spirit-world was nearly the same in Italy as elsewhere in Europe. In Italy as elsewhere there were ghosts, that is, reappearances of deceased persons; and if the view taken of them differed in any respect from that which prevailed in the North, the difference betrayed itself only in the ancient name *ombra*. Even nowadays if such a shade presents itself, a couple of masses are said for its repose. That the spirits of bad men appear in a dreadful shape is a matter of course, but along with this we find the notion that the ghosts of the departed are universally malicious. The dead, says the priest in a novel of Bandello, kill the little children. It seems as if a certain shade was here thought of as separate from the soul, since the latter suffers in purgatory, and when it appears, does nothing but wail and pray. At other times what appears is not the ghost of a man, but of an event – of a past condition of things. So the neighbours explained the diabolical appearances in the old palace of the Visconti near San Giovanni in Conca, at Milan, since here it was that Bernabò Visconti had caused countless victims of his tyranny to be tortured and stran- gled, and no wonder if there were strange things to be seen. One evening a swarm of poor people with candles in their hands appeared to a dishonest guardian of the poor at Perugia, and danced round about him; a great figure spoke in threatening tones on their behalf – it was St Alò, the patron saint of the poorhouse. These modes of belief were so much a matter of course that the poets could make use of them as something which every reader would understand. The appear- ance of the slain Lodovico Pico under the walls of the besieged Mirandola is finely represented by Castiglione. It is true that poetry made the freest use of these conceptions when the poet himself had outgrown them.

Italy, too, shared the belief in demons with the other nations of the Middle Ages. Men were convinced that God sometimes allowed bad spirits of every class to exercise a destructive influence on parts of the world and of human life. The only reservation made was that the man to whom the Evil One came as tempter could use his free will to resist. In Italy the demonic influence, especially as shown in natural events, easily assumed a character of poetical greatness. In the night before the great inundation of the Val d'Arno in 1333, a pious hermit above Vallombrosa heard a diabolical tumult in his cell, crossed himself, stepped to the door, and saw a crowd of black and terrible knights gallop by in armour. When conjured to stand, one of them said, 'We go to drown the city of Florence on account of its sins, if God will let us.' With this, the nearly contemporary vision at Venice (1340) may be compared, out of which a great master of the Venetian school, probably Giorgione,[91] made the marvellous picture of a galley full of demons, which speeds with the swiftness of a bird over the stormy lagoon to destroy the sinful island-city, till the three saints, who have stepped unobserved into a poor boatman's skiff, exorcized the fiends and sent them and their vessel to the bottom of the waters.

To this belief the illusion was now added that by means of magical arts it was possible to enter into relations with the evil ones, and use their help to further the purposes of greed, ambition and sensuality. Many persons were probably accused of doing so before the time when it was actually attempted by many; but when the so-called magicians and witches began to be burned, the deliberate practice of the black art became more frequent. With the smoke of the fires in which the suspected victims were sacrificed were spread the narcotic fumes by which numbers of ruined characters were drugged into magic; and with them many calulating impostors became associated.

The primitive and popular form in which the superstition had probably lived on uninterruptedly from the time of the Romans was the art of the witch (*strega*). The witch, so long as she limited herself to mere divination, might be innocent enough, were it not that the transition from prophecy to active help could easily, though often imperceptibly, be a fatal downward step. She was credited in such a case not only with the power of exciting love or hatred between man and woman, but also with purely destructive and malignant arts, and was especially charged with the sickness of little children, even when the malady obviously came from the neglect and stupidity of the parents. It is still questionable how far she was supposed to act by mere magical ceremonies and formulae, or by a conscious alliance with the fiends, apart from the poisons and drugs which she administered with a full knowledge of their effect.

The more innocent form of the superstition, in which the mendicant friar could venture to appear as the competitor of the witch, is shown in the case of the witch of Gaeta whom we read of in Pontano. His traveller Suppatius reaches her dwelling while she is giving audience to a girl and a serving-maid, who come to her with a black hen, nine eggs laid on a Friday, a duck and some white thread – for it is the third day since the new moon. They are then sent away, and bidden to come again at twilight. It is to be hoped that nothing worse than divination is intended. The mistress of the servant-maid is pregnant by a monk; the girl's lover has proved untrue and has gone into a monastery. The witch complains:

> Since my husband's death I support myself in this way, and should make a good thing of it, since the Gaetan women have plenty of faith, were it not that the monks balk me of my gains by explaining dreams, appeasing the anger of the saints for money, promising husbands to the girls, men-children to the pregnant women, offspring to the barren, and besides all this visiting the women at night when their husbands are away fishing, in accordance with the assignations made in daytime at church.

Suppatius warns her against the envy of the monastery, but she has no fear, since the guardian of it is an old acquaintance of hers.

But the superstition further gave rise to a worse sort of witches, namely those who deprived men of their health and life. In these cases the mischief, when not sufficiently accounted for by the evil eye and the like, was naturally attributed to the aid of powerful spirits. The punishment, as we have seen in the case of Finicella, was the stake; and yet a compromise with fanaticism was sometimes practicable. According to the laws of Perugia, for example, a witch could settle the affair by paying down 400 pounds. The matter was not then treated with the seriousness and consistency of later times. In the territories of the Church, at Norcia (Nursia), the home of St Benedict in the upper Apennines, there was a perfect nest of witches and sorcerers, and no secret was made of it. It is spoken of in one of the most remarkable letters of Aeneas Sylvius, belonging to his earlier period. He writes to his brother:

> The bearer of this came to me to ask if I knew of a Mount of Venus in Italy, for in such a place magical arts were taught, and his master, a Saxon and a great astronomer, was anxious to learn them. I told him that I knew of a Porto Venere not far from Carrara, on the rocky coast of Liguria, where I spent three nights on the way to Basle; I also found that there was a mountain called Eryx in Sicily, which was dedicated to Venus, but I did not know whether magic was taught there. But it came into my mind while talking that in Umbria, in the old duchy [Spoleto], near the town of Nursia, there is a cave beneath a steep rock, in which water flows. There, as I remember to have heard, are witches [*striges*], demons and nightly shades, and he that has the courage can see

and speak to ghosts [*spiritus*], and learn magical arts. I have not seen it,
nor taken any trouble about it, for that which is learned with sin is
better not learned at all.

He nevertheless names his informant, and begs his brother to take
the bearer of the letter to him, should he be still alive. Aeneas goes far
enough here in his politeness to a man of position, but personally he
was not only freer from superstition than his contemporaries, but he
also stood a test on the subject which not every educated man of our
own day could endure. At the time of the Council of Basel, when he
lay sick of the fever for seventy-five days at Milan, he could never be
persuaded to listen to the magic doctors, though a man was brought
to his bedside who a short time before had marvellously cured 2,000
soldiers of fever in the camp of Piccinino. While still an invalid,
Aeneas rode over the mountains to Basel, and got well on the journey.

We learn something more about the neighbourhood of Norcia
through the necromancer who tried to get Benvenuto Cellini into his
power. A new book of magic was to be consecrated, and the best place
for the ceremony was among the mountains in that district. The
master of the magician had once, it is true, done the same thing near
the Abbey of Farfa, but had there found difficulties which did not
present themselves at Norcia; further, the peasants in the latter neighbourhood were trustworthy people who had practice in the matter,
and who could afford considerable help in case of need. The expedition
did not take place, else Benvenuto would probably have been able to
tell us something of the impostor's assistants. The whole neighbourhood was then proverbial. Aretino says somewhere of an enchanted
well, 'there dwell the sisters of the sibyl of Norcia and the aunt of the
Fata Morgana'. And about the same time Trissino could still celebrate
the place in his great epic with all the resources of poetry and allegory
as the home of authentic prophecy.

After the famous bull of Innocent VIII (1484), witchcraft and the
persecution of witches grew into a great and revolting system. The
chief representatives of this system of persecution were German
Dominicans; and Germany and, curiously enough, those parts of Italy
nearest Germany were the countries most afflicted by this plague. The
bulls and injunctions of the popes themselves refer, for example, to the
Dominican Province of Lombardy, to Cremona, to the dioceses of
Brescia and Bergamo. We learn from Sprenger's famous theoretico-

practical guide, the *Malleus maleficarum*, that forty-one witches were burnt at Como in the first year after the publication of the bull; crowds of Italian women took refuge in the territory of the Archduke Sigismund, where they believed themselves to be still safe. Witchcraft ended by taking firm root in a few unlucky Alpine valleys, especially in the Val Camonica; the system of persecution had succeeded in permanently infecting with the delusion those populations which were in any way predisposed to it. This essentially German form of witchcraft is what we should think of when reading the stories and novels of Milan or Bologna. That it did not make further progress in Italy is probably due to the fact that here a highly developed *stregheria* was already in existence, resting on a different set of ideas. The Italian witch practised a trade, and needed for it money and, above all, sense. We find nothing about her of the hysterical dreams of the northern witch, of marvellous journeys through the air, of incubus and succubus; the business of the *strega* was to provide for other people's pleasure. If she was credited with the power of assuming different shapes, or of transporting herself suddenly to distant places, she was so far content to accept this reputation, as her influence was thereby increased; on the other hand, it was perilous for her when the fear of her malice and vengeance, and especially of her power for enchanting children, cattle and crops, became general. Inquisitors and magistrates were then thoroughly in accord with popular wishes if they burnt her.

By far the most important field for the activity of the *strega* lay, as has been said, in love-affairs, and included the stirring up of love and of hatred, the producing of abortion, the pretended murder of the unfaithful man or woman by magical arts, and even the manufacture of poisons. Owing to the unwillingness of many persons to have to do with these women, a class of occasional practitioners arose who secretly learned from them some one or other of their arts, and then used this knowledge on their own account. The Roman prostitutes, for example, tried to enhance their personal attractions by charms of another description in the style of Horatian Canidia. Aretino may not only have known, but have also told the truth about them in this particular. He gives a list of the loathsome messes which were to be found in their boxes – hair, skulls, ribs, teeth, dead men's eyes, human skin, the navels of little children, the soles of shoes and pieces of clothing from tombs. They even went themselves to the graveyard and fetched bits of rotten flesh, which they slyly gave their lovers to eat – with more that is still worse. Pieces of the hair and nails of the lover were boiled in oil stolen from the ever-burning lamps in the church. The most innocuous of their charms was to make a heart of glowing ashes, and then to pierce it while singing:

> Prima che'l fuoco spenghi,
> Fa ch'a mia porta venghi;
> Tal ti punga mio amore
> Quale io fo questo cuore.

There were other charms practised by moonshine, with drawings on the ground, and figures of wax or bronze, which doubtless represented the lover, and were treated according to circumstances.

These things were so customary that a woman who, without youth and beauty, nevertheless exercised a powerful charm on men, naturally became suspected of witchcraft. The mother of Sanga, secretary to Clement VII, poisoned her son's mistress, who was a woman of this kind. Unfortunately the son died too, as well as a party of friends who had eaten of the poisoned salad.

Next comes, not as helper, but as competitor to the witch, the magician or enchanter – incantatore – who was still more familiar with the most perilous business of the craft. Sometimes he was as much or more of an astrologer than of a magician; he probably often gave himself out as an astrologer in order not to be prosecuted as a magician, and a certain astrology was essential in order to find out the favourable hour for a magical process. But since many spirits are good or indifferent, the magician could sometimes maintain a very tolerable reputation, and Sixtus IV in the year 1474 had to proceed expressly against some Bolognese Carmelites, who asserted in the pulpit that there was no harm in seeking information from the demons. Very many people believed in the possibility of the thing itself; an indirect proof of this lies in the fact that the most pious men believed that by prayer they could obtain visions of good spirits. Savonarola's mind was filled with these things; the Florentine Platonists speak of a mystic union with God; and Marcellus Palingenius gives us to understand clearly enough that he had to do with consecrated spirits. The same writer is convinced of the existence of a whole hierarchy of bad demons, who have their seat from the moon downwards, and are ever on the watch to do some mischief to nature and human life. He even tells of his own personal acquaintance with some of them, and as the scope of the present work does not allow of a systematic exposition of the then prevalent belief in spirits, the narrative of Palingenius may be given as one instance out of many.

At San Silvestro, on Soracte, he had been receiving instruction from a pious hermit on the nothingness of earthly things and the worthlessness of human life; and when the night drew near he set out on his way back to Rome. On the road, in the full light of the moon, he was joined by three men, one of whom called him by name, and asked him whence he came. Palingenius made answer: 'From the wise man on the mountain.' 'O fool,' replied the stranger, 'dost thou in truth believe that anyone on earth is wise? Only higher beings [*divi*] have wisdom, and such are we three, although we wear the shapes of men. I am named Saracil, and these two Sathiel and Jana. Our kingdom lies near the moon, where dwell that multitude of intermediate beings who have sway over earth and sea.' Palingenius then asked, not without an inward tremor, what they were going to do at Rome. The answer was: 'One of our comrades, Ammon, is kept in servitude by the magic arts of a youth from Narni, one of the attendants of Cardinal Orsini; for mark it, O men, there is proof of your own immortality therein, that you can control one of us: I myself, shut up in crystal, was once forced to serve a German, till a bearded monk set me free. This is the service which we wish to render at Rome to our friend, and he shall also take the opportunity of sending one or two distinguished Romans to the nether world.' At these words a light breeze arose, and Sathiel said: 'Listen, our messenger is coming back from Rome, and this wind announces him.' And then another being appeared, whom they greeted joyfully and then asked about Rome. His utterances are strongly anti-papal: Clement VII was again allied with the Spaniards and hoped to root out Luther's doctrines, not with arguments, but by the Spanish sword. This is wholly in the interest of the demons, whom the impending bloodshed would enable to carry away the souls of thousands into hell. At the close of this conversation, in which Rome with all its guilt is represented as wholly given over to the Evil One, the apparitions vanish, and leave the poet sorrowfully to pursue his way alone.

Those who would form a conception of the extent of the belief in those relations to the demons which could be openly avowed in spite of the penalties attaching to witchcraft may be referred to the much-read work of Agrippa of Nettesheim, *On Secret Philosophy*. He seems

originally to have written it before he was in Italy, but in the dedication
to Trithemius he mentions Italian authorities among others, if only by
way of disparagement. In the case of equivocal persons like Agrippa,
or of the knaves and fools into whom the majority of the rest may be
divided, there is little that is interesting in the system they profess,
with its formulae, fumigations, ointments and the rest of it. But this
system was filled with quotations from the superstitions of antiquity,
the influence of which on the life and the passions of Italians is at times
most remarkable and fruitful. We might think that a great mind must
be thoroughly ruined before it surrendered itself to such influences;
but the violence of hope and desire led even vigorous and original
men of all classes to have recourse to the magician, and the belief that
the thing was feasible at all weakened to some extent the faith, even of
those who kept at a distance, in the moral order of the world. At the
cost of a little money and danger it seemed possible to defy with
impunity the universal reason and morality of mankind, and to spare
oneself the intermediate steps which otherwise lie between a man and
his lawful or unlawful ends.

   Let us here glance for a moment at an older and now decaying form
of superstition. From the darkest period of the Middle Ages, or even
from the days of antiquity, many cities of Italy had kept the remembrance of the connection of their fate with certain buildings, statues
or other material objects. The ancients had left records of consecrating
priests or *telestae*, who were present at the solemn foundation of cities,
and magically guaranteed their prosperity by erecting certain monuments or by burying certain objects (*telesmata*). Traditions of this sort
were more likely than anything else to live on in the form of popular,
unwritten legend; but in the course of centuries the priest naturally
became transformed into the magician, since the religious side of his
function was no longer understood. In some of his Virgilian miracles
at Naples, the ancient remembrance of one of these *telestae* is clearly
preserved, his name being in course of time supplanted by that of
Virgil. The enclosing of the mysterious picture of the city in a vessel is
neither more nor less than a genuine, ancient *telesma*; and Virgil the
founder of Naples is only the officiating priest, who took part in the
ceremony, presented in another dress. The popular imagination went
on working at these themes, till Virgil became also responsible for the
brazen horse, for the heads at the Nolan gate, for the brazen fly over
another gate, and even for the Grotto of Posillipo – all of them things

which in one respect or other served to put a magical constraint upon fate, and the first two of which seemed to determine the whole fortune of the city. Medieval Rome also preserved confused recollections of the same kind. At the church of Sant' Ambrogio at Milan, there was an ancient marble Hercules; so long, it was said, as this stood in its place, so long would the Empire last. That of the Germans is probably meant, as the coronation of their emperors at Milan took place in this church. The Florentines were convinced that the temple of Mars, afterwards transformed into the Baptistery, would stand to the end of time, according to the constellation under which it had been built; they had, as Christians, removed from it the marble equestrian statue; but since the destruction of the latter would have brought some great calamity on the city – also according to a constellation – they set it upon a tower by the Arno. When Totila conquered Florence, the statue fell into the river, and was not fished out again till Charlemagne refounded the city. It was then placed on a pillar at the entrance to the Ponte Vecchio, and on this spot Buondelmonti was slain in 1215. The origin of the great feud between Guelph and Ghibelline was thus associated with the dreaded idol. During the inundation of 1333 the statue vanished for ever.

But the same *telesma* reappears elsewhere. Guido Bonatto, already mentioned, was not satisfied, at the refounding of the walls of Forlì, with requiring certain symbolic acts of reconciliation from the two parties. By burying a bronze or stone equestrian statue, which he had produced by astrological or magical arts, he believed that he had defended the city from ruin, and even from capture and plunder. When Cardinal Albornoz was governor of Romagna some sixty years later, the statue was accidentally dug up and then shown to the people, probably by the order of the cardinal, that it might be known by what means the cruel Montefeltro had defended himself against the Roman Church. And again, half a century later, when an attempt to surprise Forlì had failed, men began to talk afresh of the virtue of the statue, which had perhaps been saved and reburied. It was the last time that they could do so; for a year later Forlì was really taken. The foundation of buildings all through the fifteenth century was associated not only with astrology but also with magic. The large number of gold and silver medals which Paul II buried in the foundation of his buildings was noticed, and Platina was by no means displeased to recognize an old pagan *telesma* in the fact. Neither Paul nor his biographer were in any way conscious of the medieval religious significance of such an offering.

But this official magic, which in many cases only rests on hearsay, was comparatively unimportant by the side of the secret arts practised for personal ends.

The form which these most often took in daily life is shown by Ariosto in his comedy of the necromancers. His hero is one of the many Jewish exiles from Spain, although he also gives himself out for a Greek, an Egyptian and an African, and is constantly changing his name and costume. He pretends that his incantations can darken the day and lighten the darkness, that he can move the earth, make himself invisible, and change men into beasts; but these vaunts are only an advertisement. His true object is to make his account out of unhappy and troubled marriages, and the traces which he leaves behind him in his course are like the slime of a snail, or often like the ruin wrought by a hailstorm. To attain his ends he can persuade people that the box in which a lover is hidden is full of ghosts, or that he can make a corpse talk. It is at all events a good sign that poets and novelists could reckon on popular applause in holding up this class of men to ridicule. Bandello not only treats this sorcery of a Lombard monk as a miserable, and in its consequences terrible, piece of knavery, but he also describes with unaffected indignation the disasters which never cease to pursue the credulous fool.

> A man hopes with *Solomon's Key* and other magical books to find the treasures hidden in the bosom of the earth, to force his lady to do his will, to find out the secret of princes, and to transport himself in the twinkling of an eye from Milan to Rome. The more often he is deceived, the more steadfastly he believes ... Do you remember the time, Signor Carlo, when a friend of ours, in order to win a favour of his beloved, filled his room with skulls and bones like a churchyard?

The most loathsome tasks were prescribed – to draw three teeth from a corpse or a nail from its finger, and the like; and while the hocus-pocus of the incantation was going on, the unhappy participants sometimes died of terror.

Benvenuto Cellini did not die during the well-known incantation (1532) in the Coliseum at Rome,[92] although both he and his companions witnessed no ordinary horrors; the Sicilian priest, who probably expected to find him a useful coadjutor in the future, paid him the compliment as they went home of saying that he had never met a man of so sturdy a courage. Every reader will make his own reflections on the proceedings themselves. The narcotic fumes and the fact that the imaginations of the spectators were predisposed for all possible terrors, are the chief points to be noticed, and explain why the lad who formed one of the party, and on whom they made most impression, saw much more than the others. But it may be inferred that Benvenuto himself was the one whom it was wished to impress, since the dangerous beginning of the incantation can have had no other aim than to arouse curiosity. For Benvenuto had to think before the fair Angelica occurred to him; and the magician told him afterwards that love-making was folly compared with the finding of treasures. Further, it must not be forgotten that it flattered his vanity to be able to say, 'The demons have kept their word, and Angelica came into my hands, as they promised, just a month later' (I, cap. 68). Even on the supposition that Benvenuto gradually lied himself into believing the whole story, it would still be permanently valuable as evidence of the mode of thought then prevalent.

As a rule, however, the Italian artists, even 'the odd, capricious and eccentric' among them, had little to do with magic. One of them, in his anatomical studies, may have cut himself a jacket out of the skin of a corpse, but at the advice of his confessor he put it again into the grave.[93] Indeed the frequent study of anatomy probably did more than anything else to destroy the belief in the magical influence of various parts of the body, while at the same time the incessant observation and representation of the human form made the artist familiar with a magic of a wholly different sort.

In general, notwithstanding the instances which have been quoted, magic seems to have been markedly on the decline at the beginning of the sixteenth century – that is to say, at a time when it first began to flourish vigorously out of Italy; and thus the tours of Italian sorcerers and astrologers in the North seem not to have begun till their credit at home was thoroughly impaired. In the fourteenth century it was thought necessary carefully to watch the lake on Mount Pilatus, near Scariotto, to hinder the magicians from consecrating their books. In the fifteenth century we find, for example, that the offer was made to produce a storm of rain, in order to frighten away a besieged army; and even then the commander of the besieged town – Niccolò Vitelli in Città di Castello – had the good sense to dismiss the sorcerers as godless persons. In the sixteenth century no more instances of this official kind appear, although in private life the magicians were still active. To this time belongs the classic figure of German sorcery, Dr Johann Faust; the Italian ideal, on the other hand, Guido Bonatto, dates back to the thirteenth century.

It must nevertheless be added that the decrease of the belief in magic was not necessarily accompanied by an increase of the belief in a moral order, but that in many cases, like the decaying faith in astrology, the delusion left behind it nothing by a stupid fatalism.

One or two minor forms of this superstition, pyromancy, chiromancy and others, which obtained some credit as the belief in sorcery and astrology was declining, may be here passed over, and even the pseudo-science of physiognomy has by no means the interest which the name might lead us to expect. For it did not appear as the sister and ally of art and psychology, but as a new form of fatalistic superstition, and, what it may have been among the Arabs, as the rival of astrology. The author of a physiognomical treatise, Bartolommeo Cocle, who styled himself a 'metoposcopist', and whose science, according to Giovio, seemed like one of the most respectable of the free arts, was not content with the prophecies which he made to the many people who daily consulted him, but wrote also a most serious 'catalogue of such whom great dangers to life were awaiting'. Giovio, although grown old in the free thought of Rome – '*in hac luce romana*' – is of opinion that the predictions contained therein had only too much truth in them. We learn from the same source how the people aimed at in these and similar prophecies took vengeance on the seer. Giovanni Bentivoglio caused Lucas Gauricus to be five times swung to and fro against the wall, on a rope hanging from a lofty winding staircase, because Lucas had foretold to him the loss of his authority. Ermes Bentivoglio sent an assassin after Cocle, because the unlucky metoposcopist had unwillingly prophesied to him that he would die an exile in battle. The murderer seems to have derided the dying man in his last moments, saying that the prophet had foretold him that he would shortly commit an infamous murder. The reviver of chiromancy, Antioco Tiberto of Cesena, came by an equally miserable end at the hands of Pandolfo Malatesta of Rimini, to whom he had prophesied the worst that a tyrant can imagine, namely, death in exile and in the most grievous poverty. Tiberto was a man of intelligence, who was supposed to give his answers less according to any methodical chiromancy than by means of his shrewd knowledge of mankind; and his high culture won for him the respect of those scholars who thought little of his divination.

Alchemy, in conclusion, which is not mentioned in antiquity till quite late under Diocletian, played only a very subordinate part at the best period of the Renaissance. Italy went through the disease earlier, when Petrarch in the fourteenth century confessed, in his polemic against it, that gold-making was a general practice. Since then that particular kind of faith, devotion and isolation which the practice of alchemy required became more and more rare in Italy, just when Italian and other adepts began to make their full profit out of the great lords in the North. Under Leo X the few Italians who busied themselves with it were called *ingenia curiosa*, and Aurelio Augurelli, who dedicated to Leo X, the great despiser of gold, his didactic poem on the making of the metal, is said to have received in return a beautiful but empty purse. The mystic science which besides gold sought for the omnipotent philosopher's stone is a late northern growth, which had its rise in the theories of Paracelsus and others.

GENERAL SPIRIT OF DOUBT

With these superstitions, as with ancient modes of thought generally, the decline in the belief of immortality stands in the closest connection. This question has the widest and deepest relations with the whole development of the modern spirit.

One great source of doubt in immortality was the inward wish to be under no obligations to the hated Church. We have seen that the Church branded those who thus felt as Epicureans. In the hour of death many doubtless called for the sacraments, but multitudes during their whole lives, and especially during their most vigorous years, lived and acted on the negative supposition. That unbelief on this particular point must often have led to a general scepticism is evident of itself, and is attested by abundant historical proof. These are the men of whom Ariosto says, 'Their faith goes no higher than the roof.' In Italy, and especially in Florence, it was possible to live as an open and notorious unbeliever, if a man only refrained from direct acts of hostility against the Church. The confessor, for instance, who was sent to prepare a political offender for death, began by inquiring whether the prisoner was a believer, 'for there was a false report that he had no belief at all'.

The unhappy transgressor here referred to – the same Pierpaolo Boscoli who has been already mentioned – who in 1513 took part in an attempt against the newly restored family of the Medici, is a faithful mirror of the religious confusion then prevalent. Beginning as a partisan of Savonarola, he became afterwards possessed with an enthusiasm for the ancient ideals of liberty, and for paganism in general; but when he was in prison his early friends regained the control of his mind, and secured for him what they considered a pious ending. The tender witness and narrator of his last hours is one of the artistic family of the della Robbia, the learned philologist Luca. 'Ah,' sighs Boscoli, 'get Brutus out of my head for me, that I may go my way as a Christian.' 'If you will,' answers Luca, 'the thing is not difficult; for you know that these deeds of the Romans are not handed down to us as they were, but idealized [con arte accresciute].' The penitent now forces his understanding to believe, and bewails his inability to believe voluntarily. If he could only live for a month with pious monks he would truly become spiritually minded. It comes out that these partisans of Savonarola knew their Bible very imperfectly; Boscoli can only say the paternoster and ave maria, and earnestly begs Luca to exhort his friends to study the sacred writings, for only what a man has learned in life does he possess in death. Luca then reads and explains to him the story of the Passion according to the Gospel of St John; the poor listener, strange to say, can perceive clearly the Godhead of Christ, but is perplexed at his manhood; he wishes to get as firm a hold of it 'as if Christ came to meet him out of a wood'. His friend thereupon exhorts him to be humble, since this was only a doubt sent him by the Devil. Soon after it occurs to the penitent that he has not fulfilled a vow made in his youth to go on a pilgrimage to the Impruneta; his friend promises to do it in his stead. Meantime the confessor – a monk, as was desired, from Savonarola's monastery – arrives, and after giving him the explanation quoted above of the opinion of St Thomas Aquinas on tyrannicide, exhorts him to bear death manfully. Boscoli makes answer: 'Father, waste no time on this; the philosophers have taught it me already; help me to bear death out of love to Christ.' What follows – the communion, the leave-taking and the execution – is very touchingly described; one point deserves special mention. When Boscoli laid his head on the block, he begged the executioner to delay the stroke for a moment: 'During the whole time since the announcement of the sentence he had been striving after a close union with God, without attaining it as he wished, and now in this supreme moment he thought that by a strong effort he could give himself wholly to God.' It is clearly some half-understood expression of Savonarola which was troubling him.

If we had more confessions of this character the spiritual picture of the time would be the richer by many important features which no poem or treatise has preserved for us. We should see more clearly how strong the inborn religious instinct was, how subjective and how variable the relation of the individual to religion, and what powerful enemies and competitors religion had. That men whose inward condition is of this nature are not the men to found a new church is evident; but the history of the Western spirit would be imperfect without a view of that fermenting period among the Italians, while other nations, who have had no share in the evolution of thought, may be passed over without loss. But we must return to the question of immortality.

If unbelief in this respect made such progress among the more highly cultivated natures, the reason lay partly in the fact that the great earthly task of discovering the world and representing it in word and form absorbed most of the higher spiritual faculties. We have already spoken of the inevitable worldliness of the Renaissance. But this investigation and this art were necessarily accompanied by a general spirit of doubt and inquiry. If this spirit shows itself but little in literature, if we find, for example, only isolated instances of the beginnings of biblical criticism, we are not therefore to infer that it had no existence. The sound of it was only overpowered by the need of representation and creation in all departments – that is, by the artistic instinct; and it was further checked, whenever it tried to express itself theoretically, by the already existing despotism of the Church. This spirit of doubt must, for reasons too obvious to need discussion, have inevitably and chiefly busied itself with the question of the state of man after death.

And here came in the influence of antiquity, and worked in a twofold fashion on the argument. In the first place men set themselves to master the psychology of the ancients, and tortured the letter of Aristotle for a decisive answer. In one of the Lucianic dialogues of the time Charon tells Mercury how he questioned Aristotle on his belief in immortality, when the philosopher crossed in the Stygian boat; but the prudent sage, although dead in the body and nevertheless living on, declined to compromise himself by a definite answer – and centuries later how was it likely to fare with the interpretation of his writings? All the more eagerly did men dispute about his opinion and that of others on the true nature of the soul, its origin, its pre-existence, its unity in all men, its absolute eternity, even its transformations; and there were men who treated of these things in the pulpit. The dispute was warmly carried on even in the fifteenth century; some proved that Aristotle taught the doctrine of an immortal soul; others complained of the hardness of men's hearts who would not believe that there was a soul at all, till they saw it sitting down on a chair before them; Filelfo in his funeral oration on Francesco Sforza brings forward a long list of opinions of ancient and even of Arab philosophers in favour of immortality, and closes the mixture, which covers a folio page and a half of print, with the words, 'Besides all this we have the Old and New Testaments, which are above all truth.' Then came the Florentine Platonists with their master's doctrine of the soul, supplemented at times, as in the case of Pico, by Christian teaching. But the opposite opinion prevailed in the instructed world. At the beginning of the sixteenth century the stumbling-block which it put in the way of the Church was so serious that Leo X set forth a constitution at the Lateran Council in 1513, in defence of the immortality and individuality of the soul, the latter against those who asserted that there was but one soul in all men. A few years later appeared the work of Pomponazzo, in which the impossibility of a philosophical proof of immortality is maintained; and the contest was now waged incessantly with replies and apologies, till it was silenced by the Catholic reaction. The pre-existence of the soul in God, conceived more or less in accordance with Plato's theory of ideas, long remained a common belief, and proved of service even to the poets. The consequences which followed from it as to the mode of the soul's continued existence after death were not more closely considered.

There was a second way in which the influence of antiquity made itself felt, chiefly by means of that remarkable fragment of the sixth book of Cicero's *Republic* known by the name of 'Scipio's Dream'. Without the commentary of Macrobius it would probably have perished like the rest of the second part of the work; it was now diffused in countless manuscript copies, and, after the discovery of typography, in printed form, and edited afresh by various commentators. It is the description of a transfigured hereafter for great men, pervaded by the harmony of the spheres. This pagan heaven, for which many other testimonies were gradually extracted from the writings of the ancients, came step by step to supplant the Christian heaven in proportion as the ideal of fame and historical greatness threw into the shade the ideal of the Christian life, without, nevertheless, the public feeling being thereby offended as it was by the doctrine of personal annihilation after death. Even Petrarch founds his hope chiefly on this Dream of Scipio, on the declarations found in other Ciceronian works, and on Plato's *Phaedo*, without making any mention of the Bible. 'Why,' he asks elsewhere, 'should not I as a Catholic share a hope which was demonstrably cherished by the heathen?' Soon afterwards Coluccio Salutati wrote his *Labours of Hercules* (still existing in manuscript), in which it is proved at the end that the valorous man, who has well endured the great labours of earthly life, is justly entitled to a dwelling among the stars. If Dante still firmly maintained that the great pagans, whom he would have gladly welcomed in paradise, nevertheless must not come beyond the limbo at the entrance to hell, the poetry of a later time accepted joyfully the new liberal ideas of a future life. Cosimo the Elder, according to Bernardo Pulci's poem on his death, was received in heaven by Cicero, who had also been called the 'father of his country', by the Fabii, by Curius, Fabricius and many others; with them he would adorn the choir where only blameless spirits sing.

But in the old writers there was another and less pleasing picture of the world to come – the shadowy realms of Homer and of those poets who had not sweetened and humanized the conception. This made an impression on certain temperaments. Gioviano Pontano somewhere attributes to Sannazaro the story of a vision, which he beheld one morning early while half awake. He seemed to see a departed friend, Ferrandus Januarius, with whom he had often discoursed on the immortality of the soul, and whom he now asked whether it was true that the pains of hell were really dreadful and eternal. The shadow gave an answer like that of Achilles when Odysseus questioned him. 'So much I tell and aver to thee, that we who are parted from earthly life have the strongest desire to return to it again.' He then saluted his friend and disappeared.

It cannot but be recognized that such views of the state of man after death partly presuppose and partly promote the dissolution of the most essential dogmas of Christianity. The notion of sin and of salvation must have almost entirely evaporated. We must not be misled by the effects of the great preachers of repentance or by the epidemic revivals which have been described above. For even granting that the individually developed classes had shared in them like the rest, the cause of their participation was rather the need of emotional excitement, the rebound of passionate natures, the horror felt at great national calamities, the cry to heaven for help. The awakening of the conscience had by no means necessarily the sense of sin and the felt need of salvation as its consequence, and even a very severe outward penance did not perforce involve any repentance in the Christian meaning of the word. When the powerful natures of the Renaissance tell us that their principle is to repent of nothing, they may have in their minds only matters that are morally indifferent, faults of unreason or imprudence; but in the nature of the case this contempt for repentance must extend to the sphere of morals, because its origin, namely the consciousness of individual force, is common to both sides of human nature. The passive and contemplative form of Christianity, with its constant reference to a higher world beyond the grave, could no longer control these men. Machiavelli ventured still farther, and maintained that it could not be serviceable to the state and to the maintenance of public freedom.

The form assumed by the strong religious instinct which, notwithstanding all, survived in many natures, was theism or deism, as we may please to call it. The latter name may be applied to that mode of thought which simply wiped away the Christian element out of religion, without either seeking or finding any other substitute for the feelings to rest upon. Theism may be considered that definite heightened devotion to the one Supreme Being which the Middle Ages were not acquainted with. This mode of faith does not exclude Christianity, and can either ally itself with the Christian doctrines of sin, redemption and immortality, or else exist and flourish without them.

Sometimes this belief presents itself with childish *naïveté* and even with a half-pagan air, God appearing as the almighty fulfiller of human wishes. Agnolo Pandolfini tells us how, after his wedding, he shut himself in with his wife, and knelt down before the family altar with the picture of the Madonna, and prayed, not to her, but to God, that He would vouchsafe to them the right use of their property, a long life in joy and unity with one another, and many male descendants; 'for myself I prayed for wealth, honour and friends, for her blamelessness, honesty, and that she might be a good housekeeper'. When the language used has a strong antique flavour, it is not always easy to keep apart the pagan style and the theistic belief.

This temper sometimes manifests itself in times of misfortune with a striking sincerity. Some addresses to God are left us from the latter period of Firenzuola, when for years he lay ill of fever, in which, though he expressly declares himself a believing Christian, he shows that his religious consciousness is essentially theistic. His sufferings seem to him neither as the punishment of sin, nor as preparation for a higher world; they are an affair between him and God only, who has put the strong love of life between man and his despair. 'I curse, but only curse Nature, since thy greatness forbids me to utter thy name . . . Give me death, Lord, I beseech thee, give it me now.'

In these utterances and the like, it would be vain to look for a conscious and consistent theism; the speakers partly believed themselves to be still Christians, and for various other reasons respected the existing doctrines of the Church. But at the time of the Reformation, when men were driven to come to a distinct conclusion on such points, this mode of thought was accepted with a fuller consciousness; a number of the Italian Protestants came forward as anti-trinitarians and socinians, and even as exiles in distant countries made the memorable attempt to found a church on these principles. From the foregoing exposition it will be clear that, apart from humanistic rationalism, other spirits were at work in this field.

One chief centre of theistic modes of thought lay in the Platonic Academy at Florence, and especially in Lorenzo il Magnifico himself. The theoretical works and even the letters of these men show us only half their nature. It is true that Lorenzo, from his youth till he died, expressed himself dogmatically as a Christian, and that Pico was drawn by Savonarola's influence to accept the point of view of a monkish ascetic. But in the hymns of Lorenzo, which we are tempted to regard as the highest product of the spirit of this school, an unreserved theism is set forth – a theism which strives to treat the world as a great moral and physical cosmos. While the men of the Middle Ages look on the world as a vale of tears, which pope and emperor are set to guard against the coming of antichrist; while the fatalists of the Renaissance oscillate between seasons of overflowing energy and seasons of superstition or of stupid resignation, here, in this circle of chosen spirits, the doctrine is upheld that the visible world was created by God in love, that it is the copy of a pattern pre-existing in Him, and that He will ever remain its eternal mover and restorer. The soul of man can by recognizing God draw Him into its narrow boundaries, but also by love of Him itself expand into the Infinite – and this is blessedness on earth.

Echoes of medieval mysticism here flow into one current with Platonic doctrines, and with a characteristically modern spirit. One of the most precious fruits of the knowledge of the world and of man here comes to maturity, on whose account alone the Italian Renaissance must be called the leader of modern ages.

Notes

PETER MURRAY

Burckhardt's *Kultur der Renaissance in Italien* was first published in 1860. It sold slowly and the second edition did not appear until 1869; it was the last to be supervised by Burckhardt himself, who was notoriously reluctant to bother with his books after they were published. This was the edition used by S. G. Middlemore for his English translation, first published in 1878 and still being steadily reprinted: it is the one used here, but without all of the notes. In his translation there are no fewer than 1,129 footnotes, taken from the second German edition – later German editions have even more – but most of them are only simple references to books cited. He also repeated the list of books most frequently cited by Burckhardt himself, as is done here. Many of the notes referred to editions of books which have now been critically re-edited, or to secondary sources now long superseded. All of these notes have been omitted, and only those which seem interesting in themselves have been retained: readers desiring to consult the original references *in extenso* will have no difficulty in obtaining the full Middlemore translation or one of the many German editions.

The Burckhardt notes retained have been further supplemented by quoting abbreviated titles in full and by inserting references to later editions, or English translations, in editorial square brackets [ ]. On a few occasions Middlemore's translations of the notes themselves have been revised, where it seemed to be necessary in the interest of clarity. Many of the notes are new, and entirely my responsibility: they also are enclosed in [ ], so there should be no possibility of confusion. Their purpose is to draw attention to things which Burckhardt perhaps took for granted, but which may be less familiar to the modern reader; and, principally, to cite modern editions (up to 1988) or English translations of the books used by Burckhardt himself – for example, the Penguin Classics versions of della Casa's *Galateo* or Castiglione's *Cortegiano*.

I hope that these will be useful to the modern reader, but the reduction from over 1,100 to under 100 notes makes it hardly necessary to stress that they are very incomplete, and indeed arbitrary.

Burckhardt's own list of most frequently quoted works is given on pp. 368–70, with fuller bibliographical details and with later editions or English translations in [ ]. These have not been cited in full in individual notes, so an abbreviated citation normally refers the reader to the list.

To Burckhardt's list it might be helpful to add J. Hale, ed., *A Concise*

Encyclopaedia of the Italian Renaissance, London, 1981, which contains brief biographies of most of the people mentioned by Burckhardt, as well as articles on topics treated by him. E. Cochrane's *Historians and Historiography in the Italian Renaissance*, Chicago, 1981, has very full bibliographical details of most of the writers cited by Burckhardt.

1. Franz Kugler, ed., *Geschichte der Baukunst*; vol. IV, part 1, on the architecture and decoration of the Italian Renaissance, is by Burckhardt. [This was first published in 1867. An English translation, ed. P. Murray, was published in 1985 (Penguin, 1987). Sections on painting and sculpture, which never got beyond brief notes, were published in the *Gesamtausgabe* of Burckhardt (1932); *The Altarpiece*, ed. P. Humfrey, was published in 1988.]

2. The rulers and their dependants were together called *lo stato*, and this name afterwards acquired the meaning of the collective existence of a territory.

3. With the parenthetical request, in reference to a previous conversation, that the prince would again forbid the keeping of pigs in the streets of Padua, as the sight of them was unpleasing, especially for strangers, and apt to frighten the horses.

4. This we find first in the fifteenth century, but their representations are certainly based on the beliefs of earlier times: L. B. Alberti, *De re aedif.*, v, 3, Franc. di Giorgio, 'Trattato', in Della Valle, *Lettere sanesi*, iii, 121. [There is a modern Latin/Italian edition of Alberti's *De re aedificatoria libri X*, by G. Orlandi and P. Portoghesi, 2 vols., Milan, 1966, and of Francesco di Giorgio's *Trattato d'architettura* by C. Maltese and L. Maltese-Degrassi, 2 vols., Milan, 1967. An English translation of Alberti (London, 1726 and 1955) has been superseded by one ed. J. Rykwert, Cambridge, Mass., 1988. For Della Valle, see note 23.]

5. The Paduan passport office about the middle of the fourteenth century is referred to by Franco Sacchetti, Nov. 117, in the words '*quelli delle bullette*' [the people of the licences]. In the last ten years of the reign of Frederick II, when the strictest control was exercised on the personal conduct of his subjects, this system must have been very highly developed. [The *Trecentonovelle* – *Three Hundred Tales* – were written before 1400 and have been reprinted many times, e.g. ed. E. Faccioli, 1970.]

6. This compound of force and intellect is called by Machiavelli *virtù*, and is quite compatible with *scelleratezza* [wickedness]. E.g. *Discorsi*, i, 10, in speaking of Septimius Severus.

7. It is uncertain whether the Venetians did not poison Alviano in 1516, cf. Prato, *Arch. stor.*, iii, p. 348. The republic made itself Colleoni's heir, and after his death in 1475 formally confiscated his property. Cf. Malipiero, *Annali veneti*, in *Arch. stor.*, vii, i, 244. It was approved of when the *condottieri* invested their money in Venice, *ibid.*, p. 351.

8. [The early Raphaels of *St Michael* and *St George* are the pictures now in the Louvre, Paris, of around 1500–1504; what Burckhardt refers to as 'the great painting of St Michael' is presumably the very late picture, also in the Louvre, dated 1518, but perhaps finished by his studio. The reference to the heavenly horseman is to Raphael's fresco of the *Expulsion of Heliodorus from the Temple*, in the Vatican, completed by 1514.]

9. [Now in the Borghese Galleria, Rome, dated 1507.]

10. Born 1466, betrothed to Isabella, herself six years of age in 1480, succeeded 1484, married 1490, died 1519. Isabella died in 1539. Her sons were Federigo (1519–40), made duke in 1530, and the famous Ferrante Gonzaga. What follows is taken from the correspondence of Isabella, with Appendices, *Archiv. stor.*, append., tom. ii, communicated by d'Arco. [J. Cartwright, *Isabella d'Este*, London, 1903 and later.]

11. The journey of Leo X when cardinal may also be mentioned here. Cf. Paul. Jov., *Vita Leonis X*, lib. I. His purpose was less serious, and directed rather to amusement and knowledge of the world; but the spirit is wholly modern. No northerner then travelled with such objects. [Paolo Giovio (Paulus Jovius), *Vita Leonis X*, Florence, 1548.]

12. [On account of weathering, Michelangelo's *David* was moved into the Accademia in 1873, but a replica made in 1905 still stands outside the Palazzo della Signoria.]

13. [The reference to Sismondi is to J. Sismondi, *Histoire des républiques italiennes au moyen âge*, 16 vols., Zurich, 1807–18; an abridged English version was published in London in 1907 and often reprinted.]

14. [The military adventures of Doge Foscari were much criticized, and just before his death he was formally deposed, an act for which there was no Venetian precedent.]

15. The statistical view of Milan, in the 'Manipulus Florum' (in Muratori, xi, 711 ff), for the year 1288, is important, though not extensive. It includes house-doors, population, men of military age, *loggie* of the nobles, wells, bakeries, wine-shops, butchers' shops, fishmongers, the consumption of corn, dogs, game birds, the price of salt, wood, hay and wines; and also the judges, notaries, doctors, schoolmasters, copying clerks, armourers, smiths, hospitals, monasteries, endowments and religious corporations.

16. Here all the houses, not merely those owned by the state, are meant. The latter, however, sometimes yielded enormous rents. See Vasari, *Vita di Jacopo Sansovino*.

17. This dislike seems to have amounted to positive hatred in Paul II, who called the humanists, one and all, heretics. Platina, *Vita Pauli*, p. 323.

18. See for this and similar facts Giov. Villani, xi, 87, xii, 54. [G. Villani (*d.* 1348), *Chroniche*, Venice, 1537, and Florence, ed. Dragomanni, 4 vols., 1844–5. A partial English translation by R. Selfe and P. Wicksteed, London, 1896,

does not include these passages. The loan to Edward III of England to pay for his wars was made in 1338; Edward reneged on it and both the Bardi and Peruzzi went bankrupt in the 1340s.]

19. Giov. Villani, xi, 92, 93. In Machiavelli, *Stor. Fiorent.*, lib. ii, cap. 42, we read that 96,000 persons died of the plague in 1348. [G. Villani, *Chroniche*; see note 18.]

20. *Ricordi* of Lorenzo, in Fabroni, *Laur. Med. Magnifici Vita*, Adnot. 2 and 25. Paul. Jovius, *Elogia*, pp. 131 ff. Cosmus. [Paolo Giovio (Paulus Jovius), *Elogia veris clarorum virorum*, Venice, 1546 and Basle, 3 vols., 1576–8. See also A. Fraser Jenkins, 'Cosimo de' Medici's Patronage of Architecture and the Theory of Magnificence' in *Journal of the Warburg and Courtauld Institutes*, xxxiii, 1970.]

21. In respect of prices and of wealth in Italy, I am only able, in default of further means of investigation, to bring together some scattered facts, which I have picked up here and there. Obvious exaggerations must be put aside. The gold coins which are worth referring to are the ducat, the sequin, the *fiorino d'oro* and the *scudo d'oro*. The value of all is nearly the same, 11 to 12 francs of our money [i.e. Swiss francs of the 1860s]. In Venice, for example, the Doge Andrea Vendramin (1476) with 170,000 ducats passed for an exceedingly rich man. About 1460 the Patriarch of Aquileia, Lodovico Patavino, with 200,000 ducats, was called 'perhaps the richest of all Italians'. Antonio Grimani paid 30,000 ducats for his son's election as cardinal. His ready money alone was put at 100,000 ducats . . . In 1522 it is no longer Venice, but Genoa, next to Rome, which ranks as the richest city in Italy . . . Bandello (*Novelle* 34 and 42) names as the richest Genoese merchant of his time Ansaldo Grimaldi. Between 1400 and 1580 Francesco Sansovino assumes a depreciation of 50 per cent in the value of money . . . At Ferrara there were people at the time of Duke Borso with 50 to 60,000 ducats. In Florence the data are exceptional and do not justify a conclusion as to averages. Of this kind are the loans to foreign princes, in which the names of only one or two houses appear, but which were in fact the work of great companies. So too the enormous fines levied on defeated parties; we read that from 1430 to 1453 seventy-seven families paid 4,875,000 gold florins. The fortune of Giovanni Medici amounted at his death (1428) to 179,221 gold florins, but of his two sons, Cosimo and Lorenzo, Lorenzo alone left at his death (1440) as much as 235,137. It is proof of the general activity of trade that the forty-four goldsmiths on the Ponte Vecchio paid in the fourteenth century a rent of 800 florins to the government. The diary of Buonaccorso Pitti [English translation in G. Brucker, ed., *Two Memoirs of Renaissance Florence*, New York, 1967] is full of figures, which, however, only prove in general the high price of commodities and the low value of money. For Rome, the income of the Curia, which was derived from all Europe, gives us no criterion; nor are statements about papal treasures and the fortunes of

cardinals very trustworthy. The well-known banker Agostino Chigi left (1520) a fortune of 800,000 ducats in all. [This long note has been abbreviated slightly and references omitted. In the present state of currencies it is almost impossible to estimate modern equivalents, but Professor Roderick Floud of Birkbeck College, London, has drawn my attention to R. W. Stevens, *On the Stowage of Ships* . . ., fourth edition, London, 1867, which gives equivalents of Swiss francs and several Italian coinages in terms of British money of the time: it seems that 11 or 12 Swiss francs would have been near enough 10 shillings in 1867, say approximately £15 or $26–$27 in 1987 terms. It is by no means clear that Burckhardt's assumption that the ducat, the sequin, the *fiorino d'oro* and the *scudo d'oro* were all approximately equal during the whole period covered by his book is correct. On this basis, the Patriarch of Aquileia, with 200,000 ducats, would be worth about £3 million, which would not make him the richest man in modern Italy.]

22. On the third Sunday in Advent, 1494, Savonarola preached as follows on the method of bringing about a new constitution: the sixteen companies of the city were each to work out a plan, the Gonfalonieri to choose the four best of these, and the Signoria to name the best of all on the reduced list. Things, however, took a different turn, under the influence, indeed, of the preacher himself.

23. How strangely modern half-culture affected political life is shown by the party struggles of 1535. Della Valle, *Lettere sanesi*, iii, p. 317. A number of small shopkeepers, excited by the study of Livy and of Machiavelli's *Discorsi*, call in all seriousness for tribunes of the people and other Roman magistrates against the misgovernment of the nobles and the official classes. [G. Della Valle, *Lettere sanesi*, 3 vols., Rome, 1782–6.]

24. Galeazzo Maria Sforza, indeed, declared the contrary (1467) to the Venetian agent, namely, that Venetian subjects had offered to join him in making war on Venice; but this is only vapouring. Compare Malipiero, *Annali veneti*, in *Archiv. Stor.*, vii, i, p. 216 ff. On every occasion cities and villages surrendered voluntarily to Venice, chiefly, it is true, those that escaped from the hands of some despot, while Florence had to keep down the neighbouring republics, which were used to independence, by force of arms, as Guicciardini (*Ricordi*, no. 29) observes. [F. Guicciardini, *Ricordi*, exists in several versions, the modern critical edition being that by R. Spongano, Florence, 1951, which is the basis of C. Grayson, *Guicciardini: Selected Writings*, Oxford, 1965.]

25. For the impression made by the blessing of Eugenius IV in Florence, see Vespasiano Fior., p. 18. For the impressive offices of Nicolas V, see Infessura (Eccard, ii, col. 1883 ff) and G. Manetti, *Vita Nicolai V* (Muratori, iii, ii, col. 923). For the homage given to Pius II, see *Diario ferrarese* (Murat., xxiv, col. 205), and *Pii II, Commentarii*, passim, esp. iv, 201, 204, and xi, 562. Even professional murderers respect the person of the pope.

The great offices in church were treated as matters of much importance by the pomp-loving Paul II (Platina, cit. 321) and by Sixtus IV, who, in spite of the gout, conducted Mass at Easter in a sitting posture (*Jac. Volaterran. Diarium*, Murat., xxiii, col. 131). It is curious to notice how the people distinguished between the magical efficacy of the blessing and the unworthiness of the man who gave it; when he was unable to give the benediction on Ascension Day, 1481, the populace murmured and cursed him (*ibid.*, col. 133). [Eccardus, i.e. J. von Eckhart, *Corpus historicum medii aevii* . . ., Leipzig, 1723; the Infessura references can also be found in Muratori, iii, 2. It is indeed 'curious' that Burckhardt seems not to have realized that the Roman Church has always asserted that the efficacy of sacraments is not affected by the worthiness of the minister.]

26. '*Ut Papa tantum vicarius Christi sit et non etiam Caesaris . . . Tunc Papa et dicetur et erit pater sanctus, pater omnium, pater ecclesiae . . .*' ['That the pope will be Christ's vicar, not Caesar's . . . Then the pope will be called, and will be, Holy Father, Father of all, Father of the Church . . .' Lorenzo Valla (1407–57) finally disproved (1440) the long-doubted 'Donation of Constantine', a forgery of the eighth century purporting to prove papal claims to the temporal power, allegedly given to them by the Emperor Constantine.]

27. According to Corio (fol. 479) Charles had thoughts of a Council, of deposing the pope, and even of carrying him away to France, this upon his return from Naples. According to Benedictus, *Carolus VIII* (in Eccard, *Scriptores*, ii, col. 1584 [see note 25]), Charles, while in Naples, when pope and cardinals refused to recognize his new crown, had certainly entertained the thought '*de Italiae imperio deque pontificis statu mutando*' [to change the dominion in Italy, reducing the pope], but soon after made up his mind to be satisfied with the personal humiliation of Alexander. The pope, nevertheless, escaped him. Details in Pilorgerie, *Campagne et bulletins de la Grande Armée d'Italie, 1494, 1495* (Paris, 1866), where the degree of Alexander's danger at different moments is discussed (pp. 111, 117, etc.). Even on his return journey Charles had no wish to harm him.

28. Corio, fol. 450. Malipiero, *Ann. veneti* in *Arch. stor.*, vii, i, p. 318. The rapacity of the whole family can be seen in Malipiero, among other authorities, *cit.*, p. 565. A *nipote* was splendidly entertained in Venice as papal legate, and made an enormous sum of money by selling dispensations; his servants, when they went away, stole whatever they could lay their hands on, including a piece of cloth of gold from the high altar of a church at Murano.

29. [The reference is to the Austrian general, Wallenstein, Duke of Friedland, whose bloody career was ended by his murder by his own officers, on suspicion of changing sides.]

30. Hence the splendour of the tombs of the prelates erected during their lifetime. A part of the plunder was in this way saved from the hands of the

popes. [Examples of such splendid tombs are those by Andrea Sansovino in Sta Maria del Popolo, Rome.]

31. [*Terribile* is a word associated with Michelangelo and implies awesome force of will, perhaps inspiring terror in lesser men.]

32. Observe the expressions '*uomo singolare*' and '*uomo unico*' for the higher and highest stages of individual development.

33. And also of their wives, as is seen in the Sforza family and among other North Italian rulers. Compare, in the work of Jacobus Phil. Bergomensis, *De plurimis claris selectisque mulieribus*, Ferrara, 1497, the lives of Battista Malatesta, Paola Gonzaga, Bona Lombarda, Riccarda d'Este and the chief women of the house of Sforza, Beatrice and others. Among them are more than one genuine virago, and in several cases natural gifts are supplemented by great humanistic culture. (See below, p. 104 ff, and Part V).

34. Trattato del governo della famiglia forms part of a work, *La cura della famiglia* (*Opere volgari di L. B. Alberti*, Florence, 1844, vol. ii). [By 1871 this was recognized as a work by Alberti, not Pandolfini, to whom the text attributes it. See now C. Grayson, ed., L. B. Alberti, *Opere volgari*, I, Bari, 1960 (*I libri della famiglia*).]

35. Ghiberti, *Secondo Commentario*, cap. xv (Vasari, ed. Lemonnier, i, p. xxix). [Ghiberti's *Commentaries*, written *c.* 1450, were first published in full by J. von Schlosser (Berlin, 2 vols., 1912). The passage quoted here is not Ghiberti's own, but is taken from Vitruvius, *De architectura*, Book vi, Preface, para. 2, and is used as an introduction to his autobiography. There is an English translation of the autobiography (excluding this passage) in R. Krautheimer and T. Krautheimer-Hess, *Lorenzo Ghiberti*, 2 vols., Princeton, N J, 1970.]

36. Codri Urcei vita, at the beginning of his works, first published at Bologna, 1502 [A. Urceus, called Codrus, *Opera*, Bologna, 1502]. This certainly comes near the old saying: '*ubi bene, ibi patria*' [where one is well-off is one's country]. The abundance of neutral intellectual pleasure, which is independent of local circumstances, and of which the educated Italians became more and more capable, rendered exile more tolerable to them. Cosmopolitanism is further a sign of an epoch in which new worlds are discovered, and men no longer feel at home in the old. We see it among the Greeks after the Peloponnesian war; Plato, as Niebuhr says, was not a good citizen, and Xenophon was a bad one; Diogenes went so far as to proclaim homelessness a pleasure, and calls himself, Laertius tells us, *apolis* [having no city].

37. In Murat., xxv, col. 295 ff, with the Italian translation in the *Opere volgari di L. B. Alberti*, i, pp. lxxxix–cix, where the conjecture is made and shown to be probable that this *Vita* is by Alberti himself. See further Vasari, iv, 52 ff. Mariano Socini, if we can believe what we read of him in Aeneas Sylvius (*Opera*, p. 622, *Epist.* 112) was a universal dilettante, and at the same time a master in several subjects.

38. This is the book [see note 34] of which one part, often printed alone, long passed for a work of Pandolfini.

39. One writer among many: Blondus, *Roma triumphans*, lib. v, pp. 117 ff, where the definitions of glory are collected from the ancients, and the desire of it is expressly allowed to the Christian. Cicero's work, *De gloria*, which Petrarch claimed to own, was stolen from him by his teacher Convenevole, and has never been seen since. [Flavio Biondo, *Roma Triumphans*, writtvn 1457–9 and published in Brescia, 1482, and later.]

40. The former in the well-known sarcophagus near San Lorenzo, the latter over a door in the Palazzo della Ragione. For details of their discovery in 1413, see Misson, *Voyage en Italie*, vol. i. [The so-called Tomb of Livy is still in the Palazzo della Ragione, but is now thought to refer to a different Livy; that of Antenor is in a niche near the Ponte S. Lorenzo, with bones discovered in 1274, which may be those of a tenth-century Hungarian soldier.]

41. In the *Casus virorum illustrium* of Boccaccio only the close of the eighth book and the last book – the ninth – deal with non-classical times. And so at a much later time in the *Commentarii urbani* of Raph. Volaterranus, in the twenty-first book; popes and emperors are treated separately in Books 22 and 23. [Raphael Maffeius (Volaterranus), *Commentariorum urbanorum*, Rome, 1506, and Paris, 1526.] In the work *De claris mulieribus* by the Augustinian Jacobus Bergomensis (printed 1497, but probably published earlier) antiquity and legend hold the chief place, but there are still some valuable biographies of Italian women [cf. note 33: Jacobus Phillipus Foresti (Bergomensis), Ferrara, 1497]. In Scardeonius (*De Urb. Patav. Antiqu.* in Graev., *Thesaur.*, vi, iii, col. 405 ff [i.e. J. Graevius and P. Burmannus, *Thesaurus antiquitatum et historiarum Italiae*, 30 vols., Leiden, 1704–23] only famous Paduan women are mentioned. First comes a legend or tradition from the time of the fall of the empire, then tragical stories of the party struggles of the thirteenth and fourteenth centuries; then notices of several heroic women; then the foundress of nunneries, the political woman, the female doctor, the mother of many and distinguished sons, the learned woman, the peasant girl who dies defending her chastity; then the cultivated beauty of the sixteenth century, on whom everybody writes sonnets; and lastly, the female novelist and poet at Padua. A century later the woman professor would have been added to these. For the famous women of the House of Este, see Ariosto, *Orlando furioso*, xiii.

42. The well-known jest of Brunellesco and the fat wood-carver, Manetto Ammanatini, who is said to have fled into Hungary before the ridicule he encountered, is clever but cruel. [The unfortunate Manetto was led to believe that he had become a man called Matteo. The story is told in a manuscript immediately preceding the manuscript of the anonymous Life of Brunelleschi, and is referred to in the *Life*. It is not contained in the English translation of the *Life* by C. Enggass, ed. H. Saalman, Pennsylvania University, 1970, but there is a modern Italian edition in C. Varese, ed., *Prosatori volgari del Quattrocento* (vol. 14 of *La letteratura italiana, storia e testi*), Milan-Naples, 1955.]

43. We find it also in the visual arts, e.g. in the famous engraving parodying the group of the *Laocoön* as three monkeys. But here parody seldom went beyond sketches and the like, though much, it is true, may have been destroyed. Caricature, again, is something different. Leonardo, in the grotesque faces in the Biblioteca Ambrosiana, Milan, represents what is hideous when and because it is comical, and exaggerates the ludicrous element at pleasure. [The *Laocoön* is a woodcut by Boldrini after Titian. It seems more likely that Leonardo's grotesque heads were made as serious studies of physiognomy, rather than for comic effect.]

44. *Il cortigiano*, lib. ii, cap. 4 ff, ed. Baude di Vesme, Florence, 1854, pp. 124 ff. For the explanation of wit as the effect of contrast, though not clearly put, see *ibid.*, cap. lxxiii, p. 136. [B. Castiglione, *Il libro del cortegiano*, Venice, 1528; modern edition by V. Cian, Florence, 1947, English translation by G. Bull, Penguin Classics, 1967.]

45. [G. della Casa, *Il galateo*, Venice, 1558; modern edition by G. Tinivella, Milan, 1954, English translation by R. Pine-Coffin, Penguin Classics, 1958.]

46. Gaye, *Carteggio*, ii, 332. [G. Gaye, *Carteggio inedito d'artisti dei secoli XIV, XV, XVI . . .*, 3 vols., Florence, 1839–40; facsimile reprint, Turin, 1961. This nauseating letter, which is constantly quoted in the Michelangelo literature, is reprinted in *Il carteggio di Michelangelo*, ed. P. Barocchi and R. Ristori, Florence, IV, 1980, p. 215; an English translation is in L. Murray, *Michelangelo, His Life, Work and Times*, London, 1984. It is not included in the selection of Aretino's letters, translated by G. Bull, in the Penguin Classics, 1976, which does contain a similar letter of 1547 (no. 95).]

47. He may have done so in the hope of obtaining the red hat or from fear of the new activity of the Inquisition, which he had ventured to attack bitterly in 1535 (*Lettere*, Venice, 1539, f. 37), but which, after the reorganization of the institution in 1542, suddenly took a fresh start, and soon silenced every opposing voice.

48. *Carmina burana*, in the *Bibliothek des literarischen Vereins in Stuttgart*, vol. xvi, Stuttgart, 1847. The stay in Pavia, the Italian local references in general, the scene with the '*pastorella*' under the olive tree, the mention of the '*pinus*' as a shady field-tree, the frequent use of the word '*bravium*', and particularly the form Madii for Maji, all speak in favour of our assumption. That he bore the name of Walther throws no light upon his origin. He was formerly identified with Gualterus de Mapes, a canon of Salisbury and chaplain to the English kings at the end of the twelfth century; since, by Giesebrecht (*Die Vaganten oder Goliarden und ihre Lieder*, in *Allgemeine Monatsschrift*, 1855) with Walther of Lille or Chatillon, who passed from France into England and Germany, and thence possibly with Archbishop Reinhold of Cologne (1164 and 1175) to Italy (Pavia, etc.). [*Carmina burana* is the name given to the songs – *carmina* –

discovered in 1803 in the Bavarian monastery of Benediktbeuren. They date from the twelfth and thirteenth centuries and are in Latin, Middle High German and Old French, and most of them are drinking songs or fairly earthy love songs. Some of them are reprinted in F. Raby, *The Oxford Book of Medieval Latin Verse*, Oxford, 1959; Helen Waddell's *Wandering Scholars*, London, 1927 and later, and her *Mediaeval Latin Lyrics*, London, 1929 and many later editions, give details of their authors.]

49. For details we must refer the reader to Roscoe, *Lorenzo Mag.* and *Leo X*, as well as to Voigt, *Enea Silvio*, Berlin, 1856–63; and to F. Papencordt, *Geschichte der Stadt Rom im Mittelalter*, Paderborn, 1857. To form a conception of the extent which studies at the beginning of the sixteenth century had reached, we cannot do better than turn to the *Commentarii urbani* of Raphael Volaterranus (ed. Basle, 1554, fol. 16, etc.) [cf. note 41]. Here we see how antiquity formed the introduction and the chief matter of study in every branch of knowledge, from geography and local history, the lives of great and famous men, popular philosophy, morals and the special sciences, down to the analysis of the whole of Aristotle, with which the work closes. To understand its significance as an authority for the history of culture, we must compare it with all the earlier encyclopedias. A complete and circumstantial account of the matter is given in G. Voigt's admirable work, *Die Wiederbelebung des classischen Alterthums*, Berlin, 1859 [third edition, Berlin, 1893; this has unfortunately never been translated into English].

50. Parenthetically we may quote foreign evidence that Rome in the Middle Ages was looked upon as a quarry. The famous Abbot Sugerius, who about 1140 was in search of lofty pillars for the rebuilding of Saint-Denis, at first thought of nothing less than getting hold of the granite monoliths of the Baths of Diocletian, but later changed his mind. See 'Sugerii Libellus Alter', in Duchesne, *Hist. Franc. Scriptores*, iv, p. 352 [see E. Panofsky, *Abbot Suger and the Abbey Church of Saint-Denis . . .*, 2nd ed., Princeton, 1976]. Charlemagne was doubtless more modest in his requirements.

51. *Poggii Opera*, fol. 50 ff, 'Ruinarum Urbis Romae Descriptio', written about 1430, shortly before the death of Martin V. The Baths of Caracalla and Diocletian then had their pillars and marble revetments. [Poggio Bracciolini, *Opera*, Argentorati (i.e. Strasburg), 1513, and Basle, 1538 (reprinted Turin, 1964–6). The passage on the ruins of Rome is reprinted in full in R. Valentini and G. Zucchetti, *Codice topografico della città di Roma*, IV, Rome, 1953, 230 ff. There is an abbreviated English translation in *The Portable Renaissance Reader*, ed. J. Ross and M. McLaughlin, New York, 1958, quoted from *Latin Writings of the Italian Humanists*, ed. F. Gragg, New York, 1927.]

52. [Blondus of Forlì (Flavio Biondo, Biondo Flavio, Flavius Blondus), *Roma instaurata*, Rome 1470(?) and later, is now available in R. Valentini and G. Zucchetti (cf. note 51), 247 ff.]

53. See on this point, Nantiporto, in Murat., iii, ii, col. 1094; Infessura, in Eccard, *Scriptores*, ii, col. 1951; Matarazzo, in the *Arch. Stor.*, xvi, ii, p. 180. [There is a contemporary drawing of this beautiful girl reproduced in F. Saxl, 'The Classical Inscription in Renaissance Art and Politics', *Journal of the Warburg and Courtauld Institutes*, IV, 1940–41, plate 5b.]

54. Quatremère [de Quincy], *Storia della vita etc. di Raffaello*, ed. Longhena, p. 531. [See now the Italian text in V. Golzio, *Raffaello nei documenti* . . ., Vatican City, 1936, 78 ff, and the abbreviated English translation and discussion in R. Jones and N. Penny, *Raphael*, New Haven and London, 1983.]

55. Polifilo (i.e. Franciscus Columna), *Hypnerotomachia*, Venice, Aldus Manutius, 1499, pages unnumbered; extracts in Temanza, p. 12. [The reference to Temanza is to *Vite de' più celebri architteti veneziani* . . ., 2 vols., Venice, 1778, but the *Hypnerotomachia Polifili*, generally attributed to Fra Francesco Colonna, is now available in modern facsimile reprints, e.g. London, 1963. It is more of an architectural fantasy-novel than a commentary, with many fine woodcuts. Burckhardt's date, 1467, occurs in the text, but the date of publication is 1499.]

56. While all the Fathers of the Church and all the pilgrims speak only of a cave. The poets, too, do without the palace. Compare Sannazaro, *De partu virginis*, book ii. [Jacopo Sannazaro's poem was published in Rome and Naples in 1526 and in Venice in 1527. The setting of the Nativity in the ruins of a palace – King David's – is especially common in Flemish painting of the fifteenth and early sixteenth centuries, e.g. the Portinari Altarpiece by Hugo van der Goes, *c.* 1475, which has been in Florence since it was painted.]

57. How the matter was provisionally treated is related in Malipiero, *Ann. Veneti*, *Arch. Stor.*, vii, ii, pp. 653, 655. [Cardinal Bessarion died in 1472; the Marciana Library opposite St Mark's was begun by Jacopo Sansovino in 1537.]

58. [The tomb of Carlo Marsuppini, called Aretino, who died in 1453, is by Desiderio da Settignano.]

59. The following words of Vespasiano are untranslatable: '*A vederlo in tavola così antico come era, era una gentilezza.*' [The general meaning is that it was a charming spectacle to see him at table, with his antique appearance; *antico* meaning 'ancient, classical', as opposed to *vecchio*, 'old'.]

60. [For Vespasiano da Bisticci, see p. 370.]

61. *Giorn. Napolet.* in Muratori, xxi, col. 1127. [See now J. Pope-Hennessy, *Italian Renaissance Sculpture* (vol. 2 of *An Introduction to Italian Sculpture*), third edition, Oxford, 1985, and G. Hersey, *The Aragonese Arch at Naples, 1443–75*, New Haven, 1973.]

62. [For the rebuilding of San Francesco see R. Wittkower, *Architectural Principles in the Age of Humanism*, third edition, London, 1962, where the use of the Triumphal Arch on the façade is interpreted as a 'glory' motive.]

63. [For Valla's exposure of the fraudulent Donation of Constantine, see note 26.]

64. Charles V, when unable on one occasion to follow the flourishes of a Latin orator at Genoa, whispered in the ear of Giovio: 'Ah, my tutor Adrian was right when he told me I should be chastened for my childish idleness in learning Latin.' Paulus Jovius, *Vita Hadriani VI*. [Adrian of Utrecht, Charles's tutor, became Pope Hadrian VI, 1522–3.]

65. Which, nevertheless, gave some offence to Jac. Volaterranus (in Murat., xxiii, col. 171) at the service in memory of Platina.

66. Vasari, xi, pp. 189, 257; *Vite di Sodoma e di Garofalo* [Milanesi edition, vi, 379, 457]. It is not surprising that the profligate women at Rome took the most harmonious ancient names – Julia, Lucretia, Cassandra, Portia, Virginia, Penthesilea, under which they appear in Aretino. It was, perhaps, then that the Jews took the names of the great Semitic enemies of the Romans – Hannibal, Hamilcar, Hasdrubal, which even now they commonly bear in Rome.

67. Paul. Jov., *Dialogus de viris litteris illustribus*, in Tiraboschi, ed. Venez., 1766, vol. vii, pt. iv. It is well known that Giovio was long anxious to undertake the great work which Vasari accomplished. In the dialogue mentioned above it is foreseen and deplored that Latin would soon altogether lose its supremacy. [G. Tiraboschi, *Storia della letteratura italiana*, 14 vols., Venice, 1772–81. Vasari's autobiography in the final volume of his *Lives* gives a somewhat coloured account of how he was pressed by Giovio, Cardinal Farnese and others to write the lives of the Italian artists (see G. Bull's Introduction to the second volume of Vasari in the Penguin Classics, 1987, pp. xi–xii). In fact, Giovio's attempt at the lives of Michelangelo, Leonardo and Raphael demonstrates how fortunate it was that Vasari undertook the task.]

68. [Vitruvius Pollio, working at the time of the Emperor Augustus, was the author of the only known ancient text on architecture, *De architectura*. It is extremely difficult, both in language and in style, but was known throughout the Middle Ages. A manuscript is supposed to have been rediscovered by Poggio Bracciolini in a Swiss monastery and to have excited the interest of the first generation of Renaissance architects. Alberti's own treatise, *De re aedificatoria*, is obviously modelled upon it, and he frequently mentions Vitruvius disparagingly: the *editio princeps* of Alberti is Rome, 1485, and that of Vitruvius, also Rome, is probably 1486. The first attempt at a critical edition of Vitruvius is by Fra Giocondo, Venice, 1511, and the first Italian translation is by Cesariano, Como, 1521. A sixteenth-century attempt at a full-scale critical edition, fully illustrated, was proposed by a special Vitruvian Academy in Rome, but got no further than an edition by Philander (1544). By far the most important edition of the sixteenth century was that by Daniele Barbaro, with woodcuts by Palladio, Venice, 1556 and later.]

69. Ariosto, *Satira*, vii. The date is 1531.

70. [Fabio Calvi made a translation of Vitruvius for Raphael, who seems to have intended to publish it with his own annotations.]

71. In the sixteenth century, Italy continued to be the home of geographical literature, at a time when the discoverers themselves belonged almost exclusively to the countries on the shores of the Atlantic. Native geography produced in the middle of the century the great and remarkable work of Leandro Alberti, *Descrizione di tutta l'Italia* [Bologna, 1550].

72. At this point a few notices on slavery in Italy at the time of the Renaissance will not be out of place. In North Italy there were no slaves; elsewhere even Christians, as well as Circassians and Bulgarians, were bought from the Turks, and made to serve until they had earned their ransom. The negroes, on the contrary, remained slaves; but it was not permitted, at least in the kingdom of Naples, to emasculate them. The word *moro* signifies any dark-skinned man; the negro was called *moro nero*. Document on the sale of a female Circassian slave (1427) – List of the female slaves of Cosimo de' Medici – Innocent VIII received 100 Moors as a present from Ferdinand the Catholic, and gave them to cardinals and other great men (1488) – Sale of slaves; negro slaves who also (for the benefit of their owner?) work as *facchini* [porters], and gain the love of the women; Moors from Tunis caught by Catalans and sold at Pisa – Manumission and reward of a negro slave in a Florentine will (1490) – Negroes as jailers and executioners of the House of Aragon in Naples – Negroes as followers of the prince on his excursions – A negro slave as a musician – A (free?) negro as swimming teacher and diver at Genoa – A negro (Aethiops) as superior officer at Venice, according to which we are justified in thinking of Othello as a negro – When a slave at Genoa deserved punishment he was sold away to Ibiza, one of the Balearic isles, to carry salt. [This note has been slightly shortened, and the references omitted.]

73. The most important passages are the following. *Pii II, Commentarii* [cf. Gragg and Gabel, *Memoirs of a Renaissance Pope*]: spring in his native country; summer residence at Tivoli; the meal at the spring of Vicovaro; the neighbourhood of Viterbo; the mountain monastery of St Martin; the Lake of Bolsena; a splendid description of Monte Amiata; the situation of Monte Oliveto; the view from Todi; Ostia and Porto; description of the Alban hills; Frascati and Grottaferrata.

74. *Jo. Pici oratio de hominis dignitate*, in his *Opera*; also printed separately [Giovanni Pico della Mirandola, *Opera*, 2 vols., Bologna, 1496; Italian translation, ed. E. Garin, Florence, 1942; see also Garin's *Portraits from the Quattrocento*, New York and London, 1972.]

75. Sansovino, *Venezia*, fol. 152: '*capelli biondissimi per forza di sole*'. ['Very blonde hair, bleached by the sun'. The famous painting by Carpaccio in the Museo Correr, Venice, of two women on a terrace, shows them with blonde hair exposed to the sun.]

76. [G. della Casa, *Il galateo*, Venice, 1558. English translation by R. Pine-Coffin in Penguin Classics, 1958.]

77. There was a limit, however, to this. The satirists introduce bits of Spanish, and Folengo (under the pseudonym Limerno Pitocco, in his *Orlandino*) of French, but only by way of ridicule. It is an exceptional fact that a street in Milan, which at the time of the French (1500–1512, 1515–22) was called Rue Belle, now bears the name Rugabella. The long Spanish rule has left almost no traces on the language, and but rarely the name of some governor in streets and public buildings. It was not until the eighteenth century that, together with French modes of thought, many French words and phrases found their way into Italian. The purism of our century is still busy removing them. [Via Rugabella still exists: it is a small street between the modern Corso Roma and Corso Italia, not far from the ancient Basilica di San Lorenzo.]

78. [i.e. *Palla*, a ball-game which has now been superseded by football.]

79. [See note 34.]

80. Vasari, iv, p. 37, *Vita di Pontormo*, tells how a child, during such a festival at Florence in the year 1513, died from the effects of the exertion – or shall we say, of the gilding? The poor boy had to represent the 'golden age'! [The Life of Pontormo, in G. Bull's second volume of Vasari, in Penguin Classics, 1987, p. 243.]

81. [The reference to Titian's *Triumph of the Cross* is not clear; it seems to refer to the woodcut, more than 12 feet long, of the *Triumph of Faith*, but there is no evidence that this was ever a painting; in any case, the description given by Burckhardt is not very close to the woodcut.]

82. [See, for example, Vasari on Piero di Cosimo, in G. Bull's second volume of Vasari, in Penguin Classics, 1987, p. 105 ff.]

83. [It is in this section that the voice of the Swiss Lutheran bourgeois is most evident; but it must be remembered that Burckhardt's view of the history of the papacy was that of Ranke, since the *History of the Popes* by Ludwig von Pastor, written from the Vatican archives, did not begin to appear until 1886. The English translation began in 1891; of the forty volumes, the first ten or twelve are relevant to our period. D. Hay, *The Church in Italy in the Fifteenth Century*, Cambridge, 1977, is an up-to-date survey of the problems in this field, and attacks the problem of the differing interpretations by Burckhardt and Pastor of the 'paganism' of the Renaissance.]

84. See extracts from his diary in Delécluze, *Florence et ses vicissitudes*, vol. ii. [Buonaccorso Pitti's *Diary* has been translated in *Two Memoirs of Renaissance Florence: The Diaries of Buonaccorso Pitti and Gregorio Dati*, ed. G. Brucker, New York, 1967.]

85. If he appeared as a corsair in the war between the two lines of Anjou for the possession of Naples, he may have done so as a political partisan, and this, according to the notions of the time, implied no dishonour. The Archbishop Paolo Fregoso of Genoa, in the second half of the fifteenth century, probably allowed himself quite as much freedom, or more. [John XXIII, Antipope,

1410–15, was certainly a pirate. He was deposed in 1415, to make way for the legitimate Martin V and is best remembered for his splendid tomb, by Donatello and Michelozzo, in the Florentine Baptistery.]

86. *L'Ordine*. Probably the tablet with the inscription IHS is meant. [This is certainly a reference to the special tablet with the letters IHS (*Iesus Hominum Salvator*), which S. Bernardino used to hold up during his sermons; see, for example, the painting by Neroccio de' Landi in Siena, Palazzo del Commune.]

87. *Ricordi*, no. 28, in the *Opere inedite*, vol. i. [For Guicciardini, see C. Grayson, ed., F. Guicciardini, *Selected Writings*, London, 1965, p. 12.]

88. Perrens, *Jérome Savonarole*, 2 vols. Perhaps the most systematic and sober of all the many works on the subject. P. Villari, *La storia di Girol. Savonarola* (2 vols., octavo, Florence). [Villari's *Savonarola* was twice translated into English (second edition London, 1897), but the modern monograph is by R. Ridolfi, English translation by C. Grayson, London, 1959. See also D. Weinstein, *Savonarola and Florence*, Princeton, 1970.]

89. We must make a further distinction between the Italian *cultus* of the bodies of historical saints of recent date, and the northern practice of collecting bones and relics of a sacred antiquity. Such remains were preserved in great abundance in the Lateran, which, for that reason, was of special importance for pilgrims. But on the tombs of St Dominic and St Anthony of Padua rested, not only the halo of sanctity, but the splendour of historical fame. [Both these shrines were major works of art: the Arca di San Domenico, in San Domenico, Bologna, was designed by Nicola Pisano and partly executed by his shop. Among others, Michelangelo helped to complete it. The Basilica of St Anthony in Padua (*Il Santo*) was built in 1232–1307 and contains his tomb in a chapel built in 1500–46; the High Altar, by Donatello, is not now in its original form.]

90. While the visual arts at all events distinguished between angels and *putti*, and used the former for all serious purposes. In the *Annal. Estens.* in Murat. xx, col. 468, the *amorino* is naïvely called *instar Cupidinis angelus* [a Cupid-like angel].

91. [This picture, which represents SS Mark, George and Nicholas saving Venice from a sea-storm raised by demons, was originally attributed to Giorgione by Vasari, who later changed his mind and gave it to Palma Vecchio. Current opinion rejects the Giorgione attribution and hesitates between Palma and Paris Bordone, following a cleaning undertaken in 1955. Formerly in the Accademia, it is now in the Biblioteca dell' Ospedale Civile in Venice.]

92. Ben. Cellini, i, cap. 64. [Cellini's *Autobiography*, translated by G. Bull, Penguin Classics, 1956.]

93. Vasari, viii, 143, *Vita di Andrea da Fiesole*. It was Silvio Cosini, who also

'went after magical formulae and other follies'. [Vasari, Milanesi edition, iv, 483; English translation by G. de Vere, London, 1913, v, 7: 'Silvio ... belonged to the Company of the Misericordia, which in that city accompanies those condemned to death ... there once came into his head, being sacristan at that time, the strangest caprice in the world. One night he took out of the grave the body of one who had been hanged the day before; and, after having dissected it for the purposes of his art, being a whimsical fellow, and perhaps a wizard, and ready to believe in enchantments and suchlike follies, he flayed it completely, and with the skin, prepared after a method that he had been taught, he made a jerkin, which he wore for some time over his shirt, believing that it had some great virtue, without anyone ever knowing of it. But having once been upbraided by a good Father to whom he had confessed the matter, he pulled off the jerkin and laid it to rest in a grave, as the monk had urged him to do.']

FULL TITLES OF WORKS MOST FREQUENTLY QUOTED BY BURCKHARDT

Anecdota literaria e mss. codd. eruta, edited by Amaduzzi and Bianconi, Rome 1773–83, 4 vols. in octavo.

Archivio storico italiano, with Appendix, Florence, Viesseux. [A periodical, published from 1842 onwards.]

Boccaccio: *Opere volgari*, Florence 1829–, presso Ign. Mountier, 17 vols. in octavo. [Boccaccio, *Opere*, ed. V. Branca, 1964 in progress; *The Decameron*, translated by G. McWilliam, 1972, is in Penguin Classics.]

Castiglione: *Il cortigiano*, Venice 1549. [B. Castiglione, *Il cortigiano* (or *cortegiano*), first published in Venice in 1528; modern edition by V. Cian, Florence, 1947; English translation by G. Bull, 1967, in Penguin Classics.]

Corio: *Historia di Milano*, Venice edition of 1554. [B. Corio, *L'Historia di Milano*, Milan, 1503; the latest edition is by A. Guerra, 2 vols., Milan, 1978.]

Fabroni: *Laurentii Medicei Magnifici Vita*. [A. Fabroni, *Laurentii Medicis Magnifici Vita*, 2 vols., Pisa, 1784 (vol. 2 contains the *Adnotationes et monumenta*).]

Fabroni: *Magni Cosmi Medicei Vita*. [A. Fabroni, 2 vols., Pisa, 1788–9.]

Firenzuola: *Opere*, Milan, 1802, in octavo. [A. Firenzuola, *Prose*, Florence, 1548, and other works also published in the sixteenth century; modern *Opere*, ed. A. Seroni, 1958.]

Tommaso Gar: *Relazioni della corte di Roma* (third volume in the second series of the *Relazioni degli Ambasciatori Veneti*, raccolte da Eug. Albèri, Florence). [T. Gar, *Relazioni della corte di Roma nel secolo XVI*, 2 vols., Florence, 1846–57.]

Machiavelli: *Opere minori*, Florence, Lemonnier, 1852. [The latest edition is

Tutte le opere, ed. F. Florio and C. Cordié, 2 vols., Milan, 1949–50. In English there are *The Historical, Political, and Diplomatic Writings*, ed. and trans. C. Detmold, 4 vols., Boston, 1882; *The Prince*, translated by G. Bull, Penguin Classics, 1967; the *Discourses*, ed. and trans. L. Walker, 2 vols., London, 1950; and the *History of Florence*, ed. M. Dunne, London, 1901, reprinted with an Introduction by Felix Gilbert, New York, 1960.]

Muratori: *Scriptores rerum Italicarum.* [L. Muratori, *Rerum italicarum Scriptores ab anno . . . 500 ad 1500*, 25 vols. (in 28), Milan, 1723–51. New edition in progress, Città di Castello, 1900–.]

Agnolo Pandolfini: *Trattato del governo della famiglia*, Turin, Pomba, 1829. [This is actually by L. B. Alberti (cf. note 34): *I libri della famiglia* are in Alberti's *Opere volgari*, vol. I, ed. C. Grayson, Bari, 1960.]

Petrarch: Complete edition of his Latin works, Basle, 1581, folio. [This is the edition still used. Earlier editions are Venice, 1501, and Basle, 1554. An *Edizione nazionale*, published in Florence, has been in progress since 1926.]

Philelphi Orationes, Venice edition of 1492, folio. [i.e. Francesco Filelfo, *Orationes cum aliis opusculis . . .*, Venice, 1492. Earlier editions are Venice, 1484, 1488.]

Pii II P.M. Commentarii, Roman edition of 1584. *Aenae Silvii Opera*, Basel edition of 1551, folio. [These are both by Aeneas Silvius Piccolomini, later Pope Pius II. The *Commentarii* were published in expurgated form in Rome in 1584 and 1589, but there is a more complete Italian edition by G. Bernetti, 4 vols., Siena, 1973, and a partial English translation by F. Gragg and L. Gabel, *Memoirs of a Renaissance Pope*, New York, 1959 and later reprints, which contains, for example, the description of Pienza and the landscape of Tuscany.]

Platina: *De vitis pontificum romanorum*, Coloniae Agrippinae [Cologne], 1626. [B. Platina, *De vitiis summorum pontificum opus*, Venice, 1479, and many later editions, including that by G. Gaida in the new Muratori, vol. III, part 1, 1913–32.]

Poesie del magnifico Lorenzo de' Medici, London, 1801. [This is probably the edition made by W. Clarke, printed in Roscoe, e.g. the tenth edition, London, 1895, as an Appendix. Lorenzo's *Opere*, ed. A. Simioni, 2 vols., Bari, 1913, is a modern edition of the poems.].

Poggii Opera, Strasburg edition of 1513, folio. [Another edition of the *Opera* was printed at Basel, 1538, and reprinted in Turin, 1963–.]

Raccolta di poesie satiriche, Milan, 1808, one volume.

Roscoe: *Life of Lorenzo Medici.* [W. Roscoe, *The Life of Lorenzo . . .*, 2 vols., Liverpool, 1795 (tenth edition, London, 1895). Burckhardt used the Italian translation, probably the four-volume one, Pisa, 1816, with additional material.]

Roscoe: *Vita e Pontificato di Leone X*, translated by Luigi Bossi, Milan 1816 seq.,

12 vols. in octavo, with many Appendices not found in the English original. [W. Roscoe, *Life and Pontificate of Leo X*, 4 vols., Liverpool, 1805, and many later editions; Burckhardt quotes from the enlarged Italian translation by L. Bossi, 12 vols., Milan, 1816–17.]

M. Anton. *Sabellici Opera*, Venice edition of 1502, folio. [M. A. Sabellicus, *De situ urbis venetae* was first printed at Venice in 1495(?).]

Trucchi: *Poesie italiane inedite*, Prato, 1846, 4 vols. in octavo.

Varchi: *Storia fiorentina*, Milan 1803, 5 vols. in octavo. [More recent editions are those by G. Milanesi, Florence, 1857, and 1963; and the *Opere*, Trieste, 1858.]

Vasari: *Le vite de' più eccellenti pittori, scultori e architetti*, Florence, Lemonnier, from 1846 onwards, 13 vols. [G. Vasari, *Le vite de' più eccellenti pittori, scultori ed architettori*, Florence, 1568. Burckhardt never quotes from the earlier, 1550, edition. The Lemonnier edition was almost immediately superseded by that by G. Milanesi, 9 vols., Florence, 1878–85 (now also in photographic reprint); this is still the standard edition, but is being replaced by P. Barocchi and R. Bettarini, 9 vols. so far, Florence, 1966–. There is a complete English translation of the 1568 edition by G. de Vere, 10 vols., London, 1912–15 (also reprinted photographically), and a selection of the *Lives* can be found in G. Bull's translation, 2 vols., in Penguin Classics, 1965 and 1987.]

Vespasiano Fiorentino: besides the edition here quoted, from the tenth volume of Mai, *Spicilegium Romanum*, a later edition by Bartoli, Florence, 1859, must be mentioned. [Vespasiano da Bisticci, *Vite di uomini illustri del secolo XV*, written at the end of the fifteenth century, was first printed by A. Mai (1839); modern editions by P. D'Ancona and E. Aeschlimann, Milan, 1951, and A. Greco, Florence, 1970; English translation by W. and E. Waters, London, 1926 and later reprints.]

Filippo Villani: *Le vite d' uomini illustri fiorentini*, Florence, 1826. [F. Villani, *De origine civitatis Florentiae et eiusdem famosis civibus*, written c. 1400; in Italian, *Le vite d'uomini illustri fiorentini*, Florence, 1747 and 1826; in Latin, Florence, 1847 and 1887.]

INDEX

READ MORE IN PENGUIN

In every corner of the world, on every subject under the sun, Penguin represents quality and variety – the very best in publishing today.

For complete information about books available from Penguin – including Puffins, Penguin Classics and Arkana – and how to order them, write to us at the appropriate address below. Please note that for copyright reasons the selection of books varies from country to country.

In the United Kingdom: Please write to *Dept. EP, Penguin Books Ltd, Bath Road, Harmondsworth, West Drayton, Middlesex UB7 0DA*

In the United States: Please write to *Consumer Sales, Penguin Putnam Inc., P.O. Box 999, Dept. 17109, Bergenfield, New Jersey 07621-0120.* VISA and MasterCard holders call 1-800-253-6476 to order Penguin titles

In Canada: Please write to *Penguin Books Canada Ltd, 10 Alcorn Avenue, Suite 300, Toronto, Ontario M4V 3B2*

In Australia: Please write to *Penguin Books Australia Ltd, P.O. Box 257, Ringwood, Victoria 3134*

In New Zealand: Please write to *Penguin Books (NZ) Ltd, Private Bag 102902, North Shore Mail Centre, Auckland 10*

In India: Please write to *Penguin Books India Pvt Ltd, 210 Chiranjiv Tower, 43 Nehru Place, New Delhi 110 019*

In the Netherlands: Please write to *Penguin Books Netherlands bv, Postbus 3507, NL-1001 AH Amsterdam*

In Germany: Please write to *Penguin Books Deutschland GmbH, Metzlerstrasse 26, 60594 Frankfurt am Main*

In Spain: Please write to *Penguin Books S. A., Bravo Murillo 19, 1º B, 28015 Madrid*

In Italy: Please write to *Penguin Italia s.r.l., Via Benedetto Croce 2, 20094 Corsico, Milano*

In France: Please write to *Penguin France, Le Carré Wilson, 62 rue Benjamin Baillaud, 31500 Toulouse*

In Japan: Please write to *Penguin Books Japan Ltd, Kaneko Building, 2-3-25 Koraku, Bunkyo-Ku, Tokyo 112*

In South Africa: Please write to *Penguin Books South Africa (Pty) Ltd, Private Bag X14, Parkview, 2122 Johannesburg*

READ MORE IN PENGUIN

A CHOICE OF CLASSICS

Jacob Burckhardt	**The Civilization of the Renaissance in Italy**
Carl von Clausewitz	**On War**
Meister Eckhart	**Selected Writings**
Friedrich Engels	**The Origins of the Family, Private Property and the State**
Wolfram von Eschenbach	**Parzival**
	Willehalm
Goethe	**Elective Affinities**
	Faust Parts One and Two (in 2 volumes)
	Italian Journey
	The Sorrows of Young Werther
Jacob and Wilhelm Grimm	**Selected Tales**
E. T. A. Hoffmann	**Tales of Hoffmann**
Henrik Ibsen	**A Doll's House and Other Plays**
	Ghosts and Other Plays
	Hedda Gabler and Other Plays
	The Master Builder and Other Plays
	Peer Gynt
Søren Kierkegaard	**Fear and Trembling**
	The Sickness Unto Death
Georg Christoph Lichtenberg	**Aphorisms**
Karl Marx	**Capital** (in three volumes)
Friedrich Nietzsche	**The Birth of Tragedy**
	Beyond Good and Evil
	Ecce Homo
	Human, All Too Human
	A Nietzsche Reader
Friedrich Schiller	**The Robbers/Wallenstein**
Arthur Schopenhauer	**Essays and Aphorisms**
Gottfried von Strassburg	**Tristan**
Adalbert Stifter	**Brigitta and Other Tales**
August Strindberg	**By the Open Sea**

m8003-JL
10